Nachum T. Gidal

JEWS
IN GERMANY
FROM ROMAN TIMES
TO THE WEIMAR
REPUBLIC

Nachum T. Gidal

JEWS
IN GERMANY
FROM ROMAN TIMES
TO THE WEIMAR
REPUBLIC

With a Preface by
Marion Gräfin Dönhoff

KÖNEMANN

Amicis et inimicis

Editing: Dieter Lang
Chief editor: Margarete Schwind
Cover design: Wolfgang Mudrak
Maps: HTG Werbeagentur, Erill Vinzenz Fritz for the English-language edition
Layout: Manfred Flöttmann, Günter Hauptmann, Raimund Post, Ute Römer

This volume contains 974 illustrations

Cover illustration:
Commemorative cloth (cotton, printed, 68 x 68 cm)
for the Service held at Yom Kippur before Metz 1870,
during the Franco-German War.

In the middle, depiction of the Service
in front of an improvised Thora Shrine,
the participants in uniform,
some wrapped in prayer shawls.

Above, in Hebrew and German, the motto:
"Do we not all have one Father? Were we not made by one God?"

In the four corner circles
a hymn by Ludwig Philippson on the Service, attended by 1200 German-Jewish soldiers.

The hymn ends with the verses:
"Uplifted through belief, encouraged for duty, they are ready for battle, they stand and falter not."

Copyright © 1998 for this English-language edition
Könemann Verlagsgesellschaft mbH
Bonner Str. 126, D-50968 Cologne

Translation from German: Helen Atkins, Patricia Crampton, Iain Macmillan, Tony Wells
Editor of the English-language edition: Michael Scuffil
Proofreader: Miriam Hurewitz
Project coordinator: Bettina Kaufmann
Typesetting: Goodfellow & Egan, Cambridge
Production: Ursula Schümer
Printed and bound by: Dürer Nyomda, Gyula
Printed in Hungary

ISBN 3-8290-0491-5
10 9 8 7 6 5 4 3 2

Contents

Acknowledgments

The author and the publisher would like to thank all those who assisted in the production of this book:

– The friends and advisers of the author, who encouraged and supported him in his work: Dr. Dietrich Andernacht, Dr. Alex Bein, Dr. Marion Gräfin Dönhoff, Jochanan Ginat, Prof. Gershom Scholem and Jochen Steinmayr. Jacov Guggenheim assisted in the preparation of the texts on the Middle Ages, Dolf Michaelis in the research on the 18th and 19th centuries. Prof. George Mosse very kindly gave valuable advice.

– Prof. Julius Schoeps, director of the Moses Mendelssohn Zentrum für europäisch-jüdische Studien at the University of Potsdam, and Dr. Johannes Wachten, head curator and deputy director of the Jüdisches Museum of Frankfurt on Main for their scholarly advice. The stimulus for the book was provided by Dr. Max Kreutzberger, director of the Leo Baeck Institute, New York.

– Directors Yeshavahu Weinberg and Aaron Doron of the Museum Bet Hatefutsot (Diaspora Museum) in Tel Aviv, where the author was curator of the 1984 "Jews in Germany" exhibition. The Central Council of the Jews in Germany provided long-term support for the exhibition. Daniel Becher was an indefatigable researcher and Mrs. Laakmann a cheerful stylist.

– The museums, archive, and private individuals who generously made available important pictorial material to the author, including: Dr. Ulrich Bauche, Museum für Geschichte der Stadt Hamburg; Dr. Veronika Bendt, director of the Jewish section of the Berlin Museum; Dr. Jutta Bohnke-Kollwitz, former director of the Germania Judaica, Cologne; Dr. Daniel Cohn and Dr. Arye Segal, directors of the Central Archives for the History of the Jewish People, Jerusalem; Dr. Rudolf Elvers, library director, Mendelssohn-Archiv, Berlin; head curator Ute Eskildsen, Fotografische Sammlung, Folkwang Museum, Essen; Dr. Falk, Stadtarchiv Mainz; Dr. Liesel Franzheim, director of the Jewish section of the Cologne Stadtmuseum; Janos Recot, director of the photographic collection of the Berlinische Galerie; Prof. Peter Freimark, director of the Institut für die Geschichte der Juden in Deutschland, Hamburg; Elisabeth von Gleichenstein, Rosgartenmuseum, Constance; director Dr. Fred Grubel and former chief archivist Dr. Sybil Milton of the Leo Baeck Institute, New York; Chief Archivist Dr. Fritz Reuter, Stadtarchiv Worms; director Prof. Josef Kruse and Head Archivist Inge Hermstrüwer, Heinrich-Heine-Institut, Düsseldorf; Dr. Michael Heymann, director of the Central Zionist Archives, Jerusalem; Frau Eva Horváth, manuscript section, Staats- und Universitätsbibliothek, Hamburg; Dr. W. van Kampen, director of the Landesbildstelle, Berlin; Dr. Jakob Katzenstein, director of the Schocken Library, Jerusalem; Michael Lenarz, Jüdisches Museum, Frankfurt am Main; Irene Lewitt, director of the Picture Archive, The Israel Museum, Jerusalem; Dr. Carole Mendleson, director of the Jewish Museum, London; the former director of the Berlinische Galerie, Prof. Eberhard Roters. Alfred Rubens, London, generously allowed the reproduction of pictures from his unique collection of Jewish iconography; Dr. Paul Sauer, director of the Hauptstaatsarchiv Stuttgart; Dr. Arno Schönberger, former director-general of the Germanisches Nationalmuseum, Nuremberg; Mr. Teutsch, of the Stadtarchiv Mannheim; former curator Dr. Leonie von Wilkens, Germanisches Nationalmuseum, Nuremberg; director Dr. Eberhard Zahn, Rheinisches Landesmuseum, Trier. I am also grateful to the following institutions: Bildarchiv des Deutschen Museums, Munich; Bildarchiv Preussischer Kulturbesitz, Berlin; Bischöfliches Ordinariat, Augsburg; Museum Bet Hatefutsot, Tel Aviv; Historisches Museum, Frankfurt am Main; Institut für Sozialgeschichte, Amsterdam; Sammlung Rosenthaliana, University Library, Amsterdam, The Jewish National and University Library, Jerusalem; Österreichische Nationalbibliothek, Vienna; Rheinisches Bildarchiv, Cologne; Staatsbibliothek, Berlin; Stadtarchiv Frankfurt am Main; Stadtarchiv Munich; Stiftung Deutsche Kinemathek, Berlin; Universitätsbibliothek Freiburg im Breisgau; Universitätsbibliothek Heidelberg; Administration of the State Castles and Parks, Berlin; numerous other private supporters.

– The editorial staff of the Bertelsmann Lexikon Verlag: Beate Assig, Hannelore Forster, Jörg Häntzschel, Dr. Jochen Kiebranz, Maria Kornhoff, Dieter Löbbert, Arno Matschiner, Karl W. Schubsky, Johannes Schulz, Dr. Simon Snopkowski, Claudia Sperr, Zuzanna Stern, Regina Wittenbrink.

– And last but not least we are very grateful to Pia Gidal. Her knowledge of Hebrew literature, her sound judgment in advice on the text and picture design, and her patience, formed an essential contribution to the realization of this book.

Preface

After Hitler had seized power and was destroying universities everywhere, many scientists, artists, Jews, and others who did not wish to conform came under pressure, and chose to leave the country. At that time the University of Basle was an ideal place for students, above all for those who were interested in economics and sociology, for it was there that Edgar Salin taught, one of the last universal scholars of this century, for whom philosophy, history and literature were a natural part of that otherwise dry course.

For three semesters Tim Gidal and I shared a bench there in Salin's lecture theater and a table in the subsequent seminars. Tim obtained his doctorate, supervised by Salin, on "Picture Reporting and the Press." He showed that there had always been a need to record special events in pictures: "Even in the army of General, later Emperor, Titus there were reporters who were sent from Rome to Palestine to document the siege and storming of Jerusalem in AD 70."

Pictures always fascinated him. He was a brilliant photo reporter, initially in order to finance his studies, but later out of passion. Finally as a member of the editorial staff of *Life*, he became a world-famous photographer. His first book on the history of photojournalism, published in 1972, is regarded in the United States and Britain as the standard work on the subject.

The theme of picture reporting has fundamentally attracted Gidal all his life: in Palestine, where he emigrated in 1936, in Great Britain with the famous *Picture Post*, and in the Second World War as the chief photoreporter for the British Eighth Army. In America, where he lived in the fifties, he lectured on "The History of Visual Communication from the Stone Age to the Television Age" at the New School for Social Research in New York. Later in Jerusalem he occupied himself with similar problems as associate professor at the Hebrew University.

And now this book, on which he has worked over a period of thirty years. His vision was to show the Germans by means of pictures – 974 of them – who the Jews actually were who lived in Germany, and what role they played from the earliest times, through the Middle Ages, and into the modern age.

The author describes the freedoms and civil rights they enjoyed under Charlemagne and the Ottonians, which made possible the flourishing of cultural and spiritual life in the Jewish communities, and then shows the switch to the oppression and destruction of the Jews by the Crusaders. The religious hatred preached by the Church had inspired the latter to extremes of cruelty: "In 1096 marauding bands of murderers moved into the Rhineland from France. They killed thousands of Jews."

When subsequently Pope Innocent III, the merciless enemy of the Jews, convoked the Fourth Lateran Council in 1215, it pushed through all the anti-Jewish regulations which, as the author says, "were to form the basis of the humiliating living conditions and evil slander of the Jews right up to our own century." Over 140 Jewish communities were destroyed in Franconia, Thuringia, Hesse, and Bavaria at the end of the 13th century. In the Middle Ages emperors and kings were frequently the patrons of the Jews, but this protection came at a high price and forced those who were exploited in this way to raise the necessary funds by means of charging extortionate interest rates: once again the "tight-fisted" Jews were at the receiving end of popular wrath.

The book takes us through the centuries and the turbulent history of this people, who usually had to endure a life of anguish and persecution, and yet who, as Gidal writes, experienced the zenith of their history – in the opinion of many Jews – in that same Germany during the Weimar era.

Nachum Tim Gidal was born in Munich in 1909. His parents were emigrants from Russia and Lithuania. It was a decidedly Jewish-Zionist world in which he grew up, one which brought him into intensive contact at an early age with the Jewish youth movement, but equally one which did not estrange him from his non-Jewish friends.

At that time, before the "Thousand Year Reich," I could well understand that it was important for him to search out his own roots, and that this wish was like a lodestar which took him further and further into the past, back to the destruction of the Temple in Jerusalem which marked the beginning of the tragic fate of the Diaspora, the scattering throughout the world of this people characterized by myth. But after all that has happened – even after this last war – it is truly awe-inspiring to have begun a life's work to explain the Jews to, of all people, the Germans. This demands a quite extraordinary openness of mind, curiosity, and concentration when reading and thinking about this book.

Marion Gräfin Dönhoff

Foreword

"The memory of a people is its history"
Isaac Leib Peretz

The inspiration for a pictorial history of the Jews in Germany goes back to lectures which I gave in the nineteen-fifties at the New School for Social Research in New York. In my researches it struck me that there was very little pictorial material deriving from Jews on their own history. The reasons for this are numerous: a theologically narrow interpretation of the Second Commandment combined with a defensive reaction to an adoration of pictures and statues by surrounding cultures, which was foreign to Judaism; religious and political pressure in the Islamic countries which did not tolerate pictures; a favoring of accounts of historical and contemporary events based on the intellect and the written word. The Bible is after all notable for its graphic language and expressiveness. In Germany during the era of emancipation and assimilation, the intention of the Jews was above all to represent themselves as German citizens. As a consequence, the Jews avoided visual documentation of their life.

In the more than thirty years which have passed since then, I have been able to collect over two thousand books on the history of the Jews in Germany. In the case of this book, then, in the beginning was not the Word, but the Picture. In my researches I tried to record all the aspects which seemed relevant to me in word and picture.

My aim is to show who these Jews in Germany actually were, how they lived, how they survived, mostly as an oppressed minority, until 1933, how they integrated, or tried to integrate, and how in the end, before the destruction of European Jewry by Hitler and his henchmen, they attained full equality as citizens. One section of them, immigrants originating from the lands in the East, lived almost without discrimination as foreigners in Germany. The descendants of baptized Jews integrated fully with the non-Jewish Germans.

While the pictorial section of this book attempts to give an insight into largely forgotten life of the Jews, the introduction provides an overview of the history of the Jews in Germany from Roman times up until the Weimar Republic.

For the pictorial section, a chronological – and at the same time thematic – division of the book into four sections proved the best arrangement, although there was some overlapping:

- The Middle Ages from the 10th to 15th centuries, in which, in spite of dreadful persecution, the German Jews experienced a religious and cultural revival which made them the legitimate and authoritative successors to the religious centers of Babylon and Spain.

- The early modern age, which for the Jews did not begin until the Enlightenment and the conquests of Napoleon.

- The Imperial Germany of the Kaisers, which brought full equality of rights to the Jews.

- The Weimar Republic, a climax in the history of Judaism. Despite growing anti-semitism, the German Jews were able to operate in all areas of public life; of equal importance was the combination of an inner Jewish renaissance, an orthodoxy which was close to life, and the ideas of Zionism which had given the Jews a new self-confidence.

The history of the Jews in Germany is a part of the history of my people. This book is dedicated to their memory.

Foreword to the Second German Edition

In 1974 I was commissioned by the Leo Baeck Institute to compile an illustrated history of the Jews in Germany.

In December 1975 I presented the first version of the text and the chronologically and thematically categorized pictorial sections of the book, which I had named "The Jews in Germany from Roman Times to the Weimar Republic."

In 1980 the newly elected chairman of the Leo Baeck Institute in Jerusalem set out new conditions for the reworking of the book according to a concept which did not correspond to mine. I considered this an attempt at censorship and broke my link with the Leo Baeck Institute.

I have sometimes been asked why I did not continue the history of the Jews until 1945. From 1933 it was no longer a history of the Jews in Germany, but a history common to all European Jews, one of humiliation, persecution and murder by an indescribably brutal dictatorship.

Jerusalem, October 1996.

Nachum T. Gidal

Nachum T. Gidal

Introduction

"The wise men of Ashkenaz ... were handed down the Torah by their forefathers in the days of the destruction of the Temple," wrote the Talmud scholar Asher ben Yehiel (c. 1250–1327), a recognized authority on the Jews in Germany.

This is one of the earliest references to the Ashkenazim as a religious and cultural entity in Europe, whose presence extended from France across the Holy Roman Empire and into Russia.

The "days of the destruction of the Temple" described by Asher ben Yehiel referred to the destruction of Herod's Temple in Jerusalem by the Roman legions under Titus in the year AD 70. This date marks the end of the Jewish state and the beginning of the Diaspora, the dispersion of the Jews to other lands.

The Middle Ages

In the year AD 321 there must have been a flourishing Jewish community in Cologne. The Roman emperor Constantine indeed may already have become acquainted with some of them when he erected a bridge over the Rhine at Cologne in the year AD 306. As emperor, Constantine sent decrees to the Cologne city council in AD 321 and 326. These dealt with the Jewish decurions (councilors) of the town and represent the earliest reference to the presence of a Jewish community in the German provinces of the Roman Empire.

Sources from the 6th to 8th centuries provide firm proof that there were Jews living in the territories of the Frankish kings, and that they were earning their living as merchants, landowners, customs officials, doctors, and master coiners.

*

With the spread of Christianity, Jews were increasingly illtreated and persecuted, particularly in the western part of the Frankish kingdom. There are no surviving documents about their life in the eastern part before the time of Charlemagne, king of the Franks, and after 800 the first Holy Roman Emperor. Charlemagne (reigned AD 768–814) united a large part of western Europe under his rule. During his reign, trade and the arts experienced a renaissance. Under his protection, his Jewish subjects were granted equal rights as citizens, enabling them to devote themselves to their religious, cultural, and economic life.

Jewish seafarers and long-distance traders undertook trade expeditions to Egypt, the Middle East, Persia, and India. There they sold eunuchs, slaves, furs, and weapons, and returned with jewels, spices, perfumes, and other easily transportable luxury goods. Trade caravans left Persia for China where there were also Jewish communities.

Under Charlemagne numerous Jewish communities were founded and existing ones were consolidated. It was this atmosphere of widespread religious freedom that laid the foundations of German Jewish culture which was to flourish over the following centuries. In AD 839, for example, it was even possible for an imperial deacon, by the name of Bodo, to convert to Judaism without running the danger of being burned alive, a fate that would have awaited any such convert a few centuries before. A few centuries later, however, that would again be the case.

This largely peaceful period continued under Ottonian rule. The imperial crown which was made for the coronation of Otto the Great in AD 962 shows portraits of Kings Solomon and David and the breastplate of the biblical high priest. Even dignitaries of the church now turned against the violent conversion of Jews to Christianity. One of the reasons must have been that the bishops were also secular rulers who dispensed justice in their territories. As rulers of the towns and cities they were also interested in the development of commercial and social life. The urbane, literate Jews with their financial acumen were welcome helpers.

*

Between the 10th and 13th centuries there were hundreds of Jewish communities both in small villages and in towns such as Bamberg, Erfurt, Regensburg, Vienna, Prague, and Cologne. The three municipalities of Speyer, Worms, and Mainz, known as the SCHUM municipalities after the initial letters of their Hebrew names, were the focus of a vibrant cultural and spiritual way of life.

The centers of Jewish learning were now no longer Babylon and the deserted Jerusalem, but Spanish, French, and German communities in Europe such as Troyes and the SCHUM municipalities, where a particular brand of pietism arose. Ashkenazi Jewry finally now became the decisive influence among the Jews of the western world.

The Bible, the prayer book, the Talmud and the commentaries were and still remain the pillars of Judaism. It was Solomon ben Isaak (1040–1105), known as Rashi, who wrote the commentaries to the Bible and the Talmud, which are still today regarded as indispensable. He had studied in Worms and at the age of 25 founded a Talmud school in Troyes.

The Ashkenazi communities developed the *kehillah* community, gathering), an institution of self-administration which was recognized by the Christian authorities. The duties of the *kehillah* included the raising of taxes, education and cultural affairs, teaching and justice. The *kehillah* was responsible for the maintenance of the synagogues, the cemetery, the *mikvah* (ritual bath), the inn, and the accommodation and care of the sick, and finally for the house where marriages and other ceremonies were held.

The students gathered in the house of the Talmud scholars and together they formed a community of learning and teaching.

The intimate atmosphere particularly of the smaller communities resulted in the members themselves largely participating in the execution of community duties. If a member of the community felt he had been wronged, he had the right to demand the interruption of prayer in the synagogue (*ikkuv hatefillah*) until the matter was settled. The *kehillah* had for its part the right to call a community member to account (*beth din*). The court could order payment as atonement for the crime and impose punishments.

The chief administrative officers (*parnassim*) and the wise men (*chachamim*) worked out the regulations and statutes (*takkanot*), whether for one or for a group of communities. Three of the best-known *takkanot* were issued by Rabbi Gershom ben Judah (ca. 965–1040), the "light of the Diaspora": the prohibition of divorce without the agreement of the wife, the prohibition of polygamy, and the privacy of correspondence.

Many of these statutes dealt with questions of everyday collective life. Some ensured that taxes imposed on the Jews by Christian authorities were allocated in a fair and humane way between rich and poor. Other statutes referred to matters of law and financial affairs. One important area was the regulation of dealings between Jews and Christians. Fraud practiced against Christians, for example, was expressly forbidden, and the consequences of such a deception could endanger the whole Jewish community. It was also forbidden to report Jews to gentile authority, except in proven cases of crime.

The statutes, regulations and community laws, which were all included in the concept of the *takkanot*, even referred to outward appearance. In the light of the persecution during the Crusades, special *takkanot* were issued which forbade the accusing of Jews if, under pain of death, they had declared themselves willing to undergo enforced baptism.

It was above all the statutes of Gershom ben Judah that became the common property of Ashkenazi Jewry. Acher ben Yehiel, a leader of German Jewry recognized by all communities, codified the works of German, French and Spanish Talmud scholars. He compiled an authoritative compendium of *halakah* (change, way of life) which evolved into a religious law for daily life which is that even today.

Despite the persecution and destruction of many communities, Jewish cultural and religious life enjoyed a golden age between the 10th and 14th centuries. Calligraphy and the art of book illustration, including Jewish micrography, also reached new heights of achievement in that period.

*

As a rule kings and emperors took a benevolent attitude towards the Jews during that period. Nevertheless their power during the Crusades mostly proved too weak to protect the Jews from attacks by the crusaders. In 1096, for example, bands of marauders from France moved into the Rhineland, killing thousands of Jews.

The church had sown religious hatred. Greed fired the fanatical crusaders in their belief that, to please God, their armed pilgrimage to conquer the Holy Land should include the murder of those Jews who refused to be baptized. Nearly all Jews preferred the alternative, the act of *kiddush hashem* (the sanctification of the name of God), and committed suicide or had themselves killed, in order to prove their faith.

Possessions which could be removed were usually shared between the crusaders. The houses became the property of the town, unless they were claimed by the rulers as compensation for not having brought the murderers to justice. There were exceptions, and some patricians, bishops and princes gave refuge to Jews or defended them in their castles against the crusaders. The later Crusades had similar, if less murderous, consequences for the Jews. Despite this, the Jews always built up their communities again; scholars and their schools continued to compile religious writings and develop the ethical principles of Ashkenazi Judaism. Thus for example Judah ben Samuel, known as Hasid (the pious one), founded German-Jewish mysticism in Regensburg.

*

In 1215 Pope Innocent III, initiator of the Fourth Crusade (1202–1204) and merciless enemy of the Jews ("sons of the crucifiers of Christ"), convoked the fourth Lateran Council. It was here that this pope pushed through the anti-Semitic regulations which formed the basis of the humiliating living conditions and malicious slandering of the Jews that lasted right into our own century.

Innocent III prohibited the charging of interest by Christians and shifted the blame for the exorbitant interest rates onto Jewish greed. The hostile laws of the Lateran Council were to expose Jews to widespread humiliation. Henceforth they were excluded from all public offices, had to sew a piece of yellow cloth on their clothing as a sign of their social degradation, and were not allowed to show themselves in public during Holy Week. The pointed Jewish hat, already introduced previously, was hardly worn in daily life, despite repeated decrees.

After 1215, church laws and similar guild regulations deprived the Jews of almost any possibility of earning their living in a Christian environment, unless it were through lending money or pawnbroking or in exceptional cases as doctors to potentates or monastic communities. Despite these canonical regulations many emperors, princes, bishops, and town councilors nevertheless maintained economic and cultural relations with the Jews in the empire.

The Hohenstaufen emperor Frederick II (reigned 1212–1250) gave the Jews the legal status of *servi camerae* (serfs of the imperial chamber). This legal status was a double-edged sword. It placed the Jews under the protection of the emperor, but at the same time made them his property. He could farm out, pledge, or sell his right of taxation entirely at his own discretion.

Against the payment of large sums of money, however, Jews were granted some invaluable rights: safety on the roads, the right to a court trial in the case of a legal dispute with a Christian, and the right not to be baptized.

The Jews were therefore caught in a vicious circle: in order to pay the extraordinarily high protection money, they had to raise the extra money by exorbitant, albeit legal, levels of interest rates. As a result, the hatred amongst the people for these profiteering Jews grew, and their situation worsened in spite of the imperial protection.

During and after the last Crusades, there were renewed massacres of the Jews in Germany. The most terrible were the slaughtering of the Jews in Frankfurt am Main around 1250 and the destruction of more than 140 Jewish communities in Franconia, Thuringia, Hesse, and Bavaria in 1298 by the impoverished knight Rindfleisch and his retinue. The excuse this time was the scurrilous slander that Jews had desecrated a host, the symbol of the body of Christ, by cutting through it.

The accusation of ritual murder was yet another tale of horror which was revived. The Jews, who are strictly forbidden any enjoyment of blood and who feel unclean by the merest contact with it, were accused of killing Christian children at the Feast of the Passover to use their blood for ritual purposes. After a thorough investigation in 1236, Emperor Frederick II had declared this accusation to be lies and nonsense.

In the years 1347 to 1352 the Black Death, the plague, killed a third of Europe's population. Once again Jews were the scapegoat: they had, it was said, poisoned the wells. In Strasbourg, for example, 2000 Jews were burned to death as a result.

Many Jews succeeded in fleeing eastward into Poland, however, where they were welcomed as merchants, artisans and founders of new towns. In 1264 King Boleslaw the Pious placed them under his protection. As early as 1200, silver coins with Hebrew inscriptions were being minted in Poland, the Jewish bracteates. Rabbi Judah ben Samuel, in his "Book of the Pious," furthermore describes the foundation of a Jewish settlement in the primeval Polish forest. The Jews from Germany brought their old customs with them, together with their German clothing and German language. With the addition of Hebrew and Slavic words, the latter developed into Yiddish.

*

By the end of the 15th and beginning of the 16th centuries the Jews in most German cities had been killed or driven out. There now began a decline in the Jewish communities and their scholarship. The cultural consequences of this development, the widespread stagnation and ossification of German Judaism, were to last until the end of the 18th century.

The majority of the survivors, particularly in the country areas, were impoverished. Thousands eked out their existence in the forests and on the roads, where they gathered together in groups to protect themselves from robbery. Many joined up with Christian vagabonds and beggars who had been rejected by society. Just how deeply integrated Jews were in the vagrant and beggar communities is shown by the *Liber vagatorum* ("Book of Vagrants") (c. 1510). It also contains a vocabulary of the vagrant and beggar language, which includes many words of Hebrew origin.

Officially it was still forbidden for Christians to charge interest, but there were many means by which the Christian merchant could circumvent the ban. Even the church no longer respected the prohibition. In the Age of Discovery Christian merchants became increasingly rich. The money of the Fuggers, a German merchant family, decided the election of Charles V (1519–1556) as Holy Roman emperor. Peasants who did not pay their tithe to their spiritual master, or could not come up with the money for an indulgence, were often obliged to borrow their money from the Jews.

In addition to the stigma of being a Jew and therefore a profiteer, there was the fact that many Christians felt insecure when confronted with their exotic culture, strange behavior and customs, odd clothing, and the incomprehensible Hebrew which Jews used in the synagogue and in sometimes quite public prayers.

The unknown often produced insecurity and mistrust. Mistrust can lead to rejection and animosity. The Jews were indeed foreigners within the Holy Roman Empire of the German nation, even if they were needed in economic life. They had not come willingly and always knew that they were living through the painful experience of the Diaspora, from which only God could redeem them through his Messiah. They put their trust in that line of the morning prayer, recited each day, which read: "Even if he should tarry, nevertheless I daily expect his coming."

On the holy Sabbath, feast days, and family events, the birth of children, the Bar Mitzvah (confirmation of the sons) and at weddings, the Jews forgot their oppressive everyday life and celebrated handsomely.

The fact that the Jews in general were very ethical in their religious, family, and daily life was of little significance for the Christian community. They were despised by the church and stood at the bottom of the social scale. In business matters it was considered that they haggled too much and demanded exorbitant interest rates. Their external appearance, "disreputable" professions, and above all their attachment to a religion which was thought to have been superseded by Christianity, all made the Jews very suspect to most Christians. The Jews were the people who, from generation to generation, carried the responsibility for the death of Christ.

Despite all the discrimination and animosity, Jews won the trust of numerous princes, bishops, and patricians in their capacity as merchants and doctors. Some rose to be financial advisers and personal physicians, while others became well-respected traders and members of the business community.

*

The beginning of the 16th century marked a milestone in Christian-Jewish relations, in that after this time the Jews rebelled openly against the attacks of their enemies. This was above all possible because the honorary position of shtadlan was set up, a spokesman for Jewish community affairs before the gentile authorities. In the course of time, therefore, a new secular order was established.

The most famous Shtadlan was Josel of Rosheim (1478–1554), initially the head of the Jewish community in lower Alsace, then, on his own initiative, the champion of the Jewish cause in the empire, and the ruler and commander of the ordinary Jews. He stood in high regard with Emperor Maximilian I and especially with Charles V. Josel defended not only the reputation of the Jews, but also their rights. He had judicial authority in disputes between Christians and Jews, and was empowered to impose fines and prohibitions. In 1525 during the Peasants' War, he successfully protected the Jews against the slanders of the apostate Anton Margaritha, who maintained that the Jews were responsible for the split of the Protestants away from the Catholic church. Josel of Rosheim wrote a tract rejecting the anti-Jewish agitation of the Reformer Martin Butzer. In 1544 he obtained confirmation from Emperor Charles V that Jews were granted permission to demand higher rates than Christians because they had to pay higher taxes, and were allowed neither to own property nor to exercise any trade. Regarding the accusation concerning blood, he obtained a certificate of protection, although only against a payment of 4400 guilders in coins and gifts.

Josel of Rosheim's stance signified a turning point in the legal and social position of the Jews in Germany. The legal status of the Jewish communities began to consolidate and become more secure. Their internal autonomy contributed significantly to this greater solidity vis-à-vis the outside world. Community leaders and *shtadlanim* were rabbis or rich merchants, often both at once, and formed a autocratic ruling class.

*

One of the most bitter opponents of the Jews was the Reformer Martin Luther. Initially he hoped to convert the Jews to his form of Christianity. In his tract *Dass Jesus Christus ein geborener Jude sei* ("That Jesus Christ Was Born a Jew"), 1523, he pleaded for tolerance and rejected the accusation of ritual murder and desecration of the Host.

Luther's struggle against the papacy aroused hopes among the Jews that there would be humane treatment and understanding for their beliefs. When however they retained their religion, Luther abused them for their "obstinacy" and suggested that "this depraved rabble of Jews, these disgusting worms" be sent into enforced labor, that they be deprived of their holy writings, and that their synagogues and houses be burned.

The Jews despised the discrepancy between the proclaimed brotherly love of the Christian churches and the means of humiliation and torture with which those of different faiths were to be converted. The threat of death meant that they did not dare to propose theological objections to Christianity during this time.

At the same time as he was attacking the Jews, Luther was translating the Bible into German with love and reverence. The version of the Old Testament he used was, where possible, the traditional Hebrew text, the Palestinian Massorah in manuscripts of the 13th and 14th centuries. With his brilliant, if occasionally flawed, work he acquainted the German people with the Bible of the Jews. For this reason, perhaps, it was a considerable time before Luther's malicious outbursts against the Jews achieved wider resonance. The Bible became an inspiration for artists, poets, and musicians. In the world of the

Christian scholars the study of the Hebrew language and the interest in Hebrew literature had already begun with the spread of humanism. The humanists rejected the scholasticism of the Middle Ages and were endeavoring to revive the universal human values of Antiquity. The Hebrew Bible, the Talmud, and the Cabala thus aroused considerable new interest.

Special studies were devoted to the Cabala, and some scholars tried to make it the basis of Christian mysticism. Johannes Reuchlin made a vital contribution through his works on the Hebrew language. Reuchlin saw in the Jews the *concives nobiscum romani imperii* ("citizens of the Roman Empire like the rest of us"). He denied the right of the church to persecute Jews because of their rejection of Christianity. The Jews could not be treated as heretics. The holy laws of the Jews are refuted neither by spiritual nor secular law, therefore they should not be snatched away from them or burned. "Above all a Christian man should love his neighbor the Jew; that is established in the law."

Into the Modern Era

In the 16th and 17th centuries, the legal situation of the Jews gradually improved, above all in cities such as Hamburg, Frankfurt am Main, Worms, Vienna, and Prague. Nevertheless, they had to put up with humiliating regulations and oppressive taxation. In towns they lived mostly in isolated areas, occasionally behind ghetto walls. Since the gates would be closed at night, the wall did at least give them the feeling of security and social and cultural unity. In a century of merciless civil wars, the towns knew how to make use of the Jews – who were neutral in the conflict between Catholic and Protestant – as traders and moneylenders whose horizons extended beyond regional boundaries.

*

In the Thirty Years' War (1618–1648), in which a large part of central Europe was devastated, the Jews, now mainly living in villages and small towns, suffered no more, and possibly even less, than the non-Jewish population. As sutlers, peddlers and money-changers, horse and corn traders, smugglers of foodstuffs and war materiel, and obtainers of ransoms, they were welcomed by all the warring parties, and thereby ensured the safety of their own communities.

Of greater significance for the Jews were the efforts of the German princes after the end of the war to revive the depressed economy of their territories as quickly as possible. This was to be done in line with mercantilist principles, according to which the prerequisite of state wealth was the amassing of gold and silver reserves. The means to this end was the development of surplus production for exports and the restriction of imports, resulting in a favorable balance of trade.

Some princes became very rich by minting coins with less silver content than previously. Through the agency of the money-changers they had these new coins exchanged throughout Europe against the old ones, which were then returned to the mints. Another method, that of the "Kipper and Wipper," involved paring the silver off the edge of the coins. The silver then went into their own pockets or into the war coffers. The result was a devaluation of money, or inflation, which was blamed on the money dealers, above all the Jewish ones.

In 1648 thousands of Jews escaped from the massacres of the Cossack commander Chmielnickij and fled to Posen, Silesia, Bohemia, Austria, and further westwards. A new wave of refugees sparked off the war between Sweden and Russia.

The refugees were totally without means to support themselves. Some could be absorbed into already existing communities, with or without the knowledge of the authorities. Some, however, without the right of abode, sank to the level of vagabonds and beggars or even fell in with bands of thieves. It took almost two hundred years before the descendants of these refugees found a normal existence, of a kind, and no longer ran the risk of being driven out of the country because they lacked means of support. A large number of the assimilated German Jews of the 19th century descended from these Polish and Russian refugees of the 17th.

Many of the new arrivals were scholars who gave a new impetus to rabbinical study in Germany. The intellectual and cultural activity in the Jewish communities of Germany had however never been totally interrupted. Even in the 17th century there were some outstanding scholars at work, among them the Talmud commentator Meïr Schiff, a rabbi in Fulda, and the Talmud teacher Yaïr Chaim Bacharach in Worms.

*

The continual persecutions and the humiliating life of the Diaspora had always kept alive the Jews' yearning for a Messiah who would lead them all back to the Holy Land. When, in 1665, the news came from Smyrna of the appearance of a Messiah, this was immediately, and all too readily, believed by a large number of Jews. A wave of hope washed through the communities. Numerous Jews sold their possessions and prepared for the journey. However Shabbetai Tzevi (1626–1676) proved to be a false Messiah. In 1666 he converted to Islam in a Turkish prison.

Despair and disillusionment spread. Shabbetai's closest supporters nevertheless remained loyal to him. They maintained that Shabbetai had only become a Muslim because this challenge to God would serve to accelerate the redemption of the Jewish people. The Shabbetaian movement survived on into the 19th century in the form of secret sects of various shapes and permutations.

*

The reconstruction of Germany in the 17th century gave many local Jews the opportunity to achieve economic wealth, especially in the new sectors of manufacturing and trade. The country people valued the Jews who traded cattle, animal skins, leather, and corn for increasingly desirable and necessary cash or textiles, linen, yarn, jewelry and other wares. Jews also gave loans against the standing corn of the coming harvest. This would be a bargain if the harvest were plentiful, but expensive if it were a bad one.

The "corn Jew" was however cursed if he sold his cheaply gotten corn at high prices in years of bad harvests. The Christian corn dealer would be labeled an exploiter in such cases, but not of course a "corn Christian." Only the estate owners in Prussia had the power to protest against the exploitation of the rural population by Christian merchants when the latter tried to exclude Jewish competition. In the words of a petition by the big landowners: "If the Jews were forbidden to trade, the Christian merchants would only give the poor farmers what they wanted to get rid of, and even that at prices which they set themselves. The consequence of this would be the ruination of the rural population."

*

In the 18th century there was a considerable and very influential number of Jewish army suppliers, moneylenders, court bankers, and agents, the so-called court Jews, who were also mostly close friends of their rulers, and on whose loyalty the lord could rely. Highly regarded court Jews, such as the Oppenheimers, Rothschilds, Behrens-Lippmanns, Ephraims, Itzigs, and Liebmanns, nevertheless often remained very protective of their Jewishness. Many schools, hospitals, schools, and synagogues owed their existence to such court Jews, who in this way contributed to the economic and cultural flowering of the Jewish communities.

The rise and fall of Josef Süss Oppenheimer (1692–1738), close friend and court Jew of Duke Karl Alexander of Württemberg was an unusual case. A farsighted economic organizer, art collector and patron, both arrogant and corruptible, Oppenheimer modernized the shattered finance system of the country, but because of the reforms which the Duke introduced on the advice of Oppenheimer he was declared an enemy of the Estates. After the death of the Duke, and at the instigation of the Estates, "Jud Süss" was accused of fraud and offenses against the coinage. When this could not be proved, he was accused of sexual intercourse with Christian women, condemned to death, and, for the delectation of a huge number of onlookers, publicly hanged. He turned down the baptism which would have saved his life.

Despite the more stable status of many communities, the majority of the Jews remained poor, and large numbers of "beggar Jews," as they were described in Prussian edicts, found it difficult to do more than eke out a paltry and humiliating existence in thoroughly miserable conditions.

A number of wandering Jews, above all in the 18th century, joined the bands of Christian beggars, thieves, and robbers which were widespread after the Thirty Years' War and which represented a very resentful underclass. Others joined purely Jewish bands which were excellently organized. They had spies, informers, professional picklocks, thieves, and receivers of stolen goods at their disposal. Killing was taboo and so they would let themselves be arrested and then try to escape. For the dependants of those who were in prison or had died, there was a kind of family insurance from the community coffers. In order to protect themselves they developed their own professional jargon made up of Hebrew and German-Jewish words which was as incomprehensible to ordinary Jews as to non-Jews and the authorities. It was in this way that the thieves' cant known as "Rotwelsch" developed and furthermore became absorbed into the professional jargon of non-Jewish robber bands.

The situation of the poorest of the "beggar Jews" was made even more desperate by the fact that they had no right of abode anywhere, and even had to leave Jewish communities after one or two days in order not to endanger them.

The Jewish beggars moved around the country roads with their families in groups of between 20 and 100 people in order to safeguard themselves against attack. So it was, for example, over a period of four months in 1721 in the small town of Harburg that more than 800 beggars were sheltered and given medical aid by the small local Jewish community. The 26 families of the village of Gochsheim similarly took care of around 1,500 Jewish vagrants and beggars in a single year. Both locations lie in southern Germany where there developed a class of settled and productive land Jews. In Prussia, however, the defenseless and homeless Jews were "whipped out of the state." In Brunswick they were locked away in the most atrocious conditions for ten to fifteen days. If they were caught a second time they were whipped, branded with a glowing iron and expelled back across the border. Being caught a third time would mean execution, as decreed by Prince Anton Ulrich in Wolfenbüttel on 31 August 1712.

Paradoxically, theft and robbery gave some Jews the opportunity to become respectable members of society. As soon as a Jew had stolen enough cash or obtained it by selling stolen goods, he could obtain the right of residence and a letter of protection from one of the poorer imperial counts or by bribing the local authority. He could even afford the costly right of residence for more than one child if he secretly continued his links with the thieving activities of a robber band.

*

At the beginning of the 18th century German Jewry consisted of three economic classes. The large majority belonged to the lower and lowest classes, a fair-sized minority to the well-off middle class, and finally there was the small upper class made up of the rich merchants, Jews attached to the court, and the many community heads who were often both scholars and merchants. The thieves and robbers were despised and were officially excluded from the Jewish community by the rabbis.

It was above all in Berlin that their elevation into Germany's high society or, more accurately, cultural elite, happened.

Many Jews driven out of Vienna and Austria in 1670 found refuge in small communities in the south and west of Germany. Fifty rich Jews and their families received permission from Elector Frederick William of Brandenburg (known as the "Great Elector") in 1671 to settle in his territories for a temporary period of twenty years.

It was not only wealth and a knowledge of the manufacturing sector that these immigrants brought with them, for they were also integrated to a certain extent into German culture. They dressed in the manner of the upper class, and some of their children and grandchildren studied at universities and were familiar with German and French language and literature. By the third generation there were already scholars of repute among them. This circle of privileged Jews, who were heavily taxed for their right of residence, also included their Jewish employees, who in contrast did not have a permanent right of abode.

One of these Jews without rights was Moses Mendelssohn (1729–1786), a poor hunchback who at the age of fourteen had followed his Talmud teacher from Dessau to Berlin. He became famous as a German philosopher of the Enlightenment and as a pioneer and symbol of the emancipation and assimilation of the Jews in Germany. In his private life he was an Orthodox Jew. His belief in the integration of the Jews into German culture and society was however shaken by one of his admirers, the Swiss theologian Lavater, when he invited Mendelssohn in an open letter to draw the obvious conclusion from his philosophical postulates, and either refute Christianity or be baptized. From then on Mendelssohn turned increasingly to Jewish themes. With the aid of friends, and above all for his five children, he translated the Pentateuch and the Psalms into German. He recommended a German education for all Jews as a preparation for being useful members of German society. Mendelssohn spoke up for the improvement of the legal status of the Jews and encouraged his non-Jewish friend, the military councilor and archivist Christian Wilhelm von Dohm, to write a tract *Über die bürgerliche Verbesserung der Juden* ("On the Civic Improvement of the Jews"), 1781/83. Dohm's suggested reforms influenced not only the Prussian reformers under Hardenberg, but also the spokesmen for the Jews in the French National Assembly.

Mendelssohn had little sympathy and understanding for the traditional way of life of Jewish communities. He took scant notice of the independent culture of Polish Jewry. The further development of a vital Jewish culture in Germany was not one of his concerns. It was at this time – as was noted later – that the split between Western and Eastern Jews occurred. For later generations Mendelssohn himself became the model for those Jews who hoped that their Jewish belief would be respected as part of their legal rights as equal citizens. They saw themselves as German citizens of the Jewish faith long after humanism and the Enlightenment had been driven out by nationalism and racism.

In Berlin the salons of Henriette Herz, Rahel Varnhagen and the de Beers became cultural centers of the German intelligentsia and the educated aristocracy. The theologian Schleiermacher, Prince Ludwig Ferdinand of Prussia, the Humboldt brothers, Brentano, the Schlegel brothers, Dorothea Schlegel, Tieck, Schadow, Count Alexander zu Dohna (who made an unsuccessful proposal of marriage to the widowed Henriette Herz), Heine and Börne were among those who moved in these circles. Nevertheless, Rahel Varnhagen later wrote that neither these nor any other baptized or unbaptized Jews were invited to the social functions held by their aristocratic guests.

The majority of German Jews during Mendelssohn's lifetime were influenced by the intellectual representatives of the

Enlightenment. The Jews on the land, on the other hand continued to cling to their traditional Jewish ways of life. After a long period of stagnation this traditional Jewry was reinforced by Polish Jews from the new Prussian provinces and Silesia.

*

The Jews had long been knocking on the doors of the modern age. These now began to open up for them. The ideas of the Enlightenment, the revolutions in America and France, and the Napoleonic era led to the Jews in western and central Europe being liberated from their physical and spiritual ghettos. With King Frederick William's edict of 11 March 1812, the Prussian state declared the Jews to be its national subjects and citizens, a right that France had granted twenty years earlier to its own Jewish population. There were however two qualifications: the offices of state remained closed to them, and the stipulations of the edict did not apply to the new or regained territories. As a result there were still Jews without rights of nationality in Prussia until 1848.

During the Age of the Restoration, however, most states of the German Federation began to reverse the concessions granted in 1812. Catholic Bavaria had, for example, introduced new restrictions even before the Congress of Vienna (1814/15). "Compulsory matriculation" was seen as particularly oppressive and discriminatory. This involved the right of settlement in a particular place being passed only on to the eldest son and his family. The remaining sons would have to wait for a "matriculation vacancy" before starting a family, which might only arise through death or the emigration of another family. There would then be a considerable sum to pay. This amounted in practice to a ban on procreation within the Christian state.

A wave of anti-Semitic laws and publications paved the way for an era of moral depression for the Jews, even in Prussia. In the Christian state envisaged by the Prussian kings Frederick William III and Frederick William IV there could be no full equality before the law unless they were baptized. Many academically trained Jews gave up the seemingly hopeless struggle and resigned themselves to an opportunistic conversion to Christianity, men such as the leading jurist Eduard Gans, the lawyer Heinrich Marx (father of Karl Marx), the poets Ludwig Börne and Heinrich Heine, and the painter Karl Bendemann.

Almost without exception it was members of the upper classes who were baptized for such reasons, and it was usually the Protestant baptism that they chose. The majority of Jews in the small towns and villages never entertained the thought of relinquishing their Jewish identity. Many began to emigrate to America where they could live as Jews and as free and equal citizens.

*

The disappointing encounter of young Jews with the German Enlightenment and the subsequent wave of jingoistic German nationalism sparked off a period of self-reflection, and an intensive debate within the Jewish community on the problems of Jewry in a modern world.

In the year of the "Hep-Hep" riots in 1819, young academics and writers in Berlin founded a "Society for Jewish Culture and Learning." The Society sought a renewal of the concept of Jewry in the values of its history, and considered its aims as part of general culture and progress.

The chairman of the society was a law student, Eduard Gans, and its secretary was the literary historian Leopold Zunz, from 1828 the editor of the *Zeitschrift für die Wissenschaft des Judentums* ("Journal of Jewish Learning") and the leading spirit of the society. Other members included the Hegelian and linguist Moses Moser and his friend Heinrich Heine, who also taught for some time in the society's school, the Hamburg educationist Immanuel Wohlwile and the orientalist Samuel Munk. Altogether there were some fifty members in the society. It campaigned against both rigid rabbinism on the one hand and the feeble attitudes of assimilation at any price on the other. However, after only four years the society disbanded itself, the main reason being the consequences of the official cultural policy which appeared to destroy any hopes of equality.

The only one who never deviated from the path was Leopold Zunz (1794–1886), the founder of the study of Judaism as a scholarly discipline. Heine's judgment of him was as "a man of deeds who wrote and acted where others dreamed and capitulated without a fight." As the unrelenting fighter for Jewish equality, Zunz demanded "justice, not rights." Zunz and his friends researched in all areas of Jewish culture: its historical development and the history of the Jewish people, rabbinical literature and the philosophy of religion, Jewish literature and poetry, and folklore and liturgical music. In the process, long-forgotten treasures were rediscovered.

Around the middle of the century, Abraham Geiger (1810–1874), the pioneer of Reform Judaism, began to make his mark as one of the most important representatives of Jewish learning together with Leopold Zunz. With Ludwig Philippson, Geiger provided the intellectual initiative for the foundation in 1872 of a teaching institute for Jewish learning, later to become a university. His researches included above all the Bible and the Mishna and spanned the whole of medieval Jewish literature.

The first Jewish history writer on a grand scale thrown up by this interest in Jewish scholarship was Heinrich Graetz (1853–1876) from Breslau, with his eleven-volume *Geschichte der Juden von den ältesten Zeiten bis auf die Gegenwart* ("History of the Jews from Ancient Times to the Present Day"). Represented here for the first time was the complete story of the Jews as one group which set the present in the context of history. Graetz' love for Judaism and his gripping presentation (despite some prejudices and errors) contributed decisively to the awakening of Jewish self-awareness.

In the years 1810–1850 decisive internal Jewish struggles took place between Orthodoxy and the Reform movement. The reformers brought the religious service closer to the German Protestant model, with a German sermon, German prayer book, the use of the organ and choir, and a new kind of rabbinical clothing, including clerical bands.

The success of the Reform movement in turn sparked off a modern Orthodoxy, as represented by the rabbis Samson

Raphael Hirsch (1808–1888) in Frankfurt am Main and Esriel Hildesheimer (1820–99) in Berlin. They wanted to preserve a Judaism which was true to the Law, while supporting the use of the vernacular in teaching (but not in the religious service), along with secular upbringing and modern dress.

Both movements spread in England and the United States and developed there into two dominant strands within Judaism. As in Germany, the Reform movement was predominantly in the moderate liberal form.

*

Around 1848, the year of revolution, a series of Jewish journals emerged, a certain number of which stood up with extraordinary courage against the official policies of the state and called for freedom and equality for the Jews. Jewish publicists concerned themselves with the clarification of questions posed by a revived and strengthened Judaism. An uncompromising champion of the equal rights of Jews and advocate of Germany unity was Gabriel Riesser (1803–1863). He was supported in this by other intrepid Jews such as Isaak Jost and Johann Jacoby, as well as by non-Jewish liberal politicians. In 1848 Riesser was elected to the National Assembly which finally granted German Jews their full rights as citizens. As vice-president of the National Assembly he belonged to the delegation which offered the Prussian king Frederick William IV the imperial crown. Riesser was shattered by the failure of the 1848 Revolution.

In the following years up to the founding of the German Empire in 1871 the rights recognized by the Frankfurt parliament were rescinded. Nevertheless Jews achieved respected positions in the economy and politics of the now increasingly industrialized country, for example: Ferdinand Lassalle, the founder and president of the General German Workers' Union (1863), the nucleus of German social democracy; Eduard Lasker, one of the leaders of German liberalism; and Ludwig Bamberger, National Liberal and from 1881 member of the Liberal party, an opponent of Bismarck's protective tariffs and colonial policies and adviser to Kaiser Friedrich (who reigned for a few weeks in 1888).

During this period German Jews ceased to view human rights as a generous gift, since they contributed just as much to the culture and economy of their homeland as did Protestants, Catholics, agnostics, and atheists. Their self-confidence both as Germans and as Jews strengthened. This was initially changed little by latent and open anti-Semitism. One of the most influential opponents of political equality for the Jews was the baptized Jew Friedrich Julius Stahl (1802–1861), who was the founder of Prussian conservatism, leader of the Conservative Party, House of Lords and member of the Upper House of the Prussian parliament. Stahl's theories decisively influenced the politics of the conservatives in Germany up until the outbreak of the First World War. In Stahl's Christian state there were indeed civil rights for all, but political rights only for those who professed the state religion. Deists, atheists, and Jews were therefore to be excluded from offices of authority. Stahl, a Lutheran, did not however share Luther's view of the Jews as obdurate and depraved.

Imperial Germany

It was not until 3 July 1869 that a law was passed giving equal rights to Jews. Initially it was binding on Prussia and the states of the North German League, but after the foundation of the empire this law was extended to the whole of Germany in 1872.

*

The freedom of trade and profession since 1848 and their almost complete legal equality gave the Jews opportunities to develop in all areas of public life, except for the army and civil service. They soon attained leading positions in banking, transport, and the newspapers. In industry Jews such as Aron Hirsch, Emil Rathenau, and Albert Ballin rose to become leading entrepreneurs through new types of organization, the introduction of modern technology, and the production of new goods. In Germany, Jews above all developed the setting up of department stores, the manufacture of ready-made ladies' and gentlemen's clothing, the tobacco, leather, and fur industries, and the new film industry. Just as their forefathers may at one time have been commentators of the Bible or the Talmud, so now many Jews took up academic posts and became scientists and above all teachers of law. Those who were baptized were then eligible to be appointed to professorial chairs. While in earlier centuries as many as half of all Jews would be peddlers or beggars, the number in 1895 amounted to no more than 12 percent of a total Jewish population of 600,000.

In the past, Christians had considered that the assimilation of the Jews was a prerequisite for their emancipation and recognition by society. After the Jews had assimilated – and they did so willingly for they considered themselves German patriots – a new wave of hatred for the Jews swept across the country. Traditional anti-Semitism was now combined with a pseudoscientific race theory which postulated the superiority of German blood. It was of no concern to the perpetrators of the German race myth that, since Roman times, the blood of the Germanic peoples had repeatedly been mixed with the blood of Italians, French, Spanish, Czechs, Hungarians, Poles, and even Jews.

The anti-Jewish animosity was not taken seriously by the majority of the Jews. Nevertheless the new anti-Semitism found many routes into the higher strata of society and into the petty bourgeoisie. The historian Heinrich von Treitschke with his slogan "Die Juden sind unser Unglück" ("The Jews Are our Misfortune") made anti-Semitism respectable in academic and officer circles.

Whether baptized or not, more than a few of those who had fully assimilated were ashamed of their origins and attacked Judaism and the Jews in order to prove to themselves and others that they belonged to the majority. Paradoxically it was some of those very people who had denied their culture (Karl Marx, Karl Kraus, Kurt Tucholsky, and others) who were attacked or praised for the Jewishness of their work.

The anti-Semitic pseudoscientific books of Paul Lagarde, Houston Stewart Chamberlain, Richard Wagner, and others had their effect. One such example was the family magazine

Die Gartenlaube, which had been founded in 1853 by Ernst Keil, initially a Liberal and subsequently a National Liberal. It had been well-disposed toward the Jews for decades, but in 1874/5 the magazine published a series of inflammatory reports, slightly censored by the editor, on allegedly disreputable Jewish speculators and stock exchange swindlers. The author, Otto Glagau, was a professional anti-Semite.

Scholars such as Theodor Mommsen and Rudolf Virchow opposed the anti-Semitism of the likes of Treitschke. Nevertheless even Mommsen advised the Jews to assimilate as rapidly as possible and give up their Jewish faith. Friedrich Nietzsche in his book "Human All-too-Human" wrote the following on the Jewish question:

"Incidentally: the whole problem of the Jews is only present within national states, as it is here that their energy, higher intelligence, and accumulated store of will and intellect, passed on in suffering from generation to generation, all combine in such excess that this incites hatred and envy. As a result literary ill manners get out of hand in nearly all the existing nations, and indeed the more they behave nationalistically, the more the Jews are made scapegoats for all possible public and internal ills and the more they are required to pay for it with their lives. Once it is no longer a matter of conserving nations, but rather of producing as powerful a mixed European race as possible, then the Jew is as useful and desirable as any other national stock. Unpleasant or even dangerous characteristics are common to every nation and human being; it is cruel to claim that the Jew should be the exception."

At the same time Jewish existence in all its forms, orthodox, liberal and supporters of Reform Judaism, experienced a new lease of life.

Moses Hess' idea of a Jewish renaissance and a return to the country of their fathers was kept alive above all among young university graduates. Although he had not read Hess before, it was Theodor Herzl who finally gave organizational shape to the Zionist movement. Herzl found enthusiastic support among the Jews of Eastern Europe whereas, with the exception of a few academics, the great majority of German Jews were skeptical toward political Zionism.

Most German Jews still believed in merging with the German people whilst still retaining their Jewish culture. Therefore the idea of a return to Palestine was often attacked by German-Jewish political commentators, leading figures in the economy, and politicians. Karl Kraus did this in Vienna in the form of hackneyed cabaret jokes. In 1897 the First World Zionist Congress took place in Basle, Switzerland. Scarcely fifty years later the state of Israel was founded.

In the Weimar Republic

Over 12,000 Jews sacrificed their lives in the First World War for the German fatherland. However, this proof of their patriotism was barely acknowledged. Even in 1916 the Ministry of War had tried to prove by means of a census of the Jews that there were more Jewish than non-Jewish shirkers. The census proved the opposite and was therefore not published.

During and after the revolution of 1918 a relatively large number of Jews played a leading role in left-wing parties, above all in Berlin and Munich. The Bavarian premier Kurt Eisner, the socialists Rosa Luxemburg, Gustav Landauer, and other Jewish politicians were murdered, while the chairman of the executive assembly of the second Munich soviet republic, Eugen Leviné, was tried by court martial and shot.

In the years of the Weimar Republic the Jews enjoyed complete equality before the law for the first time. Many were thrust into the limelight in the fields of the arts, economics, and politics. Walther Rathenau, the son and successor to Emil Rathenau, became foreign minister but, as a Jewish representative of those politicians who had advocated Germany's fulfillment of its obligations in the Treaty of Versailles, he was assassinated by members of the nationalist "Consul" organization.

The German Jews believed that their work and achievements were their contribution to a free society. Many non-Jews however saw it as the Jews imposing their will and culture on German society. In a self-confident nation such as America this would have been considered an enrichment, but in Germany it aroused hate and aversion. Some German Jews deeply felt this inner conflict and suffered under their double identity. Max Reinhardt, the integrated Austrian, wrote, for example, in a poem to Sonja Kornfeld in December 1895 how Jews would always be strangers in the midst, and would never become Christian no matter that they celebrated the Christian festivals.

That many Jews exercised justified self-criticism was also part of the psychological makeup of German Jewry. Good-natured self-ridicule was widespread, without however going beyond the bounds of loyalty. Albert Einstein, who would pen spontaneous verses in company or during boring lectures, once wrote the following: "Sehe ich meine Juden an / hab' ich wenig Freude dran / Fallen mir die Andern ein / möchte ich lieber Jude sein." Roughly translated: "When I observe my Jewish race / I don't like what I see / Yet when the others show their face / A Jew I'd choose to be."

On the subject of a Pindar translation by the poet Rudolf Borchardt, who rejected any connection with Judaism and insisted that his whole being was German, Max Brod wrote to literary critic Werner Kraft: [The Line] "So verloren ist unter den Menschen / Kein Blut, wie das sich des Heimischen schämend ..." ("Nobody is so lost among men as he who is ashamed of his own blood ...") shows clearly that Borchardt has not grasped the conflict underlying his life. He has repressed it so radically that in the translation the parallels did not occur to him. Otherwise he would not have been able to translate the piece so beautifully and would perhaps have chosen another hymn by Pindar for Hesperus I. He was guileless in his assimilation, the only one I know which has almost succeeded. Almost!"

The Zionist movement in Germany grew. Societies, student fraternities, and sports and youth groups were founded in many communities. Their representatives, such as Martin Buber, warned against overzealous assimilation and the abandonment of Jewish values instead of consciously cultivating them and treating them as a valuable contribution to German society. Goethe had with some foresight criticized the "Poems of a Polish Jew" by Isachar Bär Falkensohn, published in 1772 and whose content had nothing to do with the title of the volume. "Above all we must affirm that the title of these pages has made a very favorable impression on us ... Those for whom all is new, what emotions will stir in them and what kind of observations will they make? ... This is what we hoped, and we clutched – at thin air ... Here is yet another handsome and ostentatious young man, powdered and smooth chinned, and with a green gold-embroidered coat ..." A Polish Jew in other words who "all in all achieves no more than a Christian student of belles lettres ..."

A number of Hebrew writers now lived and worked in Germany, including the poets Hayyim Nahman Bialik and Saul Tschernichowski, Samuel Yosef Agnon, later a Nobel prize winner, Salman Rubaschow (Schasar), later president of Israel, and the leading Zionists Shmaryahu Levin, Chaim Arlosoroff, and Leo Motzkin.

Before and after the First World War a new influx of Eastern Jews had arrived in Germany; 70,000 had worked in the German war industries, 30,000 of them could not or would not move to another country. They thereby strengthened the otherwise dwindling number of German Jews. After 1918 about one-fifth of the Jews in Germany were first-, second- or third-generation immigrants from Eastern Europe. This wave of immigration aroused fear and aversion, not only amongst right-wing non-Jews but also within the German Jewish community. These sentiments were however in general not shared by the workers.

The majority of German Jews belonged to the Central Association of German Citizens of the Jewish Faith, or at least identified with its aspirations. In the manner of Moses Mendelssohn, they saw themselves primarily as Germans who belonged to the Jewish religious community, irrespective of whether they were believers or not. Of fundamental importance for the strong resonance of the Central Association was the fact that integration seemed feasible without giving up their Jewish origins, and this claim was expressed without reserve. One of the main activities of the Central Association was to counter anti-semitic defamation. Anti-Semitism, however, proved to be stronger than the forces resisting it. Most German Jews, as well as many non-Jews, did not for all that take anti-Semitism very seriously. Despite rising unemployment and poverty, Germany's Jews regarded the Weimar Republic as a high point in the history of the Jewish people.

As early as 1923, however, Hitler and his followers had attempted their putsch in Munich with the aim of seizing power. The years of the world economic crisis then helped his movement to grow at an astonishing rate. From 1933 onward Germany's Jews were humiliated, deprived of their rights, and expelled and murdered by the National Socialist rulers with the approval of the majority of the German people.

PROLOGUE

Under the Romans

The Beginnings of the Diaspora

ABOVE: The destruction of the Temple of Jerusalem by the Romans in the year AD 70. Copper engraving from *La République des Hébreux* by Jacques Basnage, Amsterdam 1713.

In the year 70, after a two-year siege, the troops of the Roman commander and future emperor Titus (reigned AD 79–81) destroyed Jerusalem, the capital city of the Jewish state and the religious center of the Jewish people.

Even during the time of the Second Temple (538 BC–70 AD) more than half the Jewish people had lived in the Diaspora: in Syria and Babylonia, then in Persia and Asia Minor, Egypt, along the coast of North Africa as far as Carthage, Spain, and in the area which is today France. Jewish communities sprang up even in Greece and Italy. Missionary efforts ensured that in many communities the number of Jews increased. It was to such communities that the Apostle Paul and Rabbi Gamaliel II traveled. The Rabbi's grandfather is referred to by the Apostle as his teacher.

The political messianism among the people experienced a revival due to the

LEFT: Objects from the Temple of Jerusalem were included in the triumphal procession of Titus. Depiction from the inside of the triumphal arch in Rome which was erected by the Emperor Domitian (reigned AD 81–96) in honor of his brother Titus. Copper engraving, 18th century.

RIGHT: Isaiah 49,17: fragment of a bible roll (mid-2nd century BC) which was found in the caves of the Wadi Qumran by the Dead Sea in 1947.

destruction of Jerusalem and the dispersion of the Jews. As early as in the 2nd century BC, the scribe Jesus ben Sirach had expressed his hope that all Jewish people would gather together in Israel, and that the city of Jerusalem would be a symbol for the glory of God, and that there would be a profession of faith by all mortals to the one and only almighty God. During the centuries that followed, this religious and politically inspired messianism became the unshakable hope of the Jewish people.

Under the leadership of Bar Kohba, the "Son of the Stars," the Jews of Palestine mounted their last rebellion. It was brutally crushed by the Romans.

It was the intention of Emperor Hadrian (reigned 117–138) to destroy the rest of the Jewish state. The emperor therefore imposed the death penalty on any Jews practicing their religious faith. The Jews were no longer allowed to live in Jerusalem, and the city was rebuilt as Aelia Capitolina. Half a million of the 1.3 million inhabitants of the country either perished or were sold as slaves. Many of the survivors were, however, later released and became Roman citizens.

In the year 212, Emperor Caracalla (reigned 211–217) granted full citizenship to the Jews throughout the Roman Empire. Many of them joined the army, including released slaves who had come to Italy as prisoners in the Jewish wars.

Others accompanied the legions on their marches to the Rhine and to Britain in their capacities as craftsmen, merchants, and doctors. The legal and, as a consequence, economic situation of the Jews did not deteriorate until the year 325, when Christianity began to establish itself as the state religion.

The Jews had lost their Jewish state. Nevertheless, by taking their Bible, they took with them into the Diaspora their sense of religious community, as a stateless spiritual nation, for they never gave up hope of returning to their home, to Eretz Israel, the land of Israel.

During the first five centuries after Christ, the Talmud was written in the

TOP: Coin of the Emperor Vespasian (reigned AD 69–79) with the circumscription "Judaea Capta." On the left below the palm tree is a Jew with his hands tied. On the right, a weeping woman is depicted.

ABOVE: Jewish coin from around AD 133, the time of the revolt against the Romans under the leadership of Bar Kohba. The coin shows the entrance to the recaptured Temple of Jerusalem and bears the circumscription "Beautiful Gateway." The back of the coin is circumscribed with the words "Salvation of Jerusalem."

teaching institutions of Babylonia and Judea. It is an interpretation of the Bible containing regulations applicable to all situations in life, a treasure of often conflicting expert opinions, narratives, legends, and wise sayings. The Bible and the Talmud became the tool that enabled the Jewish people to survive; they were supplemented during the following centuries by the commentaries of scholars in the Talmud schools. This "portable state" of religious thought guaranteed the vitality of the Torah (the doctrine), its extension and further development, especially since most Jews could read and write (in contrast to their non-Jewish contemporaries). Furthermore, the study of the holy writings was widely practiced by the laity, and there was a constant exchange of ideas between the various Talmud schools.

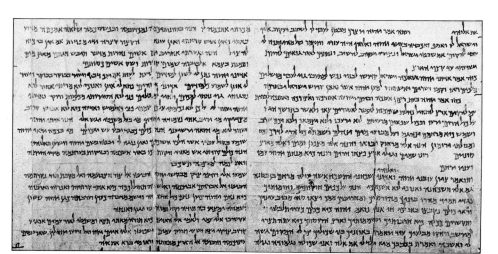

The First Communities on the Rhine

We do not know the size of the first communities on the river Rhine in the 1st and 2nd centuries AD. But we do know that there was, for example, a sizable Jewish community in Cologne by the beginning of the 4th century. Although it was a long distance from his capital city, Emperor Constantine (reigned AD 306–337) made a reference to it in a document, the original of which is still preserved in the Vatican Library. This document suggests that the community had long been in existence even then.

Constantine was the first Roman emperor to prefer Christianity to all other religions. The Jews were now regarded as enemies of the state. This is illustrated for example by a decree issued on 18 October 321. In it, the emperor ordered any Jews who "attacked with stones or by any other threatening means" and anyone who had converted from the Jewish faith to Christianity, to be "immediately consigned to the flames and burned, together with their helpers." Moreover, anyone from

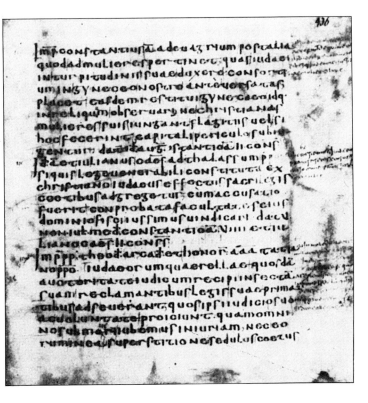

among the population who joins their abominable religion and attends their meetings, is to meet with the same well-merited punishment."

On 11 December of the same year, the emperor addressed the aforementioned letter to the Roman administration in Cologne: "We give permission by a general law to all authorities to appoint Jews to the Curia …." The offices of the Curia entailed financial burdens and a duty to extort high taxes from the population for the building of Constantinople, the new capital city of the "robber emperor." Those entrusted with the responsibility, Jews and Christians alike, therefore tended to try to excuse themselves from this honor by pleading modesty. In another imperial document dating from 1 December 331, there is, however, also mention of persons who "shall be free from any personal payment": "the rabbi … and the fathers of the synagogue, as well as all those who … hold an office in a synagogue."

The Jews were generally respected by their fellow citizens. With the increasing power of the Church, however, the situation began to change. The Church developed a system of degrading the Jews in both human and legal terms, and achieved this degradation through its influence on secular rulers and authorities. This system was largely the work of the Fathers of the Church of the 4th century, particularly the idea that the Jews were the people who had murdered Jesus. All these humiliations were finally sanctioned by Emperors Theodosius II (reigned AD 408–450) and Justinian I (reigned AD 527–565). On 31 January 439, Theodosius decreed that "no Jew … shall be allowed to hold offices or receive honors. He shall not be allowed to administer the city, neither shall he carry out the office of defending the city. We regard it as a sin that the enemies of the heavenly majesty and of the Roman law should be the executors of our laws … For the same reason we refuse permission for any synagogue to erect a new building … ."

Such imperial decrees therefore indicate that Jews did hold offices and honors, and

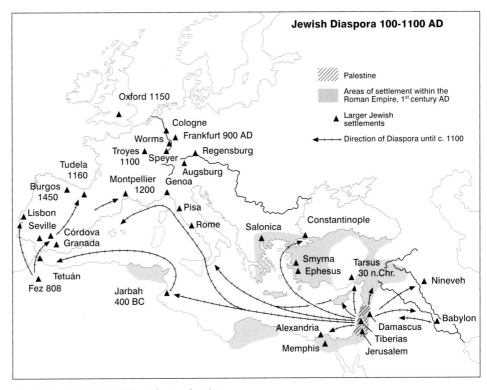

Important Jewish communities and areas of settlement between 100 and 1100 AD.

take part in the defense of the city, and build new synagogues.

THE MIDDLE AGES

*Survival and Cultural Blossoming
in a Christian Environment*

In the Frankish Empire of Charlemagne

Hardly any documents have survived from the chaotic era of the Dark Ages. However the evidence leads to the conclusion that strong Jewish communities existed in the former Roman areas of the Frankish Empire. One example is the conquest of the Moors' last stronghold in the Frankish Empire, the city of Narbonne, by Charlemagne's father Pepin III the Short (reigned 751–768) in 759. In recognition of their active help in the battle, Pippin handed over half of the city to the Jews.

Charlemagne (reigned 768–814) converted the pagans to Christianity not only by missionary activity, but also through the power of the sword. The Jews, however, were allowed to keep their religion since they were regarded as the people of the Bible. Under this emperor Jews, generally speaking, enjoyed the same rights and respect as Christians.

Like any other social groups in his empire, Charlemagne placed the Jews under his guardianship and received in return the promise of allegiance and loyalty. Imperial protection extended to life, honor, religious practice, property, and freedom of trade. Of profound consequence furthermore was the fact that the Jews were allowed to settle their civil disputes according to their own laws. This led to the establishment of a local community authority which survived until the 19th century.

Within the Frankish Empire, which stretched from the mountains of the Pyrenees to the river Elbe, the Jews continued to enjoy favorable economic conditions. After their defeat near Poitiers in 732 and Pepin's victory at Narbonne, the Muslim Arabs were largely excluded from the trade between the European Christians and the East. It was mainly Jewish merchants and seafarers who now took over caravans and trade journeys to the East as far as Palestine, Persia, India, and probably even China. The expedition members, too, were often Jews: archers for protection against enemy attacks; and craftsmen of all kinds, such as shipbuilders, coppersmiths, and sailmakers.

Around the year 870, the Arab writer Abu'l Kasim Obbaidallah Ibn Khordadbeh

Charlemagne. Contemporary portrait, detail from a mosaic in the old Lateran palace in Rome, c. AD 800.

refers to these Jewish merchant expeditions on their journey through Tabaristan where his father was governor. He calls them ar-Rhadaniya, Radanites.

"[Apart from Hebrew] the merchants speak Arabic, Persian, Latin, Frankish, Spanish, and Slavonic. They travel from west to east, from east to west, partly across country, partly across the sea. From the Occident they carry with them eunuchs, female slaves, boys, brocade, castor oil, furs of marten and other animals, and swords. They board ship in the Frankish Empire and sail to Farama [Pelusium]. There, they transfer their goods onto camels and travel across country to Suez, a journey of 25 farsakhs. They embark at the Red Sea and sail from al-Kolzom [Suez] to al-Jar [the port of Medina] and Jeddah [the port of Mecca]. Then they sail on to Sind, India, and China.

On their return from China, the merchants carry musk, aloe, camphor, cinnamon, and other products of the Orient back with them to al-Kolzom and on to Farama from where they once more cross the Western sea [Mediterranean]. Some travel to Constantinople in order to sell their goods to the Romans. Others travel to the palace of the Frankish king in order to offer their wares there.

Sometimes these Jewish merchants sail from the land of the Franks across the western sea to Antioch on the mouth of the Orontes. From there, they travel across country to al-Jabiah on the river Euphrates where they arrive after a three-day walk. They then continue their journey on the river Euphrates to Baghdad and then take the river Tigris traveling on to al-Obolla. From al-Obolla they sail to Oman, Sind, Hind, and China …

Sometimes the journey continues via Rome through the country of the Slavs to Khamlij, the capital city of the Khazars [In the 7th century, the Khazars had a powerful empire situated between the lower Volga and Don rivers. Around AD 740, their king and most of the population had converted to Judaism.] From Lake Jorjan they travel by boat to Balkh, where they cross the Oxus and continue their journey via Yurt and Toghuzghuz to China."

Other commodities which the Radanites brought to Europe included ivory, silk, rice, sugar, oranges, perfume, attar of roses, gemstones, pearls, copper, and precious glass containers. From southern Italy the traders exported silk and also the products of Venetian glassblowers.

In AD 801/02, Charlemagne sent a legation to the caliph Harun al-Rashid in Baghdad. According to the *Annales regni Francorum* ("Annals of the Kingdom of the Franks"), the delegates included a Jew named Isaac: "It was reported that the Jew Isaac, whom the Emperor had sent, along with his delegates Sigismund and Lantfrid, to the Persian king four years before, had returned laden with great gifts. Both Lantfrid and Sigismund had however died during that journey.

In October of that year, the Jew Isaac returned from Africa with an elephant and arrived in Porto Venere, a port in the Gulf of Spezia; and because he could not cross the Alps on account of the snow, he spent the winter in Vercelli. On 20 July of that year (AD 802), Isaac arrived with the elephant and the other gifts which the Persian king had sent, and presented everything to

The German imperial crown, presumed to have been made in AD 962 for Otto the Great on Reichenau (Lake Constance).

The front plate below the cross includes twelve different-colored gemstones (corresponding to the Twelve Tribes of Israel) and reproduces the breastplate of the high priest in the temple of Solomon. The figures show the biblical kings Solomon and David, who represent the good kings and whose tradition the German emperors saw themselves as following. The crown is kept in the Treasure Chamber in Vienna.

the Emperor at Aachen. The elephant bore the name Abulabaz."

Domestic trade along the Rhine was largely in the hands of the Frisians who, like the Jews, generally enjoyed imperial protection. Anglo-Saxons, Scandinavians, and Italians also came, or were summoned, to the court of the Emperor and his successors, and included both merchants and scholars.

It is likely that one of them was the Rabbi Kalonymos ben Mose from Lucca, the ancestor of the Italo-German Jewish family of Kalonymos, which produced some of the most eminent Jewish scholars in the following centuries. According to family tradition, the author Karl Wolfskehl (see page 290) and the poet Else Lasker-Schüler (see page 393) are also said to come from the Kalonymos family.

The Halcyon Days: Judaism in the 10th and 11th Centuries

The Jews continued to enjoy imperial legal protection under the Ottonians, the successors to the Carolingians. They were also granted a high degree of equality by the rulers of the Moorish-governed territories. In Moorish Spain, the foundations of a sophisticated and long-lived culture were laid by co-operation between Arab and Jewish scholars, philosophers, doctors, and diplomats.

Gradually, however, the center of the study of the Talmud shifted away from the Arab countries to the Rhine and the area which today forms northern France. Along with Lorraine, the cities of Speyer, Worms, and Mainz grew into spiritual centers for the Jews of central Europe.

Jewish scholars in that region drew up addenda to the Talmud, known as the Tosafot. Like the commentary written by the scholar Rashi of Troyes (1040–1105), they are still regarded as indispensable for the understanding of both the Bible and the Talmud.

The rich cultural period went hand in hand with a boom in the economy and a relatively long period of legal security for the Jews. It was above all Emperor Louis the Pious (reigned AD 814–840) who had granted legal protection for individuals as well as for whole groups of non-Christian inhabitants who had no legal rights. Indeed, he had even been subjected to bitter attacks by the archbishops of Mainz and Lyons because of this. But as time passed, even the bishops attracted more and more Jews to the seats of their bishoprics in order to promote the welfare of their towns. Thus Rüdiger of Speyer, for example, when he elevated the village of Speyer to the status of town in 1084, said:

BELOW: The capital of a column with a Hebrew inscription in the synagogue in Worms, 12th century. The inscription reads: The pearl decoration of "the two columns" / he produced without "casual hands" / Also the "spherical knobs," / On which he hung "the lamps" (Chronogram for 1174/75).

LEFT: A lane in the Jewish quarter in Worms near the medieval synagogue (picture taken before its destruction during World War II).

BELOW: The Rashi School in Worms (later building).

"I, Rüdiger, ... When I changed the village of Speyer into a town, I believed that I could add to the honor of our town even more by gathering all the Jews together ... and in order that they should not be disturbed by the high spirits of the rabble, I had a wall built around them." The bishop granted the Jews full freedom within the city, the right to defense and the duty of military service, and even a burial site – "laws ... that are better than any enjoyed by the Jewish inhabitants of any other town within the German kingdom." Jewish visitors were not subject to city customs duties.

This certificate of protection was endorsed by Emperor Henry IV (reigned 1056–1106) in 1090, and given further weight by his reception of a delegation of three which included a member of the respected Kalonymos family.

Treatment as generous as that was, however, not the rule. In 1012, for example, the majority of the Jewish population of Mainz, about 2000 or so people, were expelled from the city. This constituted the first known expulsion of Jews in Germany.

Despite this, thriving Jewish communities sprang up in the cities of Cologne, Bonn, Mainz, Trier, Metz, Koblenz, Strasbourg, Bingen, Speyer, Worms, Andernach, and elsewhere between the Rhine and Moselle. There is a report dating back to the 12th century by the Jewish merchant and traveler Benjamin of Tudela about those communities "in the land of Alemania." He furthermore mentions Münster, Bamberg, Freising, and Regensburg. "There are many Jews in these cities, wise and rich people." The synagogue of Worms had been built along the

ABOVE: The Emperor Henry IV's privilege for the Jews of Worms, 1074.

clear lines of Romanesque architecture in 1174/75 and survived until it was burned down on *Kristallnacht*, 9 November 1938.

The everyday language used by the Jews was Middle High German, as spoken in the towns or in the country. Hebrew was used for prayer and study, as well as for civil law documents.

It was also characteristic of the Jewish life of the time that scholars were regarded as the most important members of the community, and that the prosperous families moreover produced most of the scholars and local councilors. Talmud schools were established in the larger communities along the Rhine in the 10th and 11th centuries. Through their collaboration with similar centers in France, the Rhenish Talmud schools soon reached a status equal to that of the centuries-old institutions in Spain, North Africa, Palestine, and Babylonia, and before long even eclipsed them in importance. The school of the "Ashkenazim," the "Germans," as they were called in rabbinical literature, was to become a thriving center of Judaism for more than half a millennium. Since that time, the term "Ashkenazim" has been applied to all the Jews in Europe including those in Russia (although not those of Spain and Portugal).

All these schools were connected by a continuous exchange of teachers and expert opinions. It has already been mentioned that one of the teachers at Troyes, for example, was Rabbi Salomon ben Isaak. Known as Rashi (*Rabbi Sh*lomoh ben *Isaak*), he was the greatest medieval commentator of the Bible and the Talmud, and had studied in Mainz and Worms. The rebuilt legendary "Rashi chapel" can still be visited in Worms today. His commentaries have remained an integral part of the study of the Bible and the Talmud and hence also of religious education.

Before Rashi, it was Rabbi Gerschom ben Juda (960–1028) who had been active in Mainz. He was known as "the light of the Diaspora" and was the leading authority of the Ashkenazi Jews of the age. He banned, amongst other things, the practice of polygamy which was common until then, and any divorce against the will of the wife. He also introduced the principle of the secrecy of correspondence.

It is thanks to the Jewish academies above all of Worms, Speyer and Mainz that the Ashkenazi school of Talmud interpretation became dominant in large parts

Jewish settlement in Germany before 1238, according to "Germania Judaica"

ABOVE: Cabalistic decorations around the word "Melech" ("king, King of Heaven") in a 13th-century prayer book.

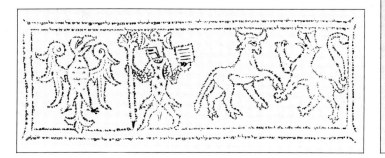

ABOVE: The four creatures (chayot) from the visions of the prophet Ezekiel: lion, bull, man, and eagle; executed in microscript. Germany, 13th century.

ABOVE: Süsskind of Trimberg, a Jewish singer, before religious dignitaries. Miniature from the Manesse manuscript (1300–1340).

LEFT: Tombstone of Meshullam ben Kalonymos in Mainz, c. 1020. The inscription reads: "Here is buried / Rabbana Meshullam / Son of Rabbana Rabbi / Kalonymos / May his soul be bound to the group of those destined for life (everlasting)."

of Europe. Instrumental in this were members of the extensive Kalonymos family. In the 12th and 13th centuries, some of this family emerged as representatives of "German Hasidism," a movement of an ascetic and mystic nature which determined the orientation and expression of Jewish piety for a long time.

The Bible, the Talmud, the commentaries, and other Hebrew books were all illuminated and illustrated by artists. A particular Ashkenazi manner of chanting the Bible and prayer melodies developed. This development continued even during the mass murders which devastated the Jewish communities after the beginning of the Crusades.

In the Lions' Den – the Age of the Crusades

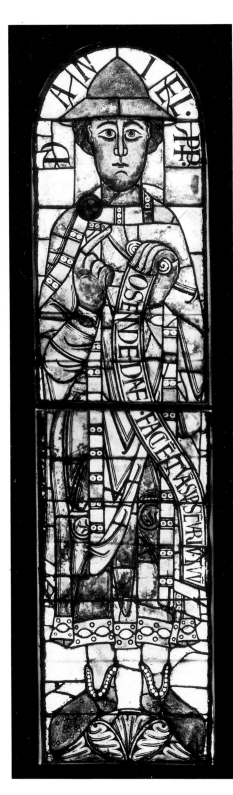

LEFT: Daniel, stained glass window in Augsburg Cathedral, c. 1130. The model for this depiction was presumably a Jew.

ABOVE: Crusaders. From an illuminated manuscript. France, 13th century.

In spite of enforced baptism and isolated instances of persecution, the 10th and 11th centuries saw a general stabilization of the situation of the Jews, both as individuals and as a group within society. They were active in many professions, not least as craftsmen and winegrowers. Their work in local, national, and international trade was therefore useful to the rulers and hence promoted.

This situation seemed to be little affected even by the fact that in the year 1078, after Emperor Henry IV's journey to Canossa, Pope Gregory VII issued a bull banning Jews from holding any official positions in Christian countries.

But only a few years later, the massacres of the Jews during the First Crusade (1090–1099) made clear just how dangerous the merely conditional toleration of the Jews was. Under the leadership of Peter of Amiens, thousands of impoverished peasants, artisans, and beggars marched to the Rhine, massacred the Jews, and stole their possessions.

From his base in Italy, Henry IV tried to stop these excesses by issuing an edict protecting the Jews. But the edict had little or no impact: those who refused to be baptized were murdered. The Emperor later allowed those who had undergone forced baptism to reconvert to Judaism.

Emperor Frederick Barbarossa as a crusader. After a miniature dating from 1188. This is the only known contemporary depiction.

The Jews defended themselves in their own areas of the towns or in the seats of the bishoprics where they had fled. If defense seemed hopeless, the community members in some towns or villages would gather together to pray and say their creed ("Shema Israel"), and then kill one another. In this way, they would not have to desecrate the name of God, according to the tradition of the "Kiddush Hashem," the "Observance of His Name."

In Speyer, the Jews got off lightly, suffering a "mere" eleven casualties and temporary evacuation. In Mainz, the Jewish community was initially protected by the archbishop, but later handed over. The 1300 expelled Jews were murdered, among them their spokesman Meshullam ben Kalonymos, who had asked Emperor Henry IV for help. Similar massacres and instances of self-sacrifice occurred in the cities of Xanten, Trier, Strasbourg, Verdun, and Worms.

The murdering of the Jews was opposed by the initiator of the Second Crusade (1147/48), Bernard of Clairvaux. This time, a significantly smaller number of Jews were massacred under the sign of the Cross.

At that time, many fled to the forests or fought their way through to Poland. They brought diligence and a commercial spirit to their new homelands, as well as the High German language of their former Rhenish and Frankish homes. Eventually, with a few additions from Hebrew, Polish and Russian, it developed into Yiddish.

After the persecutions, small groups of Jews returned to their devastated neighborhoods, often having been called back by the towns' magistrates and rulers.

In the wake of the persecution there was an increased following of the movement of "the pious in Germany," and there developed an ever stronger longing for the coming of the Messiah.

Apart from the many funeral hymns and elegies, the 13th century also saw the origin of the traditional Hanukkah song "Maos Zur": "O fortress, rock of my salvation … ." It is a plea for rapid salvation from the enemy, and an expression of the Messianic hope for the re-erection of the temple, as had once successfully been done by the Maccabees in the 2nd century BC. The Hanukkah celebration is a reminder of that recovery of the Jews' national and religious freedom. The song, however, also alludes to the persecutions by Muslims and Christians, and according to an old tradition, the sixth verse refers to Admon the Red, Emperor Frederick I (Barbarossa):

"Reveal Your Holy Power
And advance the time of help.
Take revenge for the blood of Your
    servants
On the evil people.
For we have already waited too long for
    Your help
And there is no end to our suffering.
Push out Admon in the shadow of the
    graven image
And send us the seven shepherds."

35

The Pillars of Judaism

LEFT: First page of the Schocken Bible. It was written on vellum and illuminated c. 1300 in southern Germany, probably in the Constance area. The first word of the Bible, "Bereshit" (in the beginning) is framed by 46 medallions. They show, in chronological order from top right to bottom left, events from the Pentateuch.

ABOVE: A page from the earliest completely intact manuscript of the "Babylonian Talmud," dating from 1334. The Mishna is written in large script, while the appropriate Gemara is written in small letters.

When the Jews left the devastated city of Jerusalem they took with them into the Diaspora their spiritual property, namely, their sacred writings, the Bible, the word of their One and Only God. In addition to that they had their oral traditions which were written down in the Talmud and completed in the 5th and 6th centuries.

The Bible comprises:

1. the Torah (instruction, law): the Five Books of Moses. One section of the Torah is read in the synagogue on each Sabbath over a one-year cycle in the presence of at least ten males aged over 13 (minyan);

2. the Prophets: the history books from Joshua to the Kings, the Great Prophets Isaiah, Jeremiah, and Ezekiel, and the Book of the Twelve Prophets; on the Sabbath, the reading from the Torah is followed by a section from the Prophets;

3. the Writings: the historical books, with the Psalms at the beginning.

The sacred writings in general, and the Five Books of Moses in particular, have fulfilled another function: since the intro-duction of schools prior to the destruction of the Second Temple, they have also served as readers for children. This is still the case today.

The parts of the Bible containing the Law were developed further and edited around the year AD 200 by Rabbi Judah ha-Nasi in a collection known as the Mishna ("repetition"). The Mishna was spread by word of mouth in countless scholars' pronouncements in Palestine and Babylon.

Around AD 500, the collected material was recorded in its final form in the Gemara ("final completion"). The Mishna and the Gemara together form the Talmud. Hence the Talmud is an interpretation of the traditional oral law (Mishna), accompanied by a wealth of interpretations, parables, fables, narratives, wise sayings and practical experience in fields such as psychology, astronomy, medicine, and hygiene. The Talmud has remained the fundamental source for all later versions of the Halakah, the religious law, because it contains regulations governing religious ritual as well as civil, criminal and commercial law.

From the early Middle Ages right through to the present day, the normative practice of Orthodox Judaism in the Diaspora has been determined by the Babylonian Talmud. However, the Middle Ages saw a far-reaching emancipation of the Ashkenazi Jews, away from the hierarchically autocratic Babylonian school, and towards the more democratic roots to be found in the Mishna. The Bible and the Talmud were supplemented by the prayer book for weekdays and holidays, and by the liturgy. The Mahzor ("cycle") is the prayer-book for religious holidays.

All prayers culminate in the following confession: "Shema Israel ... Hear, O Israel, the Lord our God is one Lord." (Deuteronomy 6,4). Then the devout Jew asks God for his personal welfare, the welfare of the community, the early coming of the Messiah, and peace throughout the entire world.

This was therefore the spiritual armory which the Jews brought from their home-land to the countries of the Diaspora. These were the teachings to which they adhered and which they adapted according to the requirements of their daily lives.

The Sephardi Moses ben Maimon, called Maimonides (1135 Cordoba – 1204 Tiberias), personal physician to the famous Sultan Saladin of Egypt, was the most eminent Jewish philosopher and teacher of law of the Middle Ages. Regarded as the highest authority, he corresponded extensively with Jewish communities as far apart as Yemen and Syria and southern France, advising them in matters philosophical and theological, as well as legal and practical.

Maimonides' most important works were the *Moreh Nevikhim* ("Guide for the Perplexed") and the *Mishne Thora* ("The Thora Reviewed"). In the latter, Maimonides gave a summary in clear, comprehensible Hebrew of the traditions and life experiences of the Jews, laid out according to Aristotelian systematics, a reorganization of all the legal texts contained in the Talmud according to factual categories.

In Germany, too, Maimonides' work became an integral component of the study of Jewish religion, despite the fact that

Rashi commentary on the Book of Daniel, written by Salomo ben Samuel of Würzburg, 1233.

A page from a collection of prayers (Mahzor of Worms) designed to be used by the prayer-leader. Mainz, c. 1272. The camel and elephant drivers have no connection to the text. The picture might possibly be a decorative depiction of Abulabaz, the elephant presented to Charlemagne by the Jew, Isaac, as a gift from Harun al-Rashid. The colophon (not pictured) reads: "I, Simcha bar [son of] Juda the scribe, wrote [it] in 1272 for my uncle, Rabbi Baruch bar Isaak...."

some scholars objected to the Aristotelian influence in his philosophy.

An Ashkenazi authority on Talmud interpretation was Asher ben Yehiel (c. 1250–1327). Unlike Maimonides, but in agreement with a number of other Jewish scholars, he rejected any inclusion of philosophy in religious studies. Initially Asher ben Yehiel was active in Koblenz, Cologne, and Worms.

During the beef pogrom of 1298 (see page 50), he supported his community before the Christian authorities. He escaped the massacres; but in 1303 he fled Germany in order to avoid meeting the same fate as his teacher, Rabbi Meïr ben Baruch from Rothenburg ob der Tauber (1215–1293). When he attempted to emigrate to Palestine in 1286, Rabbi Meïr was arrested on the orders of Emperor Rudolf I. Until his death in 1293, he was incarcerated first in the moated castle of Mainz and later in Ensisheim, because in agreement with the communities, he had refused to be ransomed for an enormous sum of money.

Illuminated manuscripts by Asher ben Yehiel and other contemporary scholars have survived and represent the high points of Hebrew book culture.

Ecclesia and Synagoga

ABOVE: Ecclesia with lance and shield, and Synagoga with sword (far right). Ivory reliefs on the book cover of a Gospel book from St. Godehard in Hildesheim, c. 1160–1200.

When Christianity became the official state religion of the Roman Empire in the 4th century, it was also endowed with the political and legal means to suppress other faiths. It was Saint Augustine (AD 354–430) who defined the position of Christianity toward Judaism in terms of the collective guilt of the Jews for the death of Christ, an idea that remained influential far beyond the Middle Ages.

It made no difference that this monstrous claim was repeatedly proved to be historically impossible and ethically unworthy of any religious belief. In the 18th volume of his work, "The City of God," Augustine wrote: "The Jews, however, who killed him and would not believe that he had to die and be resurrected, suffered even more greatly under the Romans. They were eradicated root and branch from their homeland, where they had

LEFT: From a prayer book dating from the 13th century: a hidden parody of the representation of Ecclesia and Synagoga found in many churches. Ecclesia, represented by a woman wearing a crown, is seen sitting in front of a young man wearing a Jewish hat. In this illustration, Ecclesia is wearing a blindfold, usually an attribute of Synagoga.

BELOW: Christ on the pillar is being tortured by the "ugly Jew." Detail from the Christ window of the Minorite church in Regensburg, around 1360.

already been living under foreign rule, and were scattered across all lands, so that they can be found anywhere. Now they must prove to us through their writings that we have not made up the prophecies of Christ." Saint Augustine's accusation has formed the foundation for the theological comparisons in art and literature between the triumphant Ecclesia and the humiliated Synagoga.

Allegorical representations of this subject can be traced back to before the 11th century. They were however usually without the outward signs of the Church triumphing over the Synagogue: with open eyes, the Synagogue is shown to turn away from the Cross, while holding its lance or banner high. Walther von der Vogelweide had still proclaimed in his praise of God: "Christians, Jews, and heathens serve HIM." It was only after the increasingly intensive religious, social, and economic suppression brought about mainly by the resolutions of the Fourth Lateran Council of 1215 that the Synagoga was finally depicted blindfold, and with a broken lance. An example of such a representation can be found in Strasbourg Cathedral.

The claim that the Jews were collectively to blame for the death of Jesus also found expression in the popular passion plays which were instrumental in shaping the anti-Semitic attitudes of the broad mass of the population. In the Passion play of Donaueschingen, dating from the second half of the 15th century, Christiana, the allegorical church (*Ecclesia militans*) addresses Judaea, the allegorical synagogue:

"As a sign that you are blind / and that you have a wrong faith / I blindfold your eyes / and break your banner in two."

In the Oberammergau passion play, which was revised by Joseph Alois Daisenberger in 1850/60, the Jewish people were again accused of murdering Christ. It was not until the 1970s that the local council saw fit to remove these absurd accusations from the script.

A Jewish prayer book from the 13th century contains a strange illustration in which the roles of the Church and the

Ecclesia and Synagoga on Strasbourg Cathedral, c. 1230.

Synagogue seem to have experienced a satirical reversal. Ecclesia, who can be recognized by her crown bearing a large cross, is shown wearing a blindfold, while the smaller figure of Synagoga is placed in front of her.

However much the Jews might have been suppressed in legal and social terms, they still insisted on their religious superi-

ority, as did Christians and Muslims. Their conviction of being the only true monotheists made them determined never to accept the fate of a Synagogue that had been the subject of religious humiliation. The Church, however, had the secular means to enforce its claim of religious superiority, at least as far as worldly consequences were concerned.

Hereticization by the Church

Berthold of Regensburg preaching. Colored pen drawing, 15th century.

"The Jewish Sow" on the wall of Regensburg Cathedral, 13th century (wood engraving, 19th century).

Hereticization by the Church was initiated by Pope Innocent III and was to have devastating consequences for the Jews. The Fourth Lateran Council of 1215 stipulated, for example, that all Jews were to be excluded from working as craftsmen. Thus, the Jews were forced into the role of pawnbrokers, money changers, and usurers, very public offices and therefore often hated. Whilst the churches were accumulating great wealth, the peasants and the common people in the cities were becoming more and more impoverished. "The poor children of God are in such a state that some of them can scarcely afford to cover their loins," preached Berthold of Regensburg (c. 1220–1272).

The guilty party was "the rich man." Since there was nothing the poor could do against the rich Christians, their spiritual and worldly rulers, and the clergy were unwilling to take any measures against those rich people, the hatred of the population was directed at the Jews, who in their positions as pawnbrokers lived almost exclusively by means of "usury," that is to say, interest. Christians were not allowed to charge interest, a ban that remained in force until 1435.

Thus "the Jew" became the tool and the scapegoat of the rising capitalist economic system. What remained hidden from the common people was the fact that the initiators and beneficiaries, the actual usurers, were not the Jews but completely different people – namely the merchants, and even the Church itself and some of its orders, such as the Templars. The financial institutions of the Templars, for example, enjoyed considerable profits from the pilgrim traffic to the Holy Land, in whose conquest and loss they had participated equally. "The Temple" in London and "Le Temple" in Paris are still monuments to the former treasure chambers of the Knights Templars. Since the Church did not allow them to charge interest, the Templars lent money to noblemen and in return received partial repayments which added up to a much higher total sum than that originally lent. They charged extortionate rates of interest, only under a dif-

Pope Innocent III (reigned 1198–1216), who among other things forced Jews to wear the distinctive pointed hats and issued a strict ban on usury for Christians, thus restricting employment possibilities for Jews to financial transactions and the charging of interest. Fresco, 13th century, in Sacro Speco, Subiaco.

A roof tile from the church of Ravensburg decorated with the head of a Jew (14th century). It is not clear whether the figure is intended to incite fear, or serve as a memorial to the murders of 1348.

ferent name; and yet nobody accused the Templars of being thieves and usurers, accusations which were leveled against the Jewish financiers and pawnbrokers. The Franciscan friar Berthold of Regensburg, the greatest popular preacher of his time, conceded that the Jews had their positive side, namely piety, religious strictness, discipline and moderation in marriage. But again and again he assured his listeners that the Jews were nevertheless robbers and thieves and, like pagans and heretics, slaves of the devil.

Since the time of the Crusades, the Commandment "Thou shalt not kill" had been largely excluded from the moral code where Jews were concerned. The general population often looked upon them as outlaws and, because of their usury, as real robbers and thieves. In the eyes of the clergy the Jews were not exactly heathens, but at least heretics if they refused to be baptized.

Jews in Christian Art

The protagonists of the Jewish sacred writings, the Old Testament, were regarded by the teachings of the Church as a prefiguration of the New Testament. Therefore they were treated sympathetically in literature and art. But the Jews of the New Testament were less fortunate. With the exception of Jesus and his family, eleven of his twelve Disciples, and his followers, Jews are represented in a distorted manner and often with repulsive features. Their portrayal is, in fact, an early form of deliberate caricature for propaganda purposes.

Where figures of the Old Testament are concerned, medieval art often depicted Jews in portraitlike fashion and in contemporary costume: women were depicted with the traditional headband, and men with their pointed hats. Features and dress are often rendered in a very realistic manner, above all in book miniatures and in naive representations.

The determining factor for the costumes were the regulations issued by both the Jewish and the Christian communities. During the 13th century, for example, the rabbinical synods of the religious community between the cities of Speyer, Worms and Mainz decided, amongst other things, that: "Nobody is to wear their hair in a non-Jewish fashion or to cut their beards … Nobody is to go to the synagogue without wearing a cape or an overcoat." And at the Fourth Lateran Council, called in 1215 by Pope Innocent III, canonical law number 68 was issued on the order of the Pope stating that all Jews and Saracens had to wear a costume which visibly distinguished them from the Christians. This would ensure that the "damned intercourse between them and the Christians" that might occur "by mistake" could be avoided. This was when Jewish symbols (such as the yellow circle on clothing) and the pointed hat became obligatory, at least in theory.

To be marked was regarded as a humiliation by the Jews. In many places the secular authorities were therefore reluctant to

LEFT: Head of a Prophet on the northwest tower of Bamberg Cathedral, c. 1240.

RIGHT: The march of the Jews through the Red Sea. Font relief in Hildesheim Cathedral, 1220. Bronze cast.

Joshua riding off to battle (Joshua 10,12: "Then spoke Joshua … in the sight of Israel, Sun, stand thou still upon Gibeon; and thou, Moon, in the valley of Ajalon"). From Rudolf von Ems, "Chronicle of the World," c.1250.

comply with the papal orders or ignored them altogether, so that the Church had to renew them constantly.

Ridiculous in appearance and highly uncomfortable to wear, the pointed Jews' hat was found in pictures more than in everyday life. In Augsburg, for example, the Jewish badge to be worn on the coat, the Jewish beard and a modified version of the Jews' hat were not made obligatory by the city council until 1434. Nuremberg and Bamberg followed suit in 1451, and Frankfurt am Main in 1452. The Jews' manner of dress, however, had been stipulated much earlier.

Towards the end of the Middle Ages, in paintings of the Gothic and Renaissance periods, it is noticeable that the Jews of the Old Testament were very often portrayed with non-Jewish features and wearing non-Jewish clothes. The Jews of the New Testament, on the other hand, continued to be depicted in a repulsive manner. This kind of depiction is responsible for the iconographical stereotype of the ugly Jew in Christian art. The outwardly visible repulsiveness was supposed to mirror the inner person, thus marking the Jews as the murderers of Jesus Christ.

ABOVE: The Betrothal of Mary. From an early 13th-century psalter.

BELOW: The Exodus from Egypt. From the "Chronicle of the World" of Rudolf von Ems.

The Legal Position of the Jews in the High Middle Ages

TOP: Seal of Emperor Frederick II (reigned 1212–1250).

LEFT: Emperor Henry VII (reigned 1308–1313) receiving a Jewish delegation outside the gates of Rome, and endorsing their old rights. Miniature from the *Codex Balduinensis*.

From the Carolingian era onward, eminent Jewish merchants were granted special privileges which raised them out of the sphere of their co-religionists to a legal position nearer to that of the Christians. The extension of such individual privileges to a whole Jewish community (as had been done for the first time in the general peace of Mainz in 1103) did not mean that the Jews were included in the generally valid common law. It did mean, however, that they were at least temporarily put on an equal footing with those unarmed groups of society which needed, and were granted, protection, namely monks and women. It is possible that this temporary protection of the Jews was a reaction to the horrors of the Crusades. This more or less protected status, which varied from place to place, remained in force for the Jews in Germany who had survived the massacres of the Crusades until well into the 13th century – at least in theory.

Some bishops associated with Jews for economic or even cultural reasons. Their attitude was shared by some secular rulers, patricians, master craftsmen, peasants, and simple ordinary people. Christian book illuminators, for example, illustrated Jewish books, an indication of the existence of cultural and probably also human relationships.

In 1236, Emperor Frederick II (reigned 1212–1250) granted a new privileged status for the Jews in his empire. On the one hand, he placed them under his imperial protection. This meant protection on country roads and lanes, freedom of movement and of residence, and exemption from special financial duties to rulers and towns.

Once again, therefore, the existence of the Jews seemed safeguarded. On the other hand, however, the Emperor declared the Jews to be his "serfs of the chamber" (*servi camerae*). In other words, they were his personal possessions with whom he could do as he pleased, an equal status with his forests and his cattle. The Jews were not included in the general common law and were in need of special protection from special payments.

Several factors accounted for the fact that the Jews largely lost their position in domestic and international trade. One was the decline of feudalism and the associated

LEFT: Seal of the Jewish community of Augsburg from the year 1298. The seal depicts the imperial double eagle, with the pointed Jews' hat between the two heads.

strengthening of merchants' associations and guilds; another the development of the cities as marketplaces for the transfer of goods. The Jews were moreover pushed out of large-scale finance because this was increasingly dealt with by monasteries and the new municipal trade companies from the 14th century onward.

Those who were in debt with interest-bearing loans from Jewish pawnbrokers increasingly tended to be impoverished knights, the poorer townspeople, and above all poor peasants. Not only did the peasants have to pay their tithes to the church, but also pay duty to the lord of the manor and do certain tasks for him.

In the eyes of the common man, the Jews became the exploiters of the people because of their function as pawnbrokers. The majority of non-Jews were hardly aware of the fact that the Jews had to pass on vast sums of money to the emperor, the princes, and the cities. On more than one occasion, when the emperors were in acute financial difficulties or needed money to finance their wars, they pawned the taxes paid by the Jews for their protection to princes and cities. These, in turn, used the money to finance special projects, such as the building of expensive churches and palaces, for which they often imposed further special taxes on the Jewish population. As a reward for having to pay these additional

RIGHT: The Jewish tower of Constance, built by the Jewish community in the 14th century for the defense of the city.

Excerpt from the laws governing trade and industry in Landshut, 1256. Paragraph 12 reads "leprous meat and meat infested by tapeworm larvae must be sold at a distance of 7 feet from the meat market; the same goes for the meat of the Jews. Anyone contravening this rule is to pay 5 pounds and stay away from the meat market for 1 year."

ABOVE: "Feiselein, the King of the Jews." Picture of a Jew in Jewish costume with hat and Torah roll from the town book of Landshut, 1361.

King Solomon, the prototype of the just ruler, and the representatives of the trades – the two depicted lowest are Jews. From a southern German collection of laws, second half of the 12th century.

Privilege of the city of Speyer for their Jewish community, 1333. The document states that the Jewish council and the "Jewish bishop" are to be elected by the Jews without any interference from the city council.

taxes, the Jews were allowed to participate in the defense of the city with their own weapons. And if they were prepared to pay yet another tax, they were sometimes even allowed to become temporary citizens.

The legal position of the Jews is recorded in the "Jews' rules" which were in force from the Middle Ages until well into the 19th century and which stipulated their rights and duties. These rules were supplemented by regulations internal to the community and applying to the Jewish population by order of rulers or municipal authorities. The Jewish communities also had their own regulations for life both inside and outside their communities.

Certain forms of the "Jewish oath" were particularly humiliating. The legal code known as the "Schwabenspiegel," for example, demanded that in order to take an oath, a Jew had to put on a belt of thorns, get into the water, spit on his penis three times, and then take the oath which included cursing himself if he had committed perjury. The legal codes of Saxony and other areas stipulated that Jews taking an oath had to stand on the fresh skin of a sow which had given birth within the previous fortnight.

Despite all this, it was possible for close cultural relationships to develop between Jews and Germans. Thus legends, like those of Gudrun and Arthur, and poems and songs were taken over into the colloquial language of the Jews and written down in Hebrew script.

The Jewish minnesinger Süsskind of Trimberg (second half of the 13th century) must have been an isolated case. A picture of Süsskind wearing the Jews' hat is recorded in the *Manessische Liederhandschrift* (a songmanuscript attributed to the Zurich collector Manesse, c. 1310/30), which also contains some songs with the heading *Sueskint der Jude von Trimperg* ("Süsskind the Jew of Trimberg"). None of the medieval lyric poems taken over by him contains a reference to the cult of Mary, a subject normally found in minnesong. There are, on the other hand, echoes of biblical and rabbinical literature. One of his poems reads:

"... and I shall grow a long gray beard.
According to the old Jewish custom
I shall live henceforth
and quietly go my own way.
My long coat shall envelop me
deep beneath my hat.
Let me now walk in humility ..."

Depictions of Jews in Eike von Repgow's *Sachsenspiegel*, a code of law written between 1220 and 1235.

A respectable Jew, either a Franconian or a Saxon, is allowed to complain before the count; a Wend (left) is not.

Like monks, clergymen, and women, Jews are under the protection of the king, who is pointing to the lily of peace.

A Christian kills a Jew and is beheaded for this crime.

A Jew is hanged because he has committed an offense.

Armed Jews and clergymen are to be treated in the same way as unarmed people, because thanks to the general peace they are not required to carry arms.

The Blood Lie, the Lie of the Host and the Black Death

LEFT: A letter from King Conrad IV to the citizens of Frankfurt, stating that on behalf of his father (Emperor Frederick II), he waives his right to damages for the murder of the Jews in the year 1241.

RIGHT: A decree by Emperor Rudolf I against the "blood libel," 1275.

BELOW: Jews being burned, 1348. Contemporary illustration.

In the first century after Christ, the Romans accused the Christians of using the blood of murdered human beings for ritual purposes – the first accusation of its kind.

A Jewish writer of the 13th century reported from the Rhineland that "Christians, out of sheer malice and in order to irritate us," used knives to cut holes into the parchment rolls of the mezuzot. The latter are small cases made from wood or metal attached to the right-hand jamb of the front door. They hold small parchment rolls containing verses from the holy scriptures, in accordance with Deuteronomy 6: 4–9, and 11: 13–21. This sacrilege might, in turn, have been responsible for the accusation that Jews had stolen the Host and drilled holes through it. The same century saw the emergence of the notorious "blood libel," which alleged that the Jews had killed a Christian child in order to use its blood for the preparation of the matzah, the Passover bread.

After carrying out a strict and thorough examination of these accusations, Emperor Frederick II sent a letter to the bishops and authorities in which he declared them to be nonsense.

For the Jews, the consumption of any blood, including that of animals, is an abominable and unforgivable act directly contravening God's commandments. It is therefore strictly forbidden. Nonetheless, the slanderous accusations leveled against the Jews continued without ever having to be proved, despite the fact that many popes, emperors, scholars, and judges repeatedly declared them to be lies. For the Jews, the slander had fatal consequences.

In 1298, an impoverished knight called Rindfleisch spread the rumor that the Host had been desecrated in Röttingen in Franconia. He claimed to have received a personal message from heaven, nominating him as the destroyer of all Jews. For six months he and his gang of murderers roamed through more than 140 villages in

Franconia and Swabia. They tortured, raped, and burned thousands of Jews, men and women, and murdered their children. In Rothenburg ob der Tauber there is still one commemorative stone reminding us of the massacre of 1298: "A bitter lamentation from a bitter soul. Because the earlier visitations have been forgotten, I have engraved into this slab of stone the names of the martyrs of Rothenburg who were beaten to death and burnt for the uniqueness of God in the year 5058 on the 19th of Tammuz. Within the fortification of the city, the citizens destroyed, burned, and murdered, and both the young and the old of our community perished … ." The citizens of Augsburg and Regensburg were the only ones to protect their Jewish fellow-citizens. A number of the persecuted managed to escape to Poland and Lithuania.

The next instance of persecution affected the Jewish communities in an area from Alsace to as far across as Swabia and Austria. In 1336, a number of impoverished peasants, robber barons, and marauding and thieving riffraff had gathered together under the leadership of the "King of the Arm Leathers," (so called because they wore a piece of leather around their arm). Calling themselves the "Judenschläger" ("Jew bashers"), they wiped out many Jewish communities. The protection pledged by Emperor Louis the Bavarian (reigned 1314–1347) failed to materialize.

Twelve years later, in 1348, another wave of persecution befell the Jews. At that time Europe was devastated by the plague, which within two years claimed the lives of 25 million people. Today we know that the epidemic was transferred via fleas from rats to humans. Then, however, a guilty party had to be found. On the orders of the Count of Savoy, a number of Jews in the Geneva region were tortured until they "confessed" to having poisoned the wells. "The Jew" had thus been established as the scapegoat for the Divine Judgment represented by the plague.

The news reached Germany via Strasbourg: "On the Saturday – it was St. Valentine's Day (February 14th) – the Jews were burned in Strasbourg in their churchyard on a wooden scaffolding. And anything owed to the Jews was regarded as settled, and any securities and letters they had referring to debts were returned. Any cash owned by the Jews was taken by the council and distributed among the craft trades… Thus it was that the Jews were burned in Strasbourg, and in the same year in all cities along the Rhine, whether they were free cities or not …"

This was reported by Jakob Twinger von Königshofen in his chronicle. Similar events took place in more than two hundred villages and towns. Even in regions which had been spared from the ravages of the plague, such as Silesia, the Jews were nevertheless burned. Where there were no Jews, those Jews who had converted to Christianity were burned instead. This time, the killings extended also to areas in Poland.

Even after this tide of persecution, the surviving Jews attempted to rebuild their lives once again. Very often they were called back because they were indispensable to the municipal economic life. For almost one hundred years, they once again lived in relative security. The accusations did not arise again until the middle of the 15th century, when the hate campaign against the Jews was above all stirred up by the Dominicans, who accused them of the desecration of the Host and of ritual child murder.

ABOVE: The Polish king Casimir III (reigned 1333–1370) welcomes the refugees from Germany with open arms. Historical painting, 19th century.

LEFT: Tombstone of a female martyr, Trier, 1348.

Survival in Town and Countryside

The text near the right edge of the image reads: *Iuden erhalten de
prepstlichen Sige*

In cities and towns, such as Magdeburg,
and in Bohemia, the Jewish communities
in all parts of the Empire formed a corpo-
ration of their own largely with internal
autonomy.

At the beginning of the 13th century,
however, the working life of the Jews began
to experience considerable restrictions, as
explained above. From then on, they were
prohibited from working in agriculture,
craft, trade, and commerce. Generally, there
remained virtually nothing but work as
pawnbrokers and moneylenders, that is,
giving credit and charging interest for it.

The interest rate that the Jews were
allowed to charge was precisely regulated by
the pope, the emperor, or the city council.

The higher the sum of the debt became, however, the more the Jewish moneylenders had
to fear for their lives. It was also fairly
common for them to lose their possessions.
Thus King Wenceslas IV (reigned
1378–1400), for example, twice (in 1385
and in 1390) granted his Christian subjects
an amnesty on paying their so-called "Jewish
debts." Instead they had to pay lower sums
of money to himself, the King. The following
passage is found in the "Limburg Chronicle"
(c. 1400): "16 September 1390 ... the King

has decided in favor of the princes and the
trades of the realm that anyone who is
indebted to a Jew shall be exempted from his
obligation to pay this debt, be it the principal
or the interest. He has further decreed that
any demand for payment a Jew made against
a Christian would not be regarded as valid
and not allowed to proceed."

For this favor, which brought in large
sums of money for both parties, the Duke
of Bavaria, the Bishop of Würzburg, and
the Count of Oettingen each paid the king
15,000 guilders. The Jews lost their money.

As early as 1356, Emperor Charles IV
had sold to the Electors the right to take in
Jews and to tax them. The only source of
income from the Jews that he kept for him-

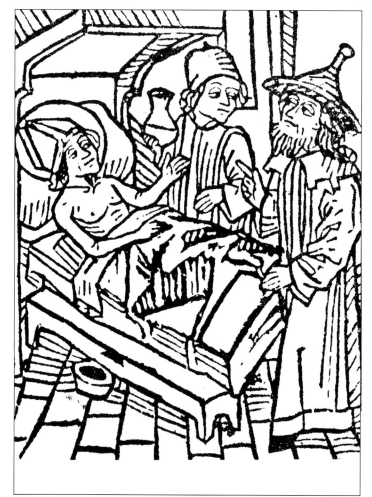

LEFT: A Jewish doctor and his patient. From : Hans Schobser (printer), *Plenarium*, Augsburg 1487.

RIGHT: A Jew in the customary Jewish costume and the "Jews' mark," a circle on the shoulder. Southern Germany, 14th century.

BELOW: Jewish beggar types. Details from a wood engraving after a pen-and-ink drawing by Hieronymus Bosch (c. 1450–1516).

self was the poll tax they had to pay, the so-called "golden penny." From then on it was very rare for princes and cities to grant residence permits to groups of Jews, since they preferred to give it to individual persons of good financial standing and potential. This led to a downgrading of many other Jews who had little money and now had to struggle through life as vagabonds and beggars. A realistic pen-and-ink drawing by Hieronymus Bosch (Albertina, Vienna) produced toward the end of the 15th century shows a number of vagrants, beggars, and minstrels, among them Jewish types who are recognizable by their headgear.

Their precarious legal and social situation led to a strong sense of insecurity

Jewish money changer, c. 1450: "Write my name and the name of my father on the (money) bag" (as guarantee).

among the Jews, making them the victims of exploitation and blackmail. At the same time, they were often wooed by merchants, towns, and princes in their role as money-lenders. Even some of Germany's cathedrals were built with the aid of special Jewish taxes. Just how precarious the situation of the Jews really was can be illustrated by the example of their history in Constance. In the 13th century, they played an influential role in the economy there. On 2 January 1349 a total of 330 Jews were burned and the others were forced to flee, although soon after these events the city council allowed Jews to return. The extremely high costs of the Church Council from 1414 to 1418 were financed largely by the Jews of Constance with the aid of Jews from the surrounding area. In 1430 they were forced to pay the still outstanding costs of the Council if they wanted to avoid being burned at the stake. Jews from Zurich and Schaffhausen helped their fellow believers in Constance

to find the money required. Between 1443 and 1448, the Jews of Constance were kept imprisoned on a charge of ritual murder, and had to leave the city again in 1448. Jews were not allowed back into Constance until 1847.

With the passage of time the Jews were increasingly separated from Christian citizens. The end of the 13th century saw the construction of the Jewish quarter surrounded by walls which was intended for the exclusive occupation of the Jews. In 1267, the Synod of Breslau decided the following: "We hereby give the strictest order that the Jews living in this diocese shall not reside together with the Christians. Instead, they are to live separately in a connected block of houses in a part of the town or village specially assigned to them. This part of the settlement occupied by the Jews must

be separated from the living quarters of the Christians by an enclosure, a wall, or a ditch." The reason for this development was the canon law of the Church and the financial interests of the princes and towns on whose land the Jews lived.

There was however one positive aspect to this, namely that the walled Jewish quarter also provided a certain security, and contributed to the strengthening of the Jewish communities.

Despite these developments, there remained some spheres of life in which Jews and Christians came into contact with one another. This was the case above all with Jewish doctors, who, from time to time, were very much in demand, despite the abuse from their Christian competitors and the clergy. Most of the Jewish doctors had studied at the University of Padua, which admitted Jewish students. From there, they either returned to Germany, where they became doctors, or migrated to other countries, sometimes as far as Turkey.

Peasants delivering tithe to their spiritual masters. If they fell into debt they often pawned objects from among their possessions to Jewish moneylenders. Woodcut, 1490.

Even emperors had Jewish personal physicians. Frederick III (reigned 1440–1493), for example, had Jakob ben Yehiel Loans as his personal physician and even on his deathbed recommended him to his son Maximilian I. Loans, was, as a matter of interest, also the Hebrew teacher of the humanist Reuchlin.

There were even a number of Jewish women doctors, such as the famous eye specialist Zerlin in Frankfurt am Main (around 1430). The woman doctor Sara was granted permission in 1419 by the Bishop of Würzburg also to practice outside the confines of the Jewish ghetto.

After the massacres of 1348/49, Jews had been readmitted to many places, or even called back, for financial reasons. But now there began a trend of an increased migration of Jews to small towns and villages. This tendency grew stronger during subsequent waves of persecution. The fragmentation of Germany into numerous sovereign small and very small states made it possible for Jews to find refuge in a

neighboring town or village under a different ruler, if they had been driven out of their hometown. Jews who were forced to leave Nuremberg, for example, could find refuge in nearby Fürth.

Some towns and cities, such as the up-and-coming commercial centers of Augsburg and Frankfurt am Main, often used the full force of the law to protect their Jewish citizens against attack. At Easter, a time when the Jews were in particular danger of their lives because of the Passion plays, these cities posted paid guards in front of the gates to the Jewish quarters. The hatred of the Jews, however, had become legitimate. Partly this was due to the fact that the Jews were forced by the Church to charge interest on the money they lent; but above all it was a result of the general hatred of the Jews within the

church itself. After many Jews had been murdered because of alleged desecration of the Host and the ritual killing of Christian children, the Frenchman Pierre de Froissard wrote in 1497:

"In Germany, the hatred of the Jews is so generally widespread that even the calmest men become agitated when the conversation turns to the subject of the Jews and their usury. I would not be at all surprised if a violent and bloody persecution of the Jews were to break out suddenly and simultaneously all over the country, as a number of them have already been subject to forcible expulsion from some German cities."

The religious and economic defamation of the Jews initiated by Pope Innocent III had brought about pogroms but had failed to lead to a mass conversion of Jews to Christianity. The majority of Germany's surviving Jewish population had fled to the east in the 14th and 15th centuries, or emigrated. In Poland, they encountered a warm welcome from the kings.

The Jewish Quarters

LEFT: The mikvah, the ritual bathing house, in Friedberg in Hesse. Since a ritual cleansing bath was only permitted in "living" water, it was necessary to dig a shaft deep enough to reach the groundwater, 30 meters (c. 1260).

ABOVE: "Wedding." From the Second Nuremberg Haggadah, c. 1470. The inscription is from Ezekiel 16:7: "And thou hast increased and waxen great."

In most towns the Jewish quarters were originally located near the cathedral precinct, the castle or the market. This was the case in Augsburg, Aachen, Trier, Worms, Brunswick and Hildesheim. Later, in towns such as Frankfurt am Main, Mannheim, Berlin, Hanover or Halberstadt, the Jews were permitted to live only on the outskirts, away from the centers of trade. Sometimes they were even obliged to live outside the towns, as was the case in Magdeburg, Meissen, and Halle.

In these autonomous communities there was a Magister Judeorum ("Master of the Jews"), the official representative who dealt with the authorities. Often this role was performed by the rabbi with the support of the parnasim, the leaders of the congregation.

In addition to his religious duties, the rabbi in the community also officiated as the judge. He was the highest authority in disputes before the public order and arbitration tribunals. The languages used in court were Hebrew and, increasingly, German.

Rabbis and parnasim were responsible for the hospital and the inn, as well as for the support of the poor. There were always a large number of poor, as well as Talmud students, passing refugees, and beggars, who had to be catered for and supported.

The dress code within the Jewish quarter was also supervised by the rabbis to ensure a sense of modesty. Outside the ghetto this was generally regulated by the town council, but not always strictly implemented.

The life of the community revolved around its two focal points, family and shul (synagogue). The culmination of the week was the eve of Sabbath and the Sabbath itself. On Friday evening the family and needy guests or Talmud students would gather around the festive table. Discussions of a worldly nature were strictly avoided on the Sabbath.

An insight into daily life is given by "The Small Book of the Pious" (1473):

"Keep cattle or poultry at all times in your house and in the morning feed them before you yourself eat … Beat neither dog

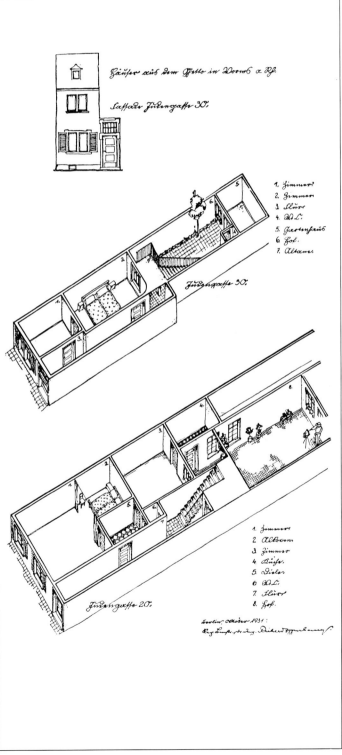

nor cat … Treat books with great reverence … place them not on the bed or on a footstool … Exercise moderation in drinking … Never be too merry except at Hanukkah and Purim, when God wills you to be cheerful … Eat not in the street – do not even taste a fruit when you buy it in the market … Try above all to fulfill everything that is written in the five Books of Moses, in the Prophets, and in the Writings … Turn towards chastity, modesty, purity, holiness, and piety … Believe not that it is merely the written commandments that are to be followed, and not the words of the sages … Serve God most punctiliously and spare no money: if a gentile has lent money in good faith and trust and has forgotten it, so remind him and pay him.

If you have a pledge from him in your hands, then do not increase the charge against him by reckoning more weeks than those that have passed, and practice no deceit or lies …"

In the event of infringements a member of the community would be summoned before the rabbinical court, and any misde-

RIGHT: Two dwellings in the medieval Jewish quarter of Worms. The ground floor and the backyard are visible. Adjoining these was the rear building which was built onto the city wall. Windows in the city wall allowed views of the countryside. A mere three-and-a-half to six meters wide, the houses were homely and built to a functional design.

meanors would have to be made good. In serious cases a ban would be imposed, that is to say, the culprit would be excluded from the community.

Neither celebration nor mourning remained a private occasion, for the community also participated. Marriages and other festivals were celebrated with dance and music in the Wedding or Bride House, known as the Judentanzhaus ("Jewish Dance House"). In most communities there were small bands of musicians for the purpose. Alternatively, wandering musicians would be hired. Sometimes Christian friends would attend these occasions, however much that might be disapproved of by the town council. Such an example is provided by the famous cosmographer Martin Behaim and the patricians Sebald Tucher and Martin Baumgartner who, shortly before the expulsion of the Jews from Nuremberg in 1499, went as guests of the bride's parents and danced in the Judentanzhaus, despite the town council's antagonism toward the Jews. They were called to account by the council and had to serve eight and four days respectively in the detention room.

A Jewess from Worms outside the confines of the Jewish quarter, and therefore obliged to wear the sign of the Jews on her cloak (16th century).

BELOW LEFT: Rabbis studying the Torah. Master of the Middle Rhine, 15th century.

BELOW RIGHT: A bird's eye view of Cologne, showing the town hall and the cathedral quarter. The Judengasse ("Jews' Lane") is marked by the Star of David. Plan by Arnold Mercator, 1571.

TOP AND TOP RIGHT: The synagogue at Regensburg. Copper engraving by Albrecht Altdorfer. According to the inscription, the synagogue was destroyed in February 1519.

RIGHT: Gravestones of the rabbi Meïr ben Baruch from Rothenburg, and of Alexander ben Salomon Wimpfen in Worms (extreme right). Meïr ben Baruch was the highest rabbinical authority of his time. From 1287 up to his death he was held prisoner by Rudolf von Habsburg because he refused to be released in return for a ransom obtained by blackmail. Fourteen years later Alexander Wimpfen redeemed his body in return for a large ransom.

Daily Life

As we have said, many Jews earned their living as moneylenders and pawnbrokers. A large group of other members of the community were dependent on these businessmen: clerks and servants, teachers and artisans, those working in the synagogues and, above all, those studying the Talmud – in other words, many local young men. Furthermore, there were the sick, the vagrants, the refugees, and the beggars.

As with the Christians, all aspects of Jewish daily life were governed by religion.

The center of community life was the synagogue, called "shul" (school), since in most cases the synagogue was also the place where school was held, and a place of study. Twice a day the congregation would go to the synagogue to pray and to hear a brief lecture. The synagogue and its entrance hall served furthermore as the court of law, sometimes for legal cases between Jews and Christians. Another important part of community life was the mikvah, the religious cleansing bath for both women and men.

In larger villages and towns, there would be a teaching institution next to the "shul." These institutions were run by the rabbi, who would also often contribute to its upkeep. Some of the Talmud teachers whose names we know were, incidentally, women, such as Miriam Luria (called Spira after the town of Speyer, c. 1300). An honorary rabbi usually came from a well-to-do family. A large part of the community's income was spent on charitable causes.

"Learning," or religious study, formed the main content of daily life. In contrast,

Circumcision scene, from a 13th-century codex.

as little time as possible was spent on the work that provided one's income. The constitution of one school in the 13th century laid down the following: "It is a duty above all of the Kohanim and the Levites to make one of their sons available for the study of the doctrine ... They may not leave the teaching institution until seven years have passed. They should be provided there with food and drink and accommodation and not waste their time on trivial matters. Every Jew is charged an annual sum of twelve hellers for the service in the teaching house [for the Talmud students] ... in order for them to be able to concentrate unceasingly on the doctrine in the name of the people, so that the kingdom of God shall not go backward ... ." The primary school is referred to as follows: "The teachers shall not accept more than ten children for each subject ... The teachers are to instruct the children not by heart, but from the books, and they are to teach them to translate the holy writings into the language of the country ... The children remain in this teaching house for seven years. For two years they study the

School scene, late 14th century. The teaching period is indicated by an hourglass. The teacher holds a whip as a sign of authority. But if he made too free use of it, he was dismissed. The pupil is reading the "Golden Rule" by the scholar Hillel, from the Talmudic period: "Do not unto thy neighbor what thou wouldst not have him do unto you." The allusion is clearly to the teacher.

צורת האיש שאל אל חביר לשלום ויבא עי חלום

example: "For reasons of self-preservation a Jewish woman who is in fear of being violated by Christians while traveling, is allowed to wear a nun's clothing so that it may protect her from being attacked. If she is in fear of being violated by Jewish lechers she is allowed to wear Christian clothes and say she is a Christian and will report them to the authorities. She is also permitted to cry for help even before such an attack has taken place, even at the risk of the Jews being beaten to death by Christians who come hurrying up to help her."

The daily life of the Jews therefore consisted in family life, prayer, study of religious writings, earning their living, and living in fear of persecution.

Five Books of Moses, for two years the Prophets and the Writings. For three years short treatises [of the Talmud]." There were also regulations governing daily life and the behavior toward non-Jews. Thus the rules of the SCHUM, the community of Speyer, Worms, and Mainz, around the year 1220, included the following:

"Firstly: no Jews are to go out in non-Jewish dress, nor are they to wear lace-up sleeves with holes, nor are they to wear their hair in a non-Jewish manner, or shave off their beards …

Thirteenth: anyone who cannot occupy himself with the Talmud is to spend half an hour every day studying according to his ability, learning statutes or midrash or the Bible or the section for the week. It is not important whether someone learns a lot or only little; what matters is whether he studies of his own free will …

Fourteenth: everyone is to leave behind any envy and jealousy on entering the house of God: there he is not to engage in idle talk, but to serve our Father in Heaven."

"The Book of the Devout" by Rabbi Judah ben Samuel Hahassid (died 1217), the head of the Talmud college in Regensburg, was generally accepted as the guide as to how one should live one's life. Paragraph 702 of the book is a good

Jews of Nuremberg in the 15th century; copper engraving after older models, from A. Würfel, *Historische Nachrichten* ("Historical News"), 1755.

Judeo-German in Colloquial Language and Popular Literature

מיין גרוסי נרה לו טטערבן אוכ' זאלט מיך זיין דר בייא גוועזן מיך
העט קיין הנאה גהאט דר פון מו וואלו אז מילונדרט דם האב מיך
דען מתרוג ניט וועזן פמול אאכן נאכלי יבן טאג וויין ער לו מיינר
אלוה הט גהערט אבר מילונדרט מן הוטענגא רבה מי כון רי אלוה
מוי דמך בין כיט געך לו עטן אוכ' מו ווינינג הנאה אלו מיך הב
פון דען טטיג מוי לו בייסן מו ווינינג העט מיך גהאט פון דען
מפכין הנאה דם דו האמט פר במטן· (ויהיו טניהם ערומים)

(דאם מיז דאז אעטה פון אדם אוכ' חוה)

In medieval Germany, the Jews were bilingual. Hebrew was the written, devotional and scholarly language, while the dialect of their Christian neighbors was used as the colloquial and business language. The latter was usually interspersed with Hebrew and some Latin loan words, such as "bentschen" which means the blessing or saying of grace, and comes from "benedicere." It was from this colloquial language, and the Rhenish in particular, that the Judeo-German language developed.

When the Jews were expelled from Germany and found refuge in Eastern Europe during the Crusades and later periods (see page 34), they took their Judeo-German language with them. In the course of time this developed into Yiddish. Yiddish was spoken by about 12 million people until the extermination of the European Jews by the National Socialists.

"Das is das Maase fon Adam un' Chawah." ("This is the story of Adam and Eve"), from the *Zena Urena* ("Come Out and See"), 16th century, written in the Judeo-German language ("Weiber-Teutsch" or "women's German"). The earliest existing edition of this devotional book for women, published in more than 200 editions, was printed in 1622 in Hanau. The *Zena Urena* is a popular adaptation with commentaries on the Five Books of Moses and other books of the Bible.

Rooted in Middle High German, the Yiddish vocabulary also includes words of Hebrew and Slavic origin (about one-eighth and one-tenth respectively).

The following comparison illustrates just how closely related the Yiddish and the Middle High German languages are. Here is the first sentence of the Song of the Nibelungs. (Hohenems Manuscript A, Staatsbibliothek Munich) together with a modern Yiddish translation: "*Uns ist in alten Maeren wonders vil geseit von helden lobebaern, von grozzer chuonheit,*" which in Yiddish reads thus: "*Uns is in alte Maysses Wunder (s) vil gesogt von Helden loibenswertike, von groisser Mutigkeit.*" (English translation: "We have often heard in old tales about laudable heroes of great bravery.")

Even today, Judeo-German and Yiddish expressions are still found in the German language. In the small village of Neroth in the Eifel region of western Germany, for example, there were old people still familiar with the following words in 1981:

Neroth Dialect	Hebrew	Standard German	English
hakdul	hakol	alles	all
mosseren	massor	angeben	to boast
Teschuwe	teshuwa	Antwort	answer
acherer	acher	anderer	other
More	mora	Angst	fear
Meloche	melacha	Arbeit	work
Tobuche	tapuach	Apfel	apple
Dalles	dalut	Armut	poverty
Ayn	ayin	Auge	eye
Suss	suss	Pferd	horse
toff	tov	gut	good

The sentence "*Das Pferd arbeitet gut*" ("the horse works well") translates into the dialect of Neroth as: "*Das Suss is toff in der Meloche.*"

Many Judeo-German expressions and Hebrew loan words entered the German language in the lowest social classes, where Jewish and Christian vagrants, beggars, receivers of stolen goods, thieves, and robbers worked or lived together. Such words

"The Book of the Fables": "… the donkey is caught and bound up whole – and they transport him on a pole." There were a number of books of fables in Judeo-German which were reprinted again and again. In Frankfurt on Main in 1697, Johannes Wüst published an illustrated edition of Moshe Wallich's "Cow Book" in which he combined Hebrew, Judeo-German, and German books of fables. The illustrations on this page show some scenes from the fable "Of the father who could not please anyone."

Ducus Horant.	dvxvs hvrnt.

Es war im deutschen Reiche ein König weit
erkannt. Ein so kühner Degen,
Etten war er genannt. Er war milde
und schön. Er trug der Ehren Krone.
Ihm dienten gewaltig alle deutschen
Lande. Lombardien und Bologna standen zu seiner
Hand. Sizilien und Toskane mussten ihm
Untertan werden. In Dänemark trug er
die Krone und es stand gar in seiner Gewalt.
Auch mussten ihm dienen in herrliche Weise alle
Spanien-lande. Der König von Ungarn war ihm
Untertan. Und musste auch die Krone von
ihm haben; Die Herren vom Lande waren ihm
alle Untertan. Ihm dienten aus einem Walde
drei Furcht erregende Riesen. Der eine war
Witolt genannt. Der war ein kühner Held;
er trug eine stahlene Stange die
war zwölf Klafter lang. Damit bezwang er für den
mächtigen König Etten alle deutschen Reiche.
Er hatte einen Bruder, der hiess Asprian. Der
hatte Wunder getan: und Wate von den

ES vvs 'ın tvžn rıxn 'ın kvnık vvıt
'rknt. 'ın degn 'lz' kvn'
'ıtn' vvs er gnnt. er vvs mıld'
'vnḏ svṇ'. er trvk der 'ırn krvn'. [:]
'ım' dıntn gvvldklıxn 'l' tvž'
lnt. lvnprtn 'vnḏ pvln stvnt gn 'n zınr
hnt. żıżılıvn 'vnḏ tvskn. mvstn 'ım'
vvern 'vndr tn: żv dınmrktn trvk er
dı krvn' 'vnḏ stvnt gr 'n zınr hnt.
'vx mvstn 'ım' dınn svn' 'l' ꝛ
spngn-lnt. der kvnık v̄vn 'vngrn vvs 'ım'
'vndr tn. 'vnḏ mvst' 'vx dı krvn' v̄vn
'ı[m'] hn: dı hırn v̄vm' lnd' vvrn 'ım'
'l' ['vn]dr tn. 'ım' dıntn 'vs 'ım'
vvld' drı rızn vrıšn. der 'ın' vvs zıx
vvıtvlt gnnt. der vvs 'ın kvnr vvıgnt:
der trvk 'ın sṯhlın' stng' dı
vvs żvvlf klvftrn lnk.d' mıt' er dem'
rıxn kvng' 'ıtn' 'l' tvž' rıx' btvvnk.
er ht' 'ınn brvdr der hıs 'sprın.der
ht' vvnd[r]s <...> gtn: 'vnḏ vvt' v̄vn den

particularly fed into "Rotwelsch," a thieves' cant with hidden meanings which were intended to be incomprehensible to normal Jews and Christians.

Some examples of words of Yiddish origin in the German language are: *Tacheles reden* ("talk straight"), *Tohuwabohu* ("ballyhoo"), *Kaff* ("dump, hicksville") Schnorrer ("scrounger"), *Pleitegeier* ("specter of bankruptcy"), *Macke* ("defect").

There are German literary texts in Hebrew script still extant which date as far back as the 14th century. Among them are

sections of the German sagas. It seems that the sagas concerning Dietrich von Bern (i.e., of Verona) were widely read in Jewish homes, too, as was the *Volksbuch von den Sieben Weisen Meistern* ("Folk Tales of the Seven Wise Masters") of which there were numerous editions in the Judaeo-German language well into the 18th century. A part of the *Gudrun-Lied* ("Song of Gudrun"), the *Dukus-Horant*, has come down to us in a version dating from 1382, also written in Judeo-German using Hebrew letters. The oldest surviving version in the German

language, on the other hand, was written about one hundred years later.

After Gutenberg's invention of printing, many German popular books and religious literature continued to be printed in Judeo-German using Hebrew letters. 1545 saw the publication in Venice by Israel Adelkind of the psalms in Judeo-German using Hebrew letters. In the preface he stated significantly that he had had the psalms "translated into German" in order that the pious girls and those men who had learned little Hebrew in their youth could

The first page of the *Dukus Horant*, a Judeo-German epic poem from the series of legends around Gudrun and Hilde, 1382.
LEFT: Judeo-German using Hebrew letters.
OPPOSITE RIGHT: transliteration;
OPPOSITE LEFT: Standard German version.
According to L. Fuks, *The Oldest Known Literary Documents of Yiddish Literature*, Leiden, 1957. The manuscript of the *Dukus Horant* is in the Cambridge University Library. It is clear from the text that in the 14th century there was little deviation from Middle High German in the language of the Jews.

jdrman kino hat un' almol gern hat was anderleut haben ..." ("Once upon a time a king was walking along when he met two men who asked the king to give them something. And the king knew both of them well. One of them was a very envious man who envied everybody and always coveted what belonged to others ...")

Printed in the Hebrew "women's script," the *Zena Urena* ("Come Out and See," a quotation from the Song of Solomon) was the most widely distributed book in the Judeo-German language. It was a popular adaptation of the Bible with commentaries, narratives, sayings, and fables from the Talmud. The book was illustrated with more than one hundred wood engravings. Other illustrated books were the book of fables *Meschal ha'kadmoni* ("Early Fables") by Isaak ben Salomo ibn Sahula, first printed c. 1490 in Italy, and the *Kuhbuch* ("Cow Book") by Moshe Wallich, published in 1697 by Johannes Wüst in Frankfurt, a collection of Hebrew and German fables in Judeo-German.

One of the most eminent translators, editors, printers, publishers, and authorities on grammar of his time was Elijah Levita (1469–1549), who counted among his friends humanists such as Sebastian Münster and Johannes Reuchlin. Works translated by him included the Anglo-French romance "Sir Bevis of Hampton" into Judeo-German. In 1542 in Isny he published a Judeo-German grammar and a Judeo-German/Hebrew dictionary which was translated into Latin and German by Paulus Fagius (1504–1549).

The German-Jewish writers included a remarkably large number of women. There was Rebecca Tiktiner in Poland, who wrote a book of customs and morals for women, the poet Taube Pan who lived and wrote in Prague; Hanna Katz, who wrote sermons; and Rösl Levi-Fischl, who translated a book of psalms in Hanover.

One book that has remained in print right up to the present day is the book of memoirs by Glückel of Hamelin (1645–1724). It includes the author's interesting reports of the Thirty Years' War and the turmoil surrounding the false Messiah Shabbetai Tzevi (see page 92) in her hometown of Hamburg.

"spend their time on the Sabbath or 'Yom Tob' (holidays) reading narratives about God rather than tales about 'Titrich von Bern' or about the happiness of the beauty" (i.e., the book of the beautiful Magelone).

For the less educated, there were also translations of the prayer book and the Bible. Aimed particularly at women and girls, epic adaptations of biblical material were printed. They included commentaries from the Talmud and were printed in the so-called "women's script," a simplified version of the Hebrew Rashi script.

In 1542, for instance, a translation of the Hebrew "Book of Customs and Morals" was published. This book does not contain any German words that have been adapted to Hebrew, nor any Hebrew words that have been Germanized. "Its orthography is at the level of German orthography." Chapter 14 begins with the story of a jealous person: "*Ain mol ging ein Melech am Weg da begegnetn im zwen mannen, di baten den melech er solt inen ezwas gebn. un' der melech kent se beid wol. der ain war ein groszer neidr, der auf*

Book Culture – the Darmstadt Haggadah

Illumination from a Talmud commentary by Asher ben Yehiel, 14th century. The seated figure might well be the commentator himself.

BELOW: page from a prayer book for the important religious festivals, Ulm, 1460 (detail).

In Jewish culture, the profession of the scribe has always been highly regarded. Ever since the earliest times there have always been, alongside bibles, various kinds of manuscripts in Jewish homes and synagogues.

Many of these handwritten and (from the end of the 15th century) printed books were destroyed during the persecutions.

One example is the mass burning of books in Paris in 1240 ordered by a decree of Pope Gregory IX during the reign of Saint Louis. On that occasion, fourteen cartloads of books (some sources say twenty-four), all copies of the Talmud, were burned on a pyre.

Most popular of all were the illustrations in the Mahzor and in the Haggadah. The name for the latter comes from the Hebrew word "haged," to tell a story. The Haggadah is the story of the Exodus from

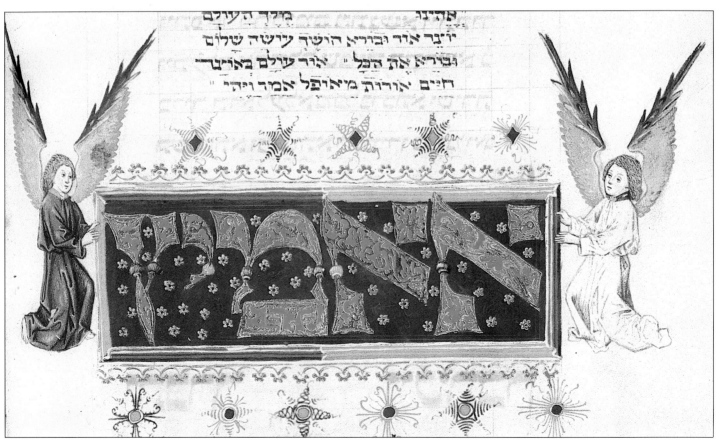

Moses receives the tablets containing the
Ten Commandments on Mount Sinai and takes
them to the Israelites (Regensburg, c. 1300).

Egypt and is interspersed with chants, secular and merry songs, parables, and prayers. Furthermore, it contains the exact order, the "seder," for the Seder evening named after it. On this the eve of the Passover, the Haggadah is read and sung jointly under the direction of the head of the household. This is in accordance with the instruction in the Bible which commands that the son be told "of that which the Lord did for me when I came out of Egypt … from bondage to freedom."

The Seder evening is dominated by the central theme of the hope of redemption for the people of Israel, as summarized in the phrase "Next year in Jerusalem!" In memory of "his" exodus from Egypt into freedom, the Jew identifies himself with all preceding and future generations of his history. In the Diaspora, the march to freedom became an event that was projected into the present and the future. In times of messianic movements among the people, hope often turned to doubt, and measures were sought that would hasten or even force the coming of the Messiah. Right up until the period of the Enlightenment, the hope for the coming of the Messiah remained the most profound source of the life energy of all Jews. It helped them to bear the persecutions and even to sacrifice their lives, an act they regarded as the "hallowing of the Name (of God)."

All this makes it clear why the illustration of the subjects became a part of the Haggadah itself, ranging from the Exodus from Egypt to the arrival of the messenger announcing the Messiah. One of the most beautiful copies of the Haggadah was written around 1400 by "Israel the Scribe," the son of Meïr of Heidelberg. It is written on 57 sheets of parchment measuring 24.5 x 35.5 cm each, and decorated with illustrations. Israel the Scribe must have lived in Heidelberg before the year 1391, since that was the year in which the Jews were forced to flee the city.

The majority of the pictures in that Haggadah deal with the everyday life of the Jew. It is striking how often there are depictions of women with books on their knees. The imaginary architecture is remi-

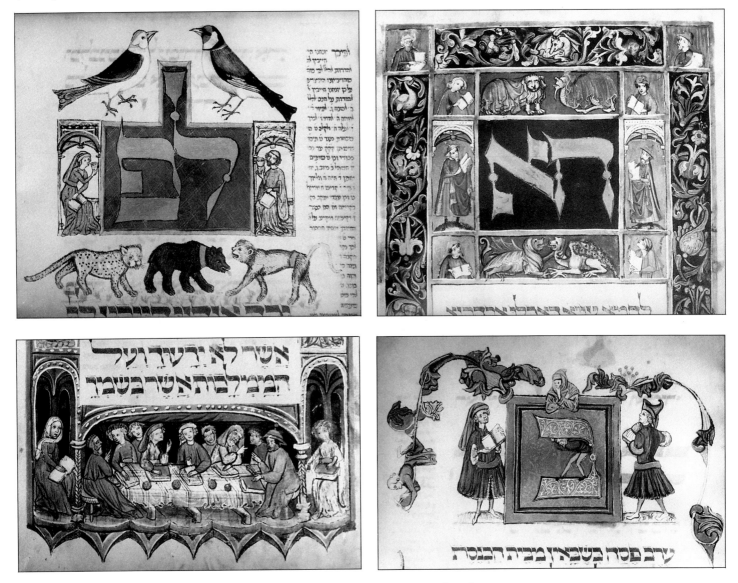

niscent of a Gothic city palace rather than the home of a middle-class citizen, a feature that might be borrowed from French illuminated books of hours and secular pictures in books owned by princes. Some members of the Jewish community in Heidelberg were descendants of refugees from France. The style is strongly influenced by or related to Christian book illumination.

Besides the Haggadah, many other illustrated manuscripts of prayer books and of Talmud commentaries have survived.

One of the full-page illustrations. On every story of the Gothic palace, men and women are engaged in the study and interpretation of the Haggadah. The text reads: "Thou hast accomplished many miracles (O Lord)."

Gutenberg and Jewish Literature

תפארת נרולתו בני אומר דברי התורה הלכו פם
יתכבר ועיניהם למעשותתיו חדר בבנים טמירים
להנדיל ספרי יתר מסטירי הלא הו כמר אברהם
ידיר יה האוזרהי יכו מקורלוני־ווי־ משר מדי שיר
קדמו להשתותנף ספר לטוכני וזמת הטראהכה מלוכה
הקודש כד הכ הטוכה עלי השם למען רייחני
הנדולים יוכנו להשלים כמונתנכ ייין־יים כליו
קדם דכתי יתן לך כלבן וכל בכתנן ישראל
ורין יודי רצון

מתתרופות
ולוה יכתותר ת
חרבותהים לאותים
ורחצונותהם לזומרו׳
ולח ישמאו גוי אל גוי חרב
ולח ילרטות כוד מלחמה והיא
המפן מטר נרטן עי כרברי רטי
ובזימריהו די כלכ״מ מינט יק׳ עה סמ״יל
כלהר כי לטולמין לת תתברכל ומרלכותה
רפם אחרון לת תכותבק והוא מטר
מטד עלי׳ ולה יהיב טלטן
דיכרוטרלו וכל מלטר״א ע
בטט״יא ולט״יא ל״ה
ילרלטן כולסנ״ת ט׳
סלטן שלס רי
לו יכרי וסי
וצלכותי׳ה די לת תתנחבל חט״ית לטשן רחמיר
ימהר יחים משטהו לטטן טר
טראה מפן מטן סלה
והיתת הטלל׳מ
חטלמותו
בכוון
הביאורו
ברברי התורה
בכלרלה והטכולות
הטמני נ אתי מעהם והתנהלה
רלי ומטר כורטו כרמהיר יס
וכהר ב חסמיע ומרסוטס על כל ב
ברכה ותתרלה מטן סלה והיה
השלמותו בכל לירה האוזר טלטת יחת
לטרט היכ השטי׳ פה בכיר האוזר יכונה
טליון מטן ברוך טכן לטיף כח ולמן אוטים
וברון ל״ לטולים מטן מטן
כבורד יי׳
אמר אברהם ס
טלמה כותל ס
ולה הנסטן וכירה רטן חברייא חכותב בכמה
קלומוט׳ס בלח מטטה נסם
בכל הדיר׳כו מטר וכט להתהי׳
ישתבה
ורהטלים זה הספר חסר
הסתורלותי בטעטסתו למפלתי ותוטרותו ויקר

TOP: Levi ben Gerson, "Commentary on the Pentateuch," printed in 1476 by Abraham ben Salomo Conat and Abraham Jedidja ha-Esrachi de Colonia: an early Hebrew incunabulum, printed in Mantua by Jewish printers from Cologne.

TOP RIGHT: A page from the book of fables *Meschal ha'kadmoni* by Isaak ibn Sahula, written in 1281 and printed in Brescia in 1490, using Hebrew Rashi script, a script often used for secular literature.

At the beginning of the 15th century, inventors in search of new technological means of text reproduction were preoccupied with the possibility of painting books using precut letters which could be exchanged when required.

Among those interested in this new art was a Jew by the name of Davin de Caderousse who lived in Avignon. It was there, around the year 1444, that a Prague goldsmith by the name of Waldvogel carried out experiments and was said to be teaching the method of "artificial writing." This was achieved by means of letters cut in tin and iron.

It is not known whether this method was familiar to Johannes Gensfleisch zur Laden, known as "Gutenberg" after an estate owned by his mother at the former "Judenberg" ("Jews' Hill") in Mainz. In any case, Gutenberg's (or Fust und Schöffer's) printing workshop existed before 1462, the year in which the Jews were driven out of Mainz.

Some of those expelled emigrated to Italy. After being allowed back into Mainz, the Jews were finally expelled for good in 1473, and again a number of them made the journey to Italy and on to Constantinople. The frequently encountered epithet "Mainzer" suggests that perhaps some of these refugees became familiar with the printer's craft in Mainz. Before long, the art of printing with movable type was heralded in Jewish writings as "the pinnacle of all sciences," or even as the fulfillment of Isaiah's prophecy (11:9): "... for the earth shall be full of the knowledge of the Lord." Gutenberg's invention contributed to a remarkable degree to the survival of the Jewish writings.

The most widely known family of Jewish book printers in Europe was a family who had fled from Speyer to Italy where they adopted the name of Soncino after their new hometown. Their first book was published in 1483 and their fame, which lasted three generations, was above all due to the outstanding typography of their printed work in Hebrew. The printing workshop was founded by Josua Salomo Soncino. His nephew Gerson ben Moses, known also as "Menzlein" ("the man from Mainz"), printed no fewer than eleven

Hebrew books before the year 1500, that is to say, in the era of the incunabula. In the words of Abbé Giovanni de Rossi, a 17th-century Hebraist and bibliophile, "He brought the art of printing with him from his homeland to Brescia." His library, which still remains in Parma, includes one of the two earliest Hebrew books dated in the imprint: namely Rashi's commentary on the Bible, printed in Reggio di Calabria in 1475.

Josef ben Jakob Gunzenhauser Aschkenasi ("the German from Gunzenhausen") and his sons Asriel and Abraham set up their printing workshop in Naples in 1487. Among the books they printed was the widely used *Canon medicinae* by Avicenna (980–1037) which was translated into Hebrew as early as the 11th century. In Mantua, the doctor and printer Abraham ben Salomo Conat and his wife Estellina had been printing since 1475. Their extraordinarily beautiful Conat

types are still used today in modern fine editions. Conat and his wife often arranged their page layout in a playful manner which today is reminiscent of modern Constructivism.

However, by far the most eminent printer of Hebrew books was a Flemish Christian named Daniel Bomberg (1470/80–1553). From 1517 onward, over 200 Hebrew works were published in his workshops in Venice under the supervision and with the cooperation of Jewish printers and proofreaders. Highlights were the monumental editions of the Jerusalem Talmud and the Babylonian Talmud. The typographical layout of Bomberg's Talmud editions are still the model used by Talmud scholars for all new editions.

Despite all the persecutions of the Jews and despite all the book burning, the survival of the Talmud remained assured, thanks to Gutenberg's invention and Bomberg's printing.

A page from the Talmud edition by Daniel Bomberg, printed in Venice in 1520. Printed in large letters in the center is the text of the Mishna and the Gemara in the traditional quadrate script. On the right is Rashi's commentary, which has remained the standard commentary since the 12th century. This column was printed in the special Rashi script. On the left are the Tosafot, the extensions and explanations of Rashi's commentaries. They were written mainly in German-French Talmud schools of the 12th to 14th centuries.

OPPOSITE: This often printed Haggadah picture shows the Messiah's arrival in Jerusalem according to the Revelation of Elija.

Persecution, Expulsion, Murder

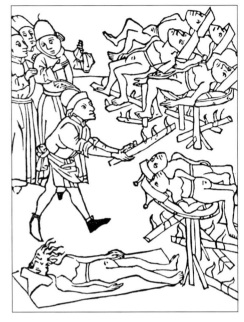

LEFT: The murder of Simon at Trent, 1475. Illustrated leaflets spread this horror story throughout Europe and led to massacres of Jews. Woodcut from Schedel's *Weltchronik* ("Chronicle of the World"), 1493.

RIGHT: Jews being tortured as a result of the Trent story. Woodcut, around 1475.

King Sigismund (reigned 1411–1437) was elected emperor in 1433 and made his coronation festivities the occasion for levying a special tax on the empire's Jews. As we have seen (p. 54), they also had to bear a major part of the costs of the Council of Constance (1414–1418) and of the later Council of Basle (1431–1449). Excluded as they were from normal occupations, they were unable to raise these enormous sums from the proceeds of the financial dealing which was permitted to them, for they had also to make payments to their local rulers, the religious authorities, and the cities or towns. Moreover, the ban on Christians lending money at interest no longer operated.

There were already several Christian banks in Paris and Florence, and the merchants in the German towns had long since been engaging in financial dealings. Trading firms from the smallest to the greatest, right up to the Fuggers and the Welsers, would lend money in return for a share in profits. This reduced the volume of financial business available to the Jews. The mass of Jews soon became impoverished, and thus unable either to raise or lend large sums of money.

Jews mourning at a cemetery. From a prayer book of 1427.

Emperor Sigismund and Pope Martin V attempted to prevent massacres of Jews in the Holy Roman Empire – after, for example, the occasion in 1421 when Duke Albrecht of Austria had two hundred or more Jews burned alive on a meadow by the Danube near Vienna, following an allegation of ritual murder. However, some religious orders continued to encourage the persecution of Jews, and their preachers in the towns and cities had a greater influence than distant rulers and popes.

Cologne, Trier, Strasbourg, and other cities expelled their Jews, though many were then allowed by neighboring clerics to settle in their areas. A large proportion of the Jews re-emigrated via Silesia and Bohemia to Poland, where, moreover, they were also allowed to practice craft trades.

The Franciscan preacher John of Capistrano (1386–1456) was the most famous pulpit orator of his day. He preached first against the Hussites and other heretics and then, as the "scourge of

The Franciscan friar and inquisitor John of Capistrano (1386–1456), the "scourge of the Jews." Contemporary woodcut.

Venice protested against it. Most of the Jews died. It later emerged that a man named Enzo Hinderbach had murdered Simon, on the instructions of the Bishop, at the start of the Passover festival.

Leaflets carried the horror story of Simon's supposed ritual murder to all parts of Europe, and this resulted in acts of violence and murder in many places. Passion plays, poems, and almanacs spread the tale of the "ritual murder" of Trent, and led to similar accusations being made right into the 20th century.

The defenseless Jewish minority knew that it was in the power of a superior and armed majority and could not defend itself. With few exceptions the Jews rejected the readily available option of safety through baptism, which would also bring economic benefits and equal rights. They felt themselves to be morally superior to the Christians, who perpetrated or condoned many atrocities in the name of their religion.

As early as the beginning of the 12th century one Jew had dared to say this openly – but only after he had allowed himself to be baptized and had become a respected cleric. This was Hermann Judaeus, later Provost Hermann of Scheda. "We endure the criticism and mockery of men with patience and equanimity, so long as we adhere to the laws of God and to his ritual commandments, for it is better for us to fall into the hands of men than to forsake the laws of God."

the Hebrews," against the Jews. In Bavaria around 1452 it was through his efforts that Jews lost their right of residence and their right to the protection of the law, so that they became outlaws. In Breslau, at his instigation, Jews were tortured until they "confessed" to having desecrated the Host, whereupon they were burned at the stake. In Poland King Casimir IV (reigned 1447–1492), after lengthy resistance, finally gave in to pressure from Capistrano, the Pope's representative, and declared the Jews to be outside the protection of the law: persecution and murder were the result. "Whether this [torturing people or burning them alive] is godly or not, I leave to the insight of the teachers of religion," was the cautious comment of the town clerk of Breslau in 1453.

When at Trent in 1475 a boy named Simon was found dead in the river Adige, a sermon was preached by Bernardinus of Feltre which led to all the town's Jews being tortured as murderers of God, even though the Duke of Tyrol and the Doge of

Flight from a German town. From a prayer book of the year 1427.

75

The Fight for the Talmud

גדל Magnificauit.magnus.fuit.magnificatus eft.ut p̄s.ciiij . Domi ne deus meus magnificatus es uehementer.&.i.Paralip.xxix.Magnificauit ergo dominus Salomonem.& Gen̄.xli.pro eo quod legimus vno tantum regni folio pr̨ecedam te.verbum e uerbo fic legitur. tantummodo fedem magnificabo fupra tuam uel fupra te.fed potius qųe a facio latine componuntur,ea ueniunt hebraice a coniugatione graui גדל q̄d poniī Efter.iij.Poft h̨ec rex Afuerus exaltauit Aman. pro magnificauit.& Genefis.xxv.pro eo quod noftra tranflatio legir, quibus adultis.hebraica ueritas habet.& magnificati funt pueri ideft creuerunt.in eo & fimilibus femp feruaī pūctus dagges. inde גדול magnus.Exodi.xi.Fuitcꝫ Moyfes uir magnus ualde.oīa eiufcemodi fignificant magnificentiā.honor̄e.pulchritudinem.ftaturam. fortitudinem et robur.Ezechielis.xvi.Et fornicata eft cum filiis Aegypti uicinis tuis magnarum carnium.ubi ponitur גדלי

גדל Magnitudo uel magnum.fubftantiuū nomen.ut Deutero.v. Ecce oftendit nobis dn̄s deus nofter maieftatem et magnitudin̄e fuā. & quandocꝫ fcribitur prima cū puncto furek.ut p̄s.ultimo . Laudate eum fecundum multitudinem magnitudinis eius. & quādocꝫ accipit he in fine cū furek in penultima.ut p̄s.cxlv.Et magnitudinis eius non eft finis. Inuenies omnia inde deriuata fupereminentiam fignificare qualitatis aut quantitatis.

מגדל Turris.Canti.iiij.Sicut turris Dauid collū tuū . & hetero-

99

While for the Christians too the Holy Scriptures of the Jews were the work of God and so remained sacrosanct, the Talmud was often attacked. The most damaging accusation was that it contained passages in which Jewish scholars had expressed anti-Christian views. This accusation led again and again to burnings of the Talmud in Europe (see p. 68).

In 1505, acting as a puppet for the Dominicans, the Cologne butcher Johannes Pfefferkorn, a convert to Christianity, demanded in several defamatory pamphlets that the Talmud be destroyed throughout the Holy Roman Empire. Indeed it was usually converts who tried to demonstrate the strength of their new religious convictions by making venomous attacks on their former faith and especially on the Talmud.

Through the influence of the Dominican Order, Pfefferkorn's efforts finally resulted in an order from Emperor Maximilian that Jewish books should be confiscated, and he at once set about confiscating copies of the Talmud in Frankfurt am Main and other towns and cities. When the Frankfurt Jews and the Archbishop of Mainz protested, the Emperor began to have doubts and sought opinions from

The prophet Isaiah depicted in the dress of a 16th-century Jewish scholar. Woodcut in Gregor Reisch's *Margarita philosophica* ("The Pearl of Philosophy"), Strasbourg, 1508.

BELOW, LEFT:
ABC-Büchlein für die christliche Jugend ("Little ABC for Christian Children"), Nuremberg, 1597.

eminent scholars, among them the humanist Johannes Reuchlin (1455–1522).

Reuchlin had studied Hebrew and had read the Talmud in that language. He published books about the Hebrew language and its grammar and also a Hebrew Bible. In his work *Der Augenspiegel*, 1511, he refuted the accusations of Pfefferkorn and of the Dominicans in the theological faculty at Cologne. The ensuing scholarly debate attracted much publicity, so much so that the Pope himself was drawn into it. It developed into a dispute about basic tenets of belief between the supporters of medieval scholasticism and the Inquisition, in opposition to the champions of the new humanistic scholarship and view of life. The Lateran Council of 1512–17 ruled in favor of Reuchlin.

Nevertheless Pope Leo X condemned the *Augenspiegel* as heretical. But the struggle for a just assessment of the Talmud continued. In the *Epistolae obscurorum virorum* ("Letters of Obscure Men"), 1514/15, Reuchlin and his friends, including Ulrich von Hutten, exposed the hypocrisy and ignorance of the Cologne Dominicans and their supporters to general ridicule. The ban on the Talmud was lifted, but the accusations continued: in 1553 and 1554, on the orders of Pope Julius III, the Talmud was publicly burned in Venice, Rome and the papal territories.

Humanism and the dispute over the Talmud had reawakened interest in Jewish literature, and many Christian scholars began to study Jewish writings. The attempt was even made to combine cabalistic teachings with Christian dogmas. In 1516 the convert Paulus Riccius, personal physician to Emperor Maximilian I and an eminent Hebrew scholar, whom the Emperor created Baron von Sperzenstein, published in

LEFT: Johannes Reuchlin and Ulrich von Hutten (detail). From Thomas Murner, *Die war Historie von den vier Ketzern Predigerordens* ("The True History of the Four Heretics of the Order of Preachers"), Strasbourg, 1509.

RIGHT: *Talmud*, Nuremberg, c. 1497. The first publication attacking the Talmud, containing a number of falsifications.

RIGHT: First (German) version of Pfefferkorn's *Defensio*, the response to Reuchlin and his friends, 1516. One sees Pope and emperor, each with his entourage. In the lower part of the picture Pfefferkorn points to Satan (Reuchlin) and his supporters, whom he has led astray by force.

LEFT: Johannes Reuchlin's *Augenspiegel*, a justification of the Talmud and response to Pfefferkorn's *Judenfeind* ("Enemy of the Jews"). Title page of the first edition, Tübingen, 1511.

Augsburg his work *Portae Lucis* ("The Portals of Light"), a Latin translation of parts of a cabalistic work of the same name (*Sha'arei ora*), which in turn influenced other Christian scholars. Riccius said that the Cabala had been the path that led to his apostasy. Finally, Reuchlin's *De arte cabbalistica* ("On the Science of the Cabala"), 1517, became the classic work of the "Christian Cabala."

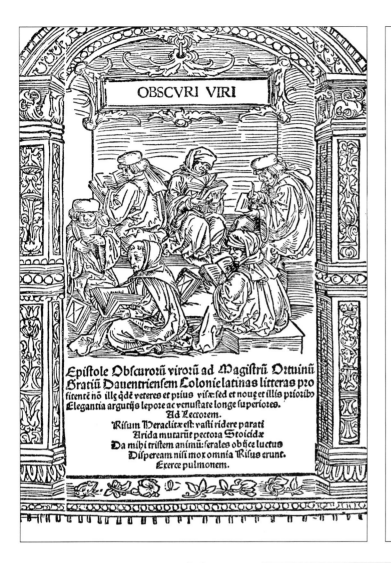

ABOVE: *Epistolae obscurorum virorum*, the famous "Letters of Obscure Men" directed against the Cologne Dominicans, 1514/15.

ABOVE RIGHT: A censored Talmud commentary. Page from Jakob ben Acher's *Arba Yoreh Deah* ("Four Sections"), printed by Soncino, 1516.

RIGHT: "Judge not, that ye be not judged." Religious discussion between a rabbi (left) and a Capuchin friar (right). Copperplate engraving, 17th century.

The Christian Cabala

Cabala (reception, that which is received) is the name given to an 11th and 12th century system of Jewish theosophy which was published in Spain in the book *Zohar* ("Radiance"). The Cabala was believed to be the secret oral tradition of this theosophical system handed down through the first man, Adam, via the patriarchs and the prophets to the present day.

According to the esoteric doctrines of the Cabala, God is boundless and stands above and outside the universe, even above being and thought. God is "En sof," without end, and cannot be comprehended by the intellect. In order to make his existence recognizable, this En sof had to reveal himself in active creativity. He did this through the medium of the ten Sefirot (countings, spheres), the ten grades of divine emanation, out of which the world is created:

1. Crown (the highest crown)
2. Wisdom
3. Understanding, intelligence
4. Grace (love, the grace of love)
5. Might, justice
6. Beauty, active compassion
7. Eternity
8. Majesty
9. Foundation (of the world)
10. Kingship

The oldest surviving work of the Cabala, the *Zohar*, says among other things: "When the Hidden One of all Hidden Ones assumed a form, He created everything in male and female form, since in no other form could things find a continuation. Therefore *wisdom*, the second Sefirah, ... radiated out into male and female, for *wisdom* spread, and *understanding* [intelligence], the third Sefirah, came into being through it, and so male and female were attained, namely *wisdom*, the father, and *understanding*, the mother." It is from the union of these two that the other pairs of Sefirot derive, through radiation. As the two Sefirot are an emanation of the first, which is the highest, they form the first triangle in the system of the Cabala.

ABOVE: *Portae Lucis* ("The Portals of Light"), by the cabalist Joseph ben Abraham Gikatilla (1248–1305), was translated into Latin by Paulus Riccius, physician to Emperor Maximilian, and printed in Augsburg in 1516. The title page shows a man holding a tree with the ten Sefirot.

The symbolist theories about the ten Sefirot were very diverse. There emerged both a theoretical and a practical Cabala, which influenced Shabbetaianism, the Frankist movement, and Hasidism. The central concern of all cabalists is the relationship of God with His creation, which they explore by a variety of mystical approaches; common to all is the assumption that nearness to God cannot be achieved by intellectual speculation and/or a religious way of life alone, but that it requires immersion into a secret tradition reaching back to the origin of man.

Unlike the theoretical Cabala, the practical Cabala occasionally adopted magical elements such as conjurations, magic formulaes, amulets, and other elements of

RIGHT: The *Cabbala denudata* ("The Cabala Unveiled"), by the mystic Baroque poet Christian Knorr von Rosenroth, was published in Sulzbach in 1667–84. Rosenroth tried to present the Cabala as reinforcing the Christian faith.

superstition. This occurred mainly in its more popular manifestations.

The late 15th century saw a movement among Christian theologians and philosophers to link the teachings of the Cabala with aspects of Christian theology, reinforcing Christian mysticism. The trinity of the first group of Sefirot seemed to them to be related to the Trinity of God the Father, Son, and Holy Ghost; they largely ignored the female component, which is fundamental to the spheres of the Cabala.

This serious movement, which was based on study of the original Hebrew texts, had its center in the Platonic Academy in Florence, with the brilliant Giovanni Pico della Mirandola (1463–1494) as its intellectual head. He maintained that the divinity of Christ could be proved with the help of magic and the Cabala. Generally, the church rejected his doctrine. The German humanist Johannes Reuchlin was stimulated by Pico's ideas, and after lengthy study of the Hebrew sources he published – the first gentile to do so – two books in Latin on the Cabala: in 1494 *De verbo mirifico* ("Of the Word That Performs Wonders") and in 1517 *De arte cabbalistica* ("On the Science of the Cabala"). This interest in the Cabala spread widely in the world of Christian scholarship. But now "popular" presentations of the subject led to the confusion of cabalistic ideas with numerology and magical powers.

The theosophical writings of Jakob Böhme (1575–1624) gave a new impetus to interest in the Cabala because of an inherent affinity between his theosophical ideas and some elements of the Cabala. It was the German scholar and theosopher Knorr von Rosenroth (1636–1689) who in his cabalistic compendium *Cabbala denudata* ("The Cabala Unveiled") introduced the world of scholarship to original texts from the *Zohar* and the Lurianic Cabala translated into Latin; Isaac ben Solomon Luria (1534–1572) had been the renewer of cabalistic thought and had given it its final received form. It was the Jesuit polymath Athanasius Kircher (1601–1680) who coined the expression "Christian Cabala." The lasting influence

of this Christian Cabala is shown for instance by the fact that in 1663 Princess Antonia of Württemberg arranged for an "instructional panel" to be put up in the church at Bad Teinach in the Black Forest, which on the outside shows the wedding procession of Shulamite and on the inside the ten Sefirot of God. This visual representation of the Christian Cabala is the only one of its kind. Gershom Scholem, the 20th-century Jewish scholar, also found traces of this Christian Cabala in the works of the philosophers Hegel and Schelling.

Martin Luther –
from Missionary to the Jews to Enemy of the Jews

LEFT: Martin Luther with a Hebrew book. After a painting by Lucas Cranach the Younger, 1560.

RIGHT: Title page of the first complete edition of Luther's Bible translation, 1534.

LEFT: *Dass Jesus Christus ein geborener Jude sei* ("That Jesus Christ was Born a Jew"), 1523. Title page of Luther's pro-Jewish work.

RIGHT: *Von den Juden und ihren Lügen* ("On the Jews and their Lies"), 1543. Title page of his anti-Jewish work.

In the struggle against the Church's medieval dogmatism in general and against Pfefferkorn's persecution of Jews in particular, Martin Luther (1483–1546) was at first, for theological reasons, on the side of Reuchlin and the humanists. His campaign against the papacy gave the Jews reason to hope for some understanding toward their faith and for humane treatment in accordance with Luther's Christian principles. For his part, Luther's attitude was shaped by the hope of being able to convert the Jews to the Christian faith.

At first Luther blamed the cruel persecutions by the Catholic Church for the fact that so few Jews had converted to the Christian faith, and that of these few the greater part had done so only in order to save their children, their wives, and themselves from acts of cruelty or death by torture. He hoped to become the great converter of Jews, indeed of Jewry in its entirety. It was in this spirit that he wrote his work *Dass Jesus Christus ein geborener Jude sei* ("That Jesus Christ was Born a Jew") in 1523. To him the Jew is a brother man who is to be called to the grace of Jesus. He rejected the accusations of ritual murder and of desecrations of the Host, both of which had, during his childhood, led to thousands of acts of torture, burnings, and expulsions: "At present we use only violence upon them and engage in lying tales ... accuse them of having a need for Christian blood ... and other such nonsense, ... If one wants to help them one must practice the law not of the Pope but of Christian charity, receive them with kindness, let them trade and work alongside us, so that they have cause and space to be with and around us, to hear and to see our Christian doctrine and way of life."

These were new sentiments to come from the Christian side, and they could have led to a normalization of the relationship between Christians and Jews. But for this Luther demanded a price from every Jew: the denial of his faith. Luther's Christian charity therefore appeared to the Jews as an attempt at religious bribery by which they might obtain humane treatment. Luther underestimated the strength of the Jews' faith, which even in the face of death and under torture permitted no betrayal of God, of the profession of faith in the uniqueness and oneness of God. He also underestimated the Jews' powers of resistance to material hardship, which had been imposed on most of them by the Christians over the centuries. In the victims the persecutions inspired a deep contempt for the armed perpetrator and often also for the religion which made it possible for him to commit these murders, and contempt, too, for the priests who quite often instigated or even led the attacks.

Luther's disappointment at the meager success of his mission turned to uncompromising rejection, indeed hatred. From now on the Jews, like the "rebellious mobs of peasants," were to be persecuted even to death. This hatred was most starkly revealed in his work *Von den Juden und ihren Lügen* ("On the Jews and their Lies"), which he published in 1542: "What are we Christians now to do with this depraved, damned Jewish people? ... We must not take revenge. I will give my sincere advice. First, that their synagogues or schools be set on fire ... Secondly, that their houses should likewise be broken up and destroyed ..." The authorities should con-

Hans Burgkmair (1473–1531): "The three Good Jews" (Joshua, King David, Judas Maccabeus) and "The three Good Jewesses" (Esther, Judith, Jael).

fiscate prayer books and the Talmud and forbid the rabbis to teach, on pain of death. And he continues: "It is not my intention to quarrel with the Jews ... Still less do I entertain the idea of converting the Jews, for that is impossible ... they are brought up from their youth in such a way that there is no hope of that, until finally by their misery they are softened and forced to confess that the Messiah has come and is our Jesus."

Luther's disillusionment was intensified by the fact that at this very time, inspired by his own Bible translation and by translations of the Talmud by humanist scholars, judaizing tendencies were appearing even among his own supporters. These tendencies had been reinforced not least by Luther's own outbursts of hatred which were so much at variance with his lip service to the Christian ideal of loving one's neighbor.

Luther had become a deadly enemy of the Jews. Because the Jews were not willing to become his brothers in Christ, they were – despite his assertion, "we must not take revenge" – to be killed. He even exhorted highwaymen and robber-knights to be his allies in such actions: they should attack the Jews who roamed homeless on the country roads. He urged princes to expel the Jews from their territories. He was still making this demand in his sermon of 15 February 1546, three days before his death in his native town of Eisleben.

John Frederick the Magnanimous, Elector of Saxony, was the first Protestant ruler to drive the Jews from his country in direct response to Luther. In 1543 he even forbade them to pass through his territory, and renewed his order "that from henceforth in our domains no Jewish man or woman ... shall reside, nor trade, live, or work in them, nor pass through." Just as in 1525 Luther had raged against the rebellious peasants with his "Stab, strike, throttle, whoever is able ... ," so now, to the very end of his life, he raged against the Jews. But his hatred of the Jews seems to have found little response either among the populace or in the world of humanist scholarship. To many people it was perfectly clear that wandering, displaced Jews suffered as much misery as wandering, displaced peasants.

Luther's Bible gave the people access to Jewish religion and history, which had previously been unfamiliar to them and had therefore inspired unease and distrust. Although his knowledge of Hebrew was imperfect, Luther nevertheless felt a close bond with the Old Testament. In this way many non-Jews were actually drawn closer to the Jews by reading Luther's Bible. Further sections of society were influenced by Luther's insistence on the freedom of the individual Christian and by the ideas of humanism. From now on Jews dared to insist publicly on their right to life, without having to fear torture and death. This is well illustrated by the case of Josel of Rosheim, an important Jewish contemporary of Luther's.

"Jewish sow" in the church at Wittenberg in Luther's day. Anonymous woodcut.

Josel of Rosheim, "Commander of the Jews"

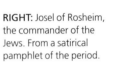

LEFT: The "Three Emperors Thaler." From left: Maximilian I, Charles V, and Ferdinand I. This coin was issued by the mint at Hall.

RIGHT: Josel of Rosheim, the commander of the Jews. From a satirical pamphlet of the period.

Emperor Frederick III was one of those rulers who, mostly for economic reasons, took the protection of the Jews seriously, especially as it was also a matter of upholding imperial rights in the diverse states which made up the Empire.

The policy toward the Jews of Frederick's son and successor, Emperor Maximilian I (reigned 1493–1519), fluctuated: that is to say, it was not always hostile. Although he had the Jews driven out of Nuremberg,

Styria, and Carinthia, he permitted them, in return for a large payment, to settle in the Burgenland. It was this same emperor who had (as mentioned on page 77) asked for an expert opinion from scholars after originally authorizing the confiscation of the Talmud by Pfefferkorn and the Dominicans.

Josel of Rosheim (c. 1478–1554) was active in the final years of Maximilian's reign and in that of Emperor Charles V

(reigned 1519–56), and his influence was to be long-lasting. A financial dealer by profession, he became the leader of the Jewish community in Alsace and soon afterward the official representative of all the Jews in the Holy Roman Empire. As such, recognized by the emperor, he confronted persecutors with all the authority of his office, and by the forcefulness of his personality was able to avert harm from Jews in many places. Josel of Rosheim was

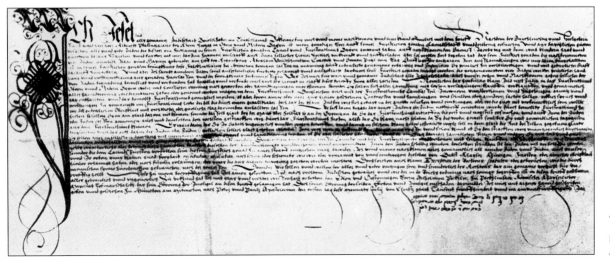

A document dating from 1551: a settlement between Josel of Rosheim and Duke Albrecht.

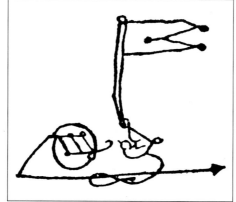

highly esteemed by Emperor Charles V. As early as 1520, at the time of Charles's coronation (as "King of Germany") at Aachen, he obtained – in return for large financial contributions to the imperial military campaigns – a guarantee of protection for all Jews in German territories.

In 1530, during the session of the Imperial Diet, Josel of Rosheim summoned the leaders of all the Jewish communities of the Empire to Augsburg with the aim of drawing up "an honorable set of rules and statutes" for Jewish congregations in cities, market towns and villages – an internal code of regulations for Jews, valid everywhere and recognized by the emperor. He had the right and the authority to enter into agreements in the name of all Jews and was the official recipient of resolutions of the Imperial Diet. The assembly at Augsburg agreed, among other things, on a "set of rules and statutes" governing the manner of doing business with Jews and with Christians, and made the congregations and their leaders responsible, on pain of severe punishment, for ensuring compliance.

Throughout the reign of Charles V, Josel von Rosheim retained his influence with the emperor. He defended the Jews against Martin Luther's attacks, against Elector John Frederick of Saxony, and against the Reformer Martin Butzer, who was threatening the safety of Jews in Hesse. In Würzburg, where an accusation of ritual

Personal device, in the form of a flag, of the cabalist and dreamer Solomon Molcho (c. 1500–1532), who saw himself as a herald of the Messiah. He won the support of Pope Clement VII for his visionary ideas of a conquest of Palestine. Though warned against it by Josel of Rosheim, Molcho went to the Imperial Diet at Regensburg and was received in audience by Emperor Charles V, but he was then handed over to the Italian Inquisition, which in 1532 condemned him to be burned at the stake.

murder had been made, he succeeded in convincing the judges that it was nonsense, thereby averting a bloodbath. A guarantee of protection from the emperor issued in 1548 states: "Josel, a Jew of Rosenheim, commander of all our Jewry in the Holy Empire of the German Nation, has brought before us a complaint that numerous Jews, beyond and contrary to their freedoms, privileges, protection, patronage, and rights of free passage ... are, by violent means, chiefly on our and the Holy Empire's roads and also in numerous cities, market towns and villages, suffering considerable hardship and damage to life and property through murder, manslaughter, robbery,

[and] expulsion from their domestic dwellings, destruction and closing of their synagogues and schools, and increased tolls and charges for free passage ..."

This was six years after Luther's proposals for the persecution of Jews. However, this imperial document also sheds light on the social situation of the majority of Jews, many of whom eked out a living as hawkers and peddlers going from one market to another or as beggars. In it, the emperor ordered that "to avoid grave disfavor and punishment by ourselves and the Empire, ... you shall let all of this our Jewry ... live and go about their business in safety."

Given the power of the emperor, such words carried weight. Josel of Rosheim also intervened successfully in various places against the accusation that the Jews shed Christian blood, and was able at least in Strasbourg to obtain an injunction preventing the printing of an inflammatory pamphlet directed against the Jews by Luther. Before town councils and princes and above all at the Imperial Diets he defended the Jews' cause, often successfully, against accusations from Catholics, Protestants, and apostates, and also attacks by the guilds, which were fighting against Jewish competition. After decades of effort he succeeded in improving the legal status of Jews: in 1548 he proved before a court that as *cives romani* the Jews possessed the rights of citizens. The arguments he deployed were based on Charles V's claim to be the legitimate successor of the Caesars. Josel also attempted to initiate a discussion with Luther, but the Reformer did not take up the offer.

Decree issued by Emperor Charles V on behalf of the Jews of Regensburg, 1541; the emperor confirms that they may conduct trade and visit towns and markets without hindrance or persecution.

Earning a Living in a Christian Environment

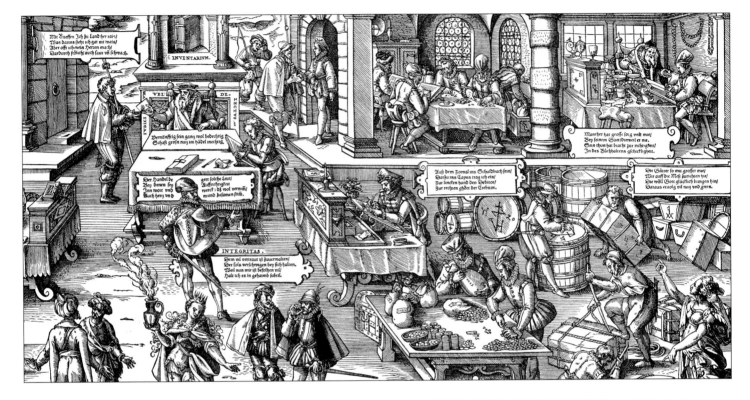

ABOVE: Christian-German commerce in the 16th century. Detail from a woodcut by Jost Amman (1539–1591).

RIGHT: Market scene in Nuremberg, 17th century. On the right, two Jewish peddlers with a boy.

LEFT: Jewish cloth merchants, 17th century. Copperplate engraving after a drawing by Georg Strauch.

The wealth that poured into Europe after the discovery of America increased the desire for gold and money and so also gave an impetus to Christian maritime trade, Christian commerce, from which Jews were excluded. Gold and money now paid for the increasing luxury enjoyed by secular and clerical rulers. Their pursuit of power burst apart the old economic order in the countryside as well as in the towns.

The land owned by the Church and its income from tithes became less significant. The Church took the decisive step from taking the tithe in kind to making money: increasingly, it sold privileges, offices and benefices, from cardinal's hats to abbacies, for hard cash. The selling of indulgences for money was one of the biggest financial enterprises of the time. The new economic practices also increased the financial pressure on peasants and craftsmen.

Martin Luther and his fellow campaigners complained bitterly about the Church's pursuit of show and money at the expense of the common man. When the common

ABOVE: Hans Sebald Beham (1500–1550), "Village Scene." On the right the debtors' prison; in front of it a Jew redeeming a Jewish debtor who is in the stocks.

BELOW: "Jewish Itinerant Musicians" (klezmorim), c. 1560 (by Hans Bol).

folk and peasants were in debt or wanted to buy an indulgence for the salvation of their souls, it was chiefly Jewish pawnbrokers, moneylenders, peddlers, and moneychangers who supplied them with money. Through the interest they received some of them became relatively prosperous – compared, that is, with the general public, not the wealthy Christian merchants.

Around 1500 the Jews were again expelled from many territories and from most of the Free Cities of the Empire. This happened at a time when Christian financial dealers and merchants were becoming powerful through the new money-based economy – the Fuggers and Welsers, the Imhofs, Hochstädters, and others. These trade barons in Augsburg and Nuremberg amassed great wealth in a short time and lent money to the emperor, to princes and cities, in return for interest or a share in profits, for instance. Like the Templars and the Lombards before them, the German merchants too either evaded or simply ignored the Church's ban on usury, once

"The lawyer with his book, the Jew with his greed, and what is under a woman's apron: these three drive the whole world mad." Woodcut by Hans Wandereisen, 1520.

"Kipper and Wipper" (degraders of the coinage). Both Jews and Christians took part in the profitable activity of collecting old coins with a higher silver content and issuing new ones containing less silver. Emperor Ferdinand II sent his "Kipper and Wipper" all around Europe. Woodcut, 17th century.

they had ousted the Jews from their role as the main dealers in money and used their political influence to have them expelled. A chronicler in Lübeck, for example, speaks in 1499 of Christian pawnbrokers providing loans at interest and taking objects as security, because there were no Jews there.

The only options that remained open to the Jews, who were for the most part impoverished as a result of special taxes, lootings, and expulsions, were those of acting as pawnbrokers to peasants and artisans, and peddling wares in the villages or on the fringes of markets. Another possibility was to trade in the towns, but this quickly aroused the envy of competing Christian traders and led to expulsions. "Insofar as one can speak of an anti-Semitic economic program in the late Middle Ages, it took the form of restricting Jews to the lowest and most demeaning occupations. This is the program that the mendicant orders had invented in the 13th century and that was later also supported by the German Reformers (Luther and his circle)." So writes the historian of medieval Jewry, Fritz Jizchak Baer, in his book *Galut* (1934).

The restriction of Jews to the occupation of lending money for interest gave them, especially among the lower economic classes, the stigma of being usurers, and also that of being receivers of stolen goods. In the turmoil of the battles of the Reformation and the Peasants' Wars, and later in the Thirty Years' War, lansquenets (hired foot-soldiers), townspeople, and highwaymen obtained booty, some of which they passed on to Jewish peddlers, pawnbrokers, and financiers in exchange for coin, which, being portable, was sought-after. It is worth noting that lansquenets and also peasants, who after all had a close relationship with their Jewish money dealers, rarely became persecutors of the Jews. "Among the lansquenets the Jews were well-liked, no [Jew] suffered the slightest maltreatment from them," states a Hebrew manuscript which records the defense of Frankfurt by Charles V's troops in 1552.

Under the influence of the clergy, however, the legendary figure of the treacher-

ous disciple Judas was transformed in the popular mind into the avaricious Jewish usurer, greedy for money and power. This image is one of the chief stereotypes of international anti-Semitism. It persisted despite the complaints of contemporary authors that Christian usurers often set far higher rates of interest than did Jews.

Jews were obliged to observe the "honorable rules and statutes" which Josel of Rosheim had managed to establish in Augsburg in 1530; in addition they adhered to the rates of interest prescribed by the Christian authorities, if only for fear of very severe penalties.

The first regulation of the Augsburg code reads: "If a Jew sells goods to a Christian on credit, he shall not (on pain of punishment) practice usury and shall not demand a higher price, even if he has to wait a year and a day for payment." The second regulation states: "If a Jew lends a smaller or larger sum of money, he may demand a moderate rate of interest, as permitted to him by the privileges granted by the Emperor and others. He shall, however, on pain of severe punishment, refrain from adding the interest to the capital sum every quarter or half year, lest the poor man be overburdened, to the detriment of his bodily nourishment."

To borrow money from a Jew was not difficult; to repay it with interest was less pleasant. When harvests were bad, it became difficult or even impossible. If there was a series of bad harvests, the promissory notes held by the Jewish mon-

eylenders piled up and the peasant found himself in difficulties. He was in debt, sometimes uncomfortably, sometimes inextricably, to "the Jew," "the Jewish usurer," "the Judas." Expelling, plundering, or killing the Jew wiped out the debt. The less protection the moneylender enjoyed, the greater was the temptation. This expedient had already been seized upon by King Wenceslas IV and other potentates in earlier centuries, and also by the burghers of some cities.

Apart from dealing in money and peddling wares, only a few other occupations were available to Jews in the Christian society. These included being showmen at fairs, quacks and doctors, or itinerant musicians (known as klezmorism, from the Hebrew *kle-zemer*, musical instruments).

As late as the 16th century many Jewish doctors, male and female, were practicing as personal physicians at the courts of princes, in towns, and also in monasteries. In Regensburg Christian doctors complained, shortly before the Jews were expelled, that when people needed treatment they nearly always went to Jewish doctors. The field of surgery in particular, which was regarded as quackery by many Christian doctors right into the 18th century, was one in which many Jews were active, in both war and peacetime. However, the opposition of the Church and of the Christian doctors meant that their number steadily declined. Among the exceptions were Marranos, ostensible Christians who had received their training in Spain and who, after fleeing from there, once again avowed their Jewish faith. One of the best-known of these was Immanuel Rosales, whom emperor Frederick III made a count of the Empire in 1647. Other Jewish doctors paid the price demanded by the Church and underwent baptism in order to be able to continue practicing their profession. Some of these were Christians in public but remained Jews in their hearts.

The Ghetto in Frankfurt am Main

In accordance with the resolutions of the Lateran Council of 1215 and of the Council of Basle (1431–1449), Emperor Frederick III had ordered the removal of all Jews from their houses in the area of the cathedral in Frankfurt. However, the city's patricians, who occupied two-thirds of the seats on the city council, were mostly on good terms with the Jews and refused to evict them. After long hesitation and despite resistance by the Jews, who in this Free City of the Empire did not lack status and influence, the city did finally carry out the emperor's orders in 1462.

By the Wollgraben, the sewer along the city wall, a second wall was now built. This created a long, narrow alley, just about 300 meters long, between the two walls; the Jews called it "New Egypt." It was closed off by three gates which were open only during the hours of daylight.

Right up to the time when Napoleon's troops marched in, this was where the Jewish community lived, with all its institutions and all its trades and activities: moneydealers and peddlers, cattle-dealers and bankers; scholars, teachers, bakers, and art collectors; butchers, tailors, shoemakers; adults and children, the sick and the well. Here lived the poor families and the rich, the Baruchs and the Rothschilds, the Sterns and the Schönbergs. It was a microcosm enclosed within two facing rows of houses.

In this muddle of narrow-fronted houses, with rooms crammed in one beside another, one inside another, one built on above another, there developed a well-ordered, multifaceted, and intensive communal life, with a schoolhouse, a house for festivities ("Jews' dancinghouse"), two guesthouses (to provide meals and accommodation for visitors and students), a bakehouse, a hospital, a public bath, and a synagogue. It was a small but prosperous community. In the 16th century it became famous far and wide through the work of its scholars and so succeeded to the preeminence that in the Middle Ages had belonged to the important Jewish communities on the Rhine.

ABOVE LEFT: Jewish couple from Frankfurt, c. 1700. Copperplate engraving by C. Weigel, Nuremberg, 1703.

Der Juden Stättigkeit, regulations imposed by the authorities, with an historical account, Frankfurt, 1614.

Frankfurt's *Judengasse* ("Jews' Lane") became the center of Jewish life in Germany and the place where the parnasim (leaders of Jewish communities) from all over the Empire would assemble. Thus during the autumn trade fair of 1603, for instance, an assembly of rabbis meeting at the same time attempted to unite the Jews of southern and western Germany in a single association, but the plan was thwarted by the particularism of some congregations and their rabbis.

Town plan showing the *Judengasse*. Copperplate engraving by Merian, 1624. All 193 houses are shown, viewed from above. The synagogue and the community hall occupy a relatively large area. The street was about 300 meters long.

However, some important resolutions were passed at that assembly, for instance that "no rabbi shall issue a rabbi's certificate in Germany without obtaining the agreement of three scholars who run rabbinical schools in Germany ...

Much harm is done in communities and small places by Jewish miscreants willfully dashing truth to the ground and making deals with new coins which are invalid or inferior but which these swindlers claim are genuine coins ... Therefore, from this day forth, anyone who is involved in such practices ... shall be excommunicated. This shall be the law in every state and every region.

If a person is proved to be doing business with thieves ... then this villain shall be punished with excommunication ...

Any person who takes a loan from a gentile or buys something from a gentile and fails to pay shall be punished with excommunication. No Jew may do business with him. If he is imprisoned for such a matter, no Jew shall come to his aid with money or by making representations on his behalf ..."

Many Jewish receivers of stolen goods, excluded in this way from all the Jewish communities in the Empire, joined bands of non-Jewish robbers and thieves.

In 1463, 110 persons were registered as living in the Judengasse itself. In 1520 there were 250, by 1580 no fewer than 1200, and by 1610 the number had risen to 2270. This means that there was one person to each square meter of space. The people lived and worked here, making use of literally every square meter and every possible way of extending the buildings. That in circumstances of such overcrowding a rich cultural life was able to develop was only made possible by the exceptional degree of individual self-discipline and discipline within the community.

The Jews were forbidden to buy land, a prohibition which also applied to building plots within the city. Outside the Judengasse they were not permitted to practice any craft trade or to sell fruit, weapons, or silk like the city's Christians. After 10 o'clock at night and on Sundays and Christian holidays they were not allowed to leave the street which was their ghetto, and at the times when they did leave it they had to wear a yellow patch on their clothing.

In the year 1612, on the occasion of the coronation of Emperor Matthias (reigned 1612–1619), the Frankfurt guilds brought a complaint about the city's patricians and

Attack on the ghetto during the Fettmilch riot, 1614. Copperplate engraving by Merian, 1628.

Jews. Many artisans and small shopkeepers were in debt to both. They demanded that the interest rate be reduced from 12 to 8 percent and that all Jews whose fortune amounted to less than 15,000 thalers be expelled. As was so often the case, the aim was to get rid not of the Jews as such but only of the poor Jews; and fifty of the poorest Jews were indeed driven out of the city. But the complaint about the interest rate was rejected as unjustified. Two years later some artisans, led by the guildmaster Vinzenz Fettmilch and aided by the city's riffraff, stormed and looted the ghetto. After five hours of resistance, during which two Jews and one attacker lost their lives, the Jews were herded together in the cemetery. For thirteen hours the mob continued its looting, until finally the mayor intervened with men in armor, under whose protection about 1400 Jews were able to leave the city.

This time the emperor took drastic measures. He placed Fettmilch under the imperial ban and had him and four others arrested and beheaded. The Jews were escorted back into their street to the sound of pipes and drums, this time with an explicit personal guarantee of safety from the emperor, who also had his coat of arms affixed to one of the gates of the ghetto.

The Jews' resistance to the attack, and the fact that even as Jews they were accorded the protection of the laws of the state, made the Fettmilch riot a turning point in the history of the Jews in Germany. Instead of leading to a wave of pogroms, as had happened on previous comparable occasions, these disturbances were followed by a period of peace. A turning point is also apparent in the way that the media of public opinion, the illustrated pamphlets, presented the Fettmilch story: for probably the first time, the Jews were not portrayed in a degrading manner.

Among the children who experienced the traumatic Fettmilch riot was Süsskind Stern (1610–1687), who was to become one of the richest of the Frankfurt Jews. A money changer, dealer in pearls, banker, and lessee of the salt mines near Bad Orb, he was also the honorary supervisor of the communal Jewish bakery with its five ovens, an active member of one of the two voluntary funeral fraternities, and a philanthropist. In addition he was the father of a scholar, which enhanced his standing in the community still further.

Most of the descendants of Süsskind Stern, among them the Paris Rothschilds, remained Jews. Their baptized descendants include the Portuguese Barons von Stern, and in England Lord Wandsworth, Lord Michelham, and Countess Rosse.

The community's rabbi up to the time of the Fettmilch riot was Isaiah Horowitz (c. 1565–c. 1630). His main work, Schene luhot ha-berit ("The Two Tablets of the Covenant") is a compendium of the doctrine and commandments of the Jewish religion. This book contributed greatly to the spread of Jewish mysticism among Jews both in Germany and in Poland and Russia.

Messianic Hope – Shabbetai Tzevi

What was the link between the Marranos on Christopher Columbus's ships and in 15th-century Spain and Portugal and the Jewish artisans and rabbis in Poland? What linked the Jewish court stewards in 17th and 18th-century Germany with the water-carriers and blacksmiths in Greece and Morocco, the Jewish tax-gatherers, distillers, and Talmud scholars of 19th-century Lithuanian Russia with the silversmiths in unexplored Yemen and the educated rabbis in Germany?

They all belonged to a minority that was often persecuted, at best tolerated, which prayed to the same God in the same language. They studied the same Bible. Their daily life was governed by the same religious laws. Their rabbis and community leaders derived their instructions to the people from a common Talmudic tradition. They shared the same memories of their ancestors from Abraham onward, and of the time when they had lived as a free people on their own land in their own country.

All of them were persistently oppressed or persecuted as a religious minority and forced into demeaning occupations. They shared the same utopian expectation of a liberation from the "Galut," their forced exile. All of them hoped for a return to Eretz Israel, the land of Israel, under the leadership of the King, the Messiah.

Nathan of Gaza, Shabbetai Tzevi's prophet. Copperplate engraving, 1665.

In the cabalistic system of rabbi Isaak Luria (1534–1572), who was active in Safed, these expectations acquired a new form and a new content. Liberation from exile was now no longer understood as a single intervention by God in the course of world history but as the task of the Jewish people and of each Jewish individual, striving for the salvation of all peoples and of the whole world.

By meticulous observance of the mitzvot (the commandments of the Torah), by good deeds, by asceticism and meditation, every Jew can take part in the "assembling of the divine sparks," that is, in the cosmic process by which the imperfect creation is improved and ultimately brought to perfection.

This was the socio-religious background of the manic-depressive scholar Shabbetai Tzevi (1626–1676), who in excessively manic periods of "illumination" regarded himself as the son of God, but in depressive states had to battle with demons. In April 1665 he traveled from Smyrna to Gaza, where he hoped to "find peace for his soul" with the famous Lurian cabalist and visionary Nathan Benjamin Levi Ghazati Ashkenazi (1644–1680). But Nathan, who had already seen the sick

man in Jerusalem, convinced him that he truly was the Messiah. Nathan himself felt that he had been called to be the prophet of the Messiah, and for the rest of his life he continued, out of true conviction, to be his follower and propagandist and the driving force of a messianic movement.

In the fall of 1665, circular letters and rumors spread reports of signs and miracles performed by a Messiah who had appeared. He was said to have declared himself king of the Jews in Jerusalem, and he would have power even over the Sultan.

In Constantinople, Smyrna, Vienna, Amsterdam, Venice, Prague, Hamburg and Fürth, Vilnius and Pinsk, and even in the smallest villages, the majority of Jews were

RIGHT, CENTER: "True portrayal of Sabetha Sebi, the appointed bringer of the Divine Kingdom," contemporary copperplate engraving.

LEFT: Departure from Vienna to the Holy Land. A satirical "New Bulletin" commenting on Shabbetai Tzevi's messianic movement, Nuremberg, 1666.

gripped by an ecstatic excitement which was accompanied by manifestations of mass hysteria. There were similar developments in Morocco and Algeria, in Egypt, in distant Yemen, and in Kurdistan.

As the messianic hope was linked with asceticism and penance, most followers fasted on three days of every week, and women and children on Mondays and Thursdays. Only a few doubters resisted the ecstatic sense that a new era was imminent. In the chronicle of the Portuguese community in Hamburg we read under the date of 1 Tevet 5426 (from the creation of the world), i.e., 9 December 1665 by the Christian calendar, "Thanks be to the Lord of creation for the tidings which have arrived from the Orient and which have received confirmation from Italy and other regions, that HE in his divine grace and mercy has given us, in the land of Israel, a prophet in the Chacham (sage) Rabbi Nathan Ashkenazi and an anointed King in the Chacham Rabbi Shabbetai Tzevi, chosen by God, to whom be praise, to liberate HIS people from exile, to the honor of HIS name which has been desecrated among the nations. We believe in these tidings because of the many signs and miracles which, it has been written to us, the Prophet and the King have performed ... May the God of Israel cause these tidings to prove true and grant us the possession of our land. May HE grant that our eyes behold this great joy!"

At the same time, Christian artists were producing pamphlets about the new Messiah illustrated with copperplate engravings or woodcuts; the accounts they gave were sometimes objective, but often mocking. A single-page leaflet by the Nuremberg copperplate engraver Paulus Fürst (1606–1666) satirically depicts and describes the Viennese Jews setting off for the Holy Land to go to the Prophet Nathan. It is a chilling document, for only four years later the Jews of Vienna were in fact driven out of the city where they had thought they enjoyed peace and safety.

Many Jews neglected or gave up all their worldly affairs und prepared to depart. Disillusionment and even despair followed

ABOVE: Shabbetai Tzevi enthroned. From a prayer book printed in Amsterdam in 1666.

RIGHT: "Shabbetai in prison in Abydos, a castle in the Dardanelles." He was held captive there by order of the Sultan, but was in fact not held in prison conditions and could receive visitors. From a contemporary German pamphlet.

very quickly. In Constantinople Shabbetai Tzevi was arrested, bound in chains and taken to the castle of Abydos, where, though under house arrest, he lived like a prince and received his followers. On 15 September 1666 he was offered the choice of a martyr's death by torture or conversion to Islam. Shabbetai Tzevi and some of his followers chose conversion.

After that he lived for ten more years, leading a relatively secluded life as both Muslim and Jew at one and the same time, and writing a number of cabalistic texts before dying suddenly in his 50th year.

To most of his followers, his conversion to Islam was a terrible betrayal and the end of the messianic dream. But his closest disciples saw his apostasy differently: he had taken evil upon himself as a means to salva-

tion. Theological speculations by Nathan, who was the first to interpret the apostasy of the Messiah in mystical terms, laid the foundations for the Shabbetaian sect, which for the next 150 years was to form the main opposition to the rabbis within the Jewish community. Following the example of Shabbetai Tzevi, groups of Orthodox Jews in Poland and Moravia went over to the local religion, which in this case was Roman Catholicism, but regarded themselves as a clandestine Jewish sect.

The majority of the German Jews probably came to terms with their disappointment that the time was not yet ripe in the same way as the Jews in Jakob Wassermann's novel *Die Juden von Zirndorf* ("The Jews of Zirndorf," i.e. Zionsdorf), who are on a pilgrimage to the Messiah when they are overtaken by news of his apostasy.

Glückel of Hamelin, a resident of Hamburg, writes in her memoirs: "The joy

when letters came [about Shabbetai Tzevi] cannot be described ... And the young men among the Portuguese [i.e., Jews from Portugal] all put on their best clothes and each of them tied on a broad green silk sash – that was Shabbetai Tzevi's livery. Thus [attired] they all went off, with drums and dancing, to their synagogue, and with joy 'like the joy in drawing water' read the letters aloud." Glückel tells how her father-in-law abandoned house and home in Hamelin and went to Hildesheim to prepare for the journey to the Messiah in Palestine: "But it was not yet the will of the Most High ... Nevertheless, dear Lord God, you will royally and graciously fulfill your promise to us!"

The Secret Sects of the Shabbetaians and the Frankists

ABOVE: Jonathan Eibeschütz (c.1690–1767), Chief Rabbi of Altona, Hamburg, and Wandsbek. He was accused of being a secret adherent of Shabbetaianism.

After the collapse of Shabbetai Tzevi's Messianic movement (see p. 92), a Shabbetaian movement came into being in various countries, a clandestine sect which influenced many orthodox rabbis and their followers.

The movement was based on the premise that Shabbetai Tzevi could not have been the ultimate Messiah, but was his precursor. A number of the Hasidic Jews in Poland turned to this movement, or at least found in a moderate form of it elements with which they could identify.

However, the followers of its extreme wing, who were suspected of heresy, united to form a religious underground movement. They were convinced that the believer is justified through his faith alone and that salvation is thus not dependent on obedience to moral laws. Breaches of the laws of the Torah could, according to these radical Shabbetaians, actually be the starting-point for salvation, the invalidating of the Torah could actually be its true fulfillment. The secret sects of the Shabbetaians had centers

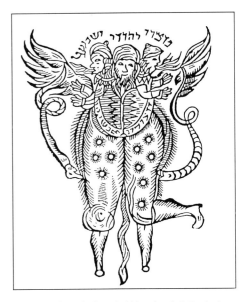

Caricature of Frank's heretical ideas in Jakob Emden's *Sefer ha' Shimmush* (Handbook), written in 1758–62 to counter Shabbetaian ideas. The three-headed figure represents, from left to right, a Muslim, a Jew, and a Christian.

all over Europe, in Turkey, in Palestine and in North Africa. In Mannheim they met from 1708 onward in an orthodox schoolroom. This group existed until 1725, the year in which Shabbetaians in Germany and in other countries were excommunicated.

One of the signatories of the declaration of excommunication was the famous cabalist and rabbi Jonathan Eybeschütz (1690–1764), who came from Prague and was appointed chief rabbi of the united communities of Altona, Hamburg, and Wandsbek. This made the scandal all the more deeply unsettling when in Altona the respected scholar Jakob Emden (1697–1776) believed he had unmasked him as a secret follower of Shabbetaianism, because Eibeschütz had distributed cabalistic amulets of a Shabbetaian character.

Eibeschütz protested against this accusation, but his opponents pointed to the

LEFT: This montage, circulated by his opponents to misrepresent him, shows Rabbi Jonathan Eibeschütz with a Shabbetaian amulet.

principle of the secret Shabbetaians that the true believer must not reveal his faith. Up to the end of the 19th century a number of rabbis and pupils remained adherents of this Shabbetaian movement.

Independently of these groups of "orthodox" Shabbetaians there grew up an extremely heretical movement under the leadership of the charismatic and autocratic Jakob (Leibowicz) Frank (1726–1791). His heresy, a ragbag of the theories of the Turkish Shabbetaians and the cabalists, lay in the assumption of a trinity of "holy antiquity," the "holy King," and the "highest female person," the Matron or the Virgin. He saw himself as an incarnation of the "holy King," with Shabbetai Tzevi as his precursor. An opponent of all religion, he demanded from his followers that they pass through all religions, destroying them all from within, in order to attain true freedom.

Frank had grown up in Czernowitz, prided himself on his imperfect Jewish education, and proclaimed a kind of transgression of religious laws on morality, including sexual morality. He and his fol-

Jakob (Leibowicz) Frank (1726–1791), the autocratic leader of a Shabbetaian Christianizing sect.

Eva Frank (d.1816), who succeeded her father at the "Frank court" in Offenbach. She sometimes claimed to be the daughter of the Tsar.

lowers converted – with reservations – to the Roman Catholic Church, and enjoyed the protection of Bishop Dembowski, who used the group for purposes of anti-Jewish propaganda. Yet the Frankists continued to regard themselves wholly as Jews, and did not marry outside Jewish families. In 1786 Jakob Frank relocated to Offenbach, where he resided in a building that was like a

palace and appeared in public with military pomp. After his death most of his followers dispersed. The three children who called themselves his successors died in poverty, the last being his daughter Eva who died in 1816. For some decades after that, however, a number of well-to-do, respected families, spread all over Europe, continued to be secret Frankists, linked by family ties.

The "Mansion of Baron de Frank" in Offenbach, with military guard and courtly ceremonial. Frank leaving the house, supported by two adjutants.

Family Life in the 17th and 18th Centuries

"Childbirth": friends, neighbors, and relatives pray in the room of the woman who has given birth and greet the newborn child with blessings. A Christian depiction in P.C. Kirchner's *Jüdisches Ceremoniell* (Jewish Ritual), Nuremberg, 1734. Copperplate engraving by Jacob Jugendas.

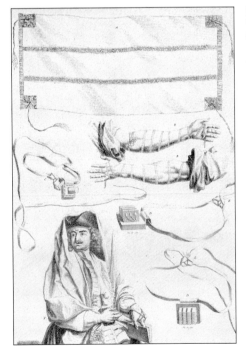

Illustration showing the tallit (prayer shawl) and the tefillin (phylacteries), which are put on for morning prayer in accordance with Exodus 13, 9. The boxes contain extracts from the Torah written on parchment. After B. Picart, *Cérémonies et coutumes religieuses de tous les peuples du monde*, Amsterdam, 1723ff.

RIGHT: Celebration of the Feast of Tabernacles (Sukkot) among the prosperous and the poor, distinguishable by the different appearance of the festive booths. Copperplate engraving by Georg Paul Nussbiegel, Nuremberg, 1738, after a drawing by Gottfried Eichler.

phylacteries (tefillin), worn wound round the left arm and on the head, with a small cube-shaped boxes at the ends containing extracts from the Pentateuch written on parchment. In the synagogue he wears the tallit, the prayer shawl. Besides this, he wears the arba kanfot (meaning "four corners"), a rectangular cloth with an opening for the head, under his clothes but with its fringes (zizit) visible.

Before every meal the pious Jew washes his hands while saying a blessing. After the main meal he thanks God for the food and drink. He says a prayer at the start of a journey, at the appearance of the new moon, when natural phenomena such as thunderstorms occur, and on many other occasions. Religiously based precepts and guidelines on sexual, hygienic, and ethical matters also

Jewish life was always informed by religion, with unconditional belief in the One and Only God at its center. Every phase of this life – and in Orthodox circles this is still true – was accompanied by ritual commandments, prayers, blessings and traditions.

Every activity, from drinking water to conjugal relations, was an occasion to thank God. Three times a day – after getting up and washing, late in the afternoon and then after sunset – prayers were and are recited, interwoven with psalms and texts from the Holy Scriptures.

Every morning from his thirteenth year onward the Orthodox Jew puts on the

contributed greatly to women's emotional well-being and thus to the harmony of family life. This is not altered by the fact that the man thanks God in his prayers for not having created him as a woman. The woman also played her part in earning a living and was almost always the center of the family.

The idea that sexuality is sinful does not exist in Judaism. In the Cabala, indeed, the sexual act is compared to God's act of creation of the world.

For Orthodox Jews the Sabbath and other Holy Days are the high points of family life.

The Sabbath begins on Friday evening at sundown. At that moment the lady of the

house lights the candles, while saying blessings. "On Friday at the approach of night every Jew is a king ... and every Jewess a queen," says an old folk song. In the synagogue the man of the family greets the Sabbath like a bride, using the traditional hymn:

"Go, my friend,
to meet the bride.
Let us welcome the Sabbath ..."

Then, at home, he blesses the children and speaks the kiddush over the wine and bread. This is the sanctification of the day of rest, which begins with Genesis, chapter 2, verse 1: "Thus the heavens and the earth were finished, and all the host of them ... And God blessed the seventh day, and sanctified it: because that in it he had rested from all his work which God created and made ..."

ABOVE: Seder night during Pesah (Passover). The prayer at table is introduced by the words "Rabosai, mir wellen benschen" (Sirs, let us say a blessing). Opposite the head of the household sits a guest, as was customary on Seder night. (18th-century depiction.)

RIGHT: An elegant wedding in Fürth. Copperplate engraving by I.C. Müller, 1735.

In the Community

The almemor, the dais (bima) from which the Torah was read out, was normally in the middle of the synagogue. The ark with the sacred scrolls of the Torah always stands against, or is set into, the east wall – the side facing toward Jerusalem, the same direction toward which Jews still turn when praying. The women sat, concealed from the eyes of the men, in the gallery, on a balcony, or at the side behind a screen of ornamental ironwork, from where they could share in the worship.

By about 1700 a kehillah, a Jewish community dating back to the time before the expulsions, survived only in a few Imperial cities. In such communities the traditional order still prevailed: they were led by a number of prosperous and respected families, who bore the main burden of taxes and were therefore well placed to deal with the city council as representatives of their community.

The Jewish communities in small towns and villages scattered throughout the

Communities generally possessed a synagogue, a school, the cemetery, a hospital, and a hostel for scholars passing through, for fugitives, and poor people. The voluntary Holy Brotherhood was responsible for burials, and membership of it was an honor for rich and poor alike. The mikvah, the ritual bath, was looked after by a couple appointed for the purpose. Schoolmasters were also appointed for children whose parents could not afford a private tutor. Other community officials were the ritual slaughterers, the cantors in the synagogue and the *shul* knocker, who knocked on the doors or window shutters twice a day to call the men to prayer in the synagogue. The time of prayers varied according to the time of sunrise. On special occasions such as weddings there was music performed by itinerant musicians. Sometimes, too, painters would be brought from other areas or even other countries to decorate a synagogue – the prayer room at Horb is an example – with decorative ornaments, animals, plants, and prayer texts. The day on which such a piece of work was completed was a day of celebration for the whole community. So was the day when a copier of the Torah had written the last word of the Five Books of Moses on a parchment scroll. When a new Torah scroll was brought into the synagogue for the first time, on a Sabbath, to be ceremonially read, it was adorned with a crown, like a king.

ABOVE: A meeting of the Jewish community council in Frankfurt am Main. Copperplate engraving, 18th century.

Cleansing in the ritual bath (mikvah) of a woman who has given birth. Copperplate engraving by J.C. Müller, c. 1730.

עשׂמו להועיל דזר מיוחד ∴ ולח"כ מתפלליך ערבית ע
עד גמירא ∴

י ואחר יציאות מב"ה יקדש הלבנה (
נקודכ קידוש הלבנה יאמר הלוייה חת"יל מן הטמיס. עד
חוק נתן ולא יעבור) ומח"כ יאמר) הריני מוכן י
ומזומן לקייס מצות לקדש הלבנה לסס יחוד קב"ה
וטכינתיה ע"י ההוא טמיר ונעלם בטס כנ יטרן:

ברוך אתה יי אלהינו מלך העולם
אשר במאמרו ברא שחקים

many petty states decided in the 17th and 18th centuries to adopt a new form of communal government. Every three years, "privileged" Jewish heads of households to whom the authorities had granted the right of residence assembled for a regional parliament (an assembly of the Jews of that state). Here the officials and representatives of the communities rendered an account of the years in which they had held office, and here every community and every member of each community was assessed with regard to the taxes to be paid by the communities to their rulers.

The parliament took place under the joint supervision of the Christian authorities and the country's chief rabbi at the time. It also took decisions regarding the conferring of the title of rabbi, and, in open voting, elected community officials for the next three years. Most important of these was the office of district shtadlan, the communities' spokesman and representative in their dealings with the authorities – the function which Josel of Rosheim had once fulfilled in such an outstanding manner (see p. 84).

Disputes between members of the well-to-do and the poorer classes were also brought before the parliament. An insuperable problem was that of the many Jews who lacked rights of residence and protection. There was probably not a single Jewish family that did not take in and support one such defenseless person, or even a whole family, as employees or tutors, but since the Thirty Years' War and the Khmelnytsky massacres the number of Jews reduced to beggary had risen so steeply that acts of charity alone were no longer enough.

In the Commercial World

During the Thirty Years' War, the fact that the Jewish community had contacts in other countries often made them useful to the military leaders as army suppliers and as providers of intelligence. They also provided services to the soldiers and peasants, changing looted coin, buying looted goods, and selling wares of many different kinds.

Under the Peace of Westphalia of 1648, the rulers agreed to a degree of mutual tolerance between Roman Catholics, Calvinists, and Lutherans. The main concern now was to rebuild the destroyed towns and villages and to strengthen the newly restored rule of law.

LEFT: Prayer when making a journey, from an illustrated prayer book, Fürth, 1738: "May it be thy will, O Lord our God and God of our fathers, to lead us in peace and accompany our steps in peace ..."

The commercially oriented period which followed provided Jews too with the chance of enjoying greater security in towns and villages and on the highways. Instead of being regarded as disreputable, trade and financial dealing were now seen as very desirable, since the trader had become indispensable to the process of reconstruction, and the pursuit of success was now the driving force. As a result many Jews were able to rise from being peddlers to being market traders. It was most notably in the matter of providing large loans that they

were able to fill a vacuum, a "gap in the market." Arranging and supplying international loans to princes and kings launched the careers of many "Court Jews."

Towards the end of the 17th century the number of Jews from German, Polish, Austrian, and Hungarian territories visiting the Leipzig trade fair each year already stood at over 750, despite the fact that Jews still had to pay high tolls for themselves and their goods. The personal and visitors' tolls imposed on Jews represented an additional source of income for the increasingly flourishing towns and for the treasuries of the princes. So it was that at Nördlingen, for instance, in response to

Abraham Höchberg, Court Jew of the Bishop of Würzburg and leader of the Jewish community. Painting attributed to Johann Kupetzky (1667–1740).

the urgent pleas of its citizens, the town's administration in 1669 once again permitted financial dealings with Jews and encouraged Jews to visit the town.

Trade with eastern Europe made Breslau a major economic center. Here, in 1630, the town council had invited Jewish traders, mostly from Poland, to settle. In later centuries, descendants of those Polish traders were to play a vital part in the economic, cultural, scholarly, and scientific life of Berlin and other cities. Even today we are reminded of their Polish-Jewish descent by such known surnames such as

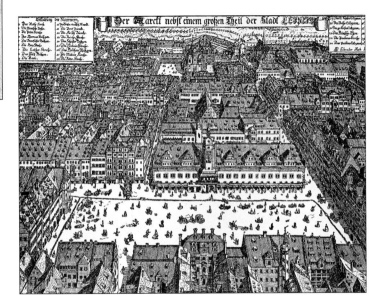

RIGHT: The marketplace in Leipzig, copperplate engraving by Johann Georg Schreiber, 1712. A considerable number of the importers of leather, hides, and furs were Jewish merchants from Poland and Russia.

Pass entitling a Jew to attend the trade fair at Nördlingen, 18th century.

Hochfürstlich und Hochgräflich
Oettingisch Gleit

Nördlinger Meß

auf fußgehende Juden.

15. Kr.

den   No. 17

"Horse-trading." Copperplate engraving by Johann Heinrich Ramberg, 1805.

Von Juden-Sachen.

No. I. Edict wegen der Pohlnischen Juden Arretirung auff denen Jahrmärckten rc. Vom 20. August. 1650.

Fr. Wilhelm.
(L.S.)

No. II. Edict wegen auffgenommenen 50. Familien Schutz-Juden, jedoch daß sie keine Synagogen halten. Vom 21. May 1671.

Tucholsky, Warschauer, Kracauer, and Witkowski.

More and more Jews were now being allowed to live in towns or at least admitted on market days on payment of a personal toll. Jewish traders who traveled from one market to another became a regular sight. They spent the time from Monday morning to Friday morning on the roads and at the markets, and then returned to their families in good time for the start of the Sabbath.

Legal powers within the community and representative status in relation to the authorities still belonged, in the 17th and 18th centuries, to the leader of a Jewish community, who was recognized by the authorities, princes and bishops as the legal representative of the Jews and was sometimes referred to as the "Jews' bishop."

Edicts issued by the Great Elector, 1650 and 1671. Edict no. 1, of 20 August 1650, prohibits the arrest of Polish Jews at fairs, and instructs that no abnormal tolls be demanded from them and that they be "allowed to pass without hindrance." Edict no. 2, of 21 May 1671, "graciously announces" that at the request of some Jews of Brandenburg and "for commercial and general benefit," fifty Jewish families are to be "most graciously taken and received into our special protection."

The Portuguese Jews in Hamburg

OPPOSITE, TOP LEFT: The Sephardic rabbi Jacob Sasportas (1610–1698) in official dress.

OPPOSITE, BOTTOM LEFT: "Jacob's dream" as depicted on a Sephardic gravestone in Altona.

Since the 14th century there had been an increase in religiously motivated persecution of Jews and enforced baptism in Spain. A climax was reached in 1492 with the expulsion of all unbaptized Jews from the territory of the "Catholic Kings" Ferdinand and Isabella.

Tens of thousands had fled into neighboring Portugal, where five years later they were forced to undergo baptism. This was the origin of the "Annussim," the "forced converts," whom the Spaniards called the "Marranos" (pigs) – Jews who had officially converted to Christianity but who inwardly remained Jews. If discovered by the Inquisition, they were burned.

Many of these Annussim and new converts to Christianity, especially wealthy holders of official positions, were able to use a journey abroad as a means of escape. They then reverted to Judaism and

A wedding in a Portuguese family, steel engraving, 19th century, after an original dating from 1725.

BELOW: Illustrated parchment scroll of the Book of Esther, which is read aloud at Purim, mid-18th century. The writing is Sephardic (from Holland); the silver case was made in Germany. Property of a Sephardic family in Germany.

founded communities in North Africa, Italy, Greece, England, South America, and Holland. They came to Hamburg as "Portuguese Christians," but later admitted to being Jews and obtained permission, in 1612, to settle there as Jews. They achieved this thanks to their skills as shipbuilders, doctors, goldsmiths, bankers, and importers of sugar, tobacco, and other goods from overseas. They also helped to encourage whaling and developed trade with Greenland. By 1600, to the delight of the Hamburg merchants, they had broken the monopoly of the Fuggers, the Welsers, and other powerful south German trading houses both in the provision of credit and in foreign and overseas trade.

An example of the highly respected Sephardic (Portuguese) families in Hamburg is the Texeira family. Abraham Texeira (1581–1666), the descendant of a family of Annussim, was the son of a lady-in-waiting to the Queen of Portugal. In 1643 he was appointed the Spanish Crown's trade representative in the Netherlands. Soon afterward he moved to Hamburg with his wife, who had now also reverted to Judaism, and had both himself and his adult son circumcised. Texeira founded an international banking house,

Henriette de Lemos, aged 14, painted in 1778 by Anna Dorothea Therbusch. Her father was a doctor in the Portuguese community in Hamburg. She later became famous as Henriette Herz.

together with Sephardic Jews in Amsterdam and England; he also served a number of terms as head of the Jewish community in Hamburg.

From 1612 onward the Sephardic Jews had had to pay an annual sum of 1000 marks to the Senate for the right to settle and stay in the city; in 1617 the amount was doubled. When, in 1697, the citizens persuaded the Senate to raise the sum to 6000 marks and also to require the Portuguese Jews to make a "once and for all" payment of 20,000 marks, while imposing severe restrictions on their worship, these humiliating demands caused some of them to emigrate to Amsterdam. A dispute arose between the Senate and the

citizens over the departure of this group that was commercially so vital to the city. An Imperial commission which was set up to resolve it arrived at a new set of regulations, confirmed by the emperor, which were more favorable to those Portuguese Jews who still remained and contained no demands for money. However, the Hamburg Sephardim became a far less significant group in the course of the 18th century. In the 1920s they numbered about 200.

There were many famous Sephardic doctors in Hamburg, and by the 17th century some of them were already becoming personal physicians to kings. "My father was a Portuguese Jew, whose grandfather had to flee from Portugal with many of his

co-religionists so as not to fall into the hands of the Inquisition," wrote the famous Henriette Herz (see p. 140) in her memoirs.

The Lowest Level of Society

In the one hundred and fifty years between the end of the Thirty Years' War and the close of the 18th century the population of Germany tripled. The number of Jews rose still more sharply.

The situation of impoverished Jews without property became particularly wretched. Because of their religious denomination they could not work their way up in the productive society, nor were they accepted into the army or the service of the state. They were not allowed to hire themselves out as laborers, to learn a trade or to do agricultural work. Worst of all, they could not obtain a permit to settle anywhere, unless they could buy their way into a village owned by a knight of the Empire; in Hesse there were about three hundred such villages. This cost a considerable sum, but less than a permit to live in a town. In some districts attached to a castle whole Jewish quarters grew up in this way, much to the benefit of the lord of the castle, whose loyal servants these Jews became.

The lowest class of Jews living on the breadline included traveling students and also younger sons of settled Jews who could not obtain a privilege enabling them to marry and whose parents could not afford to buy them a residence permit. There were also vagrants, beggars, and the masses of homeless fugitives from pogrom areas. A stratum of Jewish society was thus formed which was on the same socioeconomic level as that of déclassé Christians (for whom, however, a legal return to society was possible). For these underprivileged people there was no possibility of any legitimate activity, only of activity against society.

As people without the right to stay anywhere, the groups of Jewish beggars were exposed to especial danger. In an edict of 31 August 1712, for example, Duke Anton Ulrich of Brunswick ordered that "begging Jews ... should on the first occasion be punished by ten to fourteen days of harsh imprisonment, thrown into the worst cells fit for dogs ... the second time by flogging and branding, but the third time by the noose."

RIGHT: The robber chief Schinderhannes and his men being brought from Frankfurt am Main to Mainz on 16 June 1802; woodcut, 1802. No. 7 is "Amschel Riederburg, a Jew from Rödelheim."

A minority were received into their homes by Jews with residence permits, as domestic servants with no rights, as tutors (in the case of wandering students of the Talmud), and as employees of the community. Generally these activities were merely a pretext, for all these occupations were oversubscribed. Other homeless Jews traveled from place to place as musicians and entertainers.

The overwhelming majority wandered in groups from place to place, begging. The beggars were allowed to stay and be fed for two days in the Jewish communities' hostels for the poor, and were then sent on their way. Thus for instance in four months of the year 1721 more than 700 Jewish beggars passed through the small Bavarian-Swabian town of Harburg im Ries; in groups of "ten, fifteen or twenty together [they] lie on the hay in a Jewish house" – whereupon the chief official of the town made an order against giving shelter to Jewish beggars. Each place moved them on to the next.

In this class of people barely able to survive, some Jews formed themselves into bands of tricksters, thieves, and robbers corresponding to the non-Jewish ones. A very few non-Jews joined Jewish bands, and vice versa. Thus one of the six members of the group led by the notorious Schinderhannes was Amschel Riederburg, a Jew from Rödelheim. A Jew in the band

of the Bavarian Hiasl may have served as a model for the robber Spiegelberg in Friedrich Schiller's play *Die Räuber* ("The Robbers"), 1781. In a variant reading in the second edition Spiegelberg says to Moor, "How would it be if we became Jews and raised the subject of the Kingdom again?" Moor replies, "Ah, now I see it – now I see it – you want to make the foreskin unfashionable because the barber has already got yours?"

For communication among themselves the Jewish bands of robbers and thieves used a special thieves' cant containing garbled forms of Hebrew words, which was intended to be incomprehensible to law-abiding Jews as well as to gentiles. Many of these words and expressions were also adopted by non-Jewish bands, who naturally had social and professional contact with them. This was the origin of the argot which the police and writers but also people in general called "Rotwelsch" ("Rot" being the Middle High German form of Rotte, a gang or mob; "welsch" meaning French, foreign, unintelligible). The members of the bands themselves called it "Chochemer Loschn," a language comprehensible only to the initiated. (The Hebrew word "chochem," meaning a scholar or sage, came to mean an initiate; "laschon," language, became "loschn.")

As criminals the Jewish bands of robbers were excluded from the rest of Jewry, and this despite the fact that many of them kept the Jewish dietary and Sabbath laws, and that, when captured, Jewish thieves and robbers with very few exceptions chose hanging or being burned at the stake in preference to baptism. Captured Jewish thieves were usually tortured. Police reports noted with admiration that Jewish criminals often managed to endure torture without betraying their accomplices.

The robber bands were highly organized, so much so that individual members were able to pay a certain proportion of their booty into a communal fund which was used to provide for sick members and for the families of any who were imprisoned. For some, ironically, robbing and stealing provided the means of moving up

ABOVE: The Jewish thief Jonas Mejer. The designation "anti-Christian" refers to his refusal to receive baptism in return for a lighter punishment. He was hanged by the feet, together with a live dog that gnawed at him. Copperplate engraving by Johann Christoph Böcklin after F.T. Delius, 1699.

ABOVE RIGHT: "Hoyum Moyses, vulgo Johann Ingolstädter, an arch thief." Contemporary copperplate engraving, 1737.

BELOW: Execution of Jewish thieves in Vienna, 1642. A baptized Jewish thief, who had reverted to Judaism before his death, is hanged feet upward over a fire.

into respectable society. With the money they had stolen they could, for instance, buy a residence permit from the lord of a castle, pretend to live respectably, and let their children grow up in a normal way. "It is curious," wrote a judge who had presided over the trial of a Jewish gang, "that most Jewish thieves tend to seek the protection of lords of castles." The Jewish bands never carried out their thefts and other crimes within the territory of their patron.

The Highest Level of Society – Court Jews

Alongside the traditional elite, the biblical scholars and leaders of communities, there arose in the 17th century a new upper class consisting of secular scholars, such as doctors and natural scientists, and court factors or court Jews who acted as business agents in the service of a ruler.

What the princes and other rulers of German petty states needed above all was financiers who were not bound to the particularist interests of the nobility. Essential qualities were unconditional loyalty to the ruler, and independence of the interests of the cities, the guilds, the merchants' associations, and not least the Church. This vacuum was filled by Jewish financiers, who through their connections abroad as well as at home could obtain large sums of money and procure and sell large quantities of products.

Michael Gernsheim (c. 1705–1792), the elected head of the autonomous community at Worms. The city administration called him the "Jews' Bishop." Like most heads of communities he was a prosperous businessman, the founder of the oldest German leather firm.

Samuel Oppenheimer (1635–1703) from Heidelberg, who financed the military campaigns of Prince Eugene. Leopold I accorded him the title of "His Roman-Imperial Majesty's Chief Army Factor and Court Jew."

Thus Samuel Oppenheimer (c. 1635–1703) of Heidelberg not only supplied Prince Eugene's Austrian armies in the campaigns against France and Turkey with food, weapons, and ammunition, but also provided their pay. For this he was accorded the title of "His Roman-Imperial Majesty's Chief Army Factor and Court Jew." His successor in the Imperial service was the learned chief rabbi of Hungary, Samson Wertheimer (1658–1724) from Worms, court factor under Leopold I and Joseph I.

Jost Liebmann (c. 1640–1702), Berlin jeweler and court financier, became the Court Jew of the Great Elector and was granted permission to build a synagogue. Around 1700, with a fortune of 100,000

LEFT: Raphael Levi (1685–1779), mathematician, secretary and friend of Leibniz. Among other things Levi devised a simple method, for use in land surveying, to determine the degree of longitude.

BELOW: The doctor Gottschalk von Geldern (1726–1795), maternal grandfather of the poet Heinrich Heine.

LEFT: Marcus Elieser Bloch (1723–99), doctor in Berlin, friend of Moses Mendelssohn, and famous ichthyologist. His nine-volume "Universal Natural History of Fishes" is illustrated with many hundreds of copperplate engravings.

thalers, he was thought to be the richest Jew in Germany.

Some Court Jews, however, met with an unhappy end.

The leader of the Jewish community in Fürth, Elkan Fraenkel (1675–1720), became the Court Jew of the Margrave of Ansbach-Bayreuth. After being denounced by a baptized Jew who claimed, among other things, that he possessed anti-Christian books, he was tortured and then imprisoned for eight years until his death.

Best known of all is the fate of Joseph Süss Oppenheimer (1692–1738), which has been made the subject of a novella by Wilhelm Hauff, a novel by Lion Feuchtwanger, and plays by Paul Kornfeld

„Umſtändliche Nachricht
Von der,
Von Seiner Hochfürſtl. Durchl. zu Anhalt
etc. und Dero Durchlauchtigſten
Frau Gemahlin, auch ſämmtlichen
Hochfürſtl. Herrſchafft
Des Hochfürſtl. Güterbeſchauers bei der Accise
wie auch Aelteſten bei der Judenſchaft zu Deſſau
Jacobs Sohn
Conrad Jacob als Bräutigam,
Und
Des Hochfürſtlichen Hoff-factors daſelbſt, wie auch
Aelteſten bei gedachter Gemeine Calman Eheleiblichen
Tochter
Beſſgen Calman als Braut,
Gethanen reichlichen
Hochzeits-Ausſtattung
Und darauf am 4ten Februar 1740
Beſchehenen Trauung
Aus unterthänigſter Erkäntlichkeit vor ſothane
Hochfürſtl. Hohe Gnade
Auch zum immer währenden Gedächtniſs
dem Publico
In Druck überreichet
Von
Obbennannten neuen Ehe-Paar.

Marriage announcement: In the palace at Dessau of the Prince of Anhalt, "the Old Man from Dessau"; Conrad Jacob is to marry Bessgen Calman, "legitimate daughter of the August Prince's Court Factor, Calman" (4 February 1740).

Despite the objections of the most famous lawyer in the land, Joseph Süss Oppenheimer was sentenced to death.

First he was put on show in a cage suspended from the crossbar of a gallows. The execution was to be a public festival, and it was expected that at the last Oppenheimer would allow himself to be baptized and so save his life: this would be the climax of the spectacle. But Oppenheimer, at once a freethinker and a believing Jew, climbed the ladder to the cage of death while loudly making the Jewish declaration of belief in the one and only God. The priest standing by to baptize him shouted a curse after him.

and Eugen Ortner. He was court factor and financial adviser to Duke Alexander of Württemberg, besides which he was an esthete and a conceited dandy. "Jew Süss," as he was commonly known, succeeded by his extraordinary resourcefulness in restoring the fortunes of the bankrupt duchy, while showing an arrogant disdain for the long-established families and previous holders of power. What made him more enemies than anything else was the imposition of a five percent tax on official salaries, to boost the state's finances and pay off its debts. He also created a state monopoly on leather, salt, tobacco, and wine. He founded tobacco, silk, and porcelain manufactories and the first bank in the state. Württemberg certainly had him chiefly to thank for its financial recovery. He transferred the leases on lucrative monopolies to fellow Jews who were friends of his – sometimes in return for bribes – which caused the wealthy Christian citizens to hate him even more. Through his activities, at times involving unscrupulous manipulation, he himself became extraordinarily rich. Immediately upon the death of the duke he was arrested and charged with fraud and other crimes, without any evidence being produced.

Plate from the medical writings of Tobias Kohen. He compared the human body to a house: the head is the roof, the eyes are the windows, the mouth is the entrance door. The chest is the top floor, the lungs are the water tanks, and the legs and feet the plot of land on which the house is built.

LEFT: Joseph Süss Oppenheimer (1692–1738) in court dress.

RIGHT: Joseph Süss Oppenheimer, in prison, hears the announcement of the verdict: "The verdict has been determined, I see the staff break (signifying the death sentence), and I may not speak a word in my defense." From a contemporary illustrated account, 1738.

Das Urtheil ist verfaßt, | und ich darf doch kein Wort
ich seh den Stab zerbrechen, | Zu meinem Vortheil sprechen

RIGHT: "Jew Süss" is hanged in a cage. His corpse remained in the cage, " for the ravens to eat." Contemporary illustrated account, 1738.

TOWARD THE MODERN AGE

The Struggle for Equal Rights

From Vienna to Berlin

For the Jews in Germany the modern age began with the mercantilism of the 17th and the Enlightenment of the 18th century.

Mercantilism was based among other things on the theory that the wealth and power of a state depended on the level of its gold and silver reserves. Accordingly, efforts were made to increase domestic production for export while as far as possible depressing imports.

After the Thirty Years' War, Elector Palatine Karl Ludwig (1617–1680) returned to Heidelberg from his exile in Holland. There he had observed the considerable extent to which Jewish fugitives from Spain, Portugal, and Poland, treated with tolerance and given a large measure of commercial freedom, contributed to the country's prosperity. In 1660 he granted the first concessions to Jews living in Mannheim. In return, as part of the economic reconstruction, they were obliged among other things to build two-story dwelling houses, using Jewish as well as Christian workers. The Jews affected by this regarded the obligation as a civil privilege. Lemle Moses Rheinganum, for instance, court factor and lessee of the elector's salt monopoly, set up a model estate in nearby Mühlau. Like most of the court factors in the times that followed he was also active in the Jewish community, and his charitable foundations for the poor survived him by centuries.

Things developed differently in Brandenburg and Berlin. For the Jews here, very few in number but significant in terms of their economic influence, the beginnings of the modern age came with the admittance of fifty prosperous emigrant families from Austria in 1671. Bowing to the influence of the Church, Emperor Leopold I had on 14 April 1670 "most graciously resolved that the Jews who are here shall be removed hence and from the whole country ..." Many of them were received into existing communities in Bohemia, Moravia, and Bavaria.

Tapestry with coat of arms dating from the year 1590, with the motto "I fear God in all things," a gift made by King Frederick William I to the synagogue in Berlin on the occasion of his visit in 1718. A Hebrew inscription, the traditional blessing formula for a king, was embroidered onto this wall hanging: "Long live our lord the king Frederick William – may his radiance be increased." The tapestry served as a curtain for the ark containing the Torah.

RIGHT: The consecration of the first public synagogue in Berlin, in Heidereutergasse, 1714. The building was delayed by fiery debates within the Jewish community between those who favored modest private synagogues and those who wanted a more impressive building. Contemporary copperplate engraving.

Since the expulsions of 1573 there had been few Jews in Brandenburg. In accordance with his economic and population policies, the religiously tolerant Great Elector, Frederick William (reigned 1640–1688), brought chiefly Dutchmen and Huguenots into his underdeveloped country. By his decree of 21 May 1671, he allowed fifty of the wealthiest of the Jewish families expelled from Vienna to settle in Brandenburg, "for commercial and general benefit," as "protected Jews" with a right of residence restricted to twenty years. Here then was toleration, for a fixed period, of a financial elite which was needed for the development of the country and which could at the same time be exploited through so-called "protection charges" and other taxes.

Under his successors, Frederick I, king of Prussia from 1701, and King Frederick William I (reigned 1713–1740), the number of Jewish families in Brandenburg rose to over two hundred; about a hundred of these were "protected Jews," and the rest were "unvergleitet" (unprotected). These included the poorer Jews and the really poor, mostly servants of the privileged Jews. Until 1812, guarantees of protection were generally issued only upon proof of possession of a large fortune – to those who supplied goods to the court, to lessees of mints, jewelers, financiers, and manufacturers. In Brandenburg-Prussia as elsewhere, the guilds, whose members were financially secure, would not admit Jews. The merchants' association also remained closed to them.

According to a resolution passed by the Berlin association of German and French merchants in 1716, "Jews, culpable killers,

The protected Jew Joel (Jost) Liebmann (d. 1702), believed to have come from Halberstadt. He became a close adviser to the Great Elector. Around 1700, with a fortune of 100,000 imperial thalers, he was thought to be the richest Jew in Germany. Liebmann was the first Berlin Jew to receive permission to build a private synagogue. Oil painting by Anthoni Schoonjans.

blasphemers, and thieves" were to be kept out. The only branches of production or trade open to Jews were those in need of development or still requiring to be set up. As bankers and lessees of mints they were permitted to finance the king's economic and political enterprises through loans. In the second half of the 18th century, protected Jews in Berlin and Brandenburg founded and owned velvet and plush factories, lace-making workshops, and silk, gold and silver factories.

This small class of people, financially strong but suffering political and social discrimination, began to feel a desire to participate in the culture of their new homeland and to attain rights of citizenship. The banker and mint lessee Daniel Itzig (1723–1799) bought a large garden in Kopernikusstrasse, containing a theater and areas laid out to form a park. He had a synagogue built into his mansion in town, but also a gallery for his picture collection, which included paintings by Rubens, Terborch, Watteau, and Pesne. A son of Johann Sebastian Bach, the lonely Wilhelm Friedemann Bach, found shelter and support in the Itzig household, where he was tutor to the daughter of the house, Sara, until his death in 1784.

The everyday language spoken in these circles was standard German, with French as a second language. They took an interest in contemporary literature and music, and discussed the ideas of the Enlightenment. They became less and less involved in Jewish cultural life, which seemed to them to have become fossilized, and ever more hopeful that enlightened tolerance would bring them assimilation and eventual emancipation.

LEFT: Jews being driven out of Prague on the instructions of Maria Theresa, 1745. After a contemporary engraving.

RIGHT: A "general edict" issued by Frederick William I, King of Prussia, 1724. It caused many younger children to lose protection and residence rights, for the right to protection applied only to the eldest child.

Frederick II and his Prussian Jews

ABOVE: The mint lessee Daniel Itzig (1723–1799), chief elder of the Jews in Prussia. In recognition of his financial services to the state, Frederick the Great accorded him the rights of a Christian merchant. Pastel portrait by Joseph Friedrich August Darbes.

ABOVE: His wife, Miriam Itzig, née Wulff. Pastel portrait by Darbes.

BELOW: the Palais Ephraim on Mühlendamm, Berlin. Steel engraving after a drawing by Stock, c. 1830.

Frederick II, the Great (reigned 1740–1786), continued the mercantile policies of his predecessors, and enlarged Prussia's territories by means of wars. In both of these areas of policy he was assisted by wealthy Jews.

His religious tolerance extended to Jews, yet when it came to the Jews' civil rights he was, as his legislation relating to Jews shows, intolerant and reactionary.

His father Frederick William I had already placed new restrictions on the considerable commercial freedom which the Jews had previously enjoyed: for instance, they were not allowed to start any new businesses. In 1730, contrary to the advice of liberal ministers, the king issued the *General-Reglement* ("General Statute"), a law directed against Jews which was meant to restrict the birthrate among his Jewish subjects. Only the firstborn children of the few protected Jews had the right to settle. For a second child a permit to settle could be bought at a high price; all other offspring must remain unmarried and thus childless, or else emigrate.

ABOVE: The Jewish community's hymn of praise and prayer on the occasion of Frederick the Great's victory at Schweidnitz. Berlin, 1762.

On 17 April 1750 Frederick the Great issued a revised *General-Privilegium und Reglement* for Jews, which he later made more stringent still. It divided Jews into six classes. The richest were individually granted a privileged status which almost made them de facto citizens. Their children had the right to settle. The second class of protected Jews might settle only in the place assigned to them as a personal privilege, and this right could be inherited by only one child. Two further children could obtain a residence permit if they could show that they possessed 1000 thalers. The rights of the "extraordinary" (i.e., not fully) protected Jews were not heritable; this, the third class included above all members of the liberal professions such as doctors, lawyers, and artists. It was these first three classes which between them had to pay the Jewish taxes and other charges, and for this reason it was made very difficult for them to emigrate: they were, after all, a major source of income for the state as well as for the Jewish community.

Frederick the Great. Copperplate engraving by Salomon Bennett (1761–1838). The painter and engraver Bennett moved from Plotsk to Berlin, where he very soon became a member of the Academy. His portraits of Frederick the Great, Queen Louise, Chodowiecki, the Academy's director, and others made him a popular painter. Nevertheless, in 1800 he emigrated to England, "the land of civil liberty – for Jews too."

Visit by Frederick the Great to the Breslau trade fair, which he had instituted in 1742 as a rival to the Leipzig fair. Despite the objections of Christian merchants, Frederick allowed Jewish merchants to take part in the fair. Contemporary watercolor.

The rabbi of Potsdam. Etching by Georg Friedrich Schmidt, 1750.

Anyone who wanted to emigrate had to pay a special emigration tax. The fourth class consisted of public officials such as rabbis and higher-ranking community officials. They were not permitted to earn money either by commerce or by practicing a trade, and had the right of residence only for as long as their appointment lasted. In the fifth class were "tolerated" Jews, children of Jews of the second, third, and fourth classes who had not enough money to by a residence permit. They had no rights, and were not allowed to engage in commerce or practice a trade on their own account but were tolerated only as members of their fathers' households. For them there was also no possibility of marriage. Most of those who emigrated came from this class. The sixth class consisted of servants so long as they had a position, and also employees in businesses owned by protected Jews. One such, until 1763, was Moses Mendelssohn; in that year, because of his fame, he was made an "extraordinary" protected Jew (member of the third

class) and could now marry, unlike those in the sixth class. The large number of homeless Jewish beggars had no rights, and were persecuted and repeatedly driven out of Prussia. No Jew, incidentally, was allowed to live in the countryside, work in agriculture, or practice a craft.

Despite these laws relating to Jews, which flew in the face of the spirit of the Enlightenment, the king was respected and esteemed among them. Moses Mendelssohn, for instance, hymned the Seven Years' War as "perhaps the most wonderful campaign that has ever been conducted under the leadership of one of the world's wise men."

Among the protected Jews most favored by the king were the court banker Daniel Itzig and Veitel Heine Ephraim, lessee of the royal mint. Daniel Itzig (1723–1799), son of a rich horse-dealer and army supplier under Frederick William I, was chief elder of the Prussian Jews. For his financial services to the Prussian state the king accorded him the same rights as a Christian merchant. When a wealthy pro-

tected Jew in Magdeburg asked for similar rights, the king wrote in the margin of his letter, "This Jew had better get out of Magdeburg at once, or the Commandant will throw him out!" But Frederick did remind the courts "that Jews must be judged in the same way as Christians."

In 1763, at the end of the Seven Years' War, the king instructed his court bankers to invest their profits in factories and buildings. Itzig bought and enlarged a leather factory and an ironworks. It was he, together with his cousin Veitel Heine Ephraim (d. 1775), who had largely financed Frederick's campaigns. As lessees of the mint they had, on the king's orders, reduced the quality of the silver coins and – also at the king's behest – taken the responsibility for this upon themselves.

"Outside silver, inside tin,
Outside Frederick, inside Ephraim"
was the people's comment.

Like Daniel Itzig, Veitel Heine Ephraim served as chief elder of the Prussian Jews. Like Itzig he lived as a Jew obeying the religious laws like him he had a synagogue in his town mansion. Through his connections he was able to obtain silver for the king from Poland and overseas. He was also entrusted with a political mission, channeling bribery payments from the king to Turkey. On the king's instructions, he invested part of the profit from the degrading of the coinage in silver works and manufactories for exportable goods. To be able to hold impressive functions, he bought the house of a Berlin family and had it altered so that it became one of the most beautiful Baroque houses in the city.

The high esteem in which these few Jews were held by the king probably accounts for the fact that at this time enemies of the Jews did not succeed in stirring up the people against them, although there was no lack of humiliations, from jostling in the street to the so-called "Jews' porcelain." Frederick II ordered that whenever a Jew obtained an official permit of whatever kind – be it for a change of residence, marriage, starting a business, or whatever – he must take a certain quantity of porcelain from the Royal Porcelain Manufacture and sell it, prefer-

cerned to provide a good secular education for their children, who spoke High German and were familiar with contemporary German literature. Hebrew was still a part of their education but was increasingly neglected; the Hebrew characters were now used only in correspondence between Jews. But however closely they were involved with German culture, many Jews were painfully conscious of not being socially accepted. Conversely, they, as a more or less amorphous-seeming group with strange religious practices and customs, inspired in non-Jews a certain sense of unease, which was felt to be due to "negative Jewish characteristics."

ably abroad. The price to be paid for these concessions was generally 300 thalers, but a gravedigger, for example, was made to buy porcelain worth only 28 thalers. Between 1763 and 1775 the royal factory received 900,000 thalers for such "Jews' porcelain." These forced purchasers sometimes sold the porcelain at a loss, which in turn was not good for normal sales.

Particularly prominent businessmen like the gold dealer Markus Levin, father of Rahel Levin Varnhagen, and other protected Jews of the first class were allowed to dress and shave according to the current fashion. However, a Jew unknown to the king, named Posner, who on the grounds of having the same duties applied for the same right to shave, received his request back with a witty marginal comment from the King: "The Jew Posner is to leave me and his beard unshorn" (a play on words: to leave someone unshorn is to leave them in peace). Yet many Jews, perhaps not including Herr Posner and others similarly snubbed, appreciated the king's sense of humor and admired him deeply.

Though Frederick was a patron and friend of the fine arts and sciences, the admiration of someone like Moses Mendelssohn seemed to bring little love in return, for when in 1773 the Prussian Academy of Sciences elected "the modern Socrates, Moses Mendelssohn" to full membership, the king refused his assent.

The Prussian Jewish elite were con-

The partition of Poland by Russia, Prussia and Austria, 1772: as a result many "eastern Jews" found themselves under the rule of the Prussian, Austrian, and Russian monarchies. Satirical pamphlet, engraving by M. Lemire.

Moses Mendelssohn

ABOVE: Moses Mendelssohn (1729–1786), copperplate engraving after a painting by Anton Graff. One of the few portraits produced during Mendelssohn's lifetime.

BELOW: Berlin, houses on Spandauer Strasse, where Moses Mendelssohn lived with his family.

Letter from Moses Mendelssohn to his wife in 1762, the year of their marriage, written in German with Hebrew interpolations and in Hebrew characters. The letter begins: "Dearest Fromet! I have k'ha-jaum-[today] received a letter me- [from] R. Jaakauw Herzfeld, who is achschow b' [now in] Leipzig. He asks me to give his compliments to you and your family ..."

ABOVE: Frumet Mendelssohn (née Gugenheim) from Hamburg, wife of Moses Mendelssohn. Miniature by "Dr R. S.," 1767.

BELOW: Three of the children of Moses and Frumet Mendelssohn. From the autograph book of Herz Homberg, c. 1773.

Dorothea

Joseph

Abraham

Gotthold Ephraim Lessing (1729–1781), a leading spirit of the German Enlightenment and friend of Moses Mendelssohn. Engraving by Johann Friedrich Bause after a painting by Anton Graff.

Christoph Friedrich Nicolai (1733–1811), publisher, pamphleteer, supporter of the Enlightenment, friend of Moses Mendelssohn. Engraving by Johann Elias Haid, after a drawing by Daniel Chodowiecki.

The philosopher Salomon ben Joshua, whose admiration for Maimonides led him to call himself Salomon Maimon (1753–1800). At the age of 26 he came to Berlin, where he made his name with works on Maimonides and Kant.

Moses Mendelssohn (1729–1786) – originally Moses ben Mendel Heymann – was born in Dessau as the son of poor parents. The language spoken in the family was the usual Judeo-German. As was customary among Jews, he began from his fourth year to learn Hebrew, the language of prayers and of the Scriptures.

At that time Dessau was a center of Hebrew scholarship, with a famous Hebrew printing works. However, there was also a circle of German-speaking Jews who associated with the families of the Prince's court factors, the Calmans and Jacobs. Prince Leopold of Dessau, whom the Soldier King (Frederick William I of Prussia) referred to as his "old man from Dessau," even allowed these Jews to hold a wedding celebration in his palace, which he and his family attended.

In 1743, the fourteen-year-old Moses followed his teacher David Fränkel to Berlin, where the latter had obtained a post as rabbi. From this time on Moses ben Mendel seems hardly to have had any contact with his parents and never visited them. But in letters he mentions his mother's distinguished descent from a famous scholar, Moses Isserles of Cracow (1525–1572).

In Berlin he found work as a tutor in the house of a silk manufacturer; in 1754 he

Karl Philipp Moritz (1757–1793), author of the psychological novel of personal development *Anton Reiser*, an admirer and friend of Moses Mendelssohn.

became a book-keeper there, and was later a partner in the firm. He devoted his spare time to writing and to studying Latin, Greek, French, English, and Italian. As early as 1754 Moses ben Mendel, who now called himself Mendelssohn in the German manner, published a treatise in

Hebrew on moral philosophy. Besides Jewish scholars and writers, he met Friedrich Nicolai, Gotthold Ephraim Lessing, and other major figures in the German intellectual world, and a lifelong friendship grew up between him and Lessing (see p. 128). He also established friendly relations with Herder, Wieland, Lichtenberg, the Humboldt brothers (whom he taught Hebrew), and Kant. The fact that he was small and misshapen made no difference to his humorous and kindly personality, nor to the respect in which he was held.

Lessing had Mendelssohn's first treatise, the *Philosophische Gespräche* ("Philosophical Conversations"), 1755, printed in German. In a number of further works Mendelssohn explored the nature of esthetics. The meaning of the beautiful, he argued, lies only in the beautiful object itself and has no purpose outside itself. He felt himself to be a German philosopher and was recognized as such; a practicing orthodox Jew, he regarded religion as a private matter. Mendelssohn was convinced that the Christian world was progressively becoming more tolerant, in the spirit of the Enlightenment.

He took almost no part in the intellectual debates taking place within the Jewish

community. He rejected Judeo-German and Yiddish as demoralizing argots. He took virtually no notice of the Hasidic movement in Poland, Lithuania and Russia, which was giving a new content to the Judaism of his day. In this way he contributed to the fact that a curtain came down for more than a hundred years

Vermuthlich kennst du diese Silhouette? Ich kann dir's kaum verhelen! Sie ist mir gar zu lieb! gar zu sprechend! . . . . Kannst du sagen, kannst du einen Augenblick ansehen, ob du sagen wollest: „Vielleicht ein Dummkopf! Eine rohe geschmacklose Seele! " Der so was sagen könnte, ertragen könnte, daß ein anderer es sagte, der schließe mein Buch zu, werf es von sich — und erlaube mir, meinen Gedanken zu verwehren, daß ich nicht über ihn urtheile! Ich weide mich an diesem Umrisse! Mein Blick wälzt sich von diesem herrlichen Bogen der Stirne auf den scharfen Knochen des Auges herab . . . . In dieser Tiefe des Auges sitzt eine Sokratische Seele! Die Bestimmtheit der Nase; — der herrliche Uebergang von der Nase zur Oberlippe — die Höhe beyder Lippen, ohne daß eine über die andere hervorragt, o wie alles dieß zusammenstimmt, mir die göttliche Wahrheit der Physiognomie fühlbar und anschaulich zu machen. Ja, ich seh ihn, den Sohn Abrahams, der einst noch mit Plato und Moses — erkennen und anbeten wird, den gekreuzigten Herrn der Herrlichkeit!

1. Heil dem Manne, der nicht kömmt

In den Rath der Frevler:

Der nie betrat den Weg der Sünder:

Nie saß, wo Spötter sitzen.

2. Den nur Gottes Lehre frommt,

Der Tag und Nacht sie forschet.

3. Er grünet, wie ein Baum am Bach,

Der Früchte trägt zur rechten Zeit,

Kein Blatt zu früh abwirft:

Und was er thut, gelinget.

4. So nicht die Frevler!

Die sind wie Spreu, den jeder Wind verwehrt.

5. Die Frevler bestehn nicht im Gerichte;

Sünder nicht vor der Gemeine der Frommen:

6. Denn gottgefällig ist der Frommen Weg:

Der Sünder Weg verliehrt sich.

between the Jews of west and east. With his ideal of assimilation and emancipation came the beginning of a tendency to divide oneself between being Jewish in private and German in dealings with fellow citizens and in cultural life. Since for the children of Jewish champions of the Enlightenment the Jewish way of life had become merely formal, most of them were lost to Judaism. With few exceptions the descendants of Moses Mendelssohn, of the Itzigs, and of the Friedländers went over to the state religion.

When in 1763 the Academy of Sciences offered a prize for the best treatment of a philosophical theme, Mendelssohn won it, defeating Kant and others, with a work "On Evidence in the Metaphysical Sciences." In that year the king gave him the status of a protected Jew. In 1767 Mendelssohn published a work of far-reaching influence, his *Phaedon*, in which, arguing in the spirit of enlightened human-

Hirschel Levin (1721–1800), Chief Rabbi of Berlin. Levin approved Mendelssohn's translation of the Scripture into a secular language. Engraving by Moses Abramson the Younger, after a portrait by J.A. Krüger.

Ezekiel Landau (1713–1793), a Prague rabbi, was an opponent of the Enlightenment. He banned Mendelssohn's translation of the Scriptures.

ity against mechanistic and naturalistic philosophy, he sought to prove the immortality of the human soul.

The serenity of the German philosopher Mendelssohn received a jolt in 1769 when the Zurich Protestant pastor and theologian Johann Kaspar Lavater, in one of his publications, made fairly crude reference to his being a Jew. Lavater challenged him either to refute the proof given by the French writer Charles Bonnet of the truth of the Christian religion or to convert to Christianity.

This provocation and the many exchanges of letters and polemical writings which followed led Mendelssohn to suffer a nervous crisis. The physician, astronomer and satirist Georg Christoph Lichtenberg, who was no friend of religion, be it Christian or Jewish, was indignant at Lavater's attempt to convert Mendelssohn. "One Mendelssohn is worth a hundred Lavaters," he wrote, and championed Mendelssohn in his satire directed against Lavater, *Timorus* (1773). Goethe, too, in his memoirs, *Dichtung und Wahrheit* ("Poetry and Truth"), expressed anger at Lavater's clumsy attempts at conversion; Lavater had tried to convert him too.

Mendelssohn replied to Lavater in a polite, cautious piece of writing which avoided any theological controversy. In it he emphasized that he was and would remain a believing Jew, and contrasted

Christian missionary zeal with the Jewish doctrine of tolerance. He gave his status in society as one of the reasons why he avoided entering into a religious controversy. He felt, he said, that as a "member of an oppressed people in a Christian country" he was not in a position to raise objections to the Christian religion on an equal footing.

The Lavater affair marked a turning point in Mendelssohn's life and thought. He now took upon himself the education of the Jews in German culture but also their Jewish education, by endeavoring to renew and to refine the study of the Hebrew language and the Hebrew Bible which was being neglected in some traditional circles as well as among assimilated Jews. In 1778/79, with the help of scholars he knew in Berlin and in Poland, he translated the Pentateuch and the Psalms into German, and wrote a commentary on them. The translation was printed in Hebrew characters, so that it should also be accessible to readers who were not familiar with the German alphabet.

He never ceased to plead for Jews to be "accepted as citizens" and emancipated from discrimination. In his book *Jerusalem oder über religiöse Macht und Judentum* ("Jerusalem, or On Religious Power and Judaism"), 1782, which is his credo, he came close to demanding, on philosophical grounds, that a dividing-line be drawn

between church and state. He was thereby also challenging the claims to authority of rabbis within their communities, for in Judaism, he said, there was no compulsion to believe. The Prussian archivist and member of the military council Christian Wilhelm von Dohm, a friend of Mendelssohn's, supported his campaign for the rights of Jews in Germany, and Dohm's book, *Über die bürgerliche Verbesserung der Juden* ("On the Civic Improvement of the Jews") (vol. 1, 1781, vol. 2, 1783) attracted a great deal of attention far beyond German borders.

When Mendelssohn was presented with a plan for a Jewish state in Palestine, he rejected it on the grounds that the Jews had ceased to be a people. After more than 1500 years of oppression they were no longer receptive to the spirit of freedom and of unity in a common cause that would be required for such a task. The mass of the Jews were, moreover, far too poor, and the ratio of rich people to poor far too small; and even the prosperous Jews had far less capital than the rich among other European peoples.

Mendelssohn's philosophical ideas were soon superseded by the insights of Kant and his successors. His importance to German Jews lies in his attempt to integrate them into German culture and to justify their claim to equal rights. It was his hope that a synthesis of Jewishness and Germanness was possible. This humanistically based hope, born of the Age of Enlightenment, remained the main pillar of the aspirations of succeeding generations of Jews in Germany.

Supporters of Enlightenment, of Reform, and of Assimilation

The European Enlightenment seemed to offer a favorable climate for the Jews' efforts to achieve equality on both the political and the human levels. Such at any rate was the belief of the circle surrounding Moses Mendelssohn, who hoped to integrate Judaism and the Jews into Christian Germany through education in the German language, culture, and way of life.

At first, however, only a very small elite among the Jews could read German. As early as 1778 the "Jewish Free School" was founded in Berlin: here for the first time, as well as the narrow range of Jewish subjects, pupils were taught the German and French languages and also drawing, mathematics, and geography – subjects which would help them to assimilate to the surrounding German-Christian culture and to attain the goal of emancipation. The school was founded by the court banker Isaak Daniel Itzig (1750–1806) and his brother-in-law David Friedländer (1750–1834), who were themselves the first teachers there. Friedländer, a member of a respected family in Königsberg, a silk manufacturer and an admirer of Moses Mendelssohn, was the driving force in the modernization of Judaism. He also wrote the first German-language *Lesebuch für jüdische Kinder* ("Reader for Jewish Children"). Further reformed Jewish schools were founded, one of which, the Philantropin in Frankfurt am Main, survived until 1942.

1783 saw the publication at Königsberg of the first issue of *Ha-me'assef* ("The Collector"), a Hebrew journal in which philosophical, scientific, and political topics of the day were discussed; later some of the articles were in German and used the German alphabet. Further journals of the same kind followed, helping to spread the new ideas and to improve the education of Jews in accordance with the principles of the Enlightenment.

For some time assimilation was achieved only by a thin stratum of the Jewish community living in Berlin and other large towns. What did not take place was a genuine discussion of orthodoxy or an attempt at a renewal of the Jewish religion. The aim

ABOVE: David Friedländer (1750–1834), a well-to-do silk manufacturer and friend of Moses Mendelssohn, was a passionate campaigner for equal rights and for the assimilation of Jews in Germany. After an engraving by Caroline Bardua.

RIGHT: Philosophical explanation of the words "Or" and "Noga" from *Ha-me'assef* ("The Collector"), founded by a group of Hebrew writers in Königsberg in 1783. Besides editors such as Isaak, Abraham Euchel (1758–1804), *Ha-me'assef* counted Moses Mendelssohn, David Friedländer, and Hartwig Wessely among its contributors. The journal ran until 1811.

was to become part of German-Christian society and to obtain complete equality, and in order to achieve this Friedländer declared, "in the name of a number of Jewish heads of households," but to the horror of most Jews, that he would be prepared to convert to Christianity, albeit using an amended declaration of faith. "Heads of households" was a euphemism meaning house-owning protected Jews of the first class. The proposal was rejected by the representatives of Christianity too, but before the end of Friedländer's life a number of Jews who shared his deist philosophy did convert to Christianity.

In 1791, Frederick II's nephew and successor, Frederick William II (reigned 1786–1797), repealed a number of humiliating decrees affecting Jews which had been issued by his predecessors. The Jewish community presented the king with a memorandum expressing its "hopes of attaining equal rights." The king abolished the Jewish "body tax" and the forced purchase of porcelain by Jews, though for this exemption a high fee – in other words, another special tax imposed on Jews – had to be paid. He rejected the plea for unlimited admission of Jews to official positions and to trades and professions. Commercial activity was to be permitted only where there were not enough Christian merchants, and then only to rich Jews. However, farming was now permitted on unused land that had to be newly cultivated. Friedländer and Itzig, the leading

members of the Jewish commission, rejected "this Trojan horse" and declared that the new law contained just as many restrictions, albeit no longer humiliating ones, as the old: "The improvements offered are below all expectations."

Friedländer and his brother-in-law Isaak Daniel Itzig, as well as Israel Jacobson of Brunswick, campaigned throughout their lives for Jews to have equal rights under the laws of the state and for reforms within the Jewish communities.

Itzig, appointed "Hofbaurat" (royal architectural councilor) by Frederick William II in 1791, was one of the first Jewish officials in Prussia. But this, like his full citizenship, was a personal mark of the king's esteem and had no bearing on the claims of other Jews to the rights they sought. Despite the recognition shown to individual Jews, and the active support of many non-Jews, the efforts made to achieve equal rights during the reign of Frederick William II were unsuccessful.

Most of the leading representatives of the movement for emancipation and reform still held to their religion, though they were less committed to a belief in Jewish nationhood. Their children were brought up not in the orthodoxy of their grandparents but in a kind of deism, which

RIGHT: Naphtali Herz Wesel (1725–1805), modern Hebrew poet and friend of Mendelssohn. He collaborated with Mendelssohn on the latter's translation of the Pentateuch. In accordance with his ideals as a supporter of the Enlightenment and an early campaigner for secular education in the vernacular, he adopted the German name of Hartwig Wessely.

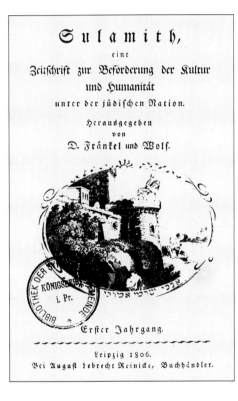

ment grew up under the name of "Haskalah" (education, enlightenment), whose supporters broke through the traditional forms to create a synthesis between Judaism and the modern world. Unlike many representatives of the German-Jewish Enlightenment, they drew just as much upon Jewish tradition, to which they had a positive attitude, as upon the culture of their own day, which they saw as enriching their Judaism. In the contemporary culture it was above all the Schillerian ideal of reconciliation between peoples and Kant's philosophy of enlightenment that influenced the movements of rebirth among the Jews of eastern Europe.

to them was often merely a formality, so that many of them had little hesitation in abandoning Judaism, in exchange, they hoped, for equal status.

The importance of these men for succeeding generations was that they were utterly convinced of their worthiness to have equal rights of citizenship. The ideas of the enlightened reformers, carried from Germany and Austria to Poland and Russia, gave rise to a fruitful development within Judaism. In those countries a move-

LEFT:
Sulamith ("Shulamite," 1806–1833), the second Jewish journal of the Enlightenment, was published in Leipzig by David Fränkel and Joseph Wolf. It was the first Jewish periodical to be written wholly in German. *Sulamith* argued for a modern form of education for rabbis and a radical reform of synagogue services, with the sermon and prayers in German.

RIGHT: "Revised rules" of the Jewish Free School in Berlin, 1796 (extract).

The Way into the Upper Middle Class

Brendel (Dorothea) Mendelssohn, Moses Mendelssohn's eldest daughter, who in 1783 married the banker Simon Veit and in 1804 Friedrich Schlegel. She was baptized as a Protestant in 1802, and as a Catholic in 1808.

Marcus Herz (1747–1803), professor and "Hofrat" (Privy Councilor, an honorific title), husband of Henriette Herz.

The overwhelming majority of Jews in Germany were virtually untouched by the developments taking place in Berlin and Königsberg. They continued to lead their lives in the spirit of Jewish tradition, with the community and the family giving ample scope for a cultural life and the warmth of human relationships. Seen from outside, however, they were still a disadvantaged class existing on the fringe of society. Their contacts with their Christian neighbors were minimal, and not always positive. Most Jews lived in very poor circumstances; but a small group, working as cattle dealers or grain merchants, had risen to the lower middle class.

In Berlin, however, an intellectual and literary elite had succeeded in gaining acceptance in cultured circles. This group included, among others, the Herz, Meyer, Beer, and Levin families.

Marcus Herz (1747–1803) had been sent by his father, a poor, "unprotected" trader in Berlin, to serve a commercial apprenticeship with some relatives in Königsberg. There Kant noticed him at his lectures, and recommended him, as one of his favorite pupils, to Moses Mendelssohn. He in turn recommended him to David Friedländer, who enabled him to study medicine. Herz became one of the most eminent physicians of his day. He superintended the newly founded Jewish hospital, and gave lectures on philosophy and experimental physics which were attended by the king and by Wilhelm von Humboldt. In 1787 Frederick William II accorded him the title of Professor.

Herz was one of the pioneers of the campaign for equality for the Jews; like Mendelssohn and David Friedländer, he wanted to encourage them to learn about and accept German culture. Herz – a committed Jew who lived in the traditional way – was the first to point a mocking finger, in one of his writings, at Jewish anti-Semitism, explaining it as a perverted way of taking revenge on fellow-Jews – but in reality on oneself – for humiliations endured. Another expression of his identification with Judaism was the part he played in the founding of the Society of Friends of the Hebrew Language and of the journal *Ha-me'assef* ("The

Amalie Beer (1767–1854). Painting by Carl Kretschmar.

Collector"). His wife Henriette was the daughter of the Portuguese-Sephardic doctor Benjamin de Lemos from Hamburg, and the couple's literary salon was a meeting place for Berlin's intellectual elite.

Amalie Beer (1767–1854) was the daughter of the banker Liebmann Meyer Wulff. Her house was an important focus of social and musical life long before and after the time of Berlin's literary salons.

Jakob Meyer Beer (1791–1864), one of the three sons of Jakob Herz Beer and his wife Amalie, later called himself Giacomo Meyerbeer and won fame as a composer, particularly of operas. One of his brothers, Wilhelm (1797–1850), became an astronomer. Between 1834 and 1836 he published, together with Johann Heinrich von Mädler, a large number of views of the moon as seen through the telescope, to produce the first complete representation of the moon. In 1846, after being baptized, he was elected to the Prussian Parliament. The youngest brother, Michael (1800–1833), became a writer and wrote the successful plays *Struensee* and *Der Paria* ("The Pariah").

Two more members of Berlin's Jewish intellectual elite Berlin were Rahel and Ludwig, the children of the gold dealer Markus Levin. Rahel (1771–1833) was the center of "a republic of creative minds"; at the age of 39 she married the diplomat and writer Karl August Varnhagen von Ense. Her brother Ludwig Levin (1778–1832), who called himself Ludwig Robert, was a translator of French plays and a writer of

ABOVE: Giacomo Meyerbeer, son of the banker Jakob Herz Beer, at the age of eleven. Painting by Friedrich Georg Weitsch, 1802.

ABOVE: A dance at the "Goldene Kugel" on Berlin's Letzte Strasse, where the Christian and Jewish jeunesse dorée met. Colored engraving.

LEFT: The Kaulla banking family of Stuttgart. On the left sits "Madame Kaulla," Kaile Raphael Kaulla (1739–1809), one of the few female court agents (Württembergische Hofbank). Gold etching by Goog, 1795.

"Singspiele" (light operas with spoken dialogue) and plays. In 1811 Goethe arranged for his play *Die Tochter Jephtas* ("Jephthah's Daughter"), printed in 1820, to be put on at Weimar, but it was not a success; *Die Macht der Verhältnisse* ("The Power of Circumstances"), printed 1819, was staged in 1815. These were probably the first plays by a Jew to be performed in Germany. Like many young Jews, Rahel and her brother Ludwig wanted to be wholly German.

The Orthodox Majority

Rabbi Abraham Ticktin (1764–1820), chief district rabbi at Breslau. Like his ancestors and his descendants, Abraham Ticktin was a representative of orthodox Judaism. A lithographic incunabulum by the four Henschel brothers, 1812.

schools, intellectual life became largely fossilized. What still remained was the traditional orthodox way of life-the observance of daily prayers, the Sabbath and holy days, and obedience to the commandments and the dietary laws. These requirements were followed even by the pedlars, traders and those traveling from one trade fair to another, who were on the road for six days of the week: they lived chiefly on bread and fruit, which were among the permitted foods, and ate hot meals and dishes containing meat or fish only when they were at home, on the Sabbath.

Whenever possible, the men gathered together – ten men was the prescribed quorum – for communal morning and evening prayers.

Meat and poultry might be eaten only if they had been killed in the ritual manner by the community slaughterer. The mixing of milk and meat dishes is strictly forbidden among orthodox Jews, in compliance

Despite the strong movement for reform, which was based mainly in the towns and cities, the majority of Jews continued until the middle of the 19th century to preserve in their way of life the traditional forms and customs of orthodox, conservative Judaism. Belief in the divine revelation received on Mount Sinai and in the coming of the Messiah to lead the people of Israel back to the Holy Land was at the heart of their religious life, as were observance of the Ten Commandments and of the ritual hygiene and dietary laws. The sign of the covenant with God was the circumcision of male children on the eighth day after birth (B'rit Mila).

The orthodox Jews took care meticulously to obey all the religious commandments and to do the required daily "studying." This meant study of the Scriptures, Bible commentaries, the Talmud and the exegeses of rabbinical precepts with a view to applying them in everyday life. Until the 17th century there was a willingness to respond to new intellectual developments and changing circumstances. But with repeated persecutions and the resultant decline of the Talmudic

Circumcision – the sealing of the covenant with God, performed on every boy since the days of Abraham, the father of the Jewish people. The blessing runs: "Praised be thou, Lord our God, King of the world; he has sanctified us with his commandments and has commanded us to practice circumcision." Illustration by Uri Pheibusch, Homburg, 1741.

with the Biblical precept, "Thou shalt not seethe a kid in his mother's milk" (Exodus 23, 19). This prohibition of mixed products was and is taken so seriously that strictly Orthodox Jews do not wear dresses or suits which contain a mixture of wool and flax. There was also strict adherence to the purifying bath "in living water," that is, in ground water or a spring.

Since children learned to read from the Bible, sexual habits and mores were no secret to them: from an early age they were aware of them as a normal part of life.

Saturday, a scene in front of the synagogue at Fürth (near Nuremberg). The women on the left are wearing Empire-style dresses, the men the German-Jewish festive clothes worn by the Jews of southern and western Germany who practiced a traditional lifestyle. Colored copperplate engraving, c. 1800.

Nathan the Good and Shylock the Bad

The theologian Theophilus Lessing gained his doctorate in 1669 with a dissertation entitled *De religionum tolerantia* ("On the Tolerance of Religions"). His grandson Gotthold Ephraim Lessing (1729–1781), born in the same year as Moses Mendelssohn, became a forceful campaigner against all intolerance and bigotry. At the age of only twenty he satirized Christian arrogance in his comedy *Die Juden* ("The Jews"). It was soon after this that his lifelong friendship and intellectual association with Mendelssohn began.

In 1779 Lessing's play *Nathan der Weise* ("Nathan the Wise") appeared; Lessing used aspects of Mendelssohn's person and character in creating the figure of Nathan.

This deliberately didactic play at once sparked off vigorous debate. But it was Schiller's adaptation in 1801 that gave it the power it still has today. Whereas Shakespeare's Shylock always remains an ambivalent figure, Lessing's Nathan represents a clear statement on behalf of tolerance in general and tolerance toward the Jews in particular – a position based on universally valid ethical principles. "The essence of religion lies not in faith but in moral behavior": this declaration of Lessing's also echoes a maxim of Judaism.

Not only groups with bigoted views, but "normal" middle-class people too, were outraged by the play, although Lessing shied away from pursuing his ideas to their logical conclusion, as Ernst Simon commented: "Lessing wants, by assimilation, to make the Jews into Germans and into human beings, but for him mixed marriage is ... not a suitable means to that end: he would rather let Recha be a Christian and even the sister of the Templar, he would rather put up with the Oedipal tension of the final scene, without resolving it, he would rather let this didactic play end just where really a human tragedy ought to be

"Nathan and the Templar," after a painting by Johann Christoph Frisch, engraved by Benedict Heinrich Bendix, Berlin, 1806. Bendix was a son of the Berlin protected Jew Hirsch Nathan Bendig. His nephew was the painter Edward von Bendemann, son of Hirsch Aron Bendix, who took the name of Anton Heinrich Bendemann.

beginning, than employ the logical and artistically necessary solution of a mixed marriage."

Lessing was accused of having taken a bribe to give a favorable portrayal of Nathan in the play. An unfathomable hatred reveals itself in this tactic of base slander with its unprovable accusations and vilifications. Here, as elsewhere, anti-semitism appealed to the lowest common denominator; perhaps this is the secret of its terrible effectiveness.

It was with these accusations against *Nathan der Weise*, and mimic and graphic caricatures of the main figure, that mockery of "the Jew" at the so-called higher cultural level began. Iffland, for instance, one of the greatest actors of his day, learned the Judeo-German of the country Jews in order to caricature it and to give a ridiculous and humiliating portrayal of the

Jewish protagonist in a play by the English writer Richard Cumberland. When it was objected that in Cumberland's play the character spoke educated English, Iffland retorted that this was an error of judgment on the author's part. He also played Shylock for laughs, stereotyping him and making the Jew of Venice, with his hybrid Jewish-German speech, a figure of much ridicule.

Among the majority of educated people, however, Lessing's hymn to tolerance found a strong echo. And what of Moses Mendelssohn, the model for Nathan the Wise? He too was respected, indeed admired, by his educated contemporaries. But in his home city Mendelssohn, like many Jews, often had to suffer contempt and mockery from the supposedly tolerant Berliners.

In 1780 he wrote, not without bitterness, to a Benedictine monk named Winkopp: "Here, in this so-called tolerant country, I nonetheless live so hemmed in by real intolerance, so restricted on all sides, that for the sake of my children I have to imprison myself all day in a silk factory just as you imprison yourself in a

ABOVE: Title page of Lessing's *Nathan der Weise* ("Nathan the Wise"), 1779. The motto reads, "Enter, for here too are gods!"

RIGHT: A caricature of Lessing's *Nathan der Weise*. Copperplate engraving from the title page of *Der travestierte Nathan der Weise* ("Nathan the Wise, Travestied"), a farce in two acts by Julius Voss, Berlin, 1804.

LEFT: The famous actor August Wilhelm Iffland (1759–1814) as Shylock in *The Merchant of Venice*, c. 1810.

monastery. I sometimes go out for a walk in the evening with my wife and children. 'Papa,' asks one child in its innocence, 'what is that boy shouting after us? Why are they throwing stones at us? What have we done to them?' 'Yes, dear father,' says another, 'they always come after us in the streets ...'."

Campaigners for Jewish Emancipation

The ideas of the French Revolution influenced European political thought far beyond the borders of France. Leading thinkers in France and Germany pointed out that the revolutionary thesis of the equality of all men, and the demand for equal rights for all which followed from it, must logically apply to the Jews too.

In 1781, eight years before the outbreak of the Revolution in France, Emperor Joseph II issued the "Edicts of Toleration" for the benefit of his Greek Orthodox and Jewish subjects. These edicts mitigated some restrictions, particularly for wealthy Jews, but they had a missionary aim, to win converts for Roman Catholicism.

Some of the Jews, particularly those in assimilated circles, saw the Edicts of Toleration as a step toward integration into the Habsburg Empire; many welcomed the ruling that religious minorities be educated in secular schools and especially the fact that they were to be admitted to universities and academies. However, the Edicts of Toleration were not tolerant of an independent Jewish way of life: their goal was the gradual dissolution of Judaism. Nevertheless, the mere fact that an emperor had uttered the word "toleration" had a positive psychological effect.

In 1781/83 the Prussian "Staatsrat" (privy councilor) Christian Wilhelm von Dohm (1751–1820) published his influential book *Über die bürgerliche Verbesserung der Juden* ("On the Civic Improvement of the Jews"). "Are we to think that many industrious and good citizens are less useful to the state because they have their origins in Asia, and because they are distinguished by their beards, by circumcision and a particular manner of worshipping the Highest of Beings bequeathed to them by their earliest forebears?" Anti-Jewish policies were in Dohm's view "a remnant of the barbarism of centuries gone by, an effect of the fanatical religious hatred which, unworthy of the enlightenment of our day, should long since have been expunged by it ... To our firmly established states every citizen must be welcome who observes the laws and by his industry increases the wealth of the state ... the Jew too has a claim to this enjoyment of civil society, to this love. His religion does not make him unworthy of this, since by punctiliously obeying his religion he can be a very good citizen ... Only the rabble which consider it permissible to deceive a Jew make the accusation that his laws permit him to defraud members of other religions,

Dancing around the Freedom Tree, Mainz, 1793: "Conversation of a Jew in Kassel near Mainz with a convinced man of freedom [i.e. a man convinced that freedom and equality are here to stay] about the Tree of Freedom in January 1793." The text of the pamphlet ends with the Jew saying skeptically: "Yes, sir, they may pull out all the hairs of my beard if the Tree of Freedom remains standing. But time will tell."

and only priests with a thirst for persecution have collected tales about Jewish prejudices which merely demonstrate their own."

Dohm's book impressed, among others, Count Mirabeau (1749–1791), who from 1789 onward was the spokesman of the French National Assembly. Mirabeau, an admirer of Moses Mendelssohn's works, had met Dohm, Schleiermacher, the Humboldt brothers, and others in the Berlin salon of Marcus and Henriette Herz; he disseminated Dohm's ideas in France. Working together with Abbé Grégoire, the "Advocate of the Jews before the French National Assembly," Mirabeau made sure that the Jewish question remained on the agenda until the Act of Emancipation was passed in 1791. Mirabeau and Grégoire were supported by Count Stanislas Clermont-Tonnerre, who demanded full and unrestricted equality for Jews, which was finally proclaimed in the session of the National Assembly on 27 September 1791. The development of French Jewry was to be affected by Clermont-Tonnerre's declaration: "To the Jews as a nation everything should be refused, but to the Jews as human beings everything should be granted!" In 1786 Mirabeau had submitted a memorandum to the Prussian king Frederick William II urging him to introduce far-reaching reforms in his state so as to bring about the general emancipation of the peasantry, the abolition of censorship, and equal civil rights for Jews. In a logical extension of Dohm's views he also advocated that Jews be allowed to hold government positions.

However, opposition from influential circles in Germany prevented the emancipation envisaged by these non-Jewish campaigners, who also included the Humboldt brothers and many other leading spirits in Germany, from being realized. Some generations were to pass before the equality of Jews before the law in Prussia and other German states became a reality.

Napoleon Brings Liberation

LEFT: "Napoleon the Great restores the cult of the Israelites, 30 May 1806." This allegorical picture shows Moses' tablets of stone with the Ten Commandments, and behind them the sacred objects of Solomon's temple and Mount Sinai. In his right hand Napoleon holds "the law given to Moses." On the left is Rabbi David Josef Sinzheim (1745–1812), president of the Sanhedrin. Copperplate engraving, Paris, 1806.

BELOW: The second Grand Sanhedrin, an assembly of Jewish notables from France, Italy, and Germany convened by Napoleon in Paris on 9 February 1807. Of the 71 members, two thirds were rabbis and one third laymen. Their main task was the separation of state and religion, which was to be one of the central demands of the movement for assimilation. Lithograph, Paris, 1807.

Inseparable from the triumphal advance of the French armies was the triumphal advance of the ideas of the French Revolution; and the concepts of liberty, equality, and fraternity had also to be applied to the Jews, for the first time in history, if they were to retain their meaning. But it was neither the decrees of the National Assembly in Paris nor the understanding shown by Christian representatives of the Enlightenment that brought the Jews in the German states equal rights of citizenship: it was the occupation by Napoleon's troops. It happened first in Westphalia under the rule of Napoleon's brother Jerome. Even before this, however, when Napoleon had conquered northern Italy in 1796, he had ordered all ghetto walls to be pulled down.

Napoleon's attitude toward the Jews fluctuated a good deal. In 1799, for instance, during his Egyptian campaign, it was probably for opportunistic reasons that he issued a proclamation to the Jews of the Orient in which he called for the restoration of a Jewish Kingdom of Jerusalem. On the other hand he often spoke contemptuously of the Jews because they had submitted to oppression by the Christian peoples without a fight. Like Count Clermont-Tonnerre, Napoleon believed that before they could be fully integrated into the state he must "liberate" them from their "Jewish" characteristics, from their attachment to their Jewish religion and nationality, and he was accordingly in favor of letting Jews and Judaism gradually disappear as a result of mixed marriages.

The Emperor convened an Assembly of Jewish Notables on 30 May 1806, "to awaken the spirit of citizenship which in a considerable proportion of this people has been weakened through having for so long endured a demeaning status which we will neither support nor renew." The Assembly of Notables was a political ploy on Napoleon's part aimed at gaining the support of world Jewry.

In the year 1807, in the hope of at last achieving human rights for Jews, the Grand Sanhedrin – Sanhedrin or

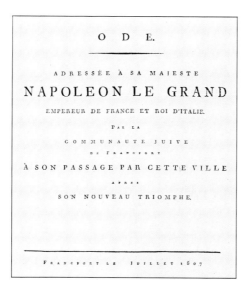

Title page of an ode to Napoleon in French, Hebrew, and German sent to Napoleon by the Jewish community of Frankfurt am Main, 1807. One stanza of the poem reads, "When from your throne you dispense blessings upon your peoples, give joy to the remnants of Israel which you have raised from the dust, and support Israel with your mighty arm of justice."

Synhedrion was the name given to the Jewish Court of Justice in Hellenistic-Roman times – declared its willingness to subordinate all the duties enjoined on Jews by their religious laws to their duties as citizens of the state.

This was agreed only with much hesitation, and a shock followed very soon after, when on 17 March 1808 Napoleon's so-called "Infamous Decree" was promulgated: for ten years all rights of Jews who engaged in trade or practiced manual crafts, including even the right to freedom of movement, were to be curtailed. It was almost exclusively the poorer Jews who were affected by this decree, which, however, was met with passive resistance and in fact largely ignored.

RIGHT: Moses Cahn pulling down the wall of the Jewish quarter in Mainz, 11 September 1798 (after an old drawing).

Equality in the Kingdom of Westphalia

LEFT: King Jerome (reigned 1807–13), brother of Napoleon. Engraving by Ludwig Buchhorn after a painting by Franziskus Kinson.

The constitution of the Kingdom of Westphalia (1807–1813) had been drawn up by Jerome's advisers. Among them were the Germans Johannes von Müller and Christian Wilhelm von Dohm (see page 130), who had entered the service of the state of Westphalia. Complete equality for the Jews was enshrined in this constitution.

Jerome, King of Westphalia and Napoleon's brother, was unshakable in his insistence on the equality of religions before the law. He made this clear in a speech immediately following his entry into Kassel on 10 December 1807: "It is my intention that they [the Jews] shall not only be citizens but also hold public positions." Such words were received with surprise and delight by Jews throughout Germany, despite the fact that the Berlin Jews were hostile to Napoleon.

The majority of the population, too, and some officials, reacted favorably to the granting of equality. Count Wentzel von Sternau, director of the Ministry of the Interior in the southern German state of Baden, expressed what was probably the view of his government: "... the bonds have been loosed by which those who profess the Mosaic doctrine were not only held back at the entrance to citizenship but

LEFT: Löw Meyer Berlin (1738–1814) was a member of the Israelite Consistory at Kassel. A well-known Talmudic scholar and writer, he represented the conservative-orthodox point of view. Portrait drawn by Salomon Pinhas (1759–1837), court painter to the Elector of Hesse.

RIGHT: Israel Jacobson (1769–1828), a determined fighter "for Jewish emancipation in the German fatherland," was the head of the Israelite Consistory in the Kingdom of Westphalia. Jacobson was both the most successful reformer of Jewish education and worship and the founder of a Jewish teacher training institute in Kassel. In nine towns modern Jewish schools were founded, among them the Jacobson School in Seesen. After the fall of Jerome in 1813, Jacobson became active in Jewish reformist circles in Berlin. Portrait drawn by Salomon Pinhas.

often consigned to the dungeon of human existence ... If one makes it in a man's interest to be good, law-abiding and useful, that is what he will be. But the Israelites have always had quite contrary interests forced upon them."

On 27 January 1808 Jerome issued a solemn manifesto laying down the fundamental principles of equal civil rights. This Magna Carta of the Jews of Westphalia was promulgated on 9 February 1808 at an audience for the Westphalian "Israelites." The speech of thanks was given by the reformer, teacher and school founder Israel Jacobson (see page 156).

In accordance with a decree by Napoleon on 17 March 1808, an Israelite Consistory was created. It was to supervise the implementation of decrees issued by the emperor and by the Sanhedrin, it confirmed the appointment of rabbis and monitored their fulfillment of their official duties, as well as the administration of communities and the management of synagogues. King Jerome let it be known that he had been pleased "that the constitution of his kingdom was entirely after his own heart with regard to the equal status of all religions." He disregarded his brother's "Infamous Decree."

The Israelite Consistory in Westphalia was led with energy and authority by Israel Jacobson, a determined fighter "for the emancipation of Jews in the German fatherland." Jacobson was court factor at Brunswick and a successful reformer of Jewish education and worship, as well as the founder of a Jewish teacher training institute in Kassel (the city where the Consistory met). Modern Jewish schools were founded in nine German towns at that time.

After the fall of Jerome in 1813 Jacobson joined the reformists in Berlin. In his synagogue there he introduced the organ and the preaching of sermons in German, following the Protestant model, as he had already done previously in the synagogue attached to his "School of Religion and Industry" at Seesen.

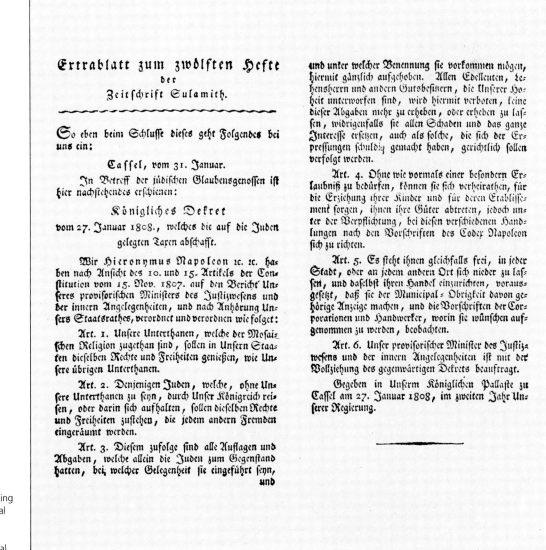

Decree of 27 January 1808 issued by King Jerome of Westphalia abolishing special taxes on Jews. This was the first comprehensive legislation passed anywhere in Germany to establish equal rights in law for Jews.

Jews in Berlin around 1800

LEFT: Aron Beer (1738–1821), cantor of the Berlin congregation. Following orthodox tradition he has the hint of a beard under his chin. The black robe and white bands show the influence of the dress of Protestant clergy. Mezzotint by B. H. Bendix, 1808.

RIGHT: The mathematician Abraham Wolff. Mezzotint by B. H. Bendix, 1797.

LEFT: The court banker Isaak Daniel Itzig (1750–1806). Together with his brother-in-law, David Friedländer, he founded the "Jewish Free School" in Berlin. Copperplate engraving by Anton Graff.

RIGHT: Blümchen Margaret Friedländer, sister of Daniel Itzig and wife of David Friedländer. Copperplate engraving by Anton Graff.

The Mühlendamm, viewed from the Kurfürstenbrücke. Behind it is a Jewish district. Drawing by Leopold Ludwig Müller, 1804.

Around the turn of the 19th century, some three thousand Jews lived in Berlin, comprising roughly two percent of the city's population. A small number of wealthy families had already attained prosperity under Frederick the Great and his successor. However, the majority, here as elsewhere, lived in poverty. They earned their living as small traders, worked as servants, community employees, butchers, and teachers, or practiced crafts such as those of seal cutters, goldsmiths, and bookbinders for which membership of a guild was not obligatory. Only registered families had civil rights. From these families came scientists, writers and musicians, bankers, and owners of large businesses, who were also reformers of Judaism and campaigners for equal rights.

In Berlin, as in all Jewish communities, there was a hostel for new arrivals and for

The Jewish hostel by the Rosenthal Gate. Colored pen-and-ink drawing by Leopold Ludwig Müller, 1807.

people passing through who could not find a bed with friends or relatives: these ranged from traveling musicians, entertainers, and the like, scholars traveling in search of a teaching appointment, itinerant folk and beggars, down to professional thieves and pickpockets. Weddings were also celebrated in the hostel, and women who had given birth were allowed to stay for more than just two or three days. In the social life of lower-class Jews, the hostel played an important part.

In Berlin, Jews coming from outside were issued by the Jewish community with passes for one of the designated city gates, but only, under the rules of the city authorities, if the community could act as guarantor for their short stay or if they could show that they had employment in the community. All other Jews might stop briefly at the "Jews' hostel" but were then made to move on.

ABOVE: Lottery ticket issued by a lottery agent named Bleichröder, Berlin.

LEFT: The old Jewish cemetery on the Grosse Hamburger Strasse in Berlin. Among the graves there is that of Moses Mendelssohn. Oil painting by Hermann Schnee.

OPPOSITE: Street plan of Berlin in 1778, with the Jewish quarter. At the top left is the Jewish cemetery; Spandauer Strasse is where Moses Mendelssohn lived and Henriette Herz had her salon; the Palais Ephraim was on the Mühlendamm.

The Salon of Marcus and Henriette Herz

Friedrich von Schlegel (1772–1829), drawn by Augusta von Buttlar, engraved by Josef Axmann, detail.

David Friedrich Schleiermacher (1768–1834). After a drawing by Johann Heinrich Lips.

Around the turn of the century the salons were focal points of intellectual and social life in Berlin society. Members of court society and the scholarly world would come together at the salon of Amalie von Imhoff or Bettina von Arnim. Bettina's guests included most notably the group of writers surrounding Ludwig Tieck, scholars like the young historian Leopold von Ranke, and the architect of royal Berlin, Karl Friedrich Schinkel. Some Jewish families, the Itzigs, Ephraims, and Meyers, also kept open house. Here Jewish and non-Jewish society met, and conversed about art, literature, politics, and the latest society gossip; the salons also acted as a marriage market for wealthy families and high-ranking aristocrats. Goethe was among those who were charmed by the pretty Sara Meyer, and Lessing and Herder also sought her friendship.

A musical evening. On the left Henriette Herz, at the piano Abraham Mendelssohn. Drawing by Johann Gottfried Schadow (1764–1850).

Count Alexander zu Dohna (1771–1831), later Prussian Minister of the Interior and General Director of the province of East Prussia. Oil painting.

Henriette Herz (1764–1847). Drawing by Wilhelm Hensel, 1823. Her salon was a center of intellectual life in Berlin.

Wilhelm von Humboldt, 1814: "While we were still children, Alexander and I were seen as protectors of the Jews." Drawing by P. E. Stroehling.

The salons of Marcus and Henriette Herz and Rahel Levin were more modest and had no such social aspirations. Rank, position, and scientific or cultural eminence took second place to originality, wit, and friendship. Thus for instance Adelbert von Chamisso, Ludwig Börne, Heinrich Heine, and other young writers were regular guests at these two salons long before their publications had brought them fame.

Schiller, Count Mirabeau, Jean Paul, and Madame de Staël did not fail to appear at the Herz and Levin salons when they came to Berlin. But not every visitor was an admirer. For instance Rahel Levin was described by one of her guests as "a philosopher ... benevolent and much sought after, but quite unnerving to me with her abstract ideas and eccentric personality. God preserve us from having a mother, sister, or daughter like her." Some visitors classed as an eccentricity the fact that Rahel Levin argued with passion for the independence of women.

Henriette Herz (1764–1847) was married at the age of fifteen to the philosopher and physician Marcus Herz, with whom she enjoyed a happy marriage until his death in 1803. While almost all of the other "beautiful, educated Jewesses" of the Berlin literary salons underwent baptism and found aristocratic husbands, Henriette Herz remained Jewish. Her

homes in Spandauer Strasse and later in Neue Friedrichstrasse became the prototype of the "Berlin salon." Among many others, the theologian, preacher, and philosopher Friedrich Schleiermacher was a frequent guest. His deep friendship with Henriette Herz, that "calm and beautiful soul," gave rise to gossip. "We talk from the depths of our being about the most important things," wrote Schleiermacher. Later, however, the famous preacher denied this aspect of their relationship. Schleiermacher had been introduced to the couple's salon by his friend, the civil servant and later government minister Count Alexander zu Dohna. The Count was a fervent admirer of Henriette Herz: "What Alexander has been to me, unreservedly, for ten years, no one will ever be to me again, nor I to anyone," she wrote in 1802 to a mutual friend.

Another familiar of the house was Friedrich Schlegel (1772–1829), the early Romantic writer and literary historian. The heroine of his novel *Lucinde*, which caused a scandal at the time, was modeled on Mendelssohn's daughter Brendel (1763–1839), who took the name Dorothea at her baptism and who was to marry Schlegel as her second husband. Later, in Cologne, she converted together with him from Protestantism to Catholicism, much to the indignation of her brothers and sisters who

had been baptized as Protestants. Schlegel and Dorothea had met at the Herz home. "She has no interest in anything in the world or out of it but love, music, wit, and philosophy. In her arms I have rediscovered my youth," wrote Schlegel to his sister-in-law Karoline.

Wilhelm von Humboldt, the statesman and founder of Berlin University and a lifelong friend of Abraham Mendelssohn and David Friedländer, was another who as a young man had a fervent admiration for Henriette Herz. He sometimes wrote letters to her in German but using Hebrew characters.

Karl Philipp Moritz, the author of the famous psychological novel of personal development *Anton Reiser*, came to know Moses Mendelssohn at the house of Henriette and her husband, who was both his friend and his physician.

A singular figure at Henriette Herz's salon was Salomon Maimon (1754–1800). Born in Lithuania, he came to Germany at the age of 26 as an educated man well versed in the Talmud, and although self-taught he attracted attention with his works on Maimonides and Kant. Maimon's autobiography, a cultural-historical document of the condition of Polish Jewry at the time, was published in 1792 by Karl Philipp Moritz, whom he had met at Henriette Herz's salon.

Rahel Levin-Varnhagen and her Circle

Rahel Levin (1771–1833) was the daughter of the Berlin gold dealer and court factor Markus Levin. In Jägerstrasse, Französische Strasse, and later in Mauerstrasse, "she, the most brilliant woman of her day, created in her modest salon a republic of creative minds."

Rahel Levin became the center and inspiration of this homogeneous circle, which cultivated an ideal of friendship and the personality. She was an early admirer of Goethe, but remained open to new movements in literature to the end of her life; thus she was seen by the "Junges Deutschland" ("Young Germany") writers as one who had prepared the way for that movement. Among her friends and guests were Chamisso, Friedrich and Wilhelm Schlegel, Henriette Herz, Dorothea Veit-Schlegel, Clemens von Brentano, Schiller, Tieck, and others. "Rahel had the art of uniting and reconciling everyone. At her salon we see warriors and diplomats, artists and scholars she did not care about the rank, position, or reputation of her guests and friends, but only about originality and naturalness: to everything else she was indifferent. It is at her home that we can best become acquainted with the many remarkable figures who in the years between 1789 and 1816 made up the society that really counted in Berlin," wrote Fritz Eberty in his *Jugenderinnerungen eines alten Berliners* ("Youthful Memories of an Old Berliner"), 1878.

At the age of 43, after liaisons – both happy and unhappy – with Prince Louis Ferdinand and Count Karl Finkenstein, Rahel Levin married the diplomat Karl August Varnhagen von Ense and at the same time converted to the Protestant faith, the Prussian state religion to which at least outward conformity was expected. Jean Paul commented after a visit to the "witty, philosophical Levi[n]" that "the

Rahel Levin (1771–1833). "The most brilliant woman in Germany," she was the focal point of intellectual Berlin society, and her friends included Börne, Heine, Franz Grillparzer, Tieck, the Humboldt brothers, Prince Louis Ferdinand, the Mendelssohns, and Marcus and Henriette Herz.

Karl August Varnhagen von Ense (1785–1858), diplomat and writer, married Rahel Levin in 1814. After her death he published her letters in a three-volume "Book of Remembrance." Drawing by Wilhelm Hensel.

Berlin Jewesses have little of the Old Testament about them and therefore always marry into the New!"

The sense of her Jewish birth as a "dagger plunged into her heart" was transformed after 1815, during a period of renewed anti-Semitism, into pride. Her Jewishness now became a fact which she "would not be without at any price."

Rahel Levin-Varnhagen also remains a significant figure because of her demand for women's liberation. She was already arguing for equality in law even for the single woman.

Mauerstrasse in Berlin, where Rahel Levin lived and had her salon after her marriage to Varnhagen von Ense. Copperplate engraving by Johann Georg Rosenberg, c. 1760.

A soireé in Berlin around 1826. Watercolor by Julius Schoppe.

Short-lived Equality in Prussia

The man chiefly responsible for the granting of almost total, though in the first instance short-lived, equality in Prussia was Chancellor Karl August, Prince Hardenberg. Despite some restrictions, the royal edict of 11 March 1812 represented the most significant victory so far in the struggle for civil rights for Jews in Germany. One humiliating element in the edict was paragraph 9, in which the

BELOW: Document conferring citizenship on the "Jewish commercial employee Sussmann Bleichröder" and his descendants. Potsdam, 30 August 1813.

ABOVE: Karl August von Hardenberg (1750–1822), the initiator of the law granting equal rights to Jews in Prussia. Painted and engraved by Johann Friedrich Bolt, 1815.

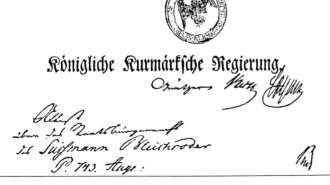

king proposed to "legislate at a future date" on the question of admitting Jews to the service of the state.

There was no uniformity among the German states in their handling of the question of emancipation. As early as 1809 the Grand Duchy of Baden had led the way with a law granting full equality to the Jews of that territory. In some states medieval ideas and laws still prevailed, while others remained progressive even after political reaction set in after 1815.

The Friedländers, Dohms, Humboldts, Varnhagens, and Jacobsons, and along with them most of the Jews in Germany, thought that they had almost reached their goal of equality. They had had to overcome a mountain of prejudices and long-established hostility toward Jews. The occupations into which Jews had been

OPPOSITE: Title page and first page of the Edict of Emancipation.

forced – commerce, petty trading, money-lending – had greatly contributed to these prejudices; a further factor was the uneasiness felt in the presence of a minority whose religion, customs and language of worship and study were alien. For centuries the Jews had been excluded from manual trades and from agriculture, and yet now they were criticized for not practicing trades or working in agriculture. It was a vicious circle which could be broken only by the granting of equal rights without restrictions.

In the event, the decisive factors in the countries of Europe were the inexorable advance of industrialization and, associated with this, the end of the guild system. In the rapidly developing railway age, with the emergence of mass production and the sophisticated organization of the business of selling goods, the "wandering Jew," a peddler carrying his wares from house to house had become superfluous.

The qualities of adaptability and astuteness that had enabled Jews to survive in times of oppression now made them receptive to economic and industrial changes. From a socioeconomic point of view, the consequences of the lost war of 1806/07 had already led to a new evaluation of the contribution that Jews could make to building up the Prussian economy. Prussia had lost half its territory, and the state and its economy needed to use all available resources.

Thus a combination of economic necessity and humanitarian ideas led the Prussian government to give serious attention to the Jews' plea for equal rights. The edict of 1812 gave them the right to settle and at last, linked to that, the possibility of obtaining rights of citizenship, though they remained excluded from the service of the state and subject to some restrictions in connection with service in the army.

Zeal for the German Fatherland

Meno Burg (1787–1853), the "Jewish major". He taught at the Schools for Artillery Officers in Danzig and Berlin. At the same time, as a committed Jew, he was a member of the governing body of the Jewish community in Berlin .

Baruch Eschwege, as a volunteer who took part in "Lützow's wild, audacious charge," 1813. Painting by Moritz Oppenheim.

Of the Jewish volunteers who fought on the Prussian side in the Wars of Liberation, one was awarded the order "Pour le Mérite," 82 received the Iron Cross, and 23 were promoted to the rank of officer. In the Battle of Waterloo 55 Jewish artillerymen were killed, but their widows received no pension, because from 1815 onward Jewish volunteers had no claim to any provision by the state.

Among the many Jews who were delighted to be able at last to follow the Prussian flag was Baruch Eschwege, a friend of the painter Moritz Oppenheim. Moritz Jonathan Itzig, son of the "Hofbaurat" Isaak Daniel Itzig, who because of his father's influential connec-

tions had been able to study agriculture, lost his life at Lützen.

One of the first Jews to choose the career of an officer was Meno Burg (1787–1853), who was known as the "Jewish major" and taught at the Schools for Artillery Officers in Danzig and Berlin. He was a member of the governing body of the Berlin community and, like most Jews, remained faithful to Judaism throughout his life. Burg had first became a land surveyor. At the beginning of the Wars of Liberation he had been rejected by the Prussian Guard on the grounds that he was a Jew. Through the intervention of Prince August, however, he was allowed to take the examinations for artillery officers, and

during the Wars of Liberation he directed the Prussian troop movements in Brandenburg and Berlin. His autobiography, the *Geschichte meines Dienstlebens* ("Story of My Life in the Service") was published posthumously in 1854.

RIGHT: "The Volunteers' Departure." In the foreground Jewish parents bid their son farewell. Contemporary wood engraving.

The Era of Reaction

The Congress of Vienna of 1814/15 redrew the map of Europe. As far as the German states were concerned, it was agreed that a German Confederation should be formed, with its seat in Frankfurt am Main. There the Federal Diet, a congress of delegates representing the states, held its sessions under the presidency of Austria.

The question of equality for the Jews was one of the matters debated by the Vienna Congress; the debate ended in a victory for the reactionary enemies of the Jews, notably the delegates from Bavaria, Saxony, Württemberg, Hanover, Hamburg, Bremen, and Lübeck. Indeed, the Hanseatic city of Lübeck soon afterward expelled Jews who had come to live there during the period of French rule. Hardenberg and Humboldt had tried in vain to extend the 1812 Edict of Emancipation to all the German states. In the end, Article 16 of the Federal Act of 1815 determined that those states which had been subject to French law were not obliged to maintain the rights conceded to the Jews; instead of the original "in," the final version stipulated only that "the rights already conceded to them *by* the individual German states" would be maintained. Thus all rights which the Jews had possessed under French rule were withdrawn.

After 1815 the civil rights conceded to Jews by Hardenberg's edict were rescinded by most of the states in the Confederation; in some they had never been implemented in the first place. It was a victory for the champions of Germanness with their Christian-Germanic nationalism, and it ushered in a wave of local pogroms and harassment of Jews in every sphere of society.

Thus for instance the Prussian Minister of Justice reported that the king was unwilling to let Jews who had been decorated with the Iron Cross enter the service of the state, on the grounds that bravery shown for a certain period in the service of the fatherland did not alter the basically low moral caliber of Jews. In 1822 King Frederick William III (reigned 1797–1840), who had come to symbolize the forces of reaction, struck a blow against the academics among the Jews, barring them from all teaching at universities and schools. Jews who were already in the state service were dismissed. With no prospect of being able to practice their profession, many Jewish lawyers converted to Christianity (see also pages 155 and 293)

In the new Prussian province of Posen, none of the provisions of the 1812 edict were put into effect. It was 1847 before the Posen Jews were placed on an equal footing with Jews elsewhere in Prussia, and it happened then at the urgent request of the provincial governor, who needed the pro-Prussian votes of the Jews as a counterweight to those of the anti-Prussian Catholic-Polish population.

In 1845 the Jews in Prussia's Westphalian and Rhine provinces succeeded, after a determined struggle, in regaining the rights taken from them in

The rights of Jews were one of the matters ruled upon by the Congress of Vienna in 1815. On the right, standing by the wall under the picture, the Secretary-General of the Congress, Friedrich Gentz, discusses a document with another delegate. Wood engraving by Jean Godefroy after a painting by Jean-Baptiste Isabey.

ABOVE: Hep-Hep disturbances in Frankfurt, 1819. Contemporary woodcut. This cry of mockery and malice directed at Jews has been interpreted, probably rightly, as a goatherd's call, addressed to Jews because of the style of their beards. (There is also another explanation, given in the text, which seeks to link this cry with the Crusades.)

BELOW, RIGHT: Caricature of Jewish emancipation. Leipzig, 1848.

RIGHT: Front page of the journal *Der Jude* ("The Jew") of 10 April 1832. Gabriel Riesser, the campaigner for equal rights for Jews, deliberately used the word "Jew," which some Jews regarded as an insult, for the title of his journal.

1815. Several of the states in the German Confederation were willing to take steps toward the emancipation of their Jewish citizens, but in the meantime the renewed uncertainty about the legal position of Jews encouraged acts of violence.

In 1819 attacks on Jewish districts took place in many states. "Let our battle cry be Hep Hep Hep!!! Death and perdition to all Jews ... ," read a student proclamation. ("Hep" is sometimes explained as an acronym of Hierosolyma Est Perdita, "Jerusalem is lost," a common taunt in the 19th century.) In Würzburg there were lootings and murders. The roughly 400 Jews had to leave the town and for several days either camped under canvas or stayed in neighboring villages.

In many places, however, the Jews now offered resistance. The strongest voice of intellectual resistance was that of Gabriel Riesser (1806–1863) of Hamburg, who was the most politically successful campaigner for equal civil rights in the 19th century.

The Stereotype of the Inferior Jew

Illustration of Jewish stereotypes based on the farce *Unser Verkehr* ("The People We Mix With") by K. B. Sessa. Picture sheet from Nuremberg, 1825. It is interesting from the social-historical point of view in that the caricatures show the limited range of professions open to the Jewish middle class.

Along with all the other consequences of this reactionary phase, the Jews had to suffer mockery and vilification. In 1803 an inflammatory pamphlet, *Wider die Juden* ("Against the Jews"), was published; its author was the lawyer Karl Grattenauer. In it he maintained that the Jews were incapable of being assimilated because of their hostility to culture.

In 1819, despite the objections of Prince Hardenberg, the farce *Unser Verkehr* ("The People We Mix With") by Karl Borromäus Sessa was performed. It achieved its comic effects by caricaturing Jewish occupations and the gestures and accent of those engaging in them. Plays which made Jews appear ridiculous on the basis of their allegedly "Jewish" manner of speech were performed at many theaters with enormous success.

The imputation that avarice was a fundamental trait of the Jewish character gave the audience a sense of moral superiority, a chance to project their own faults onto a minority, and a belated revenge for Lessing's *Nathan der Weise*.

This stereotypical representation of Jews was also spread by illustrated sheets, sold all over Germany, which at first caricatured Jews in an acceptable manner but later became vicious and calculated to stir up anti-Jewish feeling.

Plain nastiness characterized the ten successful volumes published in the 1830s by one "Itzig Feitel Stern," mocking the language and way of life of "the Jews." The man behind the pseudonym was a certain Baron Johann von Holzschuher. He invented a garbled mixture of mid-Franconian peasant dialect and Judeo-German, adding many ridiculous expressions of his own invention, and presented this as the way Jews spoke – the so-called "mauscheln," which was never spoken or written by any Jews in real life. For over a century, the "knowledge" which many non-Jews had

"Mendel Kohn goes home to keep the Sabbath."
From the title-page illustration of a book by Johann
von Holzschuher.

of "the Jews" hardly progressed beyond
the level of this kind of literature.

Another stereotype in racist propaganda
against Jews was the small, hook nosed,
crooked-legged "emancipated Jew," whose
banner bore the word "Profit" in large letters and who even had the audacity to
want to carry a gun. He was the precise
opposite of the ideal of the blond, muscu-
lar German youth, the reborn Siegfried,
with whom the new citizen of the
Romantic age wanted to identify.

RIGHT: Itzig Feitel Stern's *Gedichter, Perobeln unn
Schnoukes fer unnere Leut*, 1830. "Itzig Feitel Stern"
was the pseudonym of the anti-Semitic Baron Johann
von Holzschuher. The title, like the book, is in the non-
existent vulgar dialect which he invented and
presented as Judeo-German. His many books of
"humor" at the expense of the ordinary Jew found an
extensive readership.

Entry into the World of the Visual Arts

LEFT: Jeremias David A. Fiorino (1797–1847): miniature portrait of his father, D. A. Jeremias, c. 1830. The father had adopted the name Fiorino during the reign of King Jerome. Fiorino was one of the most gifted miniaturists of his day.

RIGHT: Salomon Bennett: "Queen Louise," copperplate engraving, 1797. The 22-year-old queen is shown as a thoughtful beauty.

Jews became involved only very gradually in the visual arts in Germany, and at first they modeled themselves closely in both content and form on the work of the Christian artists around them. It was only in the wake of the Enlightenment that more Jews turned to the visual arts. The decoration of synagogues, however, had its own independent character.

That first generation of Jewish artists in the early days of emancipation showed little originality, though several of them demonstrated great technical skill as copperplate engravers, makers of medallions, and miniature painters.

Two well-known artists were the medalists Jakob Abraham (1722–1800) and his son Abraham Abramson (1754–1811). Jakob Abraham was court medalist to Frederick the Great, who directed him to immortalize his military victories on commemorative coins. Abraham worked for decades for the Prussian mints, and he and his son jointly made medallions of Moses Mendelssohn, Lessing, Wieland, Kant and many others. There was a centuries-old tradition of Jewish medal making and seal cutting. These and similar professions practiced by Jews gave rise to surnames like Steinschneider (stone cutter), Diamant, Goldmann, Karfunkel (carbuncle) and others.

BELOW: The brothers Friedrich, August, Wilhelm, and Moritz Henschel: "Scenes from Goethe's *Dichtung und Wahrheit.*" Colored lithographs, 1819/20.

Among the early Jewish miniature painters of the 18th and 19th centuries were the Pinhas and Fiorino families. Juda Löw Pinhas (1727–1793) was court painter to the margraves of Ansbach and Bayreuth. He also spent some months at Sanssouci, the Prussian royal palace in Potsdam, where he painted members of the royal family. His son Salomon (1759–1837) was a miniature painter, etcher, and copperplate engraver. There are several known portraits by him of members of court circles and of Jewish society. David Fiorino (1797–1847), who enjoyed the

The Henschel brothers: "Our Father, Hirsch Henschel." Lithograph, c. 1825.

The Henschel brothers: "Goethe." Lithograph.

patronage of the Elector of Hesse, was a distinguished portrait painter.

References to their Jewish background can be found in the works of the four Henschel brothers from Breslau, who were copperplate engravers, painters, and lithographers; some of their early pictures are important early examples of lithography. From 1806 to 1826 the brothers worked chiefly in Berlin. Goethe admired their work, for instance their illustrations of scenes from his novel *Wilhelm Meister*, 1819. Artistically they mark a departure from the mere imitation of copperplate engraving.

Salomon Bennett (1761–1838), a Jew from Plozk in Poland, studied in Copenhagen and Berlin. In 1796 Bennett was made a member of the Berlin Academy, exhibited there and was a respected painter and copperplate engraver, but after four years he emigrated again, to England, because he found that living in Berlin was "spoiled" for him "by the oppression which the Jews had to suffer."

In 1831 Eduard von Bendemann (1811–1889) painted the picture entitled "By the rivers of Babylon, there we sat down, yea, we wept, when we remembered Zion." This picture made his name. In 1835 he converted to Christianity in order to marry the daughter of the sculptor Schadow; her mother was Jewish. After Schadow's death Bendemann, who had in the meantime been ennobled, succeeded him as director of the Düsseldorf Academy of Art.

Philipp Veit (1793–1877), a son of Brendel (Dorothea) Mendelssohn-Veit, was, like his elder brother Jonas, a leading member of the "Nazarene" school of painting. He painted many religious pictures for the cathedrals of Frankfurt, Mainz, and Naumburg, and also for the Vatican. The Veits represented the sentimentally religious and consciously German style of painting which was to have a powerful influence on the popular style of depicting religious subjects in Germany.

Eduard von Bendemann: "By the rivers of Babylon, there we sat down, yea, we wept, when we remembered Zion." Wood engraving by Ferdinand Ruscheweyh, 1832, after the oil painting by Bendemann.

Self-reflection: the Society for Jewish Culture and Learning

The efforts made to achieve emancipation had also set in train a movement for cultural assimilation, and this had split life within the Jewish communities into various opposed groups whose positions ranged from a fossilized orthodoxy, through a more enlightened orthodoxy, to the advocacy of total assimilation and absorption into the Christian-German people.

In 1819, young university graduates and scholars in Berlin from among the more assertive of the culturally assimilated Jews formed a "Society for Jewish Culture and Learning." Although the society never had more than 50 members, it had a decisive impact in developing a German-Jewish or rather Jewish-German culture that was emancipated and, in its religious aspect, not hidebound by tradition.

Among the society's founders were the brilliant Hegelian and lawyer Eduard Gans (1798–1839), the Hegelian Moses Moser (1796–1838), and the literary historian Leopold Zunz (1794–1886). Their aim

was to bring about, by scholarly research and by practical educational work, an intellectual reform of Judaism in Germany based on the humanistic-monotheistic values of Judaism.

The society had a fixed program of lectures and a learned journal, to which the early campaigner for emancipation, David Friedländer, now seventy, was a contributor. A teaching institute was also founded, at which one of the first teachers was Heinrich Heine.

After only four years of intense activity the society disintegrated. This happened partly because of its own internal weakness and partly as a result of political pressure, when in 1823 the ban on Jews working in the service of the state came into force, ushering in a period of both mental suffering and material hardship among university-educated Jews. In particular, those with a legal training, like Gans

Publications by Leopold Zunz.

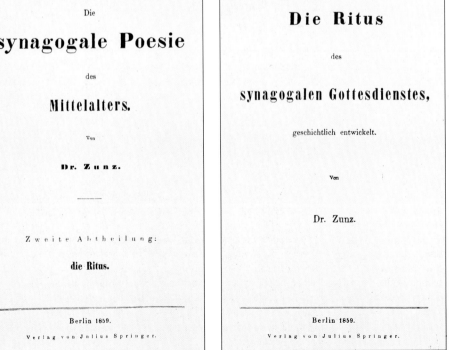

The lawyer and Hegelian Eduard Gans (1798–1839). Lithograph by G. Küstner.

Leopold Zunz (1794–1886), initiator of "Wissenschaft des Judentums" (Science of Judaism). Lithograph by Paul Rohrbach after a drawing by Julius Muhr.

and Heine, were deprived of a livelihood. Both accepted baptism in 1825. Gans was thereupon immediately appointed by the king to the chair of jurisprudence at the University of Berlin.

Without exception, those members of the association who were not lawyers remained Jewish, and they pursued their research into Jewish subjects in still greater depth. Foremost among them was Leopold Zunz, one of Germany's greatest Jewish scholars of the 19th century. His dissertation, *Etwas zur rabbinischen Literatur* ("On Rabbinical Literature"), 1818, was the first scholarly study in German of medieval Jewish culture. It made many educated Jews and non-Jews aware of the flowering of Judaism in medieval Germany, which had fallen into oblivion. His book on the most important commentator on the Bible and the Talmud, Rashi, who lived in the 11th century, and his other scholarly works, made a new generation conscious of independent Jewish intellectual achievements, thereby inspiring in them a new confidence.

Leopold Zunz became the founder of the movement known as "Wissenschaft des Judentums" (Science of Judaism), which performed an important role in researching Jewish history until its research headquarters was closed down by the National Socialists in the year 1938. Leopold Zunz inaugurated a new era in which it was possible for Jews to publish articles or books whose basis was no longer apologia but autonomous research and thought.

Politically, especially in the years of the "Vormärz" (pre-1848) and in the revolutionary days of 1848, Zunz supported both equal rights for the Jews and the Germans' aspirations for civil rights.

The Reform of Synagogue Services

The German-Jewish Enlightenment thinkers and reformers saw it as their primary task to align the outer forms of their worship with those of Christianity, in this case Protestantism. There were many who also demanded the abandonment of belief in revelation (i.e., in the revelation on Mount Sinai) and of belief in the salvation of the people of Israel and of the world through the coming of the Messiah.

After the promulgation of the short-lived edict of 1812 which gave equal rights to the Jews, David Friedländer (see p. 122) postulated a future in which the Jews would have autonomy within the state and regain their greatness as a nation, and argued that prayers for the coming of the Messiah were no longer necessary, since the Jews of Germany now had a homeland, and their natural language was German.

ABOVE: The rabbi Naftali Frankfurter of Hamburg, in the newly introduced dress of the Reform rabbi. Lithograph, c. 1845.

The scholar, publisher, and printer Wolf Heidenheim (1757–1832), though strictly conservative, removed all mystical texts from the prayer books which he was now also printing and publishing in German.

In 1810 Israel Jacobson (see page 135), who was the president of the Jewish Consistory at Kassel from 1808 and later an active reformer with his own synagogue in Berlin, pioneered the use of the organ and choral singing for synagogue worship at his school in Seesen. The official dress of rabbis was also changed to resemble that of Protestant ministers, with clerical bands and cap. The "house of study" was to be replaced by a speaker from the pulpit, and the rabbi by a preacher.

This movement to introduce reform within the synagogue reached a climax in Hamburg in 1818 with the founding of a Reform Temple there. Reform was a part of the continuing development of Judaism in modern times, but it was also, and more significantly, a break with the past.

A major reason why the reform of synagogue worship was so successful was that after centuries of oppression not only economic life but also religious scholarship among Jews was at a low ebb; expulsions had destroyed not quite all, but most, of the centers of biblical and Talmudic studies. This had contributed to a fossilizing of the religious life: for many Jews there was a linguistic barrier, since Hebrew was no longer spoken except in orthodox circles.

It was precisely these Jews whom most of the synagogue reformers aimed to bring back to the values of Judaism. They were strongly opposed by the orthodox, who saw central tenets of Jewish belief being cast aside, and viewed prayers in the German language as a desecration of the Scriptures.

The "New Temple" in Hamburg. Lithograph by Heinrich Jessen, c. 1844.

RIGHT: Title page of a German-language prayer book for women, 1839.

Salomon Heine (1767–1844), banker and philanthropist, uncle of Heinrich Heine, member of the governing body of the Reform congregation in Hamburg. Lithograph by Otto Speckter, 1842.

Gebetbuch

für

gebildete Frauenzimmer

mofaifcher Religion.

Sulzbach 1839,

Druck und Verlag von H. Frank.

Organ in the Reform Temple in Berlin built in 1854. An organ was seen as an unforgivable violation of the beliefs and principles of orthodox Judaism.

The "Judengasse" in Frankfurt am Main

ABOVE: The Judengasse in 1711. After the plan by Merian.

LEFT: The man said to be the last Jewish postman in Frankfurt, dressed in *Thurn und Taxis* livery. Drawing, painted with water colors, first half of 19th century.

RIGHT: The first page of the register of Israelite citizens, 1812.

BELOW: View along the Judengasse (detail). Steel engraving, c. 1850.

The ghetto in Frankfurt am Main was created in 1462 despite the protests of the Jews. It was built along the Wollgraben canal, just outside the old city wall dating from Hohenstaufen times (1125–1250), in a sparsely populated part of the "new town" (see also page 90).

By order of the city council, Jews might not walk more than two abreast in the city, and they were not allowed to go for walks. As late as 1769 the Frankfurt Jews petitioned "to be allowed to go for walks ... Jews everywhere [are] allowed access to the places where people walk, and we alone are to be forbidden to walk around the city gates ...". The buildings department replied that this petition was yet another proof "of

RIGHT: Houses adjoining the synagogue, after the demolition of the houses on the west side, c. 1870.

BELOW, RIGHT: Backs of houses in the Judengasse, 1872. Drawing by Peter Becker.

BELOW: Jewish sow on the Bridge Tower in Frankfurt. Goethe mentions this defamatory picture in his memoirs, *Dichtung und Wahrheit*. From J. J. Schudt's *Jüdische Merckwürdigkeiten* ("Jewish Curiosities"), Frankfurt am Main/Leipzig, 1714–17.

The Old Synagogue, interior. Watercolor by Oskar Pichler, 1855.

the boundless arrogance of these people, who do all they can to place themselves, at every opportunity, on an equal footing with the Christian population."

It was only after the French army had occupied the city that Jews were permitted to go for walks outside the Judengasse (Jews' Street). The Jews in the street traded in cloth, linen, furs, buttons, whalebone, gold, silver, jewels, tin, copper, brandy, tobacco, cheese, beer, books, coins, and antiques. Some of them were leading money changers. A number of them were prosperous, and a few became very rich indeed.

Famous inhabitants of the street include Mayer Amschel Rothschild (1744–1812), who became court factor to the Elector of Hesse, and the writer Löb Baruch (1786–1837), who upon his baptism took the name Ludwig Börne.

By about 1750 the number of dwelling houses had risen to about 350. Nevertheless, the city council refused to cover the open sewers, because that way the water was "most effective in fighting fires." It was only in 1811, after the formation of the Grand Duchy of Frankfurt, that

BELOW: Cattle market in the Judengasse in Frankfurt. Watercolor by A. Burger.

the liberal Prince Primate Karl von Dalberg ignored the protests of the city council and granted Jews the right of citizenship, though at a price of 440,000 guilders. When the Grand Duchy of Frankfurt – a Napoleonic creation – collapsed after the Battle of the Nations near Leipzig in 1813, the city council withdrew the Jews' citizenship again. But it held onto the money.

There was hardly a city or town in Germany in which religious Judaism developed so vigorously and continuously over several centuries as in Frankfurt.

In *Dichtung und Wahrheit* ("Poetry and Truth" – his memoirs) Goethe records the impression that the Judengasse and its inhabitants made on a Christian visitor:

"The lack of space, the dirt, the milling crowd, the accent of an unattractive manner of speech, all these made a most unpleasant impression even if one merely glanced in through the gateway in passing … At the same time one's young mind would darkly conjure up the old stories of the Jews' cruelty toward Christian children, which we had seen horribly illustrated in Gottfried's chronicle. And even though in more recent times people had a better opinion of them, the large picture mocking and defaming the Jews, still, unfortunately for them, fairly visible on the wall of an arch under the Bridge Tower, testified powerfully against them; for it had not been produced at the whim of some individual but put there by the public authorities.

"Yet these were still God's chosen people … Besides, they were also human beings, active, obliging, and even the obstinacy with which they clung to their customs was something one could not help respecting. Moreover, the girls were pretty … I was not content until I had visited their school several times, attended a circumcision and a wedding and formed an impression of the Feast of Tabernacles. Everywhere I was well received, given generous hospitality, and invited to come again."

Title page of the Talmud by Arie Loeb, printed by the gentile Johann Koelner in Frankfurt am Main, 1720/23.

The Rothschilds

Wilhelm IX (1743–1821), Landgrave of Hesse (from 1803 Elector Wilhelm I); Mayer Amschel Rothschild was his adviser and confidant.

Mayer Amschel Rothschild (1744–1812).

BELOW: Advertisement from Mayer Amschel Rothschild's coin catalog, 1770–1780.

Gutel Rothschild, née Schnapper (1753–1849), wife of Mayer Amschel.

BELOW: The ancestral house of the Rothschilds in the Judengasse in Frankfurt, c. 1870.

Solten von diesen schönen Münzen, welche um billige Preiße zu haben sind, und daraus verlangt werden, so beliebe man sich an den Eigenthümer zu addressiren, welcher noch mehr seltene Cabinets-Münzen, wie auch Antique-Seltenheiten und Alterthümer zu verkaufen hat.

Addresse

Mayer Amschel Rothschild

Hochfürstl. Hessen-Hanauischer Hof-Factor, wohnhaft in Frankfurt am Mayn.

The earliest documented ancestor of the Frankfurt Rothschilds was Isaak Elchanan, who died in 1585. His house bore the name *Zum Roten Schild* ("at the sign of the red shield"). In German the name "Roth-Schild" means "red shield".

Seven generations later, Mayer Amschel (1744–1812) bought house number 148, which was called "Zum Grünen (green) Schild," and also the adjoining house. This, like the other, occupied less than fifty square meters of ground. Now, with a total

of barely 100 square meters, he owned what was probably the largest house in the Judengasse. It accommodated a family of seven, servants, a shop measuring twelve square meters, and storerooms. Mayer Amschel Rothschild's activity as a dealer in

The five sons of Mayer Amschel Rothschild. Clockwise from top: Amschel Mayer (Frankfurt), Salomon Mayer (Vienna), James Mayer (Paris), Karl Mayer (Naples), Nathan Mayer (London).

coins and antiques brought him into contact with Elector Wilhelm I of Hesse, who awarded him the title of Factor to the Court of Hesse.

Wilhelm I was one of the wealthiest rulers in Germany, with a fortune estimated at 20 to 60 million reichsthalers. One significant source of income was the sale of some of his Hessian subjects as mercenaries to King George III of England – a trade initiated by his father before him.

Rothschild was a good businessman, and his dealing in coins led on to money changing and arranging loans for the Elector. Soon Mayer Amschel became Wilhelm's confidant, and the Elector also put him into contact with the English court.

At the time of the Napoleonic occupation he helped the Elector by hiding cases full of papers from the secret cabinet archive. In 1817 the five Rothschild sons were enno-

ABOVE: Nathan Rothschild (London) and his family. Painting by William Armfield Hobday, c. 1830.

Opening of the Emperor Ferdinand Northern Railway. Presentation souvenir for Nathan Rothschild, 1839.

Carl, Baron Rothschild (1820–1886), head of the Frankfurt banking house and member of the upper house of the Prussian Parliament.

bled, and in 1822 Wilhelm I made them barons. All of them cofounded and were partners in the family's international banking business: Amschel Mayer (1773–1855) in Frankfurt am Main, Salomon (1774–1855) in Vienna, Nathan (1777–1836) in London, Karl (1788–1855) in Naples, and James (1792–1868) in Paris.

Nathan Rothschild's emigration to England in 1798/99 marked the start of business dealings with that country. Nathan was the most energetic and successful of the brothers. Basing himself in Manchester, he sold cloth to Germany, but this textile business was only an episode, to be followed by the illustrious rise of the banking house of Nathan Rothschild in London.

The male descendants of Amschel Rothschild always remained committed Jews, and founded and supported Jewish institutions in many countries.

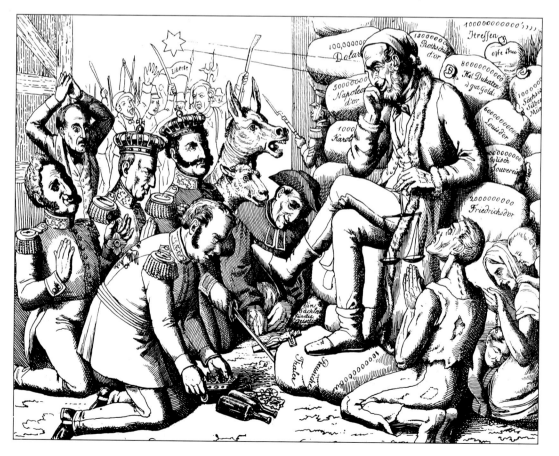

"Adoration of the Three Kings," anti-Jewish cartoon, 1848/49.

The Painter Moritz Daniel Oppenheim

LEFT: "Wedding," oil painting, 1866.

Moritz Oppenheim (1800–1882) grew up in the small town of Hanau near Frankfurt am Main, in an Orthodox lower middle-class family. From his fourth year onward, as was customary, he attended the voluntary elementary school, the "cheder," to learn Hebrew and the prayers. In his memoirs he writes: "One of my earliest memories is being taken to my first school by my eldest brother Simon; this was a small, longish room looking out on to a very small courtyard and so low that, if I remember rightly, my brother had to lower his head as he entered. Along the wall, on a bench hardly a foot high, sat boys and girls, the children of the whole Judengasse, who were called up one after another to the teacher, who was enthroned in an old armchair. On a table in front of him lay a Hebrew alphabet printed in large type, and we had to step up on to a small block of wood in order to be able to see it. The little, old, stammering teacher was called Fälkelche – 'tiny little Falk.' I suppose Falk was his real name."

In 1806, as a small boy, Oppenheim experienced the entry into Frankfurt of the French army and immediately afterward the abolition of the ghetto. His talent for drawing, encouraged by his brother Simon and his parents, led him in 1820 to the Städelsches Institut in Frankfurt and then to Paris and Munich for further study, financed by his brother. But in the very next year Oppenheim went on to Rome, where a number of German painters were living, in particular the "Nazarenes" who included Johann Friedrich Overbeck, Philipp Veit, the son of Dorothea Schlegel, Julius Schnorr von Carolsfeld, and Wilhelm Hensel, a brother-in-law of the composer Felix Mendelssohn. At first, writes Oppenheim, "I felt quite alone in this unfamiliar world. It was therefore only natural that as the time of the Jewish High Holy Days approached I should feel a greater longing for the ghetto and for the keeping of the old familiar religious customs of my parents' house than for the Vatican with all its art treasures." He did get to know some families in the Rome ghetto. But very soon he was working and living mainly among his many painter friends, some of whom tried to convert him to Christianity. "There was no lack of attempts to convert me too; of course they met with no success. On the contrary, they tended rather to make me into a more pious Jew, because they caused me to make comparisons in which my ancestral faith emerged as superior."

Oppenheim gradually moved ever further away from the Nazarenes' style of painting and from the philosophical outlook expressed in their work. Instead, especially in portraiture, he now emulated the Old Masters of the Renaissance.

The Nazarenes "despised a decent appearance, were carelessly dressed, often unkempt, ... At that time I also still came across imita-

according to the old customs." He had perhaps witnessed this scene himself as a 14-year-old at the house of the Eschwege family, for there is an obvious resemblance between the soldier in the painting and the portrait of the volunteer Baruch Eschwege,

He prepared the originals for photographic reproduction, using the grisaille technique of painting in shades of gray, which, at the stage that photography had then reached, using orthochromatic plates, could exactly reproduce every detail.

LEFT: Moses Mendelssohn in conversation with Lavater, with Lessing watching and Frumet bringing coffee. Lithograph by S. Maier after Moritz Oppenheim, 1866.

RIGHT: "Return of a volunteer from the Wars of Liberation," a picture based on the artist's memories, 1834.

BELOW: Oppenheim at his easel, c. 1860.

tors of the heroes of religious faith who had once been in vogue" (here among others he was referring to the Veit brothers, though in fact he remained on friendly terms with them) "– former Protestants who had become zealous Catholics. They would appear at the Café Greco in the old German style of coat, with a pious expression and folded hands. At home they painted stiff, clumsy, hard, wooden pictures of saints, in which the drawing itself was bad, and they believed that in these paintings they had expressed real feeling and brought about a renaissance of art."

After spending four years in Rome, Oppenheim returned to live in Frankfurt am Main. In 1839, after nine unsuccessful attempts, he finally obtained a permanent residence permit. By now he was a well-known and respected painter. After twelve further years he was granted citizenship.

As a protégé of the Rothschild family, he had become much sought after as a portrait painter by both Jews and non-Jews. Goethe, Börne, Heine, Riesser, Zunz, members of the Rothschild family and of Frankfurt society, commissioned him to paint their portraits. Starting in 1833, Oppenheim painted a series of sentimental genre pictures of Jewish family life. One of the earliest was the "Return of a Jewish volunteer to his family who still live

and the boy on the right could well be the young Moritz Oppenheim himself. The picture's bombastic title was also a protest at the fact that after the Wars of Liberation the Jews, including those who had fought as volunteers, were once again deprived of their rights; at the same time the picture and its title together suggest the consolation that was to be found in a return to the Jewish parental home.

Later Oppenheim published twenty-four pictures on the subject of Jewish family life.

Often excessively sentimental in their portrayal, these pictures, which are documents of Judeo-German social history, reflected the longing of Jews to be able to lead a Jewish style of life recognized as legitimate by the surrounding Christians. This no doubt accounts for Oppenheim's extraordinary success.

Goethe was among the many admirers of Moritz Oppenheim's paintings and portraits, and it was at his recommendation that the Grand Duke of Saxe-Weimar accorded Oppenheim the title of professor. Goethe commented on that occasion that "titles and decorations can ward off many a blow in the jostling crowd," with which Moritz Oppenheim happily concurred.

In the Villages and Towns

While in the 18th and 19th centuries Jewish society in the large cities was riven by the differences between the orthodox, liberals, and extreme reformists, and also by the gulf between rich and poor, the communities in villages and small towns remained homogeneous.

The natural focal point of the community was the rabbi, whom people could also turn to for advice, help, or adjudication in their personal problems or business disputes.

Common to all the rural communities was the, almost without exception, traditionally orthodox synagogue. In the 19th century even small towns often acquired a second synagogue for supporters of the liberal movement. Membership of charitable societies and of the burial association was honorary.

From their sixth year onward, Jewish and non-Jewish children went together to elementary school; in addition the Jewish children attended the "cheder" (see page 166) from their fourth year. Among the village children, among neighbors, at work,

ABOVE: The market place at Fürth (near Nuremberg), where Jews were not required to live in a special district and so lived side by side with Christians. No. 4 is the house of the Behrmann family. Copperplate engraving by Johann Alexander Baener, 1704.

RIGHT: Jewish beggar. Colored woodcut, c. 1830.

LEFT: "Pig dealers" in Baden agree on a sale. Colored drawing by Sohn, c. 1850.

ABOVE: "Teacher from Warsaw," etching by Ludwig Emil Grimm, 1818.
RIGHT, ABOVE: The parlor in a Jewish home in a Franconian village. On the left Keile, on the right Eleasar and Akiba Cahn. Watercolor by M. D. Harmann, 1817.
RIGHT, BELOW: An 18th-century cemetery. Graves of the Samson family in Wolfenbüttel.

and in general everyday life, hardly any distinctions were made between Jews and non-Jews.

The majority of Jews in northern and eastern Germany were small traders and in the west and south cattle dealers. In the south-west, Jews often had a cow, a small garden, a goat, and a few chickens for their own use, and sometimes they also owned a vineyard, a piece of agricultural land, or a small inn.

In the small towns Jews had the opportunity to practice craft trades, for instance as clockmakers, jewelers, spectacle makers, bookbinders, and printers, while in the villages they worked predominantly as bakers, tailors, synagogue caretakers, and teachers. In addition there were pawnbrokers, wandering Talmud students, and beggars, and the peddlers and itinerant market traders who traveled the countryside with their wares during the week. Wandering musicians, ballad singers, and conjurers also came from the country.

In villages and small towns the coexistence of Jews and non-Jews was less vulnerable to political tensions than in the cities. People met in the street or at the market, and chatted in a neighborly way

"over the fence." The children grew up together at school and spoke the same dialect.

In the villages the legal restrictions placed on Jews barely hampered them in their everyday lives; in the small towns, where there was now a considerable range of modern urban occupations, they were somewhat more disadvantaged. Nevertheless, for the most part the lives of Jews in villages and small towns flowed peacefully by with the changing round of the seasons.

LEFT: Faience tableware for the Passover, early 19th century.

OPPOSITE: Augsburg, a view looking down the Judengasse (Jews' Street), c.1700. Copperplate engraving by Karl Remshard.

Thalheim Castle on the river Neckar, the "Judenschlössle" (Jews' little castle). From 1778 to 1840 only Jewish families lived here, in return for high protection charges.

Jewish dwellings in an alleyway in Haigerloch, Württemberg. In some villages in Württemberg, Jews and Christians lived peaceably together up to the time of Hitler.

The Terracotta Figures of Zizenhausen

בְנֵי יִשְׂרָאֵל Kinder Israel

Rüstung auf den Schabis.

Around 1800 Anton Sohn, mayor of the village of Zizenhausen in southwestern Germany, began to make and paint groups of terracotta figures in semirelief. He usually worked from sketches and drawings by well-known artists such as Jacques Callot and Hieronymus Hess, but he developed his own satirical style, which was politically biting but good-natured on the human level. From Zizenhausen, itinerant traders took the small terracotta figures, each about 25 centimeters tall, with them on their travels.

Among the figures were some that caricatured Jews, but they differed from the great mass of anti-Jewish caricatures of the time in their gentle humor and their completely authentic portrayal of Jewish behavior and clothing. Anton Sohn modeled these figures during that period of deep humiliation for the Jews, the *Vormärz* (1815–1848). In Baden and Württemberg at that time many farmers and members of the lower middle class owed money to Jewish pawnbrokers. In years when the harvests were bad, interest and compound interest piled up to create a crippling burden of debt. The Jewish pawnbroker would lend money "on standing corn," and so if there was a bad harvest his risk increased – but so too did the farmer's debt.

Anton Sohn was able to observe all this at first hand and was familiar with Jews pursuing their typical occupations: they were cattle dealers and peddlers (whether selling from carts or merely from trays strapped to their fronts), commercial travelers, skilled tradesmen, teachers, money lenders, booksellers, beggars, musicians, keepers of tiny country inns, winegrowers, and, as in all border areas, smugglers of foodstuffs (into and out of nearby Switzerland).

As a result Sohn's figures, despite their satirical traits, provide an intimate picture of the ordinary Jew and of Jewish families in southwestern Germany in the early 19th century.

OPPOSITE, TOP: "Children of Israel." The Zizenhausen terracottas show south-west German country Jews in their characteristic style of dress.

OPPOSITE, BOTTOM: "Preparing for the Sabbath." The heart of life in the village was the Sabbath spent with the family.

RIGHT: The commercial traveler on horseback: "Blauschild, traveling representative for merchants, does business in all branches of trade."

RIGHT, BELOW: "As true as I stand here, she gives two full pails every ... " Country Jews often had a cow, and sometimes also a piece of farmland.

BELOW: The Jewish ribbon seller was a precursor of the department store: "I'm a businessman too, after all. Je vend en gros et en detail."

Peripheral Occupations

In general, up to the 18th century, the majority of Jews were still restricted to the occupations they had been forced into, of hawking and peddling, pawnbroking and money lending, and trading in cattle and in grain. Naturally, the fact that they were largely without legal rights often led them to disregard the law themselves: there were honest and dishonest market traders, straightforward horse dealers and tricksters, traveling tradesmen and swindlers. With the coming of mercantilism the Jews had begun to be permitted greater freedom of movement. In some territories they received permission to run small businesses, and became clockmakers, spectacle makers, and jewelers; they engaged in manufacturing and selling textiles, making

The "Jewish Exchange" in Hamburg, mid-19th century.

Jewish entertainers at a public festival in Cannstatt (near Stuttgart), lithograph, 1835.

A Jewish cattle dealer, etching by Johann Adam Klein, 1811.

Second hand clothes dealer, copperplate engraving by Chodowiecki, 1780.

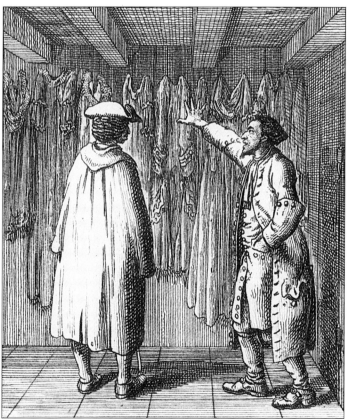

Bock's book and music shop in Unter den Linden, Berlin, c. 1850.

Fashion shop close to the Royal Palace in Berlin, painting, 1830.

leather goods, or producing tobacco, and a few even owned shops. In the 18th century, Jews already had almost a thousand stands at the Leipzig fair, even though they were generally allowed to conduct their trading only in rear courtyards, and had to pay special charges such as gate tolls. Jews from Poland and Russia brought furs, leather, bristles, and also textiles, woolen goods, and jewels. It was primarily the Jewish furriers from the east who made Leipzig into the biggest fur market in the world – an early example of the transition of Jews from exclusively peripheral occupations to participation, however limited, in normal professions. From now on it was mainly Jewish manufacturers who produced velvet and lace; the Jewish peddlers and commercial travelers were gradually superseded by representatives working for industries supported by the state; the Jewish ribbon-vendor with his tray ceased his travels and became a shop-owner.

"Walking-shticksh!": a Jewish street trader in Hamburg, colored copperplate engraving by Christoph Suhr, c. 1808.

Jewish peddler in Lübeck. Naive pen-and-ink drawing, c. 1830.

BELOW: Lübeck. Advertisement for the itinerant optician Aron Jacob from the Ansbach region, 1809.

BELOW RIGHT: The bustle of the Leipzig fair, on the Brühl. Drawing by Georg Emanuel Opiz, 1825.

Mit gnädigfter Bewilligung.

Unterzeichneter Optifer aus dem Ansbachifchen hat die Ehre einem hohen Adel und verehrungswürdigen Publifum von feiner Ankunft, wie auch daß er verfchiedene optifche Gläfer verfertiget, Nachricht zu geben.

Erftens find bei ihm verfchiedene Confervations-Gläfer zu befommen. Seine Brillen find nach Verfchiedenheit des Augenmaaßes eingerichtet, fowohl für Kurz- als Nahfichtige, als auch für folche Augen, die nicht in der Nähe, fondern nur in der Ferne fcharf fehen. Diejenige Brille, welche den Augen, je nachdem fie befchaffen find, am angemeffenften und wohlthätigften ift, wird fogleich nach den Regeln von ihm beftimmt, fobald er die Augen gefehen hat.

Licht und deutliche Unterfcheidung der Gegenftände wird unfehlbar einem jeden, über das Gefühl feiner hergeftellten Sehkraft mit Freude erfüllen, wobei niemand beforgen darf, daß die Augen angegriffen, und noch mehr gefchwächt werden. Diefe Beforgniß findet bloß bei Vergrößerungsgläfern ftatt. Vielmehr zeigt fich, wie fchon gefagt, das Gegentheil, daher diefe Brillen nicht nur Confervations- fondern auch Reftaurations-Brillen heiffen follten.

Ferner find zu haben: Verfchiedene Ferngläfer; Microfcope composita, wie auch Microfcope folara, welche von 10 bis hunderttaufendmal vergröffern; Camerae obscure, wo man einen groffen Gegenftand auf einen Viertelbogen Papier aufnehmen kann; kurze und lange Perfpective, welche mit doppelten Objectiv-Gläfern verfertigt find, und die Sonnenftrahlen verwerfen; Camerae clarae, welche alle Gegenftände im Kleinen präfentiren; Brenn- und Hohlfpiegel, mit welchen man viele Experimente durch die Sonne machen kann; Cones et prismata; verfchiedene Laternen Magica, welche kleine auf Glas gemahlte Figuren in Lebensgroße an der Wand präfentiren. Auch wer etwas Schadhaftes von folchen Waaren zu repariren hat, kann um einen billigen Preis hier bedient werden.

Wer von dergleichen Gegenftänden Etwas zu repariren hat, empfiehlt fich Unterzeichneter zu Dero Dienften.

Logirt im wilden Mann am Kornmarkt, in der erften Etage Nr. 10.

Aron Jacob.
aus dem Ansbachifchen.

In Posen, East Prussia, and Danzig

LEFT: Baer Loew Monasch (1801–1876), printer, publisher, and bookbinder in Krotoschin, Posen. Pastel portrait by the Henschel brothers, 1839.

RIGHT: Mathilde Monasch-Wiener, his wife. Pastel portrait by the Henschel brothers, 1839. Their daughter married the Jewish historian Heinrich Graetz.

Around 1800 there were about 37,000 Jews living in the Posen region, making up about six percent of the total population of Prussia. There were almost as many skilled Jewish tradesmen as Christian ones.

When in 1815 – after an interruption during the Napoleonic period – this province was returned to Prussia, together with some additional districts, there were altogether 65,000 Jews living there. Jews "lacking sufficient property and education" were now subject to severe restrictions which were not lifted until 1847. Until then they continued to have the status of nonnaturalized protected Jews, even though the great majority of them represented a group within the mainly pro-Polish population that was receptive to German culture and largely assimilated to

it in language and outlook. The decision to give the naturalized Posen Jews the same rights as the Jews in the Prussian "home" territory was a political move designed to prevent a Polish majority vote in the local elections. Many Posen Jews were quick to join the movement for emancipation, and all of them supported German culture against the Catholic-Polish section of the population; at times there were violent clashes between the two groups.

The economic and political discrimination against the Posen Jews led to waves of emigration to Berlin and to America, especially when in the second half of the 19th century the Prussian officials in Posen became still more anti-Semitic. Many Berlin Jews originating from Posen became well-known figures in the cultural and intellectual life of the capital. When Posen

became part of Poland under the Treaty of Versailles (under the name Poznan), almost all the Jews opted for Germany and migrated westward.

In Königsberg, the capital of East Prussia, there were about 300 Jews on 1756, but the community was rapidly enlarged by migration from neighboring Russia. Here too, many members of the community became supporters of the Enlightenment movement, most notably under the influence of Kant, who taught at Königsberg, and it was here that the Enlightenment journal *Ha-me'assef* (see page 122) was published. With the founding of the "Society for the Promotion of the Hebrew Language" (1783), the city became a center of Jewish Enlightenment, producing such figures as David Friedländer and Marcus Herz. It was also at Königsberg that early attempts were made to reform synagogue services. An influential role was played by the small colony of Russian-Jewish intellectuals, among them Abraham Mapu (1808–1867), whose Hebrew works dealing with biblical and contemporary themes were translated into German, Yiddish, English, and Arabic. Works of his are among the classics of modern (i.e. secular) Hebrew literature.

Danzig, which until 1919 was the capital of West Prussia, had been a center of international trade and a Free City ever since the Middle Ages. Again and again, for economic reasons, Jews were allowed to come and settle there despite the opposi-

RIGHT: Rabbi Akiba Eger (1761–1837) and two companions in the market place in Posen. Eger was a rabbi in Posen and the greatest authority on the Talmud of his day. Detail from a painting by Julian Knorr, c. 1835.

BELOW: Scene in the market place in Posen. In the foreground, right, a group of Jews including members of the Heymann Saul family. Detail from a painting by Julian Knorr, c. 1835.

LEFT: Danzig, Breitegasse. In the fourth house from the left the banker Carl Fürstenberg (1850–1933) was born. Watercolor, mid-19th century.

tion of the local merchants. Johanna Schopenhauer, the mother of the philosopher, lived in Danzig as a child and young woman from 1766 to 1793 and writes in her memoirs: "I gladly leave aside the dirty and disreputable Polish-Jewish peddlers who let neither the body tax which they had to pay, nor the oppression and mockery of all kinds which they had to suffer from Christian souls, discourage them from coming here in large numbers and plying their miserable trade here, there, and everywhere, to the accompaniment of ugly cackles and shouts.

"But besides these there were others, Old Testament figures, whose more dignified appearance contributed to making life in the public streets present a most varied picture of fascinating diversity. Rich Israelite merchants from Warsaw, Cracow, Posen and other Polish cities in their impressive national dress, who came to Danzig on business – tall men with dark, flashing eyes and truly oriental features, worlds apart from that rabble in their tatters. Their beards, well cared for, often snow-white and spreading far down and across their chests, their tall, dark sable caps, their black robes falling into picturesque folds, gave them a striking resemblance to the most effectively rendered figures of prophets and apostles in pictorial art.

"Their wives, too, sometimes accompanied them; their dress, however, had a rather odder appearance and gave a very outlandish impression – skirts of heavy silk brocade with large floral patterns, a tunic made of similar material reaching down to their knees and bordered along the hem with sable, and a golden bonnet. Over their foreheads they wore a fairly broad band made up of several rows of real pearls – large but mostly irregularly shaped, so-called baroque pearls – which kept every single hair out of sight. A quantity of heavy, old-fashioned gold chains and jewelry made of all kinds of gemstones completed the adornment of one of these daughters of Zion, which, however, suited their faces with their dark complexions and black eyes tolerably well, while they were still young."

After a varied history the city became Prussian in 1793 and granted the right of citizenship to a number of Jewish merchants. During and after the First World War the community experienced a new cultural flowering as a result of further immigration from the east.

Nachdem der Jude *Zacharias Hamburger zu Schmiegel* sich gehörig ausgewiesen, daſs er benebst seiner Familie zur Zeit als die Provinz Südpreussen denen Königlichen Preussischen Staaten einverleibt worden, sich in dieser Provinz wohnhaft *Schmiegel* befunden, und sich nach Vorschrift des General-Juden-Reglements vom 17. April 1797, als *Schutz-Wahren Händlar* künftig ehrlich ernähren kann und will; so haben Seine Königlichen Majestät von Preussen unser Allergnädigster Herr geruhet gedachten Juden *Zacharias Hamburger* nicht nur für seine Person, sondern auch für seine auswarts noch nicht etablirte, sondern unter väterlicher Gewalt stehende, und für seine künftig zu erzeugende Kinder in Allerhöchst Dero Provinz Südpreussen unter die Zahl der darinn befindlichen Schuz-Juden aufnehmen zu lassen, und wird demselben unter der Bedingung, daſs sich derselbe allen denen, im Reglement vom 17. April 1797 enthaltenen und etwa noch über die Verfassung der Juden künftig zu publicirenden Vorschriften willig und genau unterwerfen, und denen ihm vorgesezten Obrigkeitlichen Personen Gehorsam leisten werde, dieser Königliche Schuz-Brief ertheilet und demselben der Genuſs aller der Rechte und Befugniſse zugesichert, welche erwähntes Reglement denen Südpreussischen geschüzten Juden verheiſset und zusichert.

Gegeben zu *Posen 27 ten August* 1805

ABOVE: Document giving Zacharias Hamburger of Schmiegel (province of South Prussia) the status of a "protected" Jew, 1805.

RIGHT: The old Jewish cemetery in Königsberg. Lithograph by W. Behnigson, c. 1890.

In Silesia

ABOVE: Karl Georg, Count von Hoym, Minister for the Province of Silesia. A benevolent friend to the Jews and connoisseur of Jewish literature, he urged that the Jews be treated humanely and in accordance with the constitution.

In Silesia – as also, incidentally, in East and West Prussia and in Poland – the first Jewish settlers were fugitives from the bands of murderous Crusaders. Some of them settled as farmers in the Breslau area.

At the time of the Black Death, around 1348, many Jews in Breslau were murdered, and Emperor Charles IV gave their houses and synagogues to the town. Early in the 15th century their surviving descendants were invited to return, and a prosperous community grew up there. Following anti-Jewish sermons by John of Capistrano (1386–1456), the Jews were driven out again (see pages 74–75). In 1650 the town's administration once more allowed Jewish families to settle, in order to boost trade with Poland. Jewish fugitives from Poland came to Breslau after the Khmelnytsky massacres of 1648, and it was fugitives who also formed the core of other Jewish communities elsewhere in Silesia.

In the following centuries Jewish communities were founded in Brieg, Glatz, Glogau, Görlitz, Liegnitz, Schweidnitz, and some fifty other places, and these communities produced many important scholars. Late in the 17th century a Hebrew printingworks opened at Dyhernfurt near Breslau where, among other things, not only an edition of the Talmud but also the first Hebrew newspaper in Germany was printed. Religious books continued to be printed at Dyhernfurt until 1834.

After Silesia had been conquered by Frederick the Great, it too became subject to the discriminatory Prussian laws. A more humane attitude toward the Jews prevailed under the Minister for Silesia, Count Hoym, during the reign of Frederick William II. In particular, Hoym ensured that there was well-regulated secular education and a constitution that reflected the spirit of the Enlightenment. He granted full privileges of citizenship to twenty-four families, and partial privileges to a further 160.

During the 18th and well into the 19th century, Silesia's Jewish population could

LEFT: "The Jews' meeting place or flea market ... jestingly called the Jews' Exchange": a square in Breslau. Copperplate engraving after a drawing by Friedrich Bernard Werner, c. 1780.

be divided into three groups. The largest was that of the country Jews, who were mostly small tenant farmers, market traders, and employees of the community. The second group consisted of merchants, importers and exporters, and also small manufacturers in Breslau, Glogau, and Zülz. The third group was the educated upper class which, being wealthy and enjoying full legal rights, was in a special position. This group made an outstanding contribution to the development of science and technology in Prussia.

Separate from these three groups were the orthodox and liberal rabbis and Talmudic scholars and their pupils, as well as the Reformists.

From an early period and right up to the 20th century Breslau was a center for both orthodox and moderately reformist Talmudic scholars. In 1854 Zacharias Frankel (1801–1875) founded the Breslau Jewish Theological College, where many liberal rabbis received their training. The college had a profound influence on the religious development of modern Judaism in the whole of the western world.

Silesian Jews also played an ever-increasing role in German cultural life, particularly once they had attained some degree of emancipation during the more enlightened periods. Ephraim Moses Kuh (1731–1790) was one of the first Jewish poets to write in the German language, and another was Esther Gad-Bernard (1770–1820), a granddaughter of the famous scholar, Talmudist, and cabalist Jonathan Eibeschütz (c. 1690–1764). It was at Breslau that the first modern Jewish historian, Heinrich Graetz (1817–1891), taught at the Jewish Theological College, was a professor at the university, and wrote as well his eleven-volume *Geschichte der Juden von den ältesten Zeiten bis zur Gegenwart* ("History of the Jews from the Earliest Times to the Present Day"), 1835–1875.

Other famous Silesians were the politician Ferdinand Lassalle (1825–1864), the explorer Eduard Schnitzer, known as Emin Pasha (1840–1892), and the founder of modern chemotherapy and Nobel prize-winner Paul Ehrlich (1854–1915). Many scholars, scientists and writers forsook Breslau for Berlin, as did many businessmen. The four Henschel brothers (see pages 152–153) were also originally from Breslau.

In the 20th century the number of Jews in Silesia fell, through emigration, from 50,000 people in 1900 to 15,000 people in 1939. Most of those who had remained there were murdered in the years that followed.

ABOVE: Salomon Pappenheim (1740–1814), Hebrew writer, rabbinical candidate in Breslau, and leader of the community; he advocated incorporating Enlightenment principles in orthodox Judaism. Oil painting, c. 1800.

BELOW: The physician Elias Henschel of Breslau, uncle of the Henschel brothers. Lithograph, 1837.

RIGHT: Title page of an ordinance concerning the Jews "tolerated" in Silesia. Potsdam, 8 March 1780.

Synagogue Buildings around 1800

Around the year 1800, synagogues were for the most part simple buildings in the traditional style of their region. In the villages they generally had only one story and from the outside were hardly distinguishable from any other functional building. The taller synagogue buildings in small towns and cities usually had a gallery in which the women sat.

The interior walls and ceilings were normally left unpainted, except in the synagogues of Horb, Bechthofen, and some other Franconian villages, where Elieser

LEFT: The synagogue at Heidingsfeld near Würzburg, c. 1780. View of the interior during a service.

BELOW: Harburg in Bavaria. The synagogue next to the church dates from about 1800 and is located in the middle of the former Jewish quarter.

Sussmann of Brody covered them with decorative painting in the style of the eastern European wooden synagogues. He imaginatively combined sayings and prayer texts with plants and symbolic animals such as the Lion of Judah. At Horb an elephant crops up for no apparent reason, as it did in the Worms mahzor (see page 37): both of these instances perhaps represent a survival in folk memory of the elephant Abulabaz (see page 29), which was presented to Charlemagne by Isaak the Jew as a gift from Harun al-Rashid.

The Horb synagogue (now in the Israel Museum, Jerusalem).

RIGHT: Detail from the ceiling painting, with an elephant amid the design of entwined flowers.

BELOW: View of the east wall. On the left is an imaginary representation of Jerusalem.

Almemor and ark of the Torah in the synagogue at Ansbach (Bavaria). Above the ark one can find the inscription, "Know before whom you stand."

Up to the early decades of the 19th century many communities still favored a simple Baroque style of building, and the later examples of this seem almost anachronistic.

It was only after 1840 that a neoclassical style became the norm in the building of synagogues. This change was introduced by Reform communities, which wanted the synagogue to become, like a Christian church, a "House of God" (which they also called a "temple"). At around this time an effort was also made, when building synagogues, to get away from the "back courtyard" location.

RIGHT: The synagogue of Krumbach-Hürken, 1819, built in the Baroque style. It is unusual to find a clock on a synagogue building.

BELOW: Synagogue in Mannheim, c. 1800.

The Festivals

Jewish life in the course of the year is shaped by the Sabbath and the religious festivals. Despite its weekly recurrence, the Sabbath is the highest festival, for "on the seventh day God ended his work which he had made; and he rested on the seventh day from all his work which he had made. And God blessed the seventh day, and sanctified it ..." (Genesis, 2: 2,3).

On the Sabbath, the portion of the Torah prescribed for that week is read aloud from the Torah scroll in a particular style of chanting; in the course of a year all the chapters of the Pentateuch are read out. The reading of the Torah is followed by extracts from the books of the Prophets.

The Jewish year, a lunar year, begins in September/October with the festival of the New Year, Rosh Hashana ("Head of the Year"), which is celebrated with a particu-larly solemn service. On this day, according to popular belief, one's name is – or is not – entered in the Book of Life

This destiny of life or death is sealed, so people believe, ten days later on Yom Kippur, the Day of Atonement. On this day a total fast is prescribed; the believer confesses his sins, repents and hopes for the Lord's forgiveness. On Rosh Hashanah and on Yom Kippur the prayer leader in the synagogue blows the shofar, the ram's horn. It is a call to repentance and amend-ment, but it also commemorates and recalls God's rejection of human sacrifice when Abraham obediently offered up his beloved son Isaac. A ram, an animal sacri-fice, took the place, once and for all, of the human sacrifice.

Fourteen days after Rosh Hashanah, in October, comes Sukkot, the Feast of Taber-

ABOVE: On Simhat Torah (Rejoicing of the Law), the seventh day of Tabernacles, the Torah scrolls are ceremonially carried in procession around the synagogue. After a painting by Hugo Elkan.

LEFT: A blessing (after Leviticus 23: 40) being recited over a festive bunch of palm branches, an etrog (citron), myrtle twigs, and willows during the festival of Tabernacles. After a painting by Hermann Junker.

nacles. It commemorates the forty years spent by the Children of Israel in the wilderness, when, as they wandered toward the Promised Land, they lived in primitive shelters (Deuteronomy 16: 13ff.). Sukkot seems originally to have been a harvest festival, and its symbols, the palm branch and etrog (citron), survive to this day. During the eight-day Feast of Tabernacles, meals are taken in the sukkah, a wooden hut roofed with branches through which the sky remains visible.

With December comes Hanukkah (the Feast of Dedication, or Lights), the festival of the eight-day light. It commemorates the reconquest of Jerusalem through the victory of the Maccabeans over the Seleucids in the second century B.C., and the miracle when, as the Temple was rededicated, one day's supply of oil lasted for eight days. On each evening of this festival one more candle is lit, usually by the children, than on the evening before, until at last all eight candles are burning. Hanukkah is a festival of joy, celebrated with merrymaking.

Another joyful festival, especially for children, is Purim, the "Feast of Lots," in February/March. With dressing up, performances of lighthearted plays and the exchanging of gifts, Jews remember their deliverance from the Persian Haman, the persecutor of Jews, and the story of Queen Esther and her foster father Mordechai. It is called the Feast of Lots because Haman drew lots to discover in which month he could successfully carry out his attack on the Jews.

The festival of Pesah in March/April is celebrated to commemorate the exodus from Egypt, the land of bondage (see page 194). Pesah is called Passover in English, and that in fact is what it means. When killing the firstborn of the Egyptians, the angel passed over the houses of the Israelites (see Exodus 12, 1–29).

The last festival of the Jewish year is Shavuot, the Feast of Weeks, which commemorates the giving of the Ten Commandments on Mount Sinai.

ABOVE: The blowing of the shofar on Yom Kippur. After a painting by Hermann Junker.

BELOW: The kohanim (priests), their heads covered with the tallit, pronounce a blessing upon the community. After a painting by Hermann Junker.

Religion in the Family

LEFT: Bar Mitzvah ("subject to the Commandment"). When reaches the age of 13, the boy becomes subject to the law, i.e. a full member of the community. On the Sabbath following his birthday he is called up for the first time to read from the Torah scroll. In modern and liberal communities a girl becomes a Bat Mitzvah ("daughter of the Commandment").

Until the end of the 19th century the family life of most Jews was largely shaped or at least influenced by religious tradition. Children are Jewish by virtue of their descent from the mother, not from the father. A girl is a member of the Jewish community from birth, a boy becomes a member through his circumcision on the eighth day after birth.

The Bible and the prayer book provide the basis for the upbringing of children in the traditional Jewish home. The daily meals are prepared strictly according to the dietary laws, and the Sabbath is the day of rest, to be observed unconditionally; on this day all actions or thoughts relating to worldly, material things are to be avoided.

The saying of a blessing precedes every meal, even the drinking of a glass of water or the eating of a slice of bread, as well as actions like washing the hands or starting on a journey; they also accompany such natural phenomena as the appearance of the new moon or of a rainbow. The morning prayer with which each day begins is a

LEFT: Hanukkah, the festival of the eight-day light, is, like Purim, a domestic festival, geared especially to children. On this day it is traditional to play games of all kinds, including games with cards, dice or a spinning top, and to give presents to the children.

matter of course, as are the afternoon and the evening prayers.

Like birthdays, to which Orthodox families do not attach great importance, all religious festivals are also family festivals. This is especially true of the eve of the Sabbath and that of the Passover, when the festive meal is framed by readings of the biblical account of the departure from Egypt but also by stories, jolly children's songs and fables, parables, and songs in which everyone joins in. Hanukkah, the winter Festival of Lights, and Purim with its carnival-like activities are also primarily family festivals. The same is true of the Feast of Tabernacles which commemorates the primitive shelters used during the forty years spent in the wilderness after the exodus from Egypt.

The Frankfurt painter Hermann Junker the Elder, a Christian (1838–1899), captured these family festivals and the synagogue feasts and services in his pictures. They faithfully document Jewish family life and Jewish festivals as they were and still are celebrated in Orthodox communities.

RIGHT: Seder night at Passover. After a painting by Hermann Junker.

RIGHT: The festival of Purim is celebrated with exuberant merriment, with games, dressing up, and gifts. After a painting by Hermann Junker.

Ceremonial Art in the Synagogue

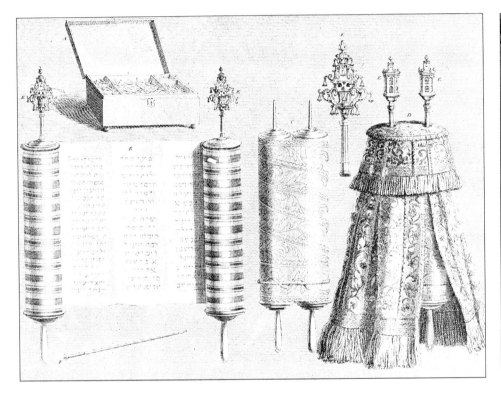

LEFT: Breastplate to adorn the Torah scroll which has been draped in a covering of cloth. Berlin, 1790. The gilded tablets bear the initial letters of the Ten Commandments. The little frame below holds interchangeable plaques with the name of the appropriate festival: here it is "Pesah."

ABOVE, LEFT: Torah scrolls and adornments for them. After a steel engraving by B. Picart, 1725.

ABOVE, RIGHT: Curtain of the ark of the Torah, 1751. Embroidered on it are, top, the seven-branched candelabrum, and to the left the table for the shewbread (ritual objects from Solomon's Temple). The two lions, symbolizing the tribe of Judah, are on either side of the crown, the symbol of the Kingdom of God. The two columns represent the columns at the entrance to Solomon's Temple.

LEFT: A silver crown, partly gilded, Germany, late 18th century. The spread hands symbolize the blessing upon the community pronounced by the priests.

BELOW: Engraved
shofar (ram's horn),
German, 18th century.
This is the wind
instrument used by Jews
since biblical times.

RIGHT: Open Torah scroll
and pointer (yad).

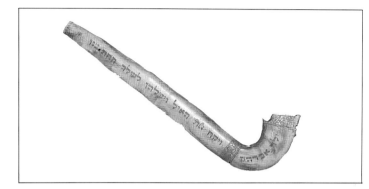

A number of objects, often produced with great artistry, are used in the synagogue, and each has a special significance. Most striking are the adornments of the Torah scroll. The Torah is the most precious possession of Jews, because it contains the Word of God revealed on Mount Sinai and which is set down in the Pentateuch, the first five books of the Bible. Handwritten on parchment, the Torah is so precious that it is protected and adorned; its text is so deeply revered that people do not touch it with their hands. It is kept in a cabinet, the "ark," standing against or set into the east wall, usually with a decorative curtain in front of it. After each use the scroll is wound on past the portion that has just been read, and before putting it away the prayer leader or a member of the community ties the binder or sash around the scroll: this is a strip of linen which has been cut by the mother from the diaper worn at a boy's circumcision, sewn together and then embroidered or painted. For protection and adornment, the scroll is covered with an embroidered mantle of velvet or silk. Over that is hung the shield or breastplate, usually finely worked in silver, which often has a holder for interchangeable small plates bearing the name of the day on which the scroll will next be taken from the ark to be read.

Lastly, the yad (Hebrew for "hand"), is hung on it by a chain: this is the pointer which the reader uses to avoid desecrating the writing by touching it with his fingers. Over the tops of the wooden rollers of the scroll are placed a crown or two rimonim ("pomegranates"), which are often adorned with bells. All these objects have been produced using the finest possible materials and workmanship, and they are usually gifts to the synagogue from individual members of the community.

During the days of penitence in the month of Elul (September/October), at the New Year (Rosh Hashana) and on the Day of Atonement (Yom Kippur) it is the practice in the traditional synagogue for the shofar to call the community to repentance and reflexion.

BELOW: *Wimple, Halberstadt*, 1737. The Torah scroll is held together by a narrow piece of cloth, the sash. This was made by a mother from the diaper used at her son's circumcision; it depicts the joyful wedding of her son for which the mother hopes

Ceremonial Art in the Home

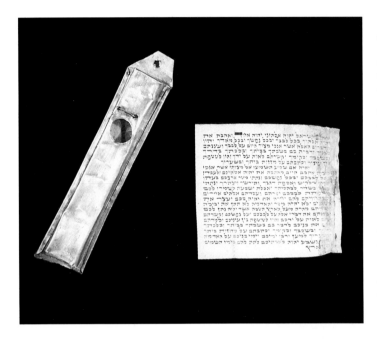

LEFT: Mezuzah ("doorpost"): a small case attached to the right-hand doorpost of the entrance door, containing a tiny parchment scroll inscribed with texts from the Book of Deuteronomy (6: 4-9 and 11: 13–21).

BELOW: Seder plate, Royal Porcelain Factory, Berlin, early 19th century. It shows figures from the Haggadah: from right to left, the wise son, the wicked one, the simple one, and the one who does not know how to ask questions. Around the edge are the actions which are to be performed on Seder night.

foods that symbolically recall the sojourn in Egypt, containers for the unleavened bread, and cups for the wine. Tradition requires that a special cup be placed for the prophet Elijah, the precursor of the Messiah.

These objects too are more or less richly decorated. Wherever Jews were not permitted to be craftsmen, the objects were made by Christians and therefore have some of the stylistic features that were usual in artifacts of the day. Often only the Hebrew inscriptions reveal that these are in fact Jewish ceremonial objects.

The festive candelabrum in the home has different forms according to the occasion. Thus at the festival of Hanukkah the eight-branched candelabrum, usually a highly prized possession of the family, is used. It is found both in the home and in the synagogue, but it is in the home that

In the home there is a great variety of religious artifacts. Some relate to the stages of life: thus in earlier times there would be amulets for the birth of a child. A plaque on the east wall of the living room indicates the direction of prayer toward Jerusalem. A mezuzah is affixed to the right-hand doorpost (see page 50), as a sign of unbounded love and dedication to the One and Only God.

The candelabrum, usually of silver, or the kiddush cup are put on the table on the Sabbath. At the end of the Sabbath, once three stars have become visible in the sky, the box of besomim ("pleasant smells") is placed on the table, filled with cloves or other sweet-smelling spices, and the father of the family says a blessing which separates the Sabbath from the other days of the week.

Of especial importance are all the objects which help to enrich Seder night, the eve of the Passover (see page 191). This festival commemorates the exodus of the people of Israel from Egypt: it is a major festival, and the Haggadah lays down precisely how it is to be celebrated. On Seder night the family uses a special set of tableware: plates bearing the names of the

this Festival of Lights is chiefly celebrated. However, this candelabrum as used in the home has taken on many different shapes and forms: thus in eastern Europe the so-called "bench" form, which often incorporates the architectural facade of a synagogue, is especially widespread.

BELOW, CENTER: Sabbath lamp, brass. Nuremberg, 18th century.

BELOW: Box for besomim ("pleasant smells"). In a short ceremony at the end of the Sabbath a prayer is spoken The sweet smells are supposed to dispel the sorrow felt at the ending of the Sabbath. Silver, Nuremberg, 1790–94.

RIGHT: Hanukkah candelabrum. Hanukkah is the festival commemorating the rededication of the Temple after the victory of the Maccabeans over King Antiochus IV Epiphanes of Syria (164 BC). Augsburg, late 18th century.

BELOW, RIGHT: Clock with Hebrew dial placed between the two columns of Solomon's Temple. Around 1830. Beneath the Star of David are the Tablets of the Law. The text on the dial reads: "Thou shalt love thy neighbor as thyself."

Printers and Printed Books

LEFT: Title page of the "Story of the Exodus of Israel from Egypt," translated and printed by Wolf Benjamin Heidenheim in Rödelheim, 1830. His printing works produced the best editions of prayer books, the Pentateuch, and other works in Hebrew.

RIGHT: The *Dyhernfurter Privilegierte Zeitung* of 1771, the first regularly-appearing Jewish newspaper in Germany. The printing works in Dyhernfurt had been in existence since 1688 and published chiefly Hebrew books destined for Poland, Lithuania, and Russia.

Gutenberg's invention of the printing press was hailed by Jewish scholars of the time as "the crown of all knowledge" and the art of printing itself as "a hallowed craft" (see page 73). Book printers had a considerable influence on the religious and cultural life of Jews, as the Bible, printed in Hebrew and in Judeo-German (in Hebrew characters) now became accessible to all.

The earliest Jewish printing works in the Holy Roman Empire was founded in Prague, and it brought out the first Hebrew books as early as 1512. There followed the towns of Oels (near Breslau; 1530) and Augsburg (1533/34). In 1534 the Christian Hebraist Paulus Fagius began to print Hebrew and Judeo-German books, in collaboration with the Jewish scholar Elia Levita (see page 67), first at Isny and later at nearby Constance.

After the Khmelnytsky massacres in Poland in 1648 and the pogroms during the Swedish-Polish war, in which the Jewish printing works in eastern central Europe were destroyed, the printing of Hebrew books moved to Amsterdam and to the German towns of Offenbach, Dyhernfurt (Silesia), Breslau, Dessau, Posen, Frankfurt am Main, Fürth, and Rödelheim.

In some towns, including Frankfurt am Main, pressure from the guilds and orders from the town council ensured that all Hebrew books were printed by Christian printers. One such book was the exemplary Frankfurt edition of the Talmud, which was printed in 1720/23 by Johann Koelner under the supervision of the Jewish scholar Arie Loeb.

A book that was printed around 1713 in Berlin was an edition of *Zena Urena* (see page 67), a retelling of the Bible (with commentaries) in a popular style, intended mainly for women, which for centuries was the most widely read book in German-Jewish homes. In 1778 David Friedländer

and his Enlightenment colleagues founded the publishing house of the Jewish Free School (see page 122), and the pupils of the Free School were taught to print. From 1796 onward a number of books were published under the imprint *Orientalische Druckerei* ("Oriental Printing House"), the adjective "oriental" perhaps being intended as a euphemism for "Hebrew" or "Jewish."

In the 19th century there were printers of Jewish books and calendars in many large and small towns in Germany.

RIGHT: Title page of *Derech Slulah* ("The Smoothed Path"), a summary of the Pentateuch with commentaries by famous writers, partly in German translation. Fürth, 1801.

דרך סלולה

הוא

חיבור כולל

חמשה חומשי תורה

עם פי׳ רש״י , ותרגום אונקלוס , ותרגום
אשכנזי , ובאור ותקון סופרים : והפטרות
וחמש מגילות , גם אלו עם פירש״י , ותרגום
אשכנזי , ובאור : והוגה על פי הוויש
של ר׳ איצק פרעמסלא הנדפס בא״ד :

תקמא לפ״ק

בפיורדא

The Struggle between Tradition and Reform

RIGHT: Samson Raphael Hirsch (1808–1888), from 1851 onward rabbi of the Orthodox "Israelite Religious Community" in Frankfurt am Main, a figure at the center of neo-orthodoxy. Lithograph by E. Schier, 1847, after a daguerreotype by Biow.

BELOW: Meeting of the governing body of the Reform congregation in Berlin, 1855. Standing, center, the founder of the "German-Jewish Church," Sigismund Stern (photomontage).

ABOVE: Students at the Jewish Theological Seminary in Breslau, 1854. Standing at left, the linguist and antiquarian Joseph Perles (1835–1894), who from 1871 onward was a rabbi in Munich; at right, Benjamin Szold (1829–1902), who from 1859 onward was rabbi of the Oheb Shalom congregation in Baltimore (USA).

BELOW: Chief Rabbi Zacharias Frankel (1801–1875), first director of the Jewish Theological Seminary in Breslau.

The Hep-Hep disturbances of 1819 and the disappointment felt by many Jews as a result of the reactionary political climate in the first half of the 19th century prompted a variety of responses.

A number of intellectuals and of those who had found a place in good middle-class society accepted baptism as a way to become part of Christian-German society. Baptism was to be, as Heinrich Heine put it, their "entry ticket to European culture." Yet Heine himself and many other Jews felt themselves to be representatives of European culture without requiring any confirmation of this from the Christian clergy. However, the external pressures caused some to re-examine their own Jewish values and to measure them against the demands of the present, and it was a surprise for many to discover that, especially for those who looked for them, the wellsprings of Judaism had by no means dried up.

This reflexion on their own culture set powerful movements in train, and those decades saw the start of vigorous inquiry into the essential nature of Judaism.

Salomon Tiktin (1791–1843) in Breslau represented old-style orthodox Judaism, which in Germany was continually reinforced above all by immigrants from the east. In the small communities of western and southwestern Germany in particular, this orthodoxy remained predominant.

However, the uncompromising stance of the Orthodox rabbis weakened their own influence once forces in the Reform movement no longer regarded their Jewishness as a private matter but felt it to be an aspect of their citizenship. Their most influential representative was Abraham Geiger (1810–1874), a supporter of reformist ideas "but without pulling up the ancient tree by the roots." For him the true essence of Judaism lay in the form and the content which it – a revealed religion – had acquired under the Prophets. Relinquishing the hope of a future for the Jewish people as an actual nation, he interpreted the idea of the Messiah in a universalistic way. Another major figure in this attempt to create a new Judaism drawing upon the ancient traditions (Leopold Zunz will be discussed elsewhere) was the Orthodox rabbi Samson Raphael Hirsch (1808– 1888). For him the imperative of the hour was not reform but regeneration, and the idea of revelation remained an inviolable axiom: "You perceive HIM in nature, in history, and in the doctrine that you received on Sinai." Commandments and customs should not be altered but should be imbued with a new spirituality. Hirsch combined modern education with strictly traditional Judaism and saw the two as complementary, not contradictory. Wherever contradictions did arise, he followed tradition. Opposed to all these efforts were the extreme assimilationist tendencies of Rabbi Samuel Holdheim (1806–1860), a reformer with an uncommonly profound knowledge of the Talmud. To many Jewish families Holdheim's Reform movement represented a way of remaining Jewish while at the same time breaking free from an orthodoxy which for them had lost its meaning.

ABOVE: Invitation to subscribe to the "Universal Church Newspaper for the Protestant, Catholic and Israelite Educated Classes," 1837.

BELOW: Masthead of the periodical *Der Orient*, the leading cultural journal, which had a literary supplement. It was published in Leipzig from 1840 onward.

Jews in the Vormärz (1815–1848)

In 1840 there were roughly 350,000 Jews living in Germany, of whom about 200,000 lived in Prussia and 150,000 in the other German states. The majority regarded themselves as being observant Jews in the traditional sense. They had often been told, and the apostate Friedrich Julius Stahl (see page 292) was later to elevate it to the level of a dogma, that "German" was synonymous with "Christian." For this reason most Jews did not want to be seen as "Jewish Germans" but as loyal sons of the fatherland who were of the Mosaic faith, or as faithful subjects of their particular ruler. In the eyes of this majority, the assimilation sought by the Enlightenment thinkers and the reformers represented a threat to their separate Jewish identity. Only after 1860 were they able to embrace German culture as an intellectual sphere of life existing side by side with Judaism, and this change was brought about not least by the granting of equal civil rights.

Opposed to this in the main "silent majority" was a militant minority, strongly aware of current developments, that argued for cultural integration. Some, like Johann Jacoby (1805–1877), Gabriel Riesser (1806–1863), and Salomon Ludwig Steinheim (1789–1866), demanded complete emancipation and equality before the law as a logical corollary of the general rights of citizens. They based their demand on the presumption that the Jews were an integral part of the German people, and that like other sections of the population they were fully entitled to insist on their own separate identity, since within Germany, their homeland, they had the same duties as non-Jews.

This view was opposed not only by some Christian theologians but also by those supporters of emancipation who regarded their Jewishness as a private matter.

The Hambach Festival, 1832: "Long live freedom! Long live Siebenpfeiffer! Long live the German freedom campaigner Ludwig Börne!"

In Hamburg, where Riesser lived, a group of such people in 1832 wanted the Senate to classify the term "Jew" as an insult. Riesser, then 24, thereupon founded the periodical *Der Jude. Periodische Blätter für Religion und Gewissensfreiheit* ("The Jew. A Periodical for Religion and Freedom of Conscience"), a publication which helped to strengthen the self-awareness and confidence of Jews all over Germany.

As a Jew, Riesser could become neither a full citizen of the Electorate of Hesse, nor a lecturer at the university in Heidelberg, nor a lawyer in his home city. These basic rights were taken for granted by any non-Jew, and to win the same rights for his Jewish fellow citizens was the goal that Riesser set himself.

He attacked the misuse of power by the economically stronger majority against the economically weaker minority, which was what really lay behind the facade of "religious" or "cultural" objections. Although there was a small, wealthy elite, the Jews as a whole were economically far below the average level of non-Jews. Economic oppression, whether exerted by discriminatory laws or by the exclusion of Jews from important areas of private commerce, prevented them from achieving more.

In 1831 Riesser published his work *Über die Stellung der Bekenner des mosaischen Glaubens in Deutschland* ("On the Position of Those who Profess the Mosaic Faith in Germany"), in which he demanded religious tolerance, absence of prejudice, and equality before the law. This prompted a flood of publications either supporting or rejecting his views. To one particularly vicious attack, Riesser replied: "Whoever seeks to deny my claim to my German fatherland denies my right to my thoughts, my feelings, the language that I speak, the air that I breathe: and for this reason I have to defend myself against him as against a murderer."

With regard to religion, Riesser defended both the right of the Reform movement to pursue its aims in the conflict over synagogue worship and that of the orthodox to let the Talmud continue to be a vital influence.

Like Riesser in Hamburg, the physician and politician Johann Jacoby in Königsberg argued for Jews to have complete equality with other citizens as a principle of a state founded on the rule of law. He succeeded in achieving for Jewish students in his own city the same status in society as that of Christian students. In 1833, in his work *Über das Verhältnis des Königlich-Preussischen Oberregierungs-rats Streckfuss zu der Emanzipation der Juden* ("On the Attitude of His Prussian Majesty's Ministerial Councilor Streckfuss to the Emancipation of the Jews"), he demanded immediate emancipation, rather than gradual emancipation which would depend on the so-called magnanimity of the giver or on "good behavior" on the part of the Jews. Jacoby too remained a committed Jew. He devoted himself above all to German politics; during the Vormärz period his campaign against censorship and a nonindependent judiciary cost him three years' loss of liberty, and under Bismarck he suffered another term of imprisonment in a fortress for urging

Dorfgeschichten ("Black Forest Village Tales"), 1843ff., and *Barfüssele* ("Little Barefoot Girl"), 1856. Together with Zunz, Riesser, and Geiger, he played an active part in the campaign for legal equality for Jews. Auerbach defined himself in this way: "I am a German, and could not be anything else; I am a Swabian, and would not like to be anything else; I am a Jew – and that has produced the right mixture." As the years passed, however, he began to doubt more and more that the prejudices of non-Jews against Jews could ever be overcome by reasoned arguments.

Unlike Riesser, Jacoby, and their many supporters, two other well-known figures of the *Vormärz* – Ludwig Börne (1786–1837) and Heinrich Heine (1797–1856) – cast off their Jewish identity when it became a

ABOVE, RIGHT:
Berthold Auerbach, author of the popular "Black Forest Village Tales". Portrait c. 1842.

Illustration of a scene from Auerbach's "Little Barefoot Girl."

people to withhold their taxes. In the 1860s he joined, as a "theoretician of the democratic movement," the activists of the new labor movement.

The writer Berthold Auerbach (1812–1882), the ninth child of a merchant's family in Nordstetten in the Black Forest, was intended for the rabbinate, but as a young man he decided instead to study the law, and later philosophy and history – and began to write. In 1837, as a member of a revolutionary students' society, he was sentenced to a term of imprisonment in the fortress of Hohenasperg in Württemberg. His first work, which he wrote as an opponent of the "Young Germany" political movement, was the patriotic "History of Frederick the Great" (1834–36), but he achieved fame with his *Schwarzwälder*

burden to them. In liberal Hamburg they associated themselves with the literary-political movement around the publisher Julius Campe, "Young Germany" and with Laube and Gutzkow, were leading militant campaigners of the *Vormärz* period against censorship, arbitrary action by the police, and all policies based on the reactionary attitudes of Metternich and Gentz.

Ludwig Börne, eleven years older than Heine, was the son of Orthodox Jews; he had been born and had grown up in the Judengasse in Frankfurt. Heine had been affected by the aftershocks of the Frankfurt pogrom in Hamburg in 1819. A year earlier Börne, a police clerk employed by the city but forced into retirement, had converted to Protestantism (a "foolish waste of baptism," he called it), in order, as he hoped, to be free

to engage in political activity. From now on he saw himself as a prophet of the idea of freedom for human beings in general, and campaigned for this in books, pamphlets, and articles. It was partly disillusionment about German politics, but mainly enthusiasm for the July Revolution, that took him to Paris, where he lived from 1830 onward. It seemed to him that freedom for the Germans would necessarily bring with it Jewish emancipation; Judaism as such did not interest him. And yet he wrote: "Hatred for the Jews is one of the Pontine Marshes which pollute the beautiful spring landscape of our freedom. One sees the most promising friends of the fatherland wandering about sick, their faces pale. And that hatred of Jews is the whetstone on which every blunt stone has tried to sharpen itself and every sharp one to become sharper still; but the stone is too hard."

As a campaigner for freedom he attended the Hambach Festival in 1832, where, with Siebenpfeiffer, he was hailed with enthusiasm by students and citizens. People greeted each other with the words "Long live freedom! Long live Siebenpfeiffer! Long live the German freedom campaigner Ludwig Börne!"

The "Young Germany" movement did not survive for long. In 1835 the governments of the German states banned the books of Gutzkow, Laube, Heine, and Börne, in part owing to the writings of Wolfgang Menzel, who, like some others, used anti-Semitic arguments. It was clear to both Heine as well as Börne in the end that their new gods had not accepted their sacrifice.

In Good Society

In the early days of emancipation, there were large numbers of Jews of the higher classes who prized their membership of the Jewish faith and the Jewish community as a most precious possession, as the appropriate religion and way of life for them.

For them baptism held no attraction, since they knew themselves to be playing a full role in European culture, and this consciousness gave them self-confidence in their dealings with non-Jews. The non-Jews, for their part, showed understanding, indeed respect, for their markedly Jewish stance, perhaps precisely because they did not feel they had to prove themselves to be Germans. This mutual respect lasted right up to the days of the Weimar Republic.

Among the members of this Jewish elite were the Rothschild and Warburg families, the publisher Rudolf Mosse, the philosopher Hermann Cohen, the religious philosopher Martin Buber, the politician Oskar Cohn, and the campaigner for women's rights Bertha Pappenheim. As respected citizens and members of good society, these Jews played a part in the public life of a Christian state.

Amalie Beer, mother of the composer Giacomo Meyerbeer, was awarded the "Luisenorden" (Queen Luise Medal) by King Frederick William III for her services during the Wars of Liberation, and the dec-

The writer Michael Beer (1800–1833), brother of Giacomo Meyerbeer.

oration was specially made for her in the shape of an oval medallion, since it was felt that as a Jewess she could not be expected to wear a cross. Meyerbeer's brother, the dramatist Michael Beer, in his one-act play *Der Paria* ("The Pariah"), performed in 1823, transposed the situation of the Jews in Germany to an Indian setting. However, he felt the three misfortunes of being "a Jew, a German, and a writer" to be not only a burden but also a

distinction. Despite all the social recognition he received – praise from Goethe and Grillparzer, the patronage of King Ludwig I of Bavaria – he continually had to fend off personal attacks, and in his despair he railed against God's injustice: "What is the reason, God, for your eternal hatred for the unhappy race that engendered me?"

Among the members of good society in Altona near Hamburg were the Warburg family. The lawyer Moritz Warburg (1810–1886) was an active politician in Schleswig-Holstein; after 1870 he became a member of the German Reichstag.

In Münster in 1825 the physician Alexander Haindorf (1782–1862) founded, with the help of his father-in-law Elias Marks, the "Society for the training of elementary school teachers and for the advancement of craftsmen and artists for the province of Westphalia." He was the first principal of the Society's school, the Marks-Haindorf Foundation, holding this position until 1845.

The Wittelsbachs' court banker and an esteemed guest of the Bavarian royal house was the Orthodox Jew Jacob von Hirsch auf Gereuth (1764–1841).

Still on view in Nymphenburg Palace in Munich is Joseph Stieler's portrait of Nanette Kaula, which King Ludwig commissioned in 1829 for his gallery of beau-

LEFT: The physician Alexander Haindorf (1782–1862) with his grandchildren Agnes and Robert Loeb. He took part in the Wars of Liberation against Napoleon, and in 1825 founded in Münster, with the help of his father-in-law Elias Marks, the "Society for the training of elementary school teachers and for the advancement of craftsmen and artists for the province of Westphalia."

RIGHT: Jacob von Hirsch auf Gereuth (1764–1841), banker to the court of the Wittelsbachs in Bavaria.

ties. Nanette, the daughter of a wholesale merchant patronized by the Bavarian king, married the wholesaler Salomon Joseph Heine from Hamburg, a relative of Heinrich Heine. Nanette Kaula was invited as a guest of honor to the unveiling of the statue of "Bavaria" on the Theresienwiese in Munich in 1850. When after the ceremony she was introduced to the aging King Ludwig I, he no longer recognized her. "Doesn't Your Majesty remember me? You had me painted by Stieler for your gallery of beauties." "I wouldn't now!" answered the once gallant king. "I wouldn't now!"

As a student in Bonn, the baptized Jew Karl Marx (1818–1883) belonged to the "Trierer Landsmannschaft," an association of students from Trier. He became one of the officers of this society, was once placed in the lockup for being drunk and disorderly, and fought a duel.

At the ceremony of homage to King Frederick William IV of Prussia in 1840, those on the platform for distinguished guests erected on the Schlossplatz in Berlin included not only the Brothers Grimm, Alexander von Humboldt and Friedrich Schelling but also the banker Abraham Mendelssohn and the composer Giacomo Meyerbeer.

The Family Photograph

In 1839, quite independently of one another, the discovery of two processes was announced, one in France and one in England, which made it possible for the latent image of the external world appearing in a camera obscura (a small square box with a small glass lens in the middle of the front) to be captured by chemical means – to be fixed. The process arrived at by William Henry Fox Talbot (1800–1877) produced a negative on waxed and therefore translucent paper, from which any number of positive prints could be made. That developed by Joseph Nicéphore Niepce (1765–1833) and Louis Jacques Mandé Daguerre (1787–1851) produced a single positive and opaque image on a small plate of silvered copper.

One of the best portrait photographers in Germany using the daguerreotype method was the Jewish photographer Hermann Biow (c. 1804–1850) of Hamburg.

What is appealing about his portraits even today is his concentration on visible character and the natural pose of the sitters – the reproduction of what the photographer saw, without pseudoartistic pretensions.

King Frederick William IV placed a large, light room in his palace in the center of Berlin at Biow's disposal, where he made portraits of the king himself, the royal family, ministers, artists such as the architect Rauch, and scholars such as Wilhelm von Humboldt. But Biow also photographed Schopenhauer and many members of the Frankfurt Parliament of 1848. He also produced the first group photograph of a Jewish family.

Just as once the family portrait in the form of a painting or drawing had been a document of the history of the family and of society, so now the photograph, a new means of portraying the family and reflecting its status, took on this role. Whereas, however, the prosperous and educated bourgeoisie in Europe and in America generally attached great importance to the family picture, whether it be a painting or a photograph, as an expression of their social standing, up to the end of the 19th century photographs of Jewish families – as opposed to portraits of individuals – are very rare.

This makes the photograph of the Hahn family all the more remarkable. Grandmother Hahn, no doubt a widow, sits enthroned as a matriarch over her children and children's children. In later Jewish family pictures, too, for instance that of the Warburgs (see page 237), the grandmother can be seen in this position.

The family photograph also indicates the social status and self-estimation of the sitters; in the case of Jewish individuals or families their outward appearance also shows the degree of their assimilation to non-Jewish society.

Mrs. Susanne Hahn (née Lazarus) with seven of her eleven children. Daguerreotype by Hermann Biow, 1843.

ABOVE: The family of Samuel Ludwig Darmstädter of Mannheim, c. 1858.

ABOVE, RIGHT: Julius Joel and Mina Levy (née Bloch) with their children, Mähringen, 1859.

RIGHT: The family of Anselm Heinrich Dülken of Deutz, c. 1860.

1848 – A Year of Liberation

For the Jews three of the demands of the 1848 revolution were especially significant:
 – total religious freedom, freedom of conscience, and academic freedom,
 – the same rights for all citizens of Germany,
 – the abolition of all privileges.

The abolition of all privileges meant that Jews were now free to work in craft trades, commerce, and agriculture, in the professions, and in the service of the state in the same way as the rest of the population. This did away with inequality before the law. All special laws and special taxes imposed on the Jewish minority, which had thereby been made socially and economically insecure, would be removed. This was all the more significant as, apart from a small number of extremely wealthy Jews and a small middle stratum, the majority were among the handicapped in society when it came to competing economically, and were therefore, compared with the Christian population, relatively, or absolutely, poor.

Complete religious freedom, freedom of conscience, and academic freedom would also have overcome the intellectual insecurity of the Jews, who always had to prove that they were of equal worth. Universal rights for all German citizens would have promoted a process of normalization for them. Such considerations meant that in 1848 the emancipation of the Jews also became an integral part of the non-Jewish liberal movement. Leopold Zunz (1794–1886), who in addition to his other work was also politically active, had demanded "not rights and freedoms, but right (justice) and freedom." As late as 1834 he had to apply for special permission from the Prussian Minister of Education in order, as a Jew, to be allowed to give public lectures. Permission was granted with the proviso that the police must be informed when the lectures were to begin.

Hopes of freedom and equality had risen among the Jews, and in 1848 many of them took part in the republican meetings, demonstrations, and fighting on the barricades.

In 1848 Leopold Zunz attracted much attention with a speech which he gave in Berlin about those killed in the events of March of that year. For Jews in those days, personal, active involvement was an expression of their will to freedom and also of their feeling of being part of the German nation.

Some Jews had been elected to the Frankfurt parliament. Gabriel Riesser became vice president of the National Assembly, and the public nature of exchanges there made it possible for him to respond with great forcefulness to the anti-Semitic attacks of Moritz Mohl and others. His speeches struck a chord with many people in the various states of the Confederation.

LEFT: Johann Gustav Heckscher (1797–1865), a lawyer from Hamburg, who was baptized a Protestant in 1808. As a member of the National Assembly he belonged to the liberal Casino Party; in the first "Reich cabinet" he became Minister of Justice and then Foreign Minister.

RIGHT: Street battles in Berlin on 18/19 March 1848. Wood engraving after a drawing by Johann Jacob Kirchhoff, *Leipziger Illustrierte Zeitung*, 1848.

LEFT: Heinrich Simon (1805–1860), from Breslau, member of the National Assembly. After the failure of the revolution he emigrated to Switzerland. An uncompromising democrat, he was condemned in his absence to life imprisonment in 1851.

BELOW: Johann Jacoby (1805–1877) at the head of a delegation sent by the National Assembly to King Frederick William IV on 3 November 1848. The king received the delegates ungraciously and dismissed them brusquely. Wood engraving from *Leipziger Illustrierte Zeitung*, 1848.

ABOVE: Gabriel Riesser (1806–1863), politician and writer, vice president of the National Assembly. Chalk lithograph by Moritz Oppenheim, c. 1848.

Disappointed Hopes

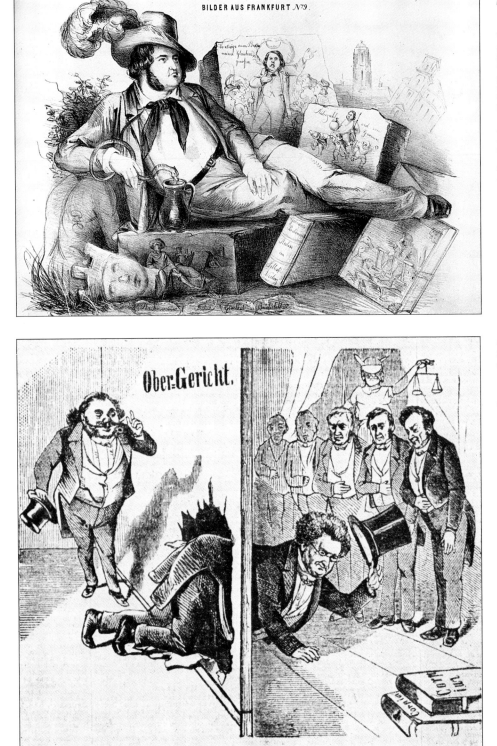

ABOVE, LEFT: Isidorius Morgenlaender, a satirical representation of the baptized Frankfurt lawyer and writer Ludwig Braunfels (1810–1885), a member of the "Young Germany" group. Cartoon by Paul Herrlich, 1849 (after Tischbein's painting of "Goethe in the Campagna").

LEFT: After protracted struggles, Gabriel Riesser breaks through the wall and so (in 1860) attains his rightful position in the High Court in Hamburg. He was Germany's first Jewish judge. Contemporary cartoon.

The hopes of the Frankfurt National Assembly for a democratic constitution were disappointed. For the Jews this disappointment was all the harder to overcome because Article 13 of the constitution had contained a statement of fundamental human rights which would have made them into citizens with equal rights.

In Bavaria, for instance, where the king had promised to improve the situation of the Jews, it actually deteriorated to such an extent in the following years that in 1851 the anti-Jewish edicts of 1813 were re-implemented. A new wave of reactionary legislation and inflammatory pamphlets followed, however much liberals and democrats, out of sincere and earnest conviction, stood up for the Jews and argued in favor of equal status for them.

In March 1849 a delegation from the Frankfurt National Assembly, led by the baptized Jew Eduard von Simson, had traveled to Berlin in order to offer King Frederick William IV (reigned 1840–1861) the imperial crown. The Prussian king declined to accept "such a meaningless circlet baked of dirt and clay." There had already been a previous occasion (3 November 1848) when a delegation under Johann Jacoby, the Jewish member from Königsberg, had described the political situation to the king, who had waved the delegation aside in a humiliating manner and abruptly left the room. Jacoby had commented, in words that have become famous, "It has always been the misfortune of kings that they will not hear the truth."

„Soll mir Gott helfen! kann ich doch fegen, ich bin geworden emanschipirt."

ABOVE: "Emancipation of the Jews in Bavaria." Contemporary cartoon.

"If you hit my Jew, I'll hit your Jew."
Illustrated proverbial saying, c. 1840.

Emigration to the Land of Freedom

In the years following 1848, Jews began to emigrate in larger numbers.

The case of Bavaria may be taken as an example. In 1848, about 12,000 Jewish families lived there, approximately 58,000 people altogether. Most of them lived by trade, while a very few were agricultural workers or artisans, for which some of them had obtained work permits.

At this time Bavaria was suffering a serious, crippling crisis. Thousands were emigrating to America each year. But the Jews were affected less by the economic crisis than by the anti-Semitism of many in the church, the government, and the people. The guilds still admitted no Jews, and it was very seldom that Jewish apprentices and journeymen could find masters prepared to train them in their workshops and give them employment. Moreover, the Edict on the Jews of 10 June 1813, with its notorious statute on residence, remained in force in Bavaria until 1861. This stated: "The number of Jewish families in the places where they live at present shall in

ABOVE: Jewish emigrants in the passenger lounge of a Prussian mail-freight office. Oil painting by Felix Schlesinger, 1857 (detail).

RIGHT: The banker Otto H. Kahn (1867–1934) in the uniform of a Mainz hussar, c. 1888. He emigrated to America in 1893; from 1903 to 1931 he was president of the Metropolitan Opera Company in New York.

general not be increased, but rather be gradually reduced if it is too large."

The head of a family had to purchase a residence permit in place of the certificate of protected status that had been valid until then; at his death the permit passed only to the eldest son, while the other sons might not marry (unless they succeeded in obtaining the right to do so by bribing a highly placed official). In this way a Catholic state imposed a partial ban on reproduction upon a minority of its inhabitants. The hopeless position in which many Jews thus found themselves, both legally and economically, led to a wave of emigration, chiefly to the United States, the land of freedom.

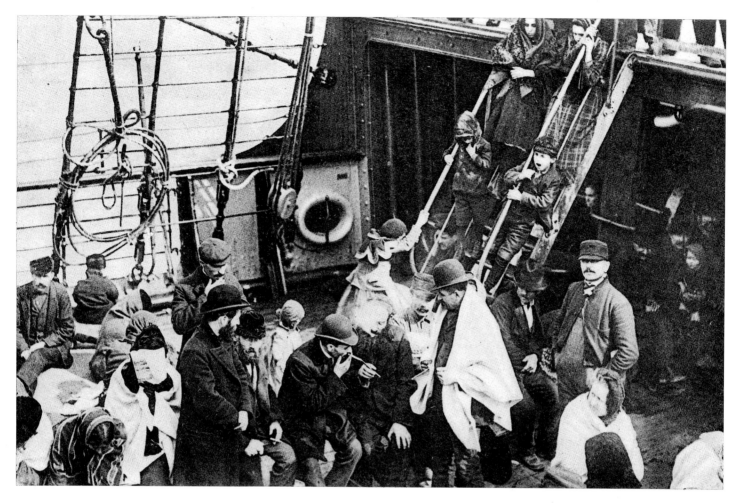

ABOVE: "On board the emigrants' steamship." Picture postcard, c. 1880.

RIGHT: Prussian passport issued for the journey to America, Marienwerder, 1866.

Title page of a miniature prayerbook "for emigrants to America," 1860. Actual size.

Their new life there often began with unskilled work – tree felling or small-scale trading in one place. Then came the life of the traveling salesman going from village to village with his pack of wares on his back, or later on with his own wagon, but returning regularly to his family on Friday evenings. Younger men often learned a craft, bred cattle, or became soldiers. Others joined the wagon trains of pioneers traveling westward. The next step for the peddlers was to open a store of their own. Some were successful enough to build up a wholesaling business, import business or department store; others found employment in banking.

It was to Australia that one son of the printer and publisher Baer Löw Monasch (see page 178) emigrated. The grandson, an active member of the Jewish community in Melbourne and an engineer by profession, was also in the Australian army and later rose to become General Sir John Monash (1865–1931). It was under his leadership that in May 1918 Australian and New Zealand troops achieved the decisive breakthrough near Amiens.

How well immigrants were able to become integrated into society in America is illustrated by the case of the family of Lazarus Straus, who went out to the Midwest in 1852 and sold his wares there. By 1854 he had saved enough to arrange for his family, from Otterberg in the Rhineland-Palatinate, to join him there. His eldest son, Isidor (1845–1912), became a businessman, a congressman and a philanthropist: in New York he financed various non-Jewish institutions and also the Jewish Theological Seminary, the center of the Jewish Conservative congregationes. In 1912 he went down with the *Titanic*. The second son, Nathan (1848–1931), also became a businessman and a philanthropist. As New York's Superintendent of Health he built up the city's health and welfare services, and in the des-

Jewish Traveling salesman in America. Wood engraving by C. G. Bush, c. 1860.

The engineer and businessman Adolph Sutro from Aachen (1830–1898), educated at the Haindorf School, emigrated to America in 1850, where he built a tunnel through Mount Davidson near Virginia City, Nevada (1869–79) to reach the Comstock lode. In 1894 he became mayor of San Francisco to which city he bequeathed his library of 200,000 books.

Julius Ochs (1826–1888) from Fürth, who emigrated to Louisville in 1845. In the American Civil War he served as an officer in the Union army; he founded the Jewish congregation in Chattanooga.
His son Adolph (1858–1935) bought the *New York Times* in 1896 and made it into a world-class newspaper.

perately hard winters of 1892/97 provided the poor with accommodation and food for five cents a night. He also provided the necessary funds for numerous health projects in Palestine, donating two-thirds of his fortune for this purpose. The town of Natanya in Israel was named after him. The youngest son, Oscar Solomon (1850–1926) was a diplomat, writer, government official and US ambassador to Turkey. An anti-imperialist and pacifist, he argued during World War I for the founding of a League of Nations, which after the war became a reality.

Not many emigrants attained such prominence, but a good number became prosperous businessmen and distinguished professionals. Among these were Austrian-born Felix Frankfurter, a member of the Supreme Court; the scholars of the Oppenheim family; the bankers Kahn, Warburg, Loeb, and Kuhn; the store magnates Straus and Altman; the publisher of *The New York Times*, Adolph Odis Sulzberger – all of them German Jews or their descendants who might use German as their everyday language and in most cases supported the introduction of German-

Jewish Reform practices into their synagogues. They often displayed a certain cultural arrogance toward the later immigrants from the "non-German" countries of eastern Europe.

In their new homeland the immigrant Jews were citizens enjoying equal rights, and so, significantly, there was no tendency to accept baptism or even to attempt to conceal their origin, as so often happened in Germany.

Heinrich Heine –
the Embodiment of the German-Jewish Dilemma

LEFT: Title page of the *Buch der Lieder* ("Book of Songs"), 1827.

RIGHT: "The Two Grenadiers," title page of Wagner's setting of Heine's famous poem celebrating the soldiers of Napoleon.

BELOW, LEFT: Heine's main works. Beneath the titles, vignette of "The Loreley," from the *Buch der Lieder*, 1827.

BELOW: Collage of sheet music of songs by Heine in settings by Mendelssohn, Meyerbeer, Schubert, Liszt, and Schumann.

Die Harzreise (1826)

Reisebilder (1826–31)

Buch der Lieder (1827)

Französische Zustände (1833)

Der Salon (1834–40)

Shakespeares
Mädchen und Frauen (1839)

Über Ludwig Börne (1840)

Deutschland.
Ein Wintermärchen (1844)

Atta Troll.
Ein Sommernachtstraum (1847)

Romanzero (1851)

"In Heine one feels the heartbeat of the German people."

Nietzsche

Harry (later Heinrich) Heine was born in 1797 in Düsseldorf; to all appearance he had a sheltered childhood and youth, but there was a growing inner rebelliousness. When, as a child, Heine asked about his grandfather, his father replied, half laughing, half angrily, "Your grandfather was a little Jew and had a big beard" (Heine, *Memoirs*). Happily repeating this piece of information at school, little Harry caused a tremendous row and was beaten unmercifully by his teacher, Father Dickerscheit, without at all understanding why. This was the first beating Heine had ever received: "I have not forgotten it."

As a child he experienced Napoleon's entry into the Rhineland: "That picture will never fade from my memory. I see him still, mounted on his horse, his eyes with a look of eternity in that marble Emperor's face, looking down, calm in the knowledge of his destiny, at the guards parading past – he was about to send them to Russia, and the old grenadiers looked up at him, so unnervingly devoted, so solemn in the knowledge they shared with him, so proud in the face of death: "Te Caesar, morituri salutant!" (Heine, *Reisebilder IV, Englische Fragmente*, "Travel Pictures IV, English Fragments"). Nor did he ever forget the beat of the drum, the call of freedom.

Heine was taught Jewish history and Hebrew. "I got on better with the Hebrew, because I always had a great liking for the Jews, although they crucify my good name to this very hour; but even so I could not make as much progress with Hebrew as my pocket watch, which had much intimate association with pawnbrokers and as a result sometimes adopted Jewish ways – for instance it would not go on a Saturday – and it learned the sacred language and practiced the grammar in later years too, for during sleepless nights I was often astonished to hear it ceaselessly ticking away to itself: katal, katalta, katalti – kittel, kittalta, kittalti – pokat, pokadeti –

Heinrich Heine: "This is how I looked this morning, 6 April 1829." Lithograph by Franz Theodor Kugler.

pikat – pik – pik." (*Ideen. Das Buch Le Grand*, "Ideas. The Book Le Grand," 1826.)

He returned again and again to the Bible. He saw the humiliations suffered by others, and often himself experienced the humiliation attendant on being a Jew in Germany. As a young poet and student he was a friend of Börne, Rahel Levin-Varnhagen, Leopold Zunz, and Eduard Gans (see page 154), was actively involved in 1819 in the reformist activities of the "Society for Jewish Culture and "Learning" and accepted baptism, so as not to remain a pariah in his beloved Germany. But the "entry ticket to European culture" (*Aufzeichnungen*, "Notes") did not help

him. When, as a Doctor of Jurisprudence, he applied for a state appointment, his application was rejected as being that of a Jew. In 1831 Heine emigrated to Paris; four years later his works were banned in the states of the German Confederation. Despite this he was soon the most widely read German author and the spokesman for "Young Germany."

Like some other writers, from 1837 onward Heine received a pension for life from the French state, and this gave him a degree of financial independence, as well as increasing the hatred felt toward him by

Maximilian Heine (1807–1879), Heine's youngest brother, a Russian imperial government minister and personal physician to the Tsar. Photograph, c. 1860.

Charlotte Heine (1800–1899, married name Embden), the poet's sister. Oil on canvas. Artist unknown.

Gustav Heine (1805–1886), Heine's brother, an officer in the Austrian army and a journalist. Editor of the Vienna *Familienblatt*.

the enthusiasts for Germanness. His much criticized uncle, the banker Salomon Heine in Hamburg, also gave him a monthly allowance. Heine, incidentally, always regarded it as his right to draw upon as many sources of money as possible, in order to be able, like other people of position or merit, to have an appropriate standard of living. His relationship with his brothers and sister was one of friendliness mixed with amusement.

From 1848 until his death in 1856 he was confined to his bed by progressive paralysis, though this never lessened his creativity. Among those who visited him during this time were Franz Grillparzer, Friedrich Hebbel (who was in receipt of a grant from the Danish state), and Richard Wagner. His admirers included Friedrich Nietzsche, Otto von Bismarck, and many of the composers of the day.

Many of his poems are imbued with a spirit of lighthearted lyricism. In others, genuine romantic feeling alternates with biting sarcasm, sometimes in a single poem, sometimes even within a single stanza. As a result his work was both widely admired and widely detested. At a time of restoration and reaction, when people who identified themselves with a

Mathilde Heine (1815–1883, née Crescence Eugénie Mirat), whom Heine married in 1841. Portrait c. 1845.

Christian Germany could feel that great writers like Tieck and Novalis reflected their attitudes, it was inevitable that Heine, swimming against the current, should inspire enmity and hatred in some circles.

Heine did not forget his Jewish origin, but his attitude to it always remained ambivalent. Occasionally he criticized it and mocked "Jewish characteristics" in other Jews. But he also wrote: "[Moses] took a poor tribe of herdsmen and created from it a people that ... was to defy the centuries, a great, eternal, holy people, a people of God, that was able to serve as a pattern for other peoples, indeed a prototype for the whole of humanity: he created Israel!" And he acknowledged: "I can see now that the Greeks were only beautiful youths, but the Jews were always men, powerful, uncompromising men, not only in olden times but right up to the present day, despite eighteen centuries of persecution and misery. I have learned to appreciate them better, and were it not for the fact that any pride in one's birth would be a ridiculous contradiction in a champion of revolution and its democratic principles, the writer of these pages could be proud that his ancestors were of the noble house of Israel, that he is a descendant of those martyrs who gave the world a God and a moral code and who have fought and suffered on all the battlefields of thought ... People think they know them, because they have seen their beards, but no more of them ever became visible, and as in the Middle Ages they are still, in modern times, a walking mystery" (*Geständnisse* "Confessions").

Many of Heine's poems have Jewish themes, and in many others the experience of being a Jew resonates beneath the surface. During his Paris years he was not interested in contemporary Judaism. Yet as late as 1842 he wrote in his *Hebräische Melodien* ("Hebrew Melodies"): "... let my right hand wither, if I should ever forget thee, Jerusalem!"

Heine's Jewish birth and consciousness of his Jewish identity had fateful conse-

Heine on his sickbed. Drawing by Charles Gleyre.

BELOW: "The New Israelite Hospital in Hamburg", founded by Salomon Heine, the poet's uncle, in memory of his wife Betty.

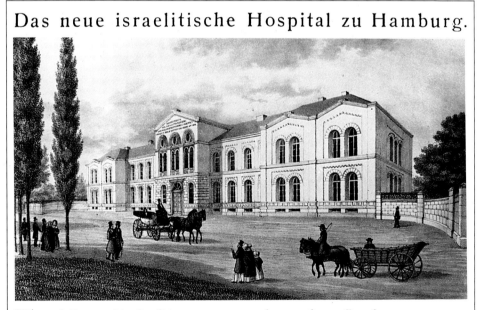

Das neue israelitische Hospital zu Hamburg.

Ein Hospital für arme, kranke Juden,
Für Menschenkinder, welche dreifach elend,
Behaftet mit den bösen drei Gebresten,
Mit Armut, Körperschmerz und Judentume!

quences for him when others made them into an obstacle to his being German:

"Das deutsche Herz in meiner Brust
Ist plötzlich krank geworden,
Der einzige Arzt, der es heilen kann,
Der wohnt daheim im Norden."

("The German heart in my breast / has suddenly become sick; / the only doctor who can heal it / lives at home in the north.")

This remained the inner leitmotif of his personal tragedy as a Jew and as a German.

The tragic relationship with his homeland, self-irony sometimes taken to the extreme of self-ridicule, unbroken pride, a positive acknowledgment of his Jewish roots, biting mockery which could at times be directed unfairly at others, and resignation: with all these discordant elements, Heine epitomizes the problem of being both German and Jewish, which was to cause anguish to many other German Jews after him.

Jews in Music

Until the 19th century there were two very different traditions of Jewish music, synagogue music and folk music.

Synagogue music was a continuation of ancient, traditional music sung by the cantors. This music perhaps goes back to biblical times; it was cultivated above all in the eastern countries, and it was from there that it influenced synagogue music in Germany.

Folk music was identified with the groups of klezmorim (a word meaning "musical instruments"), which already existed in Germany in the Middle Ages and later survived mainly in Poland and Lithuania (see page 282). They were wandering minstrels who, both in Germany and in the eastern countries, provided music on secular holidays and at weddings, but also played at fairs and for rich or well-born non-Jews. The instruments played by the klezmorim included and still include the violin, double bass, flute, and cymbal. The essence of klesmer music is free, associative improvisation, similar to that practiced, in a different form, in jazz. A well-known amateur klezmer band was the Hachenberg group in Darmstadt (c. 1840/60). The father of Giacomo Meyerbeer, the banker Abraham Beer, was also an amateur klesmer and performed with a group at concerts in private houses.

In medieval times the singing in the synagogue was an expression of mystical aspirations. Probably under the influence of the klezmorim, there developed in the 17th and 18th centuries a kind of music that did not conform to fixed rules, with improvised melodies which were often borrowed from German Baroque music. A stronger influence, however, was exerted from the 18th century onward by Hasidic melodies; in contrast to the rationalism of the Age of Enlightenment, this music evoked ideas of the liberation of the soul from its imprisonment in the body, of rising from an often miserable earthly life to spiritual worlds, of partaking in a higher form of existence. Hasidic song or sung prayer is ecstatic music.

The reform of synagogue services in the early 19th century gradually brought

about a profound change. In the Israelite Temple in Hamburg and in other Reform synagogues, Protestant hymns and Protestant choral music were taken over and adapted. It was the cantor and composer Louis Lewandowski (1821–1894) who first found the way to a new kind of synagogue music which was accepted by congregations. By making new arrangements in classical style of traditional melodies, some of them from the repertoire of Jewish liturgical music in Poland, he avoided either breaking with tradition or imitating church music. Lewandowski composed chorales and music for solo

ABOVE, LEFT: Giacomo Meyerbeer (1791–1864), the most popular opera composer of his day.

ABOVE: Felix Mendelssohn (1809–1847). Lithograph after a drawing by Dubois.

LEFT: "Elijah," oratorio by Felix Mendelssohn. Title page of the first edition, 1847. Lithograph by C. Hahn.

voice based on liturgical psalms and prayers, sometimes letting himself be influenced by contemporary German composers. His music was played above all in German synagogues, and it is still played in American synagogues today.

Of the 19th-century Jewish composers, those who still have the highest reputation today are Felix Mendelssohn, Giacomo Meyerbeer, and Jacques Offenbach. Among performing musicians the violinist Joseph Joachim (1831–1907) and the pianist Ignaz Moscheles (1794–1870) were among those who won international fame. Hermann Levi (1839–1900), kapellmeister (music director) at the court of Ludwig II in Munich, was supreme among conductors, and another celebrated composer and conductor was Friedrich Gernsheim (1839–1916).

Felix (Jakob Ludwig) Mendelssohn-Bartholdy (1809–1847), a grandson of Moses Mendelssohn, kept the latter's name although his father advised against it. In 1821, as a twelve-year-old, he played his first composition to the 72-year-old Goethe, "who loved the boy very much."

ductor, and often played at the court of Queen Victoria and Prince Albert. He died, not yet 38 years old, in 1847.

Giacomo (Jakob Liebmann Meyer Beer) Meyerbeer was a descendant of the mint master Jost Liebmann (see page 106) and was the grandfather of Leopold von Andrian-Werburg (1875–1951), the Austrian poet who was a member of the circle of Stefan George and who later became a diplomat. Meyerbeer was the composer whose symphonies and operas (*Robert le Diable*, *Les Huguenots*, *Le Prophète*) were more frequently performed in France and Germany in his day than those of any other composer. He was one of the founders of "grand opera," which inspired Richard Wagner, who was at first a fervent admirer of Meyerbeer, to develop the concept of the "Gesamtkunstwerk."

A committed Jew throughout his life, Meyerbeer reacted with sarcasm to anti-Semitic insults. He felt himself to be above

Gérolstein, but his best-known work is his dramatic opera *Les Contes d'Hoffman* ("The Tales of Hoffmann"), an apotheosis of the Romantic world of the imagination of E.T.A. Hoffmann.

Joseph Joachim was the most famous classical violinist of his day; instead of adding virtuoso elaborations he performed the work as written. Bronislaw Huberman and other well-known musicians were trained at the Academy of Music in Berlin, where Joachim was both artistic director and the most important teacher. Together with Brahms and other musicians he opposed the new "music of the future," the so-called "New German School" of which Richard Wagner was the main representative.

Ferdinand von Hiller (1811–1885) was born in Frankfurt am Main in the year in which the prohibition on Jews living outside the ghetto was lifted. A composer of oratorios, operas, songs, and chorales, he

At around this time he was vilified by other boys as a "Jew boy" and had stones thrown at him, and when he applied in 1832 for the post of director of the Berlin "Singakademie" he was rejected as a Jew. Despite all these humiliations, he never gave way – in this too he was the grandson of Moses Mendelssohn – to bitterness or despair.

Felix Mendelssohn, whose father Abraham had him baptized as a boy, became a deeply religious man who accepted elements of both Jewish and Christian belief, but not their rites. Although favoring a "purified" form of Christianity of the kind taught by Schleiermacher, he identified more strongly than his father Abraham with the people of his grandfather Moses. One of his oratorios celebrates the apostle Paul, but his greatest oratorio is dedicated to the prophet Elijah.

One aspect of Mendelssohn's love of German music was his rediscovery of the music of Bach and Handel. He himself is seen as an important composer of the early Romantic school. Many of his compositions are infused with the spirit which Romain Rolland finds in the oratorios, a factor which contributed to many of his compositions: "Jewish feeling comes to his aid with the revitalizing breath of the old prophets of his race."

In England too Mendelssohn was highly regarded both as a composer and as a con-

ABOVE, LEFT: Jacques Offenbach (1819–1880) with his family, c. 1865.

RIGHT: Ferdinand von Hiller (1811–1885), founder and first director of the Conservatory at Cologne, in his music room. Watercolor by Georg Osterwald, 1867.

both Wagner's early adulation and his later anti-Semitic attack in an essay written under the pseudonym of "Freigedank."

Jacques Offenbach (Jakob Eberscht, 1819–1880) was a son of the Cologne cantor Isaac Eberscht of Offenbach, and went to live in Paris as a boy. There he later converted to Christianity in order to be able to marry Hermine d'Accain. Throughout his life he chose not to take a Jewish theme as the subject for an operetta. His 102 operettas include *Orphée aux enfers* ("Orpheus in the Underworld"), *La Belle Hélène*, *La vie Parisienne*, and *La Grande-Duchesse de*

became, after his baptism, director of the Cologne Conservatory. He wrote a book of musical theory which reached its 25th edition shortly before 1933, and he was considered the greatest authority on music in western Germany.

Richard Wagner and "Judaism in Music"

"Reserved Seats for Jews." The caption reads: "Jews receive emergency baptism at the entrance, but in spite of this they may worship only in yellow hats." Cartoon in *Berliner Wespen*, 1876.

"Without Meyerbeer I would be nothing."
Richard Wagner, 1841

"Felix Mendelssohn-Bartholdy is the greatest musical genius since Mozart."
Richard Wagner, before 1850

"Not surprisingly, since song is the most vivid and the most incontrovertibly true expression of the whole range of personal feeling, it is in song that the peculiar quality, repulsive to us, of the Jewish nature reaches its height ..." [this refers to Mendelssohn].

"This deceiving composer [Meyerbeer] ... without being an artist, nevertheless knew how to win fame as an artist ... The period of modern Judaism in music can be historically characterized as a period of complete lack of productivity, of loss of stability ...

ABOVE: Hermann Levi (1839–1900), a celebrated Wagner conductor in his day. Among other things he conducted the first performance of Parsifal at Bayreuth (1882).

RIGHT: "Ecce Caesar nunc triumphans," cartoon satirizing the many Jewish Wagner addicts. From Puck, Leipzig, 1876.

Ecce Caesar nunc triumphans!

Triumphirend laß ich traben
Triſtan jetzt und auch Iſolden.
Hei! die Holden!

Und gefeſſelt
Folgt der Feinde
Schwarm dem Wagen.

Wogela Weia!

[Mendelssohn's compositions] give proof of dissolution and of a tragic sense of his own impotence ... An unformed, shallow mannerism, dully painted over with the appearance of solidity ... is what results from Jews involving themselves in music." (K. Freigedank, alias Richard Wagner, *Über das Judentum in der Musik*, "On Judaism in Music", 1850.)

With this essay Richard Wagner made racial anti-Semitism in music a part of "German national consciousness." The Wagner cult as a racist German movement reached its height around 1900 and was revived again in the National Socialist period. In Wagner's anti-Semitic, Germanic ideology of salvation, as Hartmut Zelinsky called it, Hitler found a model for his policies.

Many Jews were patrons of Richard Wagner and enthusiastic Wagnerians, a fact which was often derided in cartoons.

One of these passionate admirers of Wagner's music was Hermann Levi (1839–1900), who conducted the first performance of *Parsifal* in Bayreuth in 1882. This was contrary to Wagner's wishes, but King Ludwig II would not have made the Munich court orchestra available to him without its musical director, Levi. One of Wagner's chief opponents – alongside Friedrich Nietzsche, who had broken with Wagner in 1876 partly because of the latter's anti-semitism – was the music critic Eduard Hanslick (1825–1904), a half-Jew. Wagner took his revenge on him by making him the model for Beckmesser in *Die Meistersinger*.

Thomas Mann saw Bayreuth as "a miraculous grotto for the eager credulity of a decadent world."

And the socialist cultural critic Friedrich Wendel explained the attraction of Wagner's anti-Semitism sociologically:

"Wagner, a strange, late representative of our beloved Romantic movement, had dressed up the emotional world of the German capitalist bourgeoisie in Germanic costume. For everyone whose outlook was 'folkish' in the narrow Party sense of that term, it was bliss. For it was all there: the poetic rehashing of the idea of 'social' kingship, the curse on evil gold, the blue-eyed punishment of the Semitic competitor ..."

Three Jewish Socialists:
Moses Hess, Karl Marx, Ferdinand Lassalle

Moses Hess (1812–1875), founder of an ethically based form of modern socialism and a precursor of Zionism.

Moses (Moritz) Hess (1812–1875) was the son of a small manufacturer in Cologne; his father served several terms as leader of the Jewish community. Throughout his life he regarded the orthodox upbringing which he received in his parental home as a positive factor and as a decisive influence on him.

He rejected a commercial career and at the age of 20 went to Paris, against the wishes of his parents, to devote himself to intellectual work. With some interruptions, he lived in France, always in the direst poverty, for

about thirty years. In 1861 a political amnesty allowed him to return to Cologne.

In his first book, *Die heilige Geschichte der Menschheit* ("The Sacred History of Mankind"), 1837, Hess outlined a form of primitive communism in the Babeuf mold, rejecting private property as the root of all evil. He combined with it a social-messianic message: socialism as the goal of the development of the human race.

In 1840 he published a proposal for the union of the three states of Germany, France, and England as a counterweight to

Russia, the "enemy of the West." At this period Hess, the "communists' rabbi," won the support of Marx, Engels, Bakunin, and others for his idea of replacing left-wing Hegelianism with ethically based communism. He was a cofounder of the *Rheinische Zeitung*, on which Marx also worked; in 1842, because he was not safe in Prussia owing to his political views, he became the newspaper's Paris correspondent.

There, in 1847, he wrote a draft for a Communist Manifesto. In it he emphasized that the Laws of Moses and the teachings of the prophets had laid down for all time the basic principles of justice and human equality, and argued from this that all nations and races must have equal rights and independence. Religion itself, including the Jewish religion, he rejected as one of the roots of the process of human alienation. Marx and Engels mocked Hess for his "sentimental and idealistic communism," but used parts of his program in developing their own ideas. Hess became the "father of German socialism" of the communist kind with his theory of a classless society, while Marx argued for the supremacy of one class, namely the proletariat.

In the 1850s Hess recognized that nationality exerted a centripetal force which would affect any future development of socialism, and now turned his attention to the Jewish question, which hitherto had not seemed to him to present a separate problem.

With his book *Rom und Jerusalem. Die letzte Nationalitätenfrage* ("Rome and Jerusalem. The last of the nationality issues"), 1862, he became the precursor of political Zionism. He drew a comparison between the national rebirth of Italy taking place at that time and a possible rebirth of the Jewish people in its homeland of Palestine: "... with the liberation of the eternal city on the Tiber there begins also that of the eternal city on Moriah; with the rebirth of Italy there begins also the resurrection of Judea." A rebirth with which he identified himself: "Here I stand again, after an estrangement of twenty years, in the midst of my people, and take part in its festivals of joy and sorrow, in its memories and hopes, and in its intellectual battles within its own house and with the civilized peoples among which it lives but with which, although it has lived and striven together with them for two thousand years, it cannot become organically one."

Abandoning his former thesis of a total dissolution of the Jewish people, Hess thought that a combination of economically and ethically based socialism with conservatism in matters of religious tradition was a genuinely viable option: "Judaism is above all a nationality, whose history, spanning thousands of years, goes hand in hand with that of all mankind," he writes in "Rome and Jerusalem"; yet for him this Jewish nationalism was inseparable from the axiom of the equal worth of all peoples and races.

But Hess holds up to the German Jews the harsh mirror of a disagreeable truth: "The German Jew is always inclined, because of the anti-Semitism all around him, to shake off everything Jewish and to deny his race ... Even baptism does not free him from the nightmare of German anti-semitism ... What the Germans hate about the Jews is not so much their religion as their race, not so much their peculiar faith as their peculiar noses. Neither reform nor baptism, neither education nor emancipation can fully open up to German Jews the portals of German society. They therefore attempt to deny their descent." The need for a political renaissance of the Jews in their land of Palestine seemed to Hess the only possible conclusion to be drawn from these insights.

Karl Marx, who usually responded with biting irony to Hess's works, made no comment whatever on "Rome and Jerusalem". Liberal Jews rejected the book, while the orthodox warned against a secular anticipation of the messianic future.

In accordance with his antiassimilationist views, Hess changed his first name, Moritz, to Moses. Ironically, because the name Moritz was so common among Jews, it later became the stereotypical Jewish forename. Hess would no doubt have seen

Karl Marx (1818–1883), during his years in London, 1875.

this with some amusement as a confirmation of his views. After the publication of "Rome and Jerusalem" he continued to be politically active and in 1867 was a member of the First International, representing the workers of Berlin.

Karl Marx (1818–1883) came from a family which had included a number of respected Jewish scholars and rabbis from Galicia and Germany, but his father, whose brother was a rabbi, had himself and his son baptized. After his father's death Marx had serious disagreements with his mother, who refused to give him a regular

allowance, and as a result he saw her as the embodiment of Jewish avarice.

In 1842 Marx worked on the *Rheinische Zeitung*, and from 1843 onward was a close associate of Moritz Hess in Paris. At that time Hess was working on a theory to make the Jewish and Christian religions obsolete and thereby put an end to bourgeois society and thus to the oppression of human beings.

Marx probably knew this work when in the same year he wrote his first essay *Zur Judenfrage* ("On the Jewish Question"). This first essay on this subject was already

Masthead of the *Social-Demokrat*, the organ of the General German Workers' Association, with the names of the main contributors, 4 January 1865.

clearly influenced by his own emotional reaction against his Jewish background. In his second essay on the same theme, however, his dislike turned to complete rejection. "The bill of exchange," he wrote, possibly alluding to the bills of exchange he did not receive from his mother, "is the true God of the Jews." Parodying the first commandment (Exodus 20, 3), he wrote, "Money is the jealous God of Israel; thou shalt have no other gods before it." He accordingly locates "the mystery of the Jewish religion" in "its secular rite, haggling, and its secular God, money." Marx equates Judaism with bourgeois society when he says, "Judaism attains its apogee with the perfecting of bourgeois society" – purveying what is clearly a historical untruth in order to distance himself from his own Jewishness and from the Jews.

Yet Marx should have been aware of the fact that for centuries the humiliated Jews had had usury forced upon them by the Christians as almost the only possible way of earning a living. It is ironic that in later years anti-Semitic insults were directed at Marx himself by opponents, including some within the socialist camp such as Dühring and Bakunin.

He also began at that time to have friendly relationships with other Jews, and he recommended his favorite daughter Eleanor, nicknamed "Pussy," to attend lectures on the Jewish prophets. While Eleanor aided eastern Jews in slum districts, Jean Longuet, Karl Marx's grandson, became an active supporter of Zionism.

The breakthrough of German Jews into political life began with Ferdinand Lassalle, Eduard Lasker, Leopold Sonnemann, and Ludwig Bamberger.

Ferdinand Lassalle (1825–1864) was the son of Heyman Lasal, who had a textile business, and his wife Rosalie, from

Breslau. He combined the talents of an idealistic philosopher, a wily politician, a memorable writer, a speaker who could enthuse an audience, and a party organizer of exceptional vision.

In 1848 Lassalle took part in the revolutionary movements in the Rhineland. At various times he engaged in intensive exchanges of views with Heine, Hess, Engels, and Marx, and as late as 1861 Marx stayed for eleven days as a guest in Lassalle's apartment in Berlin, which he called "a luxurious focal point of interesting society." This did not, however, prevent him from referring to Lassalle in private letters as "Itzig" or "the Jewish nigger [*sic*] Lassalle": "It is now quite clear to me that – as is proved by the shape of his head and by his hair – he is descended from the negroes who joined Moses' people as they left Egypt, unless his mother or his grandmother on the father's side interbred with a nigger [*sic*]." However, after Lassalle's death in a duel his judgment was: "Lassalle called – this remains his immortal achievement – the worker's movement back to Germany."

A brilliant speaker at workers' meetings and in court, Lassalle founded in 1863 the *Allgemeiner Deutscher Arbeiterverein* ("General German Workers' Association"), thereby freeing the working class once and for all from its dependence on liberal-bourgeois groups and parties. His second great project was the formation of production cooperatives helped by credits from the state, and the third was to bring about the introduction of universal, equal, and secret suffrage.

Lassalle's negotiations with Bismarck angered Marx and Engels, because he had offered the Chancellor the support of the workers in return for the granting of the right to vote. "A common, low-down scoundrel ... a betrayal of the whole labor movement to the Prussians," was Friedrich Engels' judgment.

His Jewishness was something about which Lassalle still spoke with enthusiasm in 1848, at the age of 23: "I would even go to the scaffold if I could make the Jews into a great, respected nation once more."

Ferdinand Lassalle (1825–1864), founder of the General German Workers' Association, 23 May 1863.

Later, however, the subject no longer interested him, though he remained a member of the Jewish community.

Ferdinand Lassalle was killed in a duel in 1864. "One of the many acts of tactlessness that he committed in his life," commented Karl Marx.

"Far from having come to an end, the effects of that life continue to appear like fresh waves ... [to anyone] who is deeply concerned about social reform," wrote Hermann Oncken in 1920.

Contributing to Industrialization

The development of industry and technology enabled Jewish entrepreneurs in Germany to break down the barriers of political and economic discrimination without performing the humiliating act of "voluntary" baptism. They could now find a sphere of activity in branches of the new large-scale industries and of transport where they were not prevented from competing, and so they entered into competition with non-Jewish pioneers of the age of capitalism and played a part alongside them in building up industry in Germany. On a far more modest scale than the non-Jewish Borsigs, Thyssens, Kirdorfs, and Siemenses, Jewish entrepreneurs introduced new industries above all to Upper

LEFT: The Herminenhütte ironworks near Laband (Upper Silesia), 1860.

BELOW: The terminus at Wittenberg of the Magdeburg-Wittenberg railroad. On the right is Salomon Herz's oil factory.

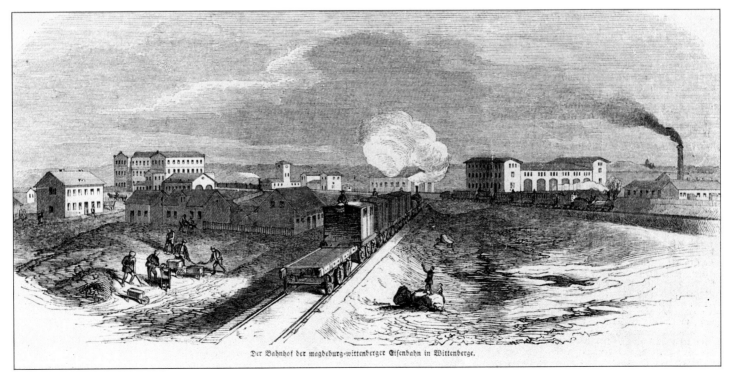

Der Bahnhof der magdeburg-wittenberger Eisenbahn in Wittenberge.

Silesia, which was then still an underdeveloped agricultural region, and pioneered major industries there, just as, for instance, Emil Rathenau (1838–1915) later did in Berlin.

Around the middle of the 19th century, German textile production was still mainly a cottage industry. The products of the weaving factories of Meyer Kauffmann in Tannhausen, Silesia, were also at first made on looms in the workers' homes. Meyer Kauffmann, who had started with a small linen store, became one of the founders of the Silesian textile industry.

"I soon recognized the inferiority of our products compared to those exhibited by England," wrote his son Salomon after visiting the Great Exhibition in London in 1851. He accordingly bought two hundred mechanical looms for his factory; at the same time he improved his workers' standard of living.

The economic and industrial upturn in Upper Silesia is linked above all with the names of Hegenscheidt, Caro and Kern. Heinrich and Aloys Kern built up the Herminenhütte (ironworks) near Laband, and their nephews Georg and Oskar Caro were also involved in the enterprise (see page 226). Wilhelm Hegenscheidt (1823–1891), who came from a Protestant family, built a cable and chain factory near Gleiwitz in 1852. In 1887 he amalgamated his firm with Caro and Kern's Herminenhütte and Julienhütte ironworks, and this new firm formed the basis of the Upper Silesian iron industry.

Salomon Herz, another of those pioneering entrepreneurs, was born in Bernburg in 1794. In October 1823 he was "graciously granted permission for business dealing, the purchase of a house in Bernburg, and marriage, on payment of the usual fee."

He soon moved to Berlin and built an oil mill in Wittenberg on the Elbe. It grew into the most important oil mill in Europe, providing Berlin and other towns with root vegetable oil for lighting at night and with other vegetable oils for cooking and for technical uses.

With the expansion of his oil mill, Herz became the first German oil exporter, espe-

Josef Liebermann, a pioneer in the field of mechanical engineering. Portrait painted in 1842.

BELOW: Liepmann's invention of the oleograph (1839), exhibited at the Great Exhibition, London, 1851.

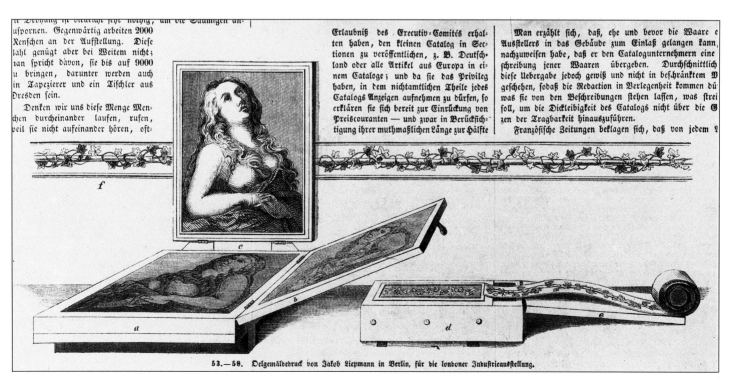

cially to North America. His son Wilhelm (1823–1914) became president of the Berlin Chamber of Commerce and received the title of "Excellency."

The enterprises of two Berlin Jews in the field of transport were also remarkable, though more for their ideas and methods than for their size. Israel Henoch, known by the nickname of "Droschkenhenoch" ("Cab Henoch"), introduced the horse cab to Berlin. Simon Kremser (1775–1851) in 1825 acquired the concession – granted to him because he had served as a volunteer in the Wars of Liberation – for a regular horse bus service in Berlin. In the early 20th century, excursion coaches in Berlin were still called "Kremser."

Jacob Liepmann was an industrial inventor-entrepreneur in yet another field free of control by the guilds. In 1840 he developed the oleograph. Some time previously he had worked on a process for mechanically duplicating images, but had abandoned it as impractical. That was a process to fix the picture in a camera obscura – photography.

Josef Liebermann, the owner of a small ironworks in Sprottau in Upper Silesia, built agricultural machinery. For years his grandson Emil Rathenau worked for him "as a proletarian in a blue overall," while a second grandson, Max Liebermann, went to art school. Josef Liebermann built up a calico factory and brought over from England the technique of machine-printing on calico. When he was made a "Kommerzienrat" (commercial councilor), he introduced himself to King William IV in broad dialect, saying, "I'm that Liebermann what chased the English off the Continent." His grandsons inherited not only a great deal of money but also his sense of humor.

While all these enterprises were built up by individuals, the development of the railroad required particularly large investments of capital which could only be raised by consortia or by means of international bank loans or complicated financial operations. The Rothschild banking house financed the Austrian and the Russian railroad in particular, while the Prussian railroads were built mainly using English capital. The authorized agent in that matter was Bethel Henry Strousberg (1823–1884), a curious character from Neidenburg (East Prussia), who had himself baptized in London, worked as a journalist editing a periodical specializing in economic statistics, and then returned to

Berlin. He soon became the most active and respected railroad builder in Europe, and in 1870 his company issued shares to the value of over 85 million thalers. In 1868 the King of Romania granted to the Duke of Ujest, a certain Count Lehndorf, and Bethel Henry Strousberg the concession for a railroad network with 9000 kilometers of track. Strousberg became a Conservative member of the parliament of the North German Confederation; he was much decorated, a multi-millionaire and had an ostentatious lifestyle; he was courted by members of the high aristocracy and had the support of the Prussian Minister for Trade. But he issued more shares than he could cover, and finally had to declare himself bankrupt, just one of many cases involving "fraudulent setting up of companies". Later on, this "bad boy of industrialization" had more far-sighted plans, such as one for a canal between the North Sea and the Baltic, but was unable to realize them.

RIGHT: Josef von Hirsch (1805–1885), banker in Munich. He financed the building of many stretches of railroad in Bavaria. Photograph by Franz Hanfstaengl.

BELOW: "For two groschen you can travel like this to Charlottenburg." Kremser's suburban transport around 1845, the beginning of public transport in cities.

So fährt man für 2 ng. nach Charlottenburg.

Equality under the Law

Law passed on 3 July 1869 providing for the equal status of the religious denominations and their equal rights.

instance on the cloth commemorating the Yom Kippur service at Metz.

"And one greets another, stretches out a brother's hand to him": this was now the hope of most German Jews.

As they saw it, German citizenship for them presupposed a willingness on their part to enter into a synthesis of Germans and Jews. However, a majority of non-Jewish, especially middle-class citizens showed no such willingness. Even a death for the Fatherland would be denied in nationalist, anti-Semitic circles, or resented as Jewish impudence, since the notion of a brave, patriotic Jew ran counter to the stereotype current in those circles. Nevertheless, in practice equal rights did on the whole become a reality, since they were imposed from above.

In the Grand Duchy of Baden, which had a long tradition of liberalism, the Jews enjoyed full equal rights from 1862 onward. The second place to enact legislation granting "equal rights for citizens who are of the Israelite religion" was a city in which the patricians, in particular, had always disregarded the prejudices of the majority – Frankfurt am Main. The measure was proclaimed as an "organic law" at the meeting of the city council on 7 October 1864.

Five years later, on 3 July 1869, Bismarck issued a law for the states of the North German Confederation "concerning equal status for the religious denominations in all civic and state matters". Unlike the Frankfurt "organic law", this law did not refer specifically to "citizens of the Israelite religion" but was framed in more general terms. After the Empire was proclaimed in 1871, this law applied in the whole of Germany.

But even before this, in 1870/71, 12,000 Jews were permitted to take part, as full citizens of the state, in the Franco-Prussian War, and they welcomed this with enthusiasm. The battles to "liberate Alsace-Lorraine" were glorified in celebratory poems and sentimental pictures, for

Meyer Dinkel (center), from Mannheim, and two comrades, Albert Gautier and Peter Metz, in the war of 1870/71.

Jewish field-service on Yom Kippur outside Metz,
1870. Commemorative cloth.

THE GERMAN EMPIRE
1871–1918

Germany my Fatherland –
Jewry my Heritage

The German-Jewish Bourgeoisie

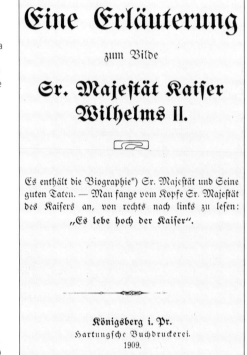

After the official introduction of equal civil status by the laws of 1869/71, the goal of the Jews in Germany seemed to have been achieved: no longer "Jews in Germany," but "German Jews." Opposition to the new equality laws for which they had fought so long was more moderate this time than during the brief periods

RIGHT: Friederike Josephy (1854–1916), wife of a grain dealer and banker. She was Walter Benjamin's aunt and insisted that his father allow him to take his school-leaving exam. She promoted the circle of young Expressionists Hoddis, Heym, and Hiller. Photograph c. 1880.

BELOW: The upper middle-class Rosenberg family in Bromberg, about 1890.

ABOVE: Georg Lichtheim, assimilated Berlin Jew in good society about 1880. He was a grain merchant, lived in the style of a prosperous member of the upper middle class and kept his own riding horses. His son Richard, who grew up without any Jewish education, saw the assimilation route as wrong and became one of the leading Zionists of German Jewry.

of equal rights in 1812 and 1848. Both internal and external security seemed incomparably greater and stronger than at that time. Of the 600,000 Jews, some 6,000 were already in agriculture, the least accessible occupation for them in 1895. No less than 130,000 made their living in craft and industry, some 40,000 working

LEFT: Walter Rathenau, later Foreign Minister, as a sergeant in a Cuirassier regiment, c. 1888.

RIGHT: Mrs. Aniela Fürstenberg, wife of the "wittiest of all bankers," Carl Fürstenberg, about 1890. Fürstenberg was a financier of German heavy industry. The couple belonged to the "peak of society" in Berlin. From a painting by Leopold Horowitz.

LEFT: German Jews in an idealized self-depiction. From the celebration of the centenary of the Philanthropin, Frankfurt am Main, 1904, founded as a school for poor Jewish children. It ultimately became a Reform grammar school (with girls' high school).

RIGHT: "Schmulchen Schievelbeiner": the Jew in Wilhelm Busch's caricature.

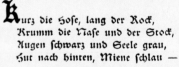

for the civil service and in the independent professions. Only just over half, in contrast to the 90 percent in previous centuries, were engaged in commerce. At the social level, especially in the smaller towns, there was increasing closeness to the Christian milieu.

In the professions of law, soldiering and education, Jews continued to be neglected

ABOVE: The upper middle-class families Schulhoff and Katzenstein at a wedding , c. 1910.

RIGHT: The German Jewish Warburg family, Hamburg 1884. The grandmother occupies the place of honor. Famous members of the family were bankers, academics and philanthropists (see pages 270 and 357).

The Kulp family in Frankfurt am Main, a photomontage from 1897. In the background the portrait of the "progenitor" Juda Michael Kulp, surrounded by his son Menko and his sons-in-law Schwabacher, Rapp and Goldschmidt. They are present only in effigy as portraits on the wall.

or excluded: with a few exceptions they were unable, unless baptized, to become full professors, officers, judges or senior civil servants. However, closer co-operation began in the fields of theater, the press, the arts and literature.

Despite waves of anti-Semitism in politics and the universities, encouraged by the theories of Treitschke and the inflammatory writings and sermons of Stoecker and Ahlwardt, the Jews felt secure in Germany. Many had risen to the middle classes, many lived prosperously. They entertained the belief that with the general progress, the last restrictions on professional and social life would fall away.

ABOVE: Coffee time on Sunday afternoon in the Munich Hofgarten café, about 1902. The Marx, Schülein, Levi and Cahnmann families met there regularly.

ABOVE RIGHT: Two sons of orthodox rabbi Marcus Horowitz in Frankfurt am Main, taken in Jerusalem in 1910.

RIGHT: China in Albert Einstein's parental home. Right, on the coffee cup, a portrait of Albert Einstein aged five. Photograph: Lotte Jacobi.

German Jews in Politics

Leopold Sonnemann leads a town councilors' meeting in Frankfurt am Main, 1880. As a Reichstag member he opposed Bismarck's anti-socialist laws.

Gabriel Riesser and Johann Jacoby were the first Jews who were able to work as German politicians, although they demanded full recognition of their Jewishness as interpreted by Leopold Zunz (see page 155). After 1848, they were followed by a number of others who also became German politicians while remaining Jews.

After their protracted battle for civil and political rights, the Jews were the obvious potential voters for the liberal and free-thinking parties in particular. Here many believed that they would find the political home that suited them. But Jews were also among the leading spirits of the rising socialist movement, although most Jewish

voters distrusted it. The Social Democrats did indeed reject anti-semitism as a demagogic diversionary tactic of Christian bourgeois society, while at the same time opposing the very economic order in which Jews could be ranked economically as free entrepreneurs.

Concern with the social issue and the promotion of liberal ideas were the leitmotif of Jewish members of parliament of all parties.

In contrast to Lassalle, Eduard Lasker (1829–1884), co-founder of the National Liberal Party, was a declared representative of bourgeois ideas. From 1865 onward, as their chief spokesman in the Prussian parliament, he came out in sup-

port of the civil rights not yet gained by German Jews. After the German empire was founded, he played a decisive part in the new legislation and as a member of the Reichstag, the imperial parliament, he sharply rejected the death penalty and Bismarck's antisocialist laws. His brother Morris (1831–1916) fought in the American Civil War on the side of the southern States and became senator for Texas.

Deeply rooted opposition to all autocratic politics or parties was represented by the banker, newspaper publisher, patron, and liberal politician Leopold Sonnemann (1831–1909). He was the most outstanding representative of the

Bismarck and Eduard Lasker in caricature. In the Prussian House of Deputies, Lasker, one of the founders of the National Liberal Party, fought for equal rights for Jews.

„Wollen wir conſtitutionell regieren, ſo bedürfen wir einer Majorität. Verweigern Sie ſie uns, ſo iſt die Regierung genöthigt, ſich auf andere Parteien zu ſtützen, mit denen ſie innerlich nicht ſo conſolidirt iſt."

Parteigenossen!

Nachdem ich Berlin verlassen habe drängt es mich, Euch noch ein Wort des Abschieds zu sagen.

Die Polizei hat mich auf Befehl des Ministers des Innern ausgewiesen.

Ich bin ausgewiesen, weil ich die Thätigkeit des Spitzelthums aufgedeckt habe und ich mußte dem Ausnahmegesetz zum Opfer fallen, weil man Leute, die ehrliche durchdringende Verbesserung der Lage des arbeitenden Volkes fordern und welche die **Scheinreform der Regierung** unerbittlich bekämpfen, die Haltlosigkeit derselben nachweisen, in Berlin nicht duldet.

Man zwingt mich, die Stätte meiner Wirksamkeit **zu verlassen.** Es ist nicht gelungen, mir das Vertrauen der Genossen zu rauben, es ist **trotz der gehässigsten Verläumdungen** nicht möglich gewesen, meine Wähler zu beeinflussen.

Parteigenossen! So wie Ihr stets darauf rechnen könnt, mich für die Befreiung der Menschheit von politischem und wirthschaftlichem Joch kämpfen zu sehen so rechne auch ich fest darauf, daß Ihr unserer Fahne treu und ergeben bleibt und daß Ihr mannhaft zusammensteht, wenn es gilt, unsere heilige Sache zu fördern.

Laßt Euch —.dies rufe ich Euch warnend zu — durch keine **Provokationen**, welche nicht ausbleiben werden, verleiten, den Gegnern gefällig zu sein, **behaltet die Köpfe klar!**

Stets das erhabene Ziel im Auge, laßt die Frucht reifen, auch für uns kommt die Zeit der Ernte!

Bis dahin unaufhörlichen Kampf gegen die Feinde auf allen Gebieten; wir müssen und werden siegen unter dem Rufe:

Hoch die Sozialdemokratie!

Paul Singer.

Verlag und Druck
Schweizerische Genossenschaftsdruckerei Hottingen Zürich.

Jewish middle class of Frankfurt am Main in the second half of the 19th century. As a free-thinking politician he became a leading member of the Democratic People's Party, which he represented in the Frankfurt City Councilors' Assembly from 1884 to 1904. In 1867 Sonnemann became the owner and publisher of the *Frankfurter Zeitung* newspaper, which became world-famous under his direction. His motto was "Politically free, ever just, and in favor of reform in social policy, ever tending to support the economically weak." The *Frankfurter Zeitung* was his weapon against the power politics of Bismarck, who hated the resolutely liberal Sonnemann.

In 1849 Ludwig Bamberger (1823–1899) was condemned to death for his participation in the revolutionary risings in Baden and Hesse, but succeeded in escaping to Switzerland. There and in Paris he became a political economist and banker. In 1866 he returned to Germany, where he became a follower of Bismarck. From 1868 he was a member of the Customs Union parliament and from 1871 to 1893 he was in the Reichstag.

Bismarck appointed Bamberger, an international authority on currency and banking affairs, as his adviser. As co-founder of the German Reichsbank he was soon known as the "father of the gold standard." At first a national liberal, from 1897 he was active in opposition to Bismarck's protective tariff policy. As a member of the Reichstag he also opposed Bismarck's colonial and military policy and moved towards the bourgeois left. In 1894, when anti-Semitic persecution increased and he found himself on the receiving end of the "ingratitude of the Fatherland," Bamberger retired from his public posts.

Ludwig Loewe (1837–1886) was at first a follower of Ferdinand Lassalle, to whom he was secretary; when Lassalle became a socialist, he left him. At the age of 24, Loewe went into politics and was elected soon afterward to the Berlin city council. He organized the muddled finances of the city and carried through modern ideas in

Masthead of the *Berliner Volksblatt* published by Paul Singer.

Masthead of the *Volkszeitung*, founded by Aaron Bernstein in 1852.

marck banned the Social Democratic Party, the hitherto independently minded Paul Singer joined it. With Bebel and Wilhelm Liebknecht he became one of its leaders, founding in 1884 the *Volksblatt*, later known as *Vorwärts*, a mouthpiece of the socialist movement. In the same year he was elected to the Reichstag in opposition to Stoecker.

In 1886, the antisocialist laws resulted in Singer's expulsion from Germany for a few years. He developed into a radical spokesman for a socialist economic and social order and later became Berlin's most popular Social Democrat.

At his funeral more than a million people followed the cortège, "and voluntarily, too," as Lenin commented. What distinguished him from Lenin was his support for the rights of the individual, for freedom of thought, and the independence of art and science.

A leading ideologue of the Social Democratic movement was Eduard Bernstein (1850–1932), the son of an enginedriver and nephew of the writer and founder of the *Berliner Volkszeitung* newspaper Aaron Bernstein (1812–1884). When he too was expelled under the antisocialist laws, Eduard Bernstein published *Die neue Zeit* in London. His goal was to put Social Democratic policy on a scientific footing. In 1901 he returned to Germany.

Bernstein was the harshest opponent of the Marxist class war theory. He founded evolutionary revisionism, which is still the basis of Social Democracy in western European countries. After the First World War Bernstein espoused the socialist-Zionist ideal.

the administration. His chief contribution was the reform of basic primary and secondary education, which achieved equal treatment for all children regardless of their parents' wealth, status, or religion.

In 1878 Loewe became a member of the Reichstag for the Progress Party. There he opposed Bismarck's antisocialist laws and from 1884, together with Virchow, he led a campaign against the exploitation of the workers. His social ideas were put into practice in his own factories, where he

began by producing sewing machines, moving on in 1872 to the mass production of precision rifles, referred to derogatorily by non-Jewish rivals and anti-Semitic journalists as "Jew guns." As an active member of the Jewish assembly of representatives in Berlin, Loewe opposed the anti-Semitic agitation of Adolf Stoecker, the court chaplain.

Berlin's most popular labor leader was the women's coat manufacturer Paul Singer (1844–1911). When in 1878 Bis-

The Science of Judaism

Title page of *Das Wesen des Judentums* ("The Essence of Judaism"), 1905, by Leo Baeck.

BELOW: A "cell," or teaching house, in Posen, where the Hebrew religious Scriptures were studied at all hours of the day until late into the night, c. 1900.

The central figure of the Jewish liberal movement was Leopold Zunz (1794–1886), founder of the "science of Judaism." Even in his first publication in 1818, the 24-year-old outlined the tasks of this form of science; in 1832 he published *Die Gottesdienstliche Vorträge der Juden* ("The Religious Discourses of the Jews"), which raised the study of Judaism to a scientific discipline.

An uncompromising researcher, he generally earned his living as a house tutor, writer, and preacher. "A man of speech and action, he created and worked where others dreamed and floundered helplessly," as Heinrich Heine wrote of Zunz at 40.

The science founded by Zunz was concerned with Talmudic, historical, literary, linguistic, liturgical, Islamic, philosophical, statistical, and economic investigations, insofar as they affected Judaism either centrally or marginally.

The significance of Zunz and his fellow campaigners is that they uncovered the literary and historical sources of Judaism and studied its many and varied achievements in terms of a historical critique. Nevertheless, the science of Judaism was also accused of being more of a cataloging and explanation of significant works than a living, let alone a fighting, force. For instance, important areas which were "not for the drawing room" were excluded: the Jewish gangs of crooks and robber bands of the 18th and 19th centuries.

Also excluded as unexplained or irrational incidental phenomena were such essential features as Jewish mysticism, the Cabala, Shabbetaianis, and Hasidism. Only the later, more open, attitude of Zionism brought about a change here. Critical objections of this kind, which recognized at the same time the extraordinary achievements of Leopold Zunz as certainly the most important representative of the science of Judaism, were raised in particular by Gershom Scholem.

Conservative Judaism found its research center in the Jewish theological seminary in Breslau. This was founded in 1854 by Zacharias Frankel (1801–1875) and con-

ABOVE LEFT: Azriel Hildesheimer (1820–1899), leader of Orthodox Jewry in Germany, founder and principal of the Rabbinical Seminary in Berlin.

ABOVE RIGHT: Heinrich Graetz (1817–1891), author of the first comprehensive "History of the Jews from the Earliest Times to the Present Day" (11 volumes, 1853–75), lecturer at the Jewish Theological Seminary and professor at Breslau University.

Geschichte der Israeliten

von

ihren Uranfängen

(um 1500)

bis zum

Tode des Königs Salomo

(um 977 vorchr. Zeit).

Nebst synchronistischen Zeittafeln.

Von

Dr. H. Graetz,
Professor an der Universität Breslau.

Leipzig,
Oskar Leiner.

LEFT: Title page for "History of the Israelites," 1853, by Heinrich Graetz.

tinued until 1938 to train rabbis and scholars, who built up centers for a Jewish religion of the modern era in Germany, the United States and other countries. Important research results of the new science were published in the *Monatsschrift für Geschichte und Wissenschaft des Judentums* ("Monthly Gazette for History and Science of Judaism"), founded in 1851, which continued to appear until 1939. In 1872 this was followed by the foundation of the Teaching Institute (University from 1922) for the Study of Judaism in Berlin, which remained until 1942, when the last generation of Jewish scholars had fled from Germany or, like Rabbi Leo Baeck, were in concentration camps.

While for liberal Judaism there were always upheavals in the spiritual area and humiliations in the battle for civil rights to be overcome, Orthodox Judaism was not affected by such attacks on the alleged inferiority of the Jews. Its proponents felt superior to anti-Semitic attacks from whatever quarter, knowing themselves secure in the fulfillment of the religious commandments which made extreme ethical demands on the faithful. Even the epithet "medieval," bestowed on them by reform Jews, was not regarded by the Orthodox as demeaning, since after all, in the Middle Ages, orthodox Judaism (there was no other kind) had produced spiritual values of the highest rank. There were orthodox teaching centers in many communities. Besides Orthodox training schools for rabbis (yeshivot), many cities still had east European Jewish prayer rooms, where scholars and laymen met for the common study of the Bible and the Talmud.

One of the outstanding spiritual leaders of Orthodox Judaism was Azriel Hildesheimer (1820–1899). He took his doctoral degree at Halle and linked the long despised secular sciences with the study of the Talmud. Together with Samson Raphael Hirsch (1808–1888), Hildesheimer became the founder of modern Orthodoxy far beyond the frontiers of Germany. In 1851, as a rabbi in the little Austrian town of Eisenstadt, he founded, in the face of bitter hostility from "old orthodox" circles, a seminary in which nonreligious subjects were taught. In 1869 Hildesheimer was called to Berlin, where in 1873 he founded the Orthodox Rabbinical Seminary.

New Synagogues

Frankfurt a/M

Die neue Synagoge
der israelit. Gemeinde

eingeweiht am 23 März 1860.

Until the beginning of the 19th century there were only a few large synagogues in Germany. In most towns services took place in small synagogues and prayer rooms. At the same time, with the gradual fulfillment of the moves toward assimilation, the need grew for the kind of imposing houses of God seen in the Christian milieu.

A want of individual creativity was typical of almost all architecture from the middle of the 19th to the beginning of the 20th century. Instead of developing a contemporary style, architects imitated the styles of the past. Neo-gothic and neo-romanesque became the customary styles for prestigious buildings such as churches, theaters, museums, town halls, and railroad stations.

Imitation was also characteristic of the synagogue building of that era, for which Byzantine, romanesque, or, as an expression of "Jewishness," Moorish stylistic elements were used. The "Moorish" style was intended to display an individually "Jewish" architectural tradition in contrast to Christian sacred architecture.

In earlier days, synagogues and houses of prayer stood in side streets, but now, especially in large cities, they were built in the center, and faced onto the road, expressing once again the newly won sense of freedom and awareness of equality.

The interior of the new synagogues was sometimes "Moorish," sometimes scarcely distinguishable from Protestant churches, with a long nave, strictly ordered rows of seating for the congregation, a lectern set in the apse and reached by steps. This was a distinct change from the earlier arrangement, when the lectern stood in the middle, symbolizing its significance in the service. Most of these buildings were designed by Christian architects, as there were scarcely any Jewish ones until the 19th century.

The new synagogue in Frankfurt am Main, dedicated on 23 March 1860. Marginal figures: Emperors Joseph II and Leopold II, lithograph, 1864.

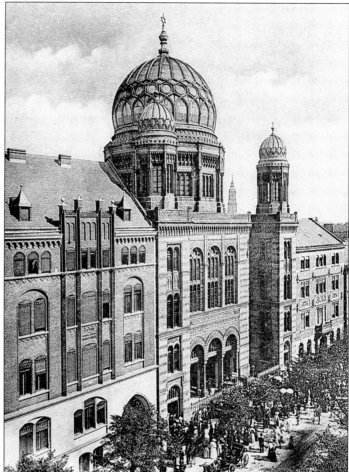

ABOVE LEFT: New synagogue in Berlin, Oranienburger Strasse 30. It was designed in 1857–59 by Eduard Knoblauch and built in 1859–66 under the direction of August Stüler. Wood engraving from "Over Land and Sea," 1866.

ABOVE RIGHT: Exterior view of the synagogue in Oranienburger Strasse 30, Berlin. Steel engraving by J. Kolb, 1883.

LEFT: The new synagogue in Dresden, built by Gottfried Semper 1838–40.

The building of the Dresden synagogue began even before the New Temple in Hamburg. Gottfried Semper drew up the plans after the King of Saxony had approved the building of a synagogue in 1837. Semper retained early models: the facade was kept in the romanesque style and Moorish motifs were used in the interior. The seating arrangement, the Torah shrine, and the women's gallery were traditionally Jewish. The synagogue was consecrated in 1840. The next large synagogue was built in Frankfurt am Main in 1855–60, replacing the Old Synagogue, in the former Judengasse, later renamed Börnestrasse.

The "non-style" of the German-imperial era also influenced synagogue architecture. Buildings arose that radiated ceremony and dignity, but the warmth and intimacy of the country synagogues and prayer rooms were lost. Most of these remained traditionally Jewish in their architecture and decoration.

ABOVE: The main synagogue in Munich, completed 1887 from Albert Schmidt's plans.

LEFT: The synagogue in Fasanenstrasse, Berlin. Architect: Ehrenfried Hessel, 1912.

ABOVE: The synagogue on Börneplatz, Frankfurt am Main, c. 1925.

ABOVE RIGHT: Wilhelm Cremer and Richard Wolffenstein among the floral decorations for the silver jubilee of their architectural business, Berlin 1917. They also built synagogues in Königsberg (1896) and Posen (1907).

RIGHT: The main synagogue in Essen, dedicated on 25 September 1913. Architect: Edmund Körner.

Attachment to the Community

ABOVE: Israelite school and town hall in the Wangen district of Öhningen. Drawing, c. 1870.

RIGHT: Memorial sheet for the celebration of Rabbi Marcus Horowitz's 25 years in office, Frankfurt am Main, 1903.

LEFT: Title page of the "Hanover Calendar for Israelites," 1904/05.

RIGHT: A prayer book as used in Germany, written in Hebrew and German.

BELOW: Transfer of two rolls of the Torah into the newly built synagogue of Künzelsau, 1907. All the houses in the little town showed flags on the day of dedication. The rabbi and the leader of the community are holding the Torah scrolls in their arms: "The bride of Israel is led home."

LEFT: Berlin-Moabit, after the service in the synagogue in Levetzowstrasse, c. 1912.

BELOW: Laying the foundation stone of the synagogue on Bornplatz, Hamburg, on 23 March 1905. Besides the chief rabbi and the congregation of the new synagogue, members of all the synagogues and Jewish institutions take part in the celebration.

ABOVE: In the "Jewish Reading Room" in Berlin, 1905.

LEFT: Mastheads of a selection of Jewish papers in Germany.

After the founding of the German Empire in 1871, local Jewish communities in Germany were recognized and their self-government was encouraged, yet at the same time policy tended toward a very gradual and non-universal inclusion of Jews in the state. Thus the Federation of German-Israelite Congregations, founded in 1869 and known as the Synod, was approved by the state only as a private association. Life in the community was almost without exception well-ordered and despite voluntary membership and relatively large financial obligations, supported by the loyalty of most members, whether poor or rich, Orthodox or Reform.

The members of the synagogue congregations also had close connections among themselves. Contributory factors were the sporting, choral, and school associations, but above all the extremely large number of charitable societies, whose aims were to fulfill the ethical demands of Judaism in accordance with social justice and social assistance.

"The Jews Are our Misfortune"

"The song of the wicked Jew – presented by the Kreuz-Zeitung," from the *Berliner Wespen*, 1875.

BELOW: "Automobile, patent Schmul, cheapest to run! Totally harmless!" Caricature, 1900.

late 1870s; pulpits and teachers' desks now became the soapboxes of a religious, political, or racist style of anti-Semitism. Adolf Stoecker (1835–1909), Berlin's court chaplain, founded in 1879 the anti-Semitic Christian Social Workers' Party. The word "Workers" was dropped when he met no response from the workers and lost an election against the Jewish workers' leader Paul Singer.

The Berlin professor of history Heinrich von Treitschke (1834–1896), a passionate Prussian patriot of Saxon origin, was the initiator of the politically nationalist anti-Semitism of the educated classes. In his speeches as a member of parliament (1871–1874) and in publications, he described "the Jew" as the repository of the democratic ideas he hated and as the ringleader of social democracy, this "bestial mob movement which is upsetting the God-given German Christian concept of masters and subjects." Treitschke demanded humility from the Jews and accused them of arrogance and slandering Christianity.

Treitschke and Stoecker were corrected by the doyen of German historians, Theodor Mommsen (1817–1903): "… and am in general of the opinion that Providence understood far better than Herr Stoecker why a small percentage of Israel was to be alloyed to the German

Like every minority, the Jewish minority in Germany constantly gave rise to feelings of insecurity in the majority surrounding it, which in times of economic crisis often turned into enmity and hatred.

The efforts of the Jews to achieve civic equality and social recognition were opposed by a countermovement: the nationalists above all feared that "the Jews" constituted a dangerous "foreign body" within the German people. The strange, the unknown, the unusual, often interpreted as too clever and overconfident, became the negative, mistrusted, and feared.

Thus hatred of the Jews began to flare up again with the collapse of firms in the

Germany. Only the social democratic workers, Treitschke's "bestial mob movement," were not impressed by the anti-Jewish agitation.

Even *Die Gartenlaube*, the most-widely read weekly, with a circulation of over 300,000, now published crudely anti-semitic articles, though in milder form. Sentimental tales such as Eugenie Marlitt's *Goldelse* (1867) and politically liberal articles, including some by Jews, had at first been the main content – along with romantic illustrations – of the paper. Its founder Ernst Keil (1816–1876) originally had liberal educational goals. A former 1848 revolutionary, in the 1870s he followed the mood of the time to become a national liberal, but still wanted to work, in an educational sense, "philosemitically." But even

in the 60s he had allowed unfair attacks on Jews to be printed in *Die Gartenlaube*, and with Otto Glagau's (1834–1892) continuing series in 1874/75 on the "stock exchange and funding swindle in Berlin," the paper was steering unmistakably in the wake of anti-Semitism. The fact that Keil censored the most furious outbursts in Glagau's series can be ascribed either to his still liberal views, or to consideration for his Jewish daughter-in-law.

With Treitschke, *Die Gartenlaube*, and its competitor *Daheim*, anti-Semitism soon became part of the ideology of a now racist nationalism, to which large sections of the German upper and middle classes adhered.

metal for its formulation." Mommsen, who already foresaw in Treitschke's "aimless great words" the danger of a civil war of the majority against the minority, nevertheless advised the Jews to be baptized as a means of becoming completely German. This was rejected by almost all Jews as a debasement of their moral and religious convictions.

The Jewish historian Heinrich Graetz, whose *Geschichte der Juden von den ältesten Zeiten bis auf die Gegenwart* ("History of the Jews from the Earliest Times to the Present Day" 11 vols, 1853–75), Treitschke had taken as one motivation for his anti-semitic outbursts, replied sharply, sarcastically correcting Treitschke's historical inaccuracies. Others, such as the philosopher Hermann Cohen (1842–1918), reacted apologetically. Bismarck was silent. No anti-Semite, he could nevertheless make good political use of the Stoeckers and Treitschkes in his battle against Liberals and Social Democrats.

But Treitschke's racist arrogance gained a following. He and his fellow campaigners bred generations of anti-Semites, including many senior officials, judges, academics, officers, the future leaders of

Wahlaufruf.

Zu den Waffen!

Am 16. Juni finden die Reichstagswahlen statt. An den deutschen Reichstagswählern liegt es, mit dem Stimmzettel in der Faust eine Aenderung der trostlosen und unhaltbaren Zustände in Deutschland anzubahnen und den energischen Willen kundzugeben, daß unser Volk aus den Klauen des Kapitalismus, des internationalen Ausbeutertums gerettet und die Ketten gesprengt werden, mit welchen das Judentum und dessen Dienstmann, "der Judenliberalismus", in schmählicher Gemeinschaft, mit allen Mitteln der Hinterlist und feigen Grausamkeit unser Volk gefesselt.

Wer noch ein Freund des vaterländischen Bodens, deutscher, christlicher Kultur ist, und wer nicht zugeben will, daß Deutschland zum Versuchskaninchen freihändlerischer, sozialdemokratischer und internationaler Phantasten und Theoretiker herhalten soll, wem es darum zu tun ist, die schaffenden Stände vor dem nahestehenden, vollkommenen Ruin zu retten, wer der reellen, nationalen und produktiven Arbeit den gebührenden Lohn sichern will, der kann nur den Kandidaten der christlich-sozialen Partei seine Stimme geben.

Katholiken und Protestanten! Vereinigt euch in brüderlicher Liebe gegen den Todfeind des Deutschtums, den Judenkapitalismus und die asiatische Geldmoral! Zeigt den Mut des stolzen Germanen, indem Ihr Alle, die Ihr unter der skrupellosen Konkurrenz des Judentums und der furchtbaren Geißel des Großkapitals leidet, am 16. Juni für diejenige Partei eintretet, von welcher das fremde Parasitenvolk mit Entschlossenheit und nach Gebühr bekämpft wird.

Christlich-sozial

muß jeder Arbeiter, Bürger und Bauer, jeder Künstler, Litterat und Lehrer, jeder Richter, Offizier, Arzt und Rechtsanwalt, jeder Staatsbeamte und Bedienstete, Kaufmann und Handwerker, jeder Kleriker, Philosoph und Forscher sein, der arischen Blutes ist und der seine Muttersprache und seine Heimat liebt!

Nieder mit allen Schwächlingen und Humanitätsduslern, die dem Freiheitskampf des deutschen Volkes hinter dem Ofen zusehen wollen!!

Nieder mit denjenigen Parteien, welche zur Schutztruppe des Judentums herabgesunken, mit derselben in volksverräterischen Beziehungen stehen oder liebäugeln!!

Nehmt Euch Alle ein Beispiel an dem Heldenmut der Christlich-sozialen Wiens und deren Feldherrn, und sorgt dafür, daß von den Frauentürmen Münchens am 16. Juni das christlich-soziale Banner weht!

Zu den Waffen!

Das Programm
der
Christlich-sozialen Partei

Distortion of the Jewish Image: *Simplicissimus*

The alien "uncanniness" of the Jews in the perception of unsettled, aggressively nationalist Germans was expressed both in fiction and in racist, distorted caricatures.

Thus the image of the bow-legged, hook-nosed, ugly Jew, who pursues money by dirty means ("as one can see from his face") and lies in wait for innocent blond girls, became a stereotype for many Germans, even if, or because, they had never seen such a person.

The deliberate equation of the term "Jew" with something contemptible and unclean stemmed mainly from the projection of the accusers' own negative characteristics onto members of a minority whose helplessness played a greater role than their foreignness.

As in Gustav Freytag's *Soll und Haben* ("Debit and Credit"), 1855, or in Felix Dahn's *Ein Kampf um Rom* ("A Battle for Rome"), 1876, the Jew was contrasted as a negative phenomenon with the honest, noble Teutonic German, who must resist the cunning intrigues of the Jews and who

is guided in business life only by high ideals.

Wilhelm Busch's "good-humored" caricature of Schmulchen Schievelbeiner (see page 236) was the kind of racist distortion which would never have entered the brilliant humorist's head in any of his "ethnic German" stereotypes. Through its broad circulation it influenced the concept of the Jews in the minds of many Germans and was also noted with amusement by many Jewish readers as a caricature of other Jews. In the humorous *Fliegende Blätter* (after 1850) and other papers, stereotypical caricatures of Jews constantly reappeared in similar variations. Presented in a repulsive, contemptuous, and sometimes pornographic way, this kind of racist distortion appeared (after 1896) in *Simplicissimus*, the artistically prestigious satirical weekly, which also carried literary contributions by Thomas Mann, Rainer Maria Rilke, Hermann Hesse, and other writers.

The *Simplicissimus* caricaturists, who were also among its shareholders, took a derogatory view of Munich's bohemian scene; modern painters such as Paul Klee, Franz Marc, Wassily Kandinsky, August Macke and their circle, who also lived and worked in Munich, were the butt of their condescending mockery – a mockery which was reciprocated by the artists, who appreciated their talents as caricaturists, if not their business behavior.

Simplicissimus selected, among others, the Roman Catholic clergy and "the Prussians" as the target of its biting wit, but never in the vulgarly malicious manner that it used toward Jews. The newspaper's great caricaturists treated Jews in their drawings often with no more than the same satirical wit that they applied to other groups. Occasional exceptions to this came from Eduard Thöny and, other than for writers such as Heinrich Heine or victims of the tsarist pogroms, Thomas Theodor Heine (1867–1948). The son of a Jewish father, he seemed to wish to hide his origins by strikingly racist ridicule of Jews.

When in the spring of 1933, *Simplicissimus* immediately toed the line opportunistically, as it had in 1914, T. T. Heine, now suddenly a Jew, was driven out of the editorial office by men who had been his friends for decades, and fled via Prague to Oslo, where he hid for nine months to avoid being murdered, like philosopher and writer Theodor Lessing

(1872–1933), by emissaries of the German government. He later succeeded in escaping to Sweden.

The tasteless Jewish caricatures brought in new subscribers to *Simplicissimus* from various strata of the population. The business policy of the editor, Albert Langen, and those colleagues who were financially involved, played a decisive role in this. Conclusions about its readers can also be drawn from the advertisements which often took up a third of its pages. Besides cameras and bicycles, sexual aids for men were regularly promoted, digestive pills against obesity, erotic books and picture postcards, hair restorers to help grow a dashing Kaiser Wilhelm mustache, and love potions. Full-page announcements were only for champagne. Sexual and business suspicions about Jews, depicted in a repellent way, brought higher profits to the shareholders of *Simplicissimus*.

On the other hand, in the caricatures of Prussian officers (many of whom were subscribers), while the captions were certainly critical and satirical, similar commercial considerations led to the officers themselves, from lieutenant upward, being shown with generally pleasant, distinguished features.

In one caricature the Jewish boss is telling two young female employees: "Vun iss not happy vid your vork," and then continues, the point having been made, in normal speech: "You will probably be dismissed on the first, but you can pick up the final decision from me tonight in my flat." "The Jew" as type, supplied with a repulsive-sounding, invented speech and disgusting appearance, is here exploiting a relationship of economic dependence for sexual purposes. Sexual exploitation of positions of dependence was regularly portrayed by *Simplicissimus*, sometimes with a sly enjoyment, sometimes with satirical criticism. "Aryan" exploiters, on the other hand, were without exception portrayed in such circumstances as distinguished gentlemen from good society.

In 1918, with the end of the Prussian officer caste, the number of subscribers fell from 65,000 to 30,000. *Simplicissimus* decided to recognize the fait accompli as usual and became mildly republican; on top of that, Jewish editorial staff were taken on again.

In April 1933, at a meeting with Julius Streicher, the artist-owners of *Simplicissimus* submitted to the Nazi demand for

Monsieur le directeur: "Vun iss not happy vid your vork. You will probably be dismissed on the first, but you can pick up the final decision from me tonight in my flat." Drawing by Adolf Münzer, *Simplicissimus*, 1899.

Gleideschaltung ("conformity"), thus guaranteeing the further existence of the paper. It became a propaganda sheet for the Third Reich.

The anti-Semitic movement of the last thirty years of the 19th century had largely trickled away in the course of the economic revival, but it remained alive notably in the middle class as well as among officers and civil servants. *Simplicissimus* directed the Jewish caricatures above all at subscribers from these circles. Along with sporadic hate pictures in other papers, they formed the bridge between the theoretical rantings of Treitschke and his ilk and the murderous anti-Semitism of the Nazi *Völkischer Beobachter* and *Stürmer*.

Resistance

Im Deutschen Reich, newspaper of the Central Association of German Citizens of the Jewish Faith.

people. The fact that we Jews are despised, hated and at the least regarded as foreigners and not as equal citizens among broad sections of the public cannot be doubted … Thanks to the continuous interrelations between young people and their teachers, racial hatred will become traditional …; a sum of tension will be built up which can only be discharged upon our heads with elemental force."

The situation of Jewish students at the universities is humiliating, states the Viadrina manifesto: many students conceal their Jewish descent, others even limit their association with their Jewish friends "in order not to attract attention." A small number of student associations … do accept Jews, but then, owing to the whole unhealthy set of circumstances, something

Students' duel between members of two KC societies, Berlin, 1912.

Anti-Semitism had become increasingly implanted in student circles, in dueling societies and fraternities. To the old slogans was now added a new one about the "cowardly" Jewish student. This was first vehemently opposed by the historian Ludwig Quidde in an anonymous paper *Die Antisemitenagitation und die deutsche Studentenschaft* ("Anti-Semitic Agitation and the German Student Body") published in 1881. In 1866 Jewish students at Breslau University founded the first exclusively Jewish student society, "Viadrina" (after the name of Breslau University). Their first manifesto stated: "Anti-Semitism seems to be in its final throes. This movement which for almost a decade has aroused the pas-

sions of the mob to an incredible degree and disseminated a new ferment of hatred, envy, and discontent among the population, has apparently grown weaker and seems at last to be near extinction … that apostle of intolerance [i.e., Stöecker] has stopped preaching racial hatred in 'people's assemblies' to the applause of the populace … If depravity and moral defects of the originators [some anti-Semitic leaders had been condemned to imprisonment or penal servitude for sexual or other offenses] is proof of the badness of the matter … then anti-Semitism should simply belong to the history of human confusion … but it only seems so … The seed came up and struck root in the German

arises which is as undeniable as it is regrettable: the Jewish members themselves, as time passes, oppose the entry of their fellow believers in order not to compromise their society by a surplus of the Jewish element … proof that these elements are ashamed of their Jewishness. That is the basic damage which undermines the vitality of Judaism … The remedy to bring about change … is the foundation of a society of Jewish students which sets up the standard of independent Judaism." These are the kind of statements which a few years later were to be written by the student Theodor Herzl.

Self-confidence, self-assurance, and self-respect were the driving forces and the

Six program points from "Token Jews or Citizens?" by Raphael Löwenfeld, Berlin, 1893.

BELOW LEFT: Title page of the "Report on the first general meeting of the Central Association," Berlin 1893.

BELOW: Moritz Lazarus (1824–1903), founder of comparative psychology, active politician in the struggle against racial anti-Semitism.

Bericht

über die

erste General-Versammlung

des

Centralvereins

deutscher Staatsbürger

jüdischen Glaubens

am 30. December 1893

im Saale der „Gesellschaft der Freunde"

W. Potsdamerstrasse 9.

BERLIN W.

Kronenstrasse 22.

goal of this first Jewish student society. In its second year, training on the fencing floor had already given its members the potential to respond to anti-Semitic provocation with a challenge to a duel, as laid down in the student code of honor.

The accusation of cowardice then turned into its reverse. The Viadrines were declared aggressive ruffians – but the anti-Semitic molestation largely stopped. When it was found that Jewish students were often superior in duels to their Christian opponents, the Jewish student association Viadrina was dissolved by the university authorities in 1894 for no stated reason. But Jewish students immediately founded a successor association in Breslau and also, on 8 August 1896, a "Kartell Convent" (KC), a union of five Jewish student societies which had meanwhile come into being in other universities.

In 1890 a "Society to Resist anti-Semitism" was formed in Berlin by non-Jews. The foundation proclamation was signed by Gustav Freytag, Paul Heyse, Theodor Mommsen, and Hermann Sudermann, among others.

Then, on 26 March 1893, with the participation of many subsequent "KC-ers," the "Central Association of German Citizens of the Jewish Faith" was founded. Its purpose was "to gather together German citizens of the Jewish faith, regardless of religious and political outlook, in order to strengthen them in the active preservation of their civic and social equality and in the unwavering cultivation of German convictions."

The Central Association rejected the idea of a Jewish nation and regarded Judaism exclusively as a religious community. It saw its chief task in opposing anti-semitism along the lines of Gabriel Riesser (see page 200). Foreign Jews were regarded as their fellows in religion and descent, but, as foreigners, could not become members. The healing of the pathological hatred of Jews was to be achieved by systematic enlightenment. So the proud declaration of the Viadrina in 1866 was diluted into an apologetic defensive declaration.

Participation in the Economy

ABOVE: Advertisement for Manoli cigarettes.

In the last quarter of the 19th century, economic development in Imperial Germany progressed rapidly, intensively, and sometimes with volcanic force.

With the rising living standards, the consumers' desire also grew, both for more and for new goods. Until about the middle of the century, demand was still covered exclusively by small shops, but with the economic structural change came a new, competitive form of commerce: the department store.

The concept of the department store had originally been developed by non-Jews in France and the United States. In Germany, Jews were the first to set their spirit of enterprise to work in this area. Among them, the Tietz, Israel, Wertheim and Gerson families were the most successful.

The brothers Hermann (1837–1907) and Oscar (1858–1932) Tietz, who from

Advertisements by Jewish firms, about 1900.

ABOVE LEFT: Stationery shop, A. Liebmann, Berlin: The Crown Prince and his secretary after a shopping trip.

ABOVE: Dolls and dolls' heads by the firm of Hermann Landshut & Co., Waltershausen in Thuringia, 1904.

LEFT: Electric delivery van from the Gerson department store, Berlin.

Market place in Neumark (West Prussia) with the Jewish shops of S. H. Landshut, Israel, and Cohn. A market day in 1916.

BELOW: A. Wertheim department store, Berlin, large light well.

1882 owned a drapery business in Gera in Thuringia, had gathered experience in New York and Paris. Equipped with family capital, they opened a store in 1895 in Munich, followed by others in Cologne and Berlin.

It was also Jews in particular who moved from hand-sewing to the machine manufacture of ready-made clothing. This area called for completely new methods, from the work of the fabric pattern artists and fashion designers, through the manufacture of the materials, to marketing and sales. This was the basis of the new women's ready-made clothing sector, in which Germany soon ruled the world market. Hausvogtei Square in Berlin became the center of this new sector, which employed many thousands of people. At the same time, the ready-made clothing manufacturer became the despised stereotype of the half-educated nouveau riche among the non-Jewish and even in the Jewish upper class.

It was again Jewish ready-made clothing merchants who, with their newly acquired capital, ventured into risky territory: the cinema – and later on film production in Germany and Hollywood, which was co-founded by Carl Laemmle (1867–1939) from Laupheim.

The Beginnings of Agricultural and Craft Training

In 1909 the Simon Foundation started a teaching farm for Jewish farm workers in Steinhorst near Celle.

BELOW: View of the Ahlem horticultural school near Hanover, a charitable Jewish foundation, 1896.

The great majority of the people of Palestine had been agriculturalists and livestock farmers from biblical times. Even today a number of religious festivals go back to agricultural festivals in ancient Palestine or are connected with them. The Hebrew word "mikneh," property, also means herd; trade was originally regarded as having a lower status than agriculture, stock-breeding, and crafts.

However, the ordinances of the church, based on religious policy, excluded the Jews in the Diaspora from agriculture, stock breeding, and crafts, and forced them into money dealing (see page 40). In the early days of their settlement in Germany there were Jewish farmers and vintners even under the tolerant Carolingians and Ottonians. This era ended with the Crusades. Only during the fight for emancipation did Jews again make individual attempts to find a footing in agriculture. For instance, the Jacobson School in Seesen (see page 135) trained farmers, as did the Israelite Horticultural College of Ahlem, founded near Hanover. But owing to the structure of the German village, any integration into the farming village community was out of the question. In 1819 Ernst Philip Sensburg, a reactionary in political and Jewish affairs who after his baptism rose to become a baron and Minister for the Interior in Baden, was still glossing over anti-Jewish risings by pointing out that the public was indignant at the Jewish desire to be admitted to agriculture and handicraft. Yet in Bavaria, Baden, and Württemberg, Jewish villagers succeeded in attaching strips of arable land to their houses and gardens, on which they could practice agriculture. Since the beginning of the 20th century there had also been a few Jewish estate owners with whom Jews could find opportunities for training and work.

ABOVE RIGHT: Fruit plantation in Ahlem, 1901.

Carpentry workshop in Ahlem, 1910.

In Large-Scale Industry

LEFT: Wilhelm Herz (1823–1914), industrialist, first President of the Berlin Chamber of Commerce and member of the Board of the Jewish Community.

BELOW: Hirsch brass and copper works, founded in Halberstadt in 1820 by Aron Hirsch (1783–1842).

Numerous Jewish industrialists helped to build up the German economy, especially after the foundation of the German Empire.

The Hirsch copper works in Halberstadt, founded in 1820 by the metal merchant Aron Hirsch, were expanded by his sons to become the most important copper and brass works in Europe. The works were still owned by the Orthodox family until 1933.

In the basic materials industry Fritz von Friedländer-Fuld (1858–1917) was outstanding, with his Silesian enterprises which were nicknamed "Oberkoks" and comprised a group of major firms. Friedländer-Fuld was responsible for building up the coke industry in Germany, having recognized the necessity for international involvement at an early stage.

Closely linked with the coke industry was the petroleum industry, led by general director M. Melamid (born 1883), whose process for the conversion of oils for technical purposes was named after him.

The founder of the Silesian iron industry (Caro-Hegenscheidt) was Georg von Caro (1849–1913). His brother Oskar Caro (died 1931) is regarded as the founder of the German enamel industry (see also page 227). Moritz van der Porten headed the Vereinigte Aluminiumwerke, which spearheaded the aluminum sector in Germany. In the eighties Carl Reichstein built a bicycle factory in Brandenburg an der Havel, which soon became the leading enterprise in the sector.

The combination of trade and production played a major role in Ludwig Loewe und Co. A.G., a company for electrical enterprises (from 1869), managed by Ludwig Loewe (see page 242). Besides machines, the firm mainly produced weapons. Through Loewe's brother Isidor (1848–1910) and jointly with the firm of Mauser, an order of unprecedented magnitude was obtained for equipping the Turkish army.

Many Jewish industrialists rose to high office, received honors, and were ennobled. At the court of Kaiser Wilhelm II some of them were esteemed for more than their

advisory positions. Among the "Kaiser Jews" were the shipowner Albert Ballin, the Hamburg banker Max M. Warburg, and Emil Rathenau, founder of AEG, in which other prominent Jews held leading positions. In 1880 Rathenau had installed the first telephone in Berlin. AEG (Allgemeine Elektricitäts-Gesellschaft) rose to be, with the Siemens works, the largest electricity company in Germany. Rathenau's son Walther (1867–1922) became president of AEG and played a decisive part in the expansion of the firm, but is remembered above all for his political activity. In 1922, after holding office briefly as Foreign Minister, he was murdered on political and racist grounds (see also page 326 f.)

Philipp Rosenthal (1855–1937), founder of the world-famous porcelain factory in Selb in Bavaria, was also responsible for the reorganization of the Leipzig Fair in the years following the end of the First World War. He was known as the second founder of the Fair.

ABOVE: Test run of an electric train on the AEG factory grounds, c. 1885.

ABOVE LEFT: Emil Rathenau (left) and Thomas Alva Edison in the AEG electricity works, 1911.

Oberspree central transmission center near Berlin with the AEG cable works.

Albert Ballin

Albert Ballin and Kaiser Wilhelm II during the Kiel regatta week, 1913.

BELOW: Emigrants on HAPAG steamer. Photograph Joseph Byron, about 1908.

Albert Ballin (1857–1918) played an outstanding part in building up the German merchant fleet. Even as a young man he was far-seeing and a knowledgeable director of the passenger branch of the Hamburg-America Line (HAPAG). He also built up HAPAG's freight traffic; in 1899 he became its general director. Under his guidance HAPAG developed into Europe's leading shipping company.

The Kaiser saw Ballin as the potential founder of German world power at sea, and he became a frequent guest and confidant of the Kaiser, who also entrusted him with political missions because of his international connections. Even just before the outbreak of World War I, which Ballin tried to stop, he was sent to England for confidential talks. When he openly warned the Kaiser against unleashing a submarine war, he fell into disfavor. On the day after

the Kaiser's flight to Holland on 10 November 1918, Ballin committed suicide. He was unable to cope with the collapse of Imperial Germany and also, no doubt, with the undignified flight of his beloved Kaiser.

Albert Ballin was a practicing Jew. In contrast to many academics and scholars, whose advancement in their professions was generally made dependent on baptism even after 1868/71, the majority of merchants, artists, actors, doctors, bankers, and lawyers remained true to the Jewish faith. They could make their careers without baptism, which Heine, as we know, called the "entrance ticket to European culture."

RIGHT: HAPAG advertisement for passages in the Imperator, the largest passenger liner in the world. *From Ost und West*, 1913.

Bankers

Banker Carl Fürstenberg (1850–1933), financier of heavy industry.

Banker Max M. Warburg (1867–1946), Hamburg.

Gerson von Bleichröder (1822–1893), adviser to Bismarck, court banker to Kaiser Wilhelm I.

Since Jews began to settle in Germany they played a sometimes small, sometimes outstanding role in the circulation of goods and money.

In the 18th century the position of court factor developed; he served the prince as supplier, financier, and mint lessee (see page 106); in the 19th century the free enterprise banker developed from this. Experience, talent and also family and business connections in many countries contributed to the fact that a large number of Jews rose to leading positions in the finance system.

This explains the fact that the number of Jews in the banks growing up in the second half of the 19th century in Europe and North America was extraordinarily high. The best-known Jewish bankers in Germany came from the families of Oppenheim, Bleichröder, Wertheim, Heine, Mendelssohn, Arnhold, von Hirsch, Fürstenberg, Rothschild, and Warburg, of whom in fact only one converted to Christianity.

Gerson von Bleichröder (1822–1893) is a typical example of the history of the rise of a small banker to become an international financier in the middle of the 19th century.

He was financial adviser and confidant to Bismarck. The closeness of the link between the Prussian statesman and the Jewish banker emerges from many letters exchanged by the two. They bear witness to almost daily contact spanning the period from Prussia's battle for pre-eminence in Germany to the new German Empire. But in countless works on Bismarck, Bleichröder's contribution is mentioned either marginally or not at all. His financial abilities and his advice were used by Bismarck and his circle, but they preferred not to acknowledge the link openly. Later generations also quickly forgot Bleichröder. This was thanks mainly to Bismarck himself, who mentions the name Bleichröder only once in his memoirs, although he never took a step without his banker in the administration of his fortune, and

asked for his advice even in the financing of the war and the budget.

Even when in 1871 there were discussions on the amount and methods of payment of French war reparations, Bleichröder was called in. The payments were made through the Rothschild Bank in Paris and the bank of S. Bleichröder in Berlin.

Bleichröder was ennobled without having to be baptized. His city mansion was often the venue for brilliant festivities to which anyone of rank and name was invited. Yet this did not mean that Bleichröder was accepted in "society," for whom, as a Jew, he was not of equal birth. Nevertheless, Bleichröder remained a Jew; he repaid humiliations with contempt for the hypocrisy of the nobility. Bleichröder too became the target of anti-Semitic attacks, so that his last years were overshadowed by disillusionment and bitterness.

Even Jews in the highest positions were not socially acknowledged. The example of Gerson von Bleichröder demonstrates with particular force that the concept of

Advertisement for the Mendelssohn & Co. banking house, Berlin.

the emancipation of the Jews, even when assimilation had gone so far, brought no solution to the Jewish question in Germany. "We may be the salt in the soup of nations," a witty representative of Zionist thinking in Germany was to comment later, "but to the nations that soup often tastes too salty."

"'Pon my honor, I'm sorry your Papa was not admitted to the Nobles' Club. Well, it's not so bad, he sees the whole membership at his home every evening." Mockery of the Berlin Nobles' Club which, though unable to admit "Papa," were delighted to be invited to dinner (or endured) by him. Drawing by Eduard Thöny, *Simplicissimus*, 1905.

271

Ullstein, Mosse, Reuter

bought the insolvent *Berliner Zeitung*, thus laying the foundations of the Ullstein empire: in 1887 he founded the *Berliner Abendpost*, for which he introduced the cheap weekly subscription (10 pfennigs per week), thanks to which the circulation soon rose to 200,000; in 1894 the *Berliner Illustrirte Zeitung* appeared and in 1914 he acquired the famous *Vossische Zeitung*. 1907 saw the foundation of a book publishing house, which with its novels and multivolume illustrated series opened up new paths of visual presentation. Five of his sons worked on this expansion. All the Ullsteins were democratic in outlook and acknowledged no Jewish problem. They left Judaism or were baptized.

The second authoritative Jewish newspaper publisher was Rudolf Mosse (1843–1920), a doctor's son. From 1867 with his friend Emil Cohn he built up an advertising bureau which soon overtook the former leaders, the English advertising agencies, and had 275 branches worldwide.

In 1872 Rudolf Mosse founded the independently minded *Berliner Tageblatt*, which under the editorship of his nephew Theodor Wolff (1868–1943) became the "German world newspaper." Mosse also published the *Berliner Volkszeitung*, the *8-Uhr-Abendblatt*, and the *Berliner Morgenzeitung*. The house also published directories, telephone books, popular scientific works, and books in Esperanto and Russian. Rudolf Mosse was a member of the board of the Reform community. He acquired Ludwig Phillipson's *Allgemeine Zeitung des Judentums* and later continued to publish it as *C. V. Zeitung*.

Mosse's son-in-law Hans Lachmann-Mosse (1885–1944) joined the business in 1910 and expanded it. He gave the young architect Erich Mendelsohn his first big commission: modernization of the original building on Jerusalemer Strasse. In 1933 the Mosse publishing firm was expropriated by the National Socialists.

The telegraph agencies were the papers' chief source of news outside the local area. The most important international telegraph agency was founded by Paul Julius

ABOVE LEFT: Rudolf Mosse (1843–1920). Painting by Karl Stauffer-Bern, 1882.

ABOVE RIGHT: Advertisement for the *Berliner Tageblatt*, 1904.

ABOVE CENTER: Rudolf Mosse publishing and printing building, Berlin, c. 1910.

The rapid growth of trade, industry, and traffic resulted in an increased need for means of communication.

Leopold Ullstein (1826–1899), son of a Fürth paper manufacturer, recognized the signs of the times early and founded a newspaper in 1867. Ten years later he

Reuter in 1851 in London, in competition with the French Havas agency. Reuter, born Israel Beer Josaphat in Kassel in 1816, died in Nice in 1899. Temporarily employed by Havas, Reuter started his own agency by sending carrier pigeons from Paris to Brussels and Aachen for news. In 1865, on his initiative and with his financial participation, jointly with the Anglo-American Telegraph Company, the first telegraph cable was laid between the continent of Europe and America.

A neutral agency in his lifetime, "Reuter's" later developed into the propaganda instrument of the British government. In the Franco-Prussian War of 1870/71, however, Reuter influenced world opinion in favor of Prussia. For this he was ennobled in 1871 by the Duke of Saxe-Coburg-Gotha and called himself Baron de Reuter from then on. Reuter did not like remembering his origins, which he regarded as an embarrassing accident.

Besides the *Vossische Zeitung* (Ullstein) and the *Berliner Tageblatt* (Mosse), the third (out of eight or ten influential daily papers in Germany) in Jewish ownership was the respected liberal *Frankfurter Zeitung*, founded in 1856 by Leopold Sonnemann (see page 240).

LEFT: Advertisement for the *Berliner Illustrirte Zeitung.*

RIGHT: Israel Beer Josaphat, after baptism Paul Julius Reuter (1816–1899). Caricature in *Vanity Fair*, London, 1896.

B. Z. zam Mittag (from 1904) and *Berliner Morgenpost* (from 1898) advertising posters.

Inventors

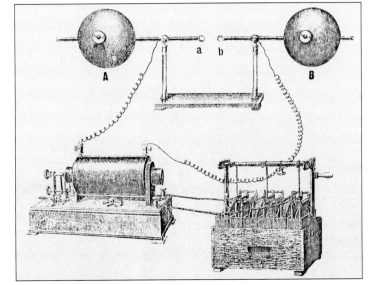

LEFT: Physicist Heinrich Hertz (1857–1894), discoverer of radio waves. The physical unit of frequency is named after him.

RIGHT: Hertz's experimental apparatus, with which in 1886 he proved the existence of long-wave electromagnetic waves (radio waves).

BELOW: Motor car by Siegfried Marcus, 1875.

Soon after the emancipation, Jews in all spheres of life had found opportunities for development, in line with their numbers in the population.

As well as successful leading personalities in industry, we also find German Jews among the inventors. Siegfried Marcus (1831–1898) was one of the pioneers of the motor car. People still marvel at his 1875 automobile in Vienna's Technical Museum. No less important was David Schwarz (1845–1897) with his invention of the rigid airship, which flew for the first time in 1897 in Berlin; after his death Graf Zeppelin acquired his patent.

Particularly numerous are the inventions by German Jews in communications technology. The production of the electric wave, the basis of wireless telegraphy, began with Heinrich Hertz (1857–1894).

Georg Wilhelm A. Graf Arco (1869–1940), whose mother was Jewish, also took part in the development of wireless telegraphy. From 1903 to 1931 he was a leader in the industry, as director of the Gesellschaft für drahtlose Telegraphie mbH System Telefunken in Berlin.

Innovations in news transmission were promoted by Arthur Korn (1870–1945), who taught at the universities in Munich and Berlin (only until 1935). His chief works, *Elektrische Fernphotographie* ("Electrical Telephotography"), 1904, and *Bildtelegraphie* ("Picture Telegraphy"), 1923, were significant steps in the invention of the wireless transmission of pictures. In aircraft design the outstanding figure was the engineer Edmund Rumpler (1872–1940), designer of the Rumpler Dove (1910), the most important German aircraft in World War I.

In science and education a major role

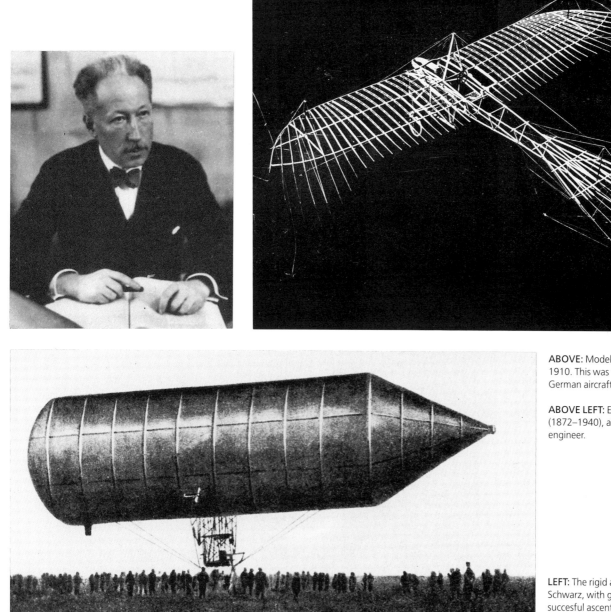

ABOVE: Model of the Rumpler Dove, 1910. This was the most important German aircraft in World War I.

ABOVE LEFT: Edmund Rumpler (1872–1940), aircraft builder and engineer.

LEFT: The rigid airship invented by David Schwarz, with gasoline engine, before the succesful ascent from Tempelhof Field, Berlin, 3 November 1897.

was played by electrical engineer Reinhold Rüdenberg (1883–1961), whose books *Kommutation in Gleichstrom-Dynamomaschinen* ("Commutation in Direct-Current Dynamos") in 1907, and *Elektrische Schaltvorgänge* ("Electrical Switch Processes") in 1923, were basic textbooks. Among other things, he was the inventor of the electron microscope.

Electrical engineer and industrialist Emil Berliner (1851–1929) was educated at the famous Samson School in Wolfenbüttel. In 1870 he moved to the United States, where he invented the gramophone, gramophone record, and microphone. Among the promoters of the Deutsche Grammophon-Gesellschaft, started by his brother Joseph in Hanover, he also achieved importance in quite different fields, such as the sterilization of milk. One of the most important inventors of his day, he died in Washington in 1929.

Benno Strauss (1873–1944) should be mentioned in another technological context. Made a professor in 1912, and from 1921 to 1934 one of the directors of Krupp AG, he played a decisive part in the development of stainless steel.

Explorers

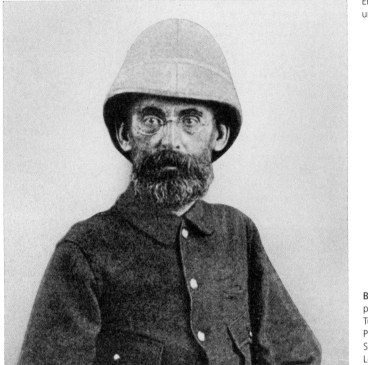

Emin Pasha in German uniform, 1891.

BELOW: Emin Pasha prevents a revolt in the Turkish Equatorial Province (Egyptian Sudan). Illustrated London News, 1888.

The most important of the early Jewish explorers was Benjamin of Tudela, who traveled from Spain in the 12th century through Mediterranean countries, north and north-west Africa, the Near East and India, and left detailed reports of Jewish communities there.

Around 1700, Dr. Tobia Kohen from Metz (1653–1729) traveled through China; in 1865 Heinrich A. Bernstein (1828–1865) from Breslau explored New Guinea and the Moluccas, where he died.

Heidelberg polar explorer Emil Bessels (1847–1888) was a member of the failed North Pole expedition led by the American Charles Francis Hall, who in 1871 attempted to reach the Pole from northern Greenland.

Eduard Schnitzer (1840–1892) worked as a doctor first for the Turks, then for the Egyptians, and in 1878 became governor of the Equatorial Province. After his conversion to Islam he called himself Mehmed Emin Pasha, defeated the rebellious Mahdists at Dufili in 1878, and explored large areas of Uganda and Arabia. Wherever he could, he opposed the slave trade. When nothing had been heard of Emin Pasha for some time, the British-American journalist H. M. Stanley equipped a rescue expedition, whose adventures he described in newspaper reports and in his book *In Darkest Africa*, 1890.

In 1890 Emin Pasha entered the German service, commissioned to explore the East African lakes and to found a German colony there. Kaiser Wilhelm II called him a "great son of his people." In 1892 Emin Pasha was murdered in Kanema (Congo) by slave-traders.

A pioneer of modern anthropology was Franz Boas (1858–1942). As a professor at New York's Columbia University he studied the Indian tribes of North America on his travels and published vital discoveries on the influence of the environment on physical development – a scientific refutation of racial theories.

In four expeditions to southern Arabia, Eduard Glaser (1855–1908) uncovered the ancient kingdoms of the Sabaeans, Minaeans, and Qatabani.

RIGHT: Sana in Yemen, photograph by explorer Hermann Burchardt, 1904.

The prehistorian and ethnologist Baron Max von Oppenheim (1860–1946), founder of the German Orient Institute, became famous through his discovery of the ruins of Tell Halaf in Syria.

The geographer and alpinist Gottfried Merzbacher (1843–1926) from Baiersdorf explored areas in the Caucasus, Arabia, Persia, India, and the Tien Shan mountains, where one range bears his name.

Hermann Burchardt, a Berliner (1859–1909), made expeditions to northeast Africa, the Near East, and Central Asia, collecting popular legends and photographing monuments and the everyday life of Islamic peoples. His photographs are of documentary value to historical research today. Burchardt was murdered in 1909 on an expedition in the Yemen.

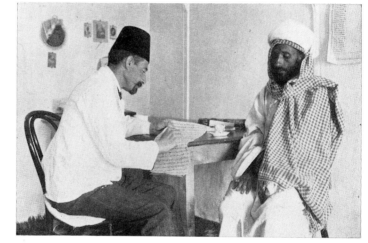

RIGHT: Hermann Burchardt with his Arab guide in Sana, 1904. Photograph Hermann Burchardt.

BELOW: Yemeni Jews on a visit to the synagogue. Photographed by Hermann Burchardt, 1905.

In Science

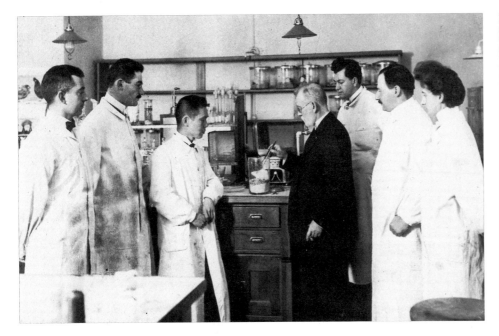

ABOVE: Chemist and bacteriologist Paul Ehrlich (1854–1915) in his laboratory in Frankfurt am Main, c. 1914.

ABOVE RIGHT: Anatomist Jacob Henle (1809–1885), Robert Koch's teacher.

LEFT: Chemist and Nobel Prize winner Otto Wallach (1847–1931).

RIGHT: Chemist and Nobel prize winner Fritz Heber (1868–1934) in front of the design sketch of a firedamp pipe.

LEFT: Title page of "The Foundation of the General Theory of Relativity" by Albert Einstein, Leipzig, 1916.

RIGHT: Albert Einstein, c. 1925.

BELOW: Nikodem Caro (1871–1935) developed a process for the manufacture of calcium cyanide in collaboration with Adolf Frank.

The rise of Jews in all areas of science began as soon as the opportunity arose in the second half of the 19th century. A centuries-old injunction to learn, and the abstract thought practiced through many generations, may have been factors which equipped Jews for special achievement in worldly knowledge as well.

Four men will be listed here to represent all the many important German-Jewish scientists.

The chemist and bacteriologist Paul Ehrlich (1854–1915) was equally important as a researcher and as a scientific innovator. Together with Weigert, he found a method of dyeing blood cells which is still used in blood tests to determine whether and which cells in the blood are diseased. Hematology, the science of the composition of the blood, is based on these research results. Ehrlich's patience in his experiments over many years was expressed by his colleagues in the research institute in the joking phrase "Ehrlich dyes last longest."

With the help of two other researchers he initiated treatment with chemical remedies: chemotherapy – and hence modern pharmaceutics. He discovered Salvarsan, the first effective remedy for syphilis. In 1908 Paul Ehrlich received the Nobel Prize for Medicine. In 1905 he joined the honorary committee for a future Hebrew university planned in Jerusalem.

Albert Einstein (1879–1955) was the author of the theory of relativity, the foundation of the whole of modern physics. Youthful experiences made Einstein a pacifist; anti-Semitic harassment at school in Munich made him a convinced Jew; historical considerations led to his stance as a Zionist. A friend and supporter of Jewish Palestine, he nevertheless refused to be considered for the presidency (of Israel) after Weizmann's death.

Nikodem Caro (1871–1935) developed with Adolf Frank in 1899 an industrial process for the manufacture of calcium cyanide (Frank-Caro process). Caro became the head of the Bavarian Nitrogen Works in Trostberg, but emigrated to Switzerland in 1933.

The chemist Fritz Haber (1868–1934) converted to Protestantism as a student under the influence of Theodor Mommsen (see page 254). In 1911 Haber was appointed to the Kaiser Wilhelm Institute for Physical Chemistry in Berlin-Dahlem, which under his direction became the most important research institute in this field. His method, developed with Carl Bosch, for the synthetic manufacture of ammonia made Germany independent of the import of artificial fertilizers in World War I. Haber received the Nobel Prize for Chemistry in 1918.

Being "descended from Jewish parents and grandparents" he applied for retirement in 1933. He recommended all his Jewish colleagues to emigrate, and left Germany after finding them posts at foreign universities. Emancipation and assimilation, he stated, had been useful to Germany, but weakened the Jews. Despite his indestructible love of German culture, he accepted the consequences of emigration.

In the Humanities

Many, many German-Jewish scholars excelled in the humanities.

Hermann Cohen (1842–1918) was the decisive transformer of Kant's philosophy, the founder of neo-Kantianism, or the "Marburg School," called after the university city where he worked (1873–1912). He was one of the very few German academics to become a professor before 1918, and this despite the fact that he was emphatically Jewish in character. In his last years he lectured in Berlin at the liberal College for the Science of Judaism on general and Jewish philosophy.

For Cohen the Jewish nation was the earthly representative of monotheism, but needed no special nation state in the Zionist sense. Cohen's most important pupil was Ernst Cassirer (1874–1945), a professor at Hamburg from 1919 to 1933, then in Oxford (1933–1935), in Göteborg, Sweden (1935–1941) and finally in the United States – in Yale (1941–1944) and Columbia (1944–1945).

Edmund Husserl (1859–1938), born a Jew, baptized at 27, was a professor at Göttingen and Freiburg. His pupil and successor Martin Heidegger, initially a member of Hitler's party, became rector at Freiburg on 27 May 1933. The dedication of his principal work *Sein und Zeit* ("Being and Time"), 1927, to Husserl was omitted from the fifth edition onward (1941). Husserl saw in his phenomenology, the doctrine of phenomena, the logical foundation for "philosophy as a strict science." This is based on his *Logische Untersuchungen* ("Logical Investigations"), 1900–1901.

The philosopher of religion Julius Guttmann (1880–1950), a stern critic of Heidegger, was a supporter of neo-Kantianism.

Moritz Lazarus (1824–1903) played a decisive part in the development of psychology, introducing the concept of *Völkerpsychologie* ("folk," or comparative, psychology). Together with his brother-in-law Heymann Steinthal (1823–1899), he published the *Zeitschrift für Völkerpsychologie und Sprachwissenschaft* ("Journal of Comparative Psychology and Linguistics") from 1859 to 1890. In his

great three-volume work *Das Leben der Seele* ("The Life of the Spirit"), Lazarus interpreted cultural phenomena from the psychological aspect.

Lazarus was an influential personality in the Jewish spiritual life of his time and was among the founders of the College for the Science of Judaism, whose piety vis-à-vis the Jewish tradition, coupled with liberalism vis-à-vis orthodoxy, he represented. He regarded it as his life's work to promote "the intimate fusion of the German and Jewish spirit." In 1864 he was dean, and then rector of Bern University. But since he wanted to live in Germany "as a German citizen," he returned to Berlin, where he was never offered a full professorship. His principal work is *Die Ethik des Judentums* ("The Ethics of Judaism"), 1898.

Heymann Steinthal (1823–1899), Lazarus's collaborator on the *Zeitschrift für Völkerpsychologie und Sprachwissenschaft*, was professor of linguistics at the University of Berlin. His book *Der Ursprung der Sprache* ("The Origin of Language"), 1851, was regarded as the standard work of linguistics. Other books were concerned with biblical scholarship and with the religious Judaic world of ideas. At the Institute for the Science of Judaism he held the chair of biblical scholarship and religious philosophy.

Moritz Steinschneider (1816–1907) was the 19th-century authority on the bibliography of Jewish literature and culture of the Middle Ages and the modern age. Born in Moravia, he was forbidden by the Aus-

trian Jewish laws to attend the Oriental Institute in Vienna. Moving for this reason to Berlin in 1885, he was recognized as the "father of Jewish bibliography." Among other things, he edited the catalogue of Hebraic manuscripts of the libraries in Leiden, Munich, Hamburg, and Berlin, and documented the part played by Jews in the development of the secular sciences (mathematics, natural science, philology, philosophy) and the general culture of the Middle Ages. These facts, which had been forgotten over the centuries, demonstrated the continuity of Jewish research in the secular field.

The philosopher and sociologist Georg Simmel (1858–1918), whose parents were already baptized, became an independent lecturer in Berlin in 1885. Highly respected as he was, it was fifteen years before he gained a professorship. When he was proposed for a chair in 1908 by Max Weber and Eberhard Gothein in Heidelberg, a pupil of Treitschke wrote in an assessment neighbour what is hateful to you. That is the substance of the teaching. Everything else is commentary. Go and learn." Up to the present day Jewish writings have been based on commentaries on the Pentateuch. order to be appointed to the chair of jurisprudence at a German university. Among them were Georg Jellinek (1851–1911) (general political science); Heinrich von Friedberg (1835–1895) (imperial and

Indian scholar Theodor Benfey (1809–1881), translator of the Vedas, pioneer of fairy-tale research.

Philosopher Edmund Husserl (1859–1938), founder of phenomenology.

Bibliographer Moritz Steinschneider (1816–1907).

Philosopher and sociologist Georg Simmel (1858–1918).

for Baden's Minister of Education: "He [Simmel] is … an Israelite through and through, in his external appearance, in his manner, and in his cast of mind." Simmel was not given the chair. In 1914, aged 56, he was finally appointed professor in Strasbourg, a demotion to the provinces. The academic teacher was often credited with positively magnetic power of attraction, and with his books, including *Einleitung in die Moralwissenschaft* ("Introduction to Moral Science"), 1892–93, *Philosophie des Geldes* ("Philosophy of Money"), 1900, *Soziologie* ("Sociology"), 1908, *Goethe*, 1913, and *Rembrandt*, 1916, he stands even today as an important philosopher and writer, one of the fathers of German sociology.

Simmel wrote the volume on religion for Martin Buber's collection of monographs entitled *Die Gesellschaft* ("Society"). The living spiritual power of religion he calls religiosity: "Until now religiosity has always survived religions, as the tree survives the repeated plucking of its fruit."

The disproportionately large number of lawyers of Jewish origin is sometimes attributed to the scholarly tradition of Judaism. For instance, the saying is quoted from Hillel the Elder (c. 30 BC–10 AD), the most respected scholar in the period of the Second Temple: "Do not do to your

Literary and legal commentary was the most particular field of the Jewish scholar. Nevertheless especially large numbers of Jews in jurisprudence were baptized in

Philosopher Hermann Cohen (1842–1912) in his circle of pupils, Marburg University. Drawing by Leonid Pasternak.

military penal code, Prussian Minister of Justice); his nephew Emil Friedberg (1837–1910) (ecclesiastical law); Edgar Loening (1843–1919) (administrative law); Eduard Rosenthal (1853–1926) (constitutional law); and Paul Laband (1838–1918), who wrote the fundamental legal work of Imperial Germany, *Das deutsche Staatsrecht* ("German Constitutional Law").

Hermann Staub (1856–1904), the author of important commentaries on commercial law, remained true to his Judaism and was therefore not awarded a chair; neither was Philipp Lotmar (1850–1922), whose major work *Der Arbeitsvertrag* ("The Labor Contract") became the basis of German labor law. Lotmar went to Switzerland, where he received a chair in Bern. In 1862 Hermann Makower (1830–1897), a judge in Berlin from 1856 to 1866 and chairman of the Berlin Jewish congregation from 1870, wrote the commentary on the general German commercial code. Though he was the first Jew to belong to the academic examining committee for jurists from 1876, he never obtained a professorship.

In Music

RIGHT: Louis
Lewandowski
(1821–1894),
choirmaster and
composer, reviver of
synagogue music.

Joseph Joachim, one of
the greatest classical
violin virtuosi, c. 1890.
Photograph by
D. Downey.

LEFT: Otto von Bismarck
and Pauline Lucca, 1864.
From 1861 Pauline Lucca
worked at the Royal
Opera in Berlin and was a
celebrated singer of her
day (photo Studio Adèle,
Bad Ischl).

Music as the expression of religious and spiritual feeling has played a significant role in the liturgy and folk life of the Jewish people. In Eastern Europe this found expression in countless folk songs, and the "klezmorim" (see page 218) also remained an integral part of Jewish folk life there.

One of the best-known of the Russian klezmorim, Michael Josef Guzikov, gave concerts in Kiev, Odessa, Vienna, and Leipzig. Felix Mendelssohn reported to his mother in 1836 on one such performance: "He really is a phenomenon ... equal to any virtuoso in the whole world. ... It is a long time since I have taken such pleasure in a concert, for the man is a genius."

While klezmorim continued to play a role in folk life in Eastern Europe, they slowly disappeared in Germany as a result of emancipation and the associated assimilation. One of the last groups was the Hertz Quartet, which was still known and loved in and around Darmstadt in the middle of the 19th century.

The composer and conductor Gustav Mahler (1860–1911) came from Bohemia, where the klezmorim tradition was still alive in his childhood and youth. His world fame was based in Austria and Germany. He was, wrote Oswald Jonas, "the composer between yesterday and tomorrow ... perfect interpreter, faithful to the style of all operas and symphonies from Gluck to Richard Strauss. ... His compositions are the creative Stations of the Cross of a mind and heart shaken in the heritage of the millennia, of this soul so profoundly Jewish in its emotions."

Louis Lewandowski remained the most important composer of synagogue music, still influential in Western Europe and America (see page 218). In 1871 he published in *Kol rinna utefilla* ("Voice of

Rejoicing and Prayer") a collection of songs for cantor and choir from old motifs. His setting of the hymn *Lecho Dodi* ("Go, my Friend") by Salomo Halevi (c.1540) is still sung on Friday evening

LEFT: Children's symphony at the house of the painter Sophie Koner (front right), wife of portrait painter Max Koner. In the middle of the group, heads bent over the music, the Wolffenstein sisters; between them the son of Prof. Klemperer, their neighbor: Otto Klemperer, aged 11. Photograph c. 1910.

ABOVE RIGHT:
Composer and conductor Gustav Mahler (1860–1911).

Mahler as conductor of the Vienna Opera, 1897. Silhouettes by Otto Böhler.

throughout the Western world in the family circle, when the candles are lit to greet the Sabbath.

As well as Hermann Levi (see also page 221), Leo Blech (1871–1958) was of particular importance among Jewish conductors of this period. Being baptized, he was appointed in 1906 to the Royal Opera House in Berlin; in 1913 he received the title of general musical director. Both under the kaiser and in the Weimar Republic Leo Blech was Berlin's authority on operatic policy.

Bronislaw Huberman, then 10 years old, a pupil of Joseph Joachim, became famous in 1902 when he "fiddled down" the great singer Adelina Patti at a concert. Lauded by her and by Brahms, he began his rise as a violin prodigy.

Among singers of Jewish descent the soprano Pauline Lucca (1841–1908) – especially in her star role, Carmen – and baritone Friedrich Schorr (1888–1953) from Nagyvárad in Hungary, became world-famous. Schorr sang Wagner in Berlin, Prague, New York, and Bayreuth, where he became a celebrated Wotan.

The New Theater

The revival of the theater at the turn of the century was not concerned with set, "theatrical" gestures, but with the natural behavior of present-day people, the expression of inner tension in the melody of speech. Above all, producers of Jewish descent such as Otto Brahm and Max Reinhardt assisted the breakthrough of this new stage art, the necessary preliminary to Ibsen's and Hauptmann's naturalist theater.

Otto Brahm (1856–1912) began as a theater critic and then became a producer and theater director. From 1889, as head of the *Freie Volksbühne*, he staged works by the then unknown naturalist writers such as Strindberg, Hauptmann and Ibsen. From 1894 to 1912, subject to the hostility of the kaiser and the "ruling class," he directed the *Lessing Theater* in the same spirit. Bassermann, Triesch, his later opposite number Max Reinhardt, and many other great actors emerged from Brahm's school of naturalism, which became the leading school for German dramaturgy and theatrical art of the period.

Ludwig Barnay (1842–1924), born in Hungary, became a main prop of the famous "Meininger Truppe," regarded before the period of naturalism as *the* German theater company, even in Berlin, London and St Petersburg. The coopera-

tive of German theater members came into being on his initiative. In 1888 he founded the Berlin Theater. From 1906 he directed the Royal Theater in Berlin and from 1908 to 1912 the Court Theater in Hanover, which he turned into centers of the "Court Theater style."

Max Reinhardt (1873–1943) was "the magician of the German theater, who brought appearance and reality to the stage in magical representations, transformations, and marriages of gestures, words, music, and scenery," a master of musically moved crowd scenes. His classical productions were regarded as tours de force. Many critics called the *Reinhardt Theater*

RIGHT: Fritzi Massary (1882–1969), the great soubrette of the German operetta stage, with Joseph Gianpietro.

LEFT: Ludwig Barnay as Mark Anthony in Shakespeare's *Julius Caesar*, 1909, at the Berliner Theater.

a box of tricks, but acknowledged its enchantment (see also page 386).

Irene Triesch (1877–1964) came to Otto Brahm's Deutsches Theater in 1902. With him and Max Reinhardt she became the great interpreter of the female roles of Ibsen and Strindberg. But her starring roles also included Goethe's Iphigenie, Schiller's Maid of Orleans, and Shakespeare's Lady Macbeth. In 1933 she fled to Switzerland.

Rudolph Schildkraut, born in Constantinople, became a celebrated exponent in Germany of the plays of Shakespeare, Lessing, Ibsen and others. In 1918 he went to America, where he became a director and leading actor at a Yiddish theater, before becoming a film actor in Hollywood.

Max Pallenberg (1877–1934) acted with the same explosive intensity, a mingling of tragedy and comedy, the good soldier Schweik, the comic father Schimek, Molière's Tartuffe and imaginary invalid, and roles in the operettas of Jacques Offenbach. His King Menelaus, in Reinhardt's production, with his wife Fritzi Massary as the beautiful Helena, was a high point of German theater.

Most of Berlin's theater critics were Jews. As in all theater cities of the world, here too the critics played an influential role. In Berlin, and therefore in Germany, they successfully promoted Gerhart Hauptmann, Frank Wedekind, and many other modern dramatists against the established bourgeoisie and the imperial court.

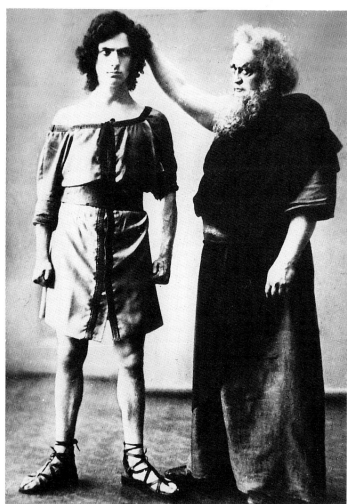

Joseph and Rudolph Schildkraut in Erich Schmidtbonn's *Der verlorene Sohn* ("The Prodigal Son").

Painters and Sculptors

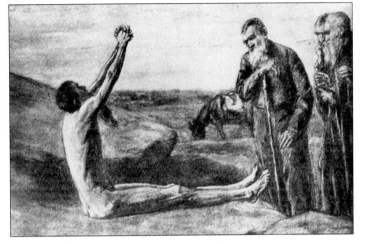

ABOVE: Max Liebermann, "Job," oil painting, about 1905.

LEFT: Lesser Ury: *Jeremiah*, 1902.

RIGHT: The old Max Liebermann under a portrait of his parents in his house on Pariser Platz in Berlin, May 1931. Photograph Dr. Erich Salomon.

In the 1890s Max Liebermann (1847–1935) introduced the French Impressionists to Germany and stood up for them against the historical painting of the Academy in Berlin, of which he was a member. As Germany's best-known Impressionist at that time, his credo was: "Any renaissance in art ... can be accomplished only on the basis of naturalism."

When the president of the Academy, Anton von Werner, closed down an exhibition of paintings by Edvard Munch, Liebermann left with others of like mind, and with them founded the Secession in 1894. By so doing, together with the art dealer Paul Cassirer, he made it possible for painters such as Lovis Corinth, Max Slevogt, Hans Baluschek, Lesser Ury, and others to exhibit publicly and find artistic recognition. Early paintings by Liebermann show biblical motifs and genre scenes. But when in 1878 he showed his painting "Jesus before the Scribes' in Munich, he unleashed an anti-Semitic scandal. His models were inmates of Christian hospitals in Munich. "Liebermann has depicted the ugliest know-all Jewboys imaginable ... the picture offends not just our feelings but even our noses ..." There were protests in the provincial parliament and the picture was moved to an inconspicuous position.

Liebermann was deeply surprised and hurt. From then on he avoided scenes from the Gospels. Previously famous for his Berlin wit and repartee, he reacted almost with fear: "Although I have unfortunately often enough been persuaded to the contrary, I imagine that – as the Constitution states – every citizen is equal before the law."

Twelve years later he exhibited again in Munich, this time "The Woman with the

Goats". For this he was awarded the grand gold medal, and the State of Bavaria bought the painting for its collection.

Meanwhile Kaiser Wilhelm II was equally convinced of Liebermann's importance: "But all the same, the chap's an anarchist!" he commented.

Liebermann became the portraitist of high society – and its mocking commentator. When one big industrialist complained that his portrait did not look much like him, the painter replied: "What, you don"t think it's like you? It's *very* like – disgustingly like!"

"Although throughout my life," he once wrote, "I have felt myself to be German, my adherence to Judaism was no less alive in me …" Liebermann died in 1935. In 1943 his widow committed suicide to avoid being deported to a concentration camp.

The painter and graphic artist Lesser Ury (1861–1931) from Birnbaum (in Posen) had a harder time than Liebermann. Little valued, and often in financial need until he was very old, he is now regarded as a great master of Impressionism. He also painted biblical themes, Adam and Eve, Jerusalem, Moses, Jeremiah, David, Ruth and Boaz. However, his international fame was founded on his paintings, drawings and engravings of the capital, Berlin, and its surroundings: landscapes in Brandenburg, reminiscent of those described by the novelist Theodor Fontane, coffee-house life and human types, night scenes with horse-drawn carriages and cars back-lit by street lamps and reflected in the wet streets. His last self-portrait is moving and reminiscent of Rembrandt.

Other important painters and graphic artists were Ernst Oppler, Eugen Spiro, Jakob Nussbaum, Jakob Steinhardt, Joseph Budko, Emil Orlik, Ephraim Mose Lilien, Hermann Struck, Laser Segall, and Max Oppenheim. The painter Hans von Marées and the sculptor Adolf von Hildebrandt (1847–1921), creator of the Wittelsbach fountain in Munich, were of Jewish descent on one side (see also page 295).

The sculptor Hugo Kaufmann from Hesse (1868–1919) produced a large

ABOVE: Lesser Ury: *Tiergarten, Berlin*, 1922.

RIGHT: Hugo Kaufmann: Unity memorial in Frankfurt am Main.

number of naturalistic figures, which grace many German cities to this day: for instance, in Munich, "Art" on the Ludwigsbrücke (badly damaged in World War II), the bronze figure of the Mercury fountain (now in the street "Im Tal"), and the stone figures above the portico of the Bavarian army museum; and in Augsburg the "Goldsmith fountain."

ABOVE: Ephraim Mose Lilien: *Sulamith*, drawing c. 1905.

German Jewish Writers

Montage from a catalogue of the S. Fischer publishing house, Berlin 1913.

No writer experienced the problems of German-Jewish existence as dramatically as Jakob Wassermann, a merchant's son from Fürth in Franconia, whose landscapes he often and lovingly described.

In 1897 he published his first book, *Die Juden von Zirndorf* ("The Jews of Zirndorf"): in about 1660 many Jews cast aside their possessions in messianic euphoria and set out on the road to the Promised Land and Shabbetai Tzevi (see page 92). In the Fürth area a group of these travelers to the Holy Land were shocked by the news that Shabbetai Tzevi had gone over to Islam. They stopped, and founded Zionsdorf, which later became Zirndorf.

Wassermann's fundamental conflict, his battle for justice and against the "inertia of the heart," is most strongly expressed in his autobiographical work *Mein Weg als Deutscher und Jude* ("My Path as German and Jew"), 1921. "What is left? Self-destruction? A life in twilight, awkwardness and discontent? It is better not to think about it!" But then, he goes on: "I am German, and I am Jewish, the one as much and as completely as the other, neither can be canceled out by the other." In his often negative attitude to "other Jews," Wassermann occasionally actually put forward anti-Jewish arguments and tried to make the "East European Jews" a scapegoat for German anti-Semitism. In 1933, a year before his death, having been deprived by law of his German nationality, he gave lectures to Jewish religious communities on "German Jews in a German landscape," which after all was to most Jews, whether of German or East European descent, their beloved and natural home. Jakob Wassermann was one of the most-read novelists, especially in the 1920s. Thomas Mann called him a "world star of the novel."

On the other hand, Georg Hermann (1871–1943 – murdered in Auschwitz) in his popular light novels *Jettchen Gebert* (1906) and *Henriette Jacoby* (1908) idealized allegedly Jewish family life in Berlin of the Biedermeier period. Jettchen, unhappily in love with a Christian, commits suicide.

In the security of his spiritual heritage, the world of Old Testament prophecy, Alfred Mombert (1872–1942) became a poet of mystical penetration; for him poetry was a "constant revelation of the spiritual," an oft-repeated manifestation of universal harmony.

Else Lasker-Schüler (1869–1945) transformed feelings and experiences, religions and events into a picturesque poetic tapestry of enthusiastic rhapsodies. Coming from an Orthodox family in Elberfeld, her spiritual home was within the circle of the German literary avant-garde. She spent her last years in Jerusalem, but she was always at home in her own world, using the biblical stories of her childhood as its building blocks just as uninhibitedly as her amorous experiences and friendships, her violent likes and dislikes. She was known as a German poet in the Hebrew language – of which she did not know a single word – or as an oriental poet in the German language, in which she poured out the beauty and bitterness of her life.

In contrast to the German Jews in the Reich, the Jewish writers of Vienna and Prague, with the exception of Kafka and Brod, felt themselves to be members of the German-Austrian cultural circle in a multinational state in which they were "a minority just like others – if with less entitlement." Arthur Schnitzler (1862–1931) saw the position of the individual Jew as an Austrian and world citizen becoming more and more frequently jeopardized. In his novel *Der Weg ins Freie* ("The Road to the Open"), 1908, and the play *Professor Bernhardi*, 1912, he dealt with the situation of the Jewish intellectual and the Jewish bourgeoisie in a non-Jewish milieu. At the same time he described the Viennese of the fading imperial age, the erotically elated, brightly elegiac atmosphere of the Austrian capital.

Jakob Julius David (1858–1906) was regarded by many readers as a "Moravian Dostoevsky" (*Am Wege Sterben* ("Dying by the Roadside"), 1899; *Der Übergang* ("The Transition"), 1903). Peter Altenberg

(1859–1919) and Alfred Polgar (1873–1955) cultivated the short form, Altenberg in egomaniac showers of sparks, Polgar in worldly and mockingly philosophical reflexions and theater reviews. To both, their Jewishness was mere chance. For Egon Friedell (1878–1938), actor and art historian (*Kulturgeschichte der Neuzeit* ("Cultural History of the Modern Age"), 1927–1932), and the satirist Karl Kraus (1874–1936) their Jewish origins were a millstone around their necks, which they tried vainly to cast off by attacking the Jews.

Standing astride the three races of Prague, Franz Kafka (1883–1924) and his friend Max Brod were the only ones of those referred to who were familiar with Jewish literature and participated in the contemporary Jewish movement. Kafka's "Diaries" show that the Jewish national character, incorporated in Yitzhak Löwy's

ABOVE: The poet Richard Beer-Hofmann (1866–1945).

BELOW: Franz Kafka (left) with Albert Ehrenstein, Otto Pick and Lise Kaznelson in the Prater fairground in Vienna, 1913.

RIGHT: The poet Alfred Mombert (1872–1942), painting by Carl Hofer, about 1913.

Yiddish acting ensemble, made a lasting impression on him. The thought of an unredeemed world, the concept of a court constantly in session, and the dream world of Kafka's prose are unmistakably rooted in rabbinical Judaism and Hasidism.

The best-known works of Felix Salten (1869–1945) are his animal stories: *Bambi* became a famous Walt Disney film; but Salten also wrote novels for adults, including the erotic novel *Josephine Mutzenbacher*, now a classic.

Finally, Richard Beer-Hofmann (1866–1945), the aristocrat among Viennese writers, read the Jewish future from its (and his own) origins, in *Jakobs Traum* ("Jacob's Dream"), *Der Junge David* ("The Young David"), and *Schlaflied für Miriam* ("Lullaby for Miriam"), 1919.

The Group around Stefan George

ABOVE: George in the circle of his disciples: Left to right: Wolfskehl, Schuler, Klages, George, Verwey. Photograph K. Bauer, Munich 1902.

ABOVE RIGHT: Literary historian Friedrich Gundolf, c. 1904.

LEFT: On the park steps, Heidelberg, c. 1920. Some of the members of the George circle about that time were Percy Gothein, Norbert von Hellingrath, Edgar Salin, Friedrich Gundolf, Max Kommerell, and Ernst Bertram, who, like a few of George's other disciples, celebrated Hitler in 1933 as Germany's salvation.

A number of young Jews lived and worked under the spell of Stefan George (1868–1933). Most of them were "no-longer-Jews," searching for a new inner center of law, perhaps even for a new divinity. But Karl Wolfskehl (1869–1948), lifelong herald of the Master, was proud of the long "Tuscan-Rhenish line of his ancestors" and at the same time always felt himself to be the "codefender of the German spirit." "In truth and fire he was most reminiscent of the prophets of his race, drunk on the wine of holy rage from all the vessels of time to our own day," wrote Karl Wolters, a member of George's inner circle.

The fact that Jews and, during the Munich period of the "Cosmic Circle," anti-Semites like Ludwig Klages and Alfred Schuler could foregather in the same circle for years is inexplicable. Perhaps George's lines were meant as explanation:

"Blond or black
sprung from the same womb/
Unrecognized brothers
seeking yourselves and hating/
You ever wandering
and hence never fulfilled!"

The Jewish writer and poet Margarete Susman (1874–1966) left the George circle "because there the Dionysian turned into the cruelly demonic, even into treachery, the age-old Germanic treachery … I have often wondered how Germanic treachery differs from that of Judas, and have become convinced that in the Germanic tradition of the Edda via the Nibelungenlied and Kleist's Hermannsschlacht through to National Socialism, treachery is not only allowed but celebrated, whereas Judas, after his treachery, took his own life."

Members of George's inner circle included the literary historian Friedrich Gundolf (1880–1931) and his brother Ernst, the historian Ernst Kantorowicz (1895–1963); also Heinrich Friedemann, Percy Gothein, Edith Landmann, Gertrud Kantorowicz, Ernst Morwitz, and Richard Perls. Georg Bondi, a Berliner, published George's books and the *Blätter für die Kunst* ("Pages for Art") (from 1892) and had a special typeface designed for them, as suggested by George. The economist and Plato expert Edgar Salin (1892–1974) also belonged to the George circle in Heidelberg and wrote the book *Um Stefan George* ("Around Stefan George"), 1948.

George's poems also met with a powerful response in the Jewish youth movement.

Ida Coblenz, the only woman who played a role in George's life. She later married the poet Richard Dehmel.

BELOW LEFT AND CENTER: Karl Wolfskehl: *Saul* (1905). Title page and dedication to the Jordania Zionist Student Club in Munich, 1906.

BELOW RIGHT: Title page for Ernst Kantorowicz's history of Emperor Frederick the Second, 1931.

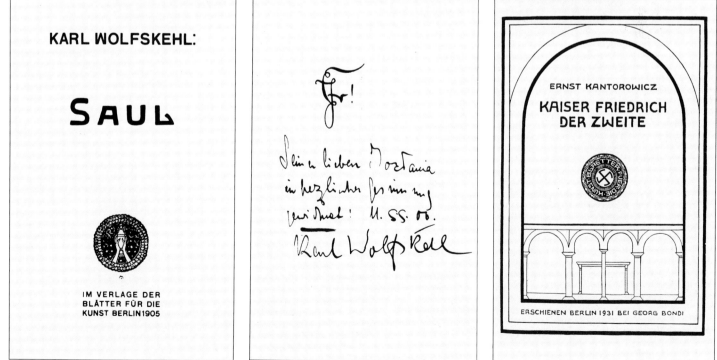

KARL WOLFSKEHL:

SAUL

IM VERLAGE DER BLÄTTER FÜR DIE KUNST BERLIN 1905

ERNST KANTOROWICZ

KAISER FRIEDRICH DER ZWEITE

ERSCHIENEN BERLIN 1931 BEI GEORG BONDI

Break with the Past

ABOVE LEFT: Criminal lawyer and publisher Julius Eduard Hitzig (1780–1849). Lithograph after a drawing by Franz Krüger, 1837.

ABOVE: Friedrich Julius Stahl (1802–1861), spokesman for the Prussian conservatives. Contemporary lithograph.

LEFT: Eduard von Simson (1810–1899) , president of the National Assembly 1848/49, at the head of the imperial delegation before Frederick William IV, 3 April 1849. Wood engraving, *Leipziger Illustrierte Zeitung*.

Theodor Mommsen (see page 254) saw in the merging of Germany's Jews with the German people a positive contribution to their culture.

Being part of the German people, which was a matter of course to non-Jews, whether Christians, agnostics, or atheists, was granted to a Jewish inhabitant of the country only if he entered a Christian church. Mommsen's idea of a mass move to Christianity on worldly grounds, however well-meant, disregarded a positive attitude to Judaism on the part of the great majority of Jews. The historian Heinrich Graetz expressed this view when he wrote that the Jews had contributed at least as much to European culture as gentiles.

Although after the Enlightenment there were many conversions to Christianity, these were in general by Jews to whom their Jewishness no longer implied any purpose in life. The ideals of the Enlightenment had taken its place. Here Enlightenment, deism, and readiness to be assimilated became pioneers of the move to the religion of the majority, which the Christian-German State largely saw as the condition for social and professional equality under the law.

The fact that for the members of the Mendelssohn Enlightenment the revealed Jewish law was no longer the sole authority in metaphysical, moral, and humanitarian issues often made the conversion to Christianity easier. Thus Enlightenment ideas and state pressure (see page 148) combined in regarding baptism simply as a formality, to avoid the prejudices of the majority. Herschel Marx, father of Carl Heinrich (later Karl) Marx, became the respected attorney Heinrich Marx. The lawyer Eduard Gans, president of the Society for Jewish Culture and Learning, early champions of a united Germany under Prussian leadership,· converted to Christianity in 1835 and was immediately made professor and dean of the Faculty of Law of Berlin University. "The state only wants lip service from me, after all," he said.

Gans's friend Heinrich Heine wrote *Einem Abtrünnigen* ("To an Apostate"):

Theologian Johann August Neander (1789–1850). Lithograph after a drawing by the Henschel brothers.

"The New Peter of Amiens and the Crusaders," caricature of Stahl and the new Kreuzzeitung from *Kladderadatsch*, 4 November 1849.

Allgemeine Geschichte der christlichen Religion und Kirche ("General History of the Christian Religion and Church"), 1826, and *Das Leben Jesu* ("The Life of Jesus"), 1837, were standard works of Protestant theology.

The lawyer and politician Julius Schlesinger (1802–1861) called himself Friedrich Julius Stahl after his conversion to Lutheranism. Professor of constitutional and ecclesiastical law in Würzburg and Erlangen from 1832, in 1840 Stahl was appointed to the most respected legal chair in Germany, at Berlin University, occupied before him by Eduard Gans.

The Prussian member of the high consistory, member of the upper chamber and spokesman of the conservatives, he supported in his writing the divine right of the monarchy and demanded holy orders for the teaching profession. There was no place for Jews in the administration of Stahl's Christian state. With his conservative Christian constitutional doctrine, Stahl had a great influence on conservatism in Prussia and Germany after the foundation of the German Empire.

Many of the Jewish neo-Christians may still inwardly have felt attached to

"And you have crawled to the Cross,
To the Cross that you despise,
That only a few weeks ago
You thought to tread in the dust!
Oh! that's what comes of much reading
of a Schlegel, a Haller, a Burke –
Yesterday still a hero
Today already a rogue."

This accusation was aimed by Heine not only at Gans but also at himself: in that year he too was baptized in order to obtain an appointment as a lawyer.

A small number of Jews also converted to Christianity from conviction. Chief among these were Neander and Stahl.

David Mendel (1789–1850) took the name Johann August Wilhelm Neander when he was baptized in 1806. In 1813 Schleiermacher appointed him to the chair of theology at Berlin University. Neander's

The poet and Nobel Prize winner Paul Heyse (1830–1914), after a painting by Franz von Lenbach.

Judaism. We know this to be true of Felix Mendelssohn, the painter Eduard von Bendemann, and the composer Jacques Offenbach, who refused to parody a Jewish theme on the stage. Others, such as Julius Stahl and Karl Marx, became opponents of Judaism, whether for purposes of concealment or from a psychologically based hatred of one parent or of origins they saw as inferior, projected back from an anti-Jewish milieu. Concealment of origins admits of this interpretation. In the course of the generations, in any case, especially when a Jewish-sounding name had been discarded or a German-sounding name acquired by marriage, the partly Jewish origin became a distant memory, sometimes suppressed, sometimes forgotten. The individual merged with the non-Jewish population.

For instance, the two painters Hans von Marées and Franz Marc came from Jewish families, the latter from that of a Waldeck court agent, Moses Nathan Marcus. The imperial admiral Felix von Bendemann (1848–1915), son of the painter Eduard von Bendemann, became chief of the German naval staff in 1899. Felix von Bendemann was disappointed when his daughter-in-

Chemist and Nobel Prize winner Adolf von Baeyer (1835–1917), inventor of synthetic indigo.

BELOW LEFT: "Darwinistics" from *Der Schlemiel*, January 1904.

BELOW RIGHT: Hans von Marées (1837–1887, front) painted by his friend Franz von Lenbach, 1863 (inset). Hans von Marées was descended from the Halberstadt Sussmann family on his mother's side.

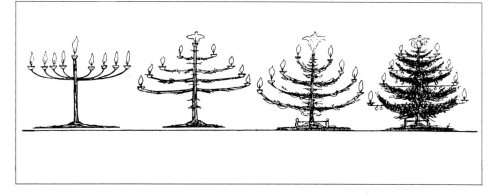

law, the well-known Jewish writer and poet Margarete Susman, refused baptism.

All the descendants of the court factor Daniel Itzig (see page 114) were baptized and some of them married into the aristocracy.

In the 19th century, when there was a total of about 530,000 Jews in 1875, some 30,000 were baptized.

"No Kaddish Will Be Said"

RIGHT: "How Mother Germany Honors her Poet Heinrich Heine." Drawing by Olaf Gulbransson in *Simplicissimus*, 1906, on the 50th anniversary of the poet's death.

BELOW: A German male voice choir sings the popular setting of *Die Lorelei* (written by Heine) by the poet's grave in Montmartre cemetery, 1901.

No other German poet was ever so involved in passionate polemic as Heine. For most people he was and remained the great poet, whose love of Germany was expressed even in his sharpest criticism. For others he was the French vassal and Jewish foreigner who praised Napoleon in his *Zwei Grenadieren* ("Two Grenadiers") – a traitor to the fatherland. "Had I been in his place," commented one of the admirers of this

RIGHT-HAND PAGE: For the 50th anniversary of Heinrich Heine's death. Drawing and poem by Wilhelm Schulz in *Simplicissimus*, 12 February 1906.

Zu Heinrich Heines 50. Todestag

(Zeichnung und Gedicht von Wilhelm Schulz)

Sie äußern derb ihre Meinung,
Doch ihnen es nie behagt,
Wenn grade heraus ein andrer
Sie ihnen auch einmal sagt.

Von Heinrich Heine, dem Dichter,
Sie fühlen sich grob verletzt,
Laut alle Philister schwören:
Kein Denkmal wird ihm gesetzt!

Sie saßen beisamm' und tranken,
Der Mond ging am Himmel bleich,
Da ward von dem vielen Biere
Das Herz den Philistern weich.

Leis fingen sie an zu singen
Und seufzten so still dabei.
Sie sangen mit süßer Stimme
Das Lied von der Lorelei.

"traitor to his country," Otto von Bismarck, "I would not have acted otherwise. Could I have accepted, if born as a Jew, as Heine was, that at eight in the evening the gates of the Jewish town were barred and Jews in general placed under the severest laws of exclusion? In the man who brought French law to the Rhineland, removed all the exclusion laws, a Heine must naturally praise a savior from agonizing oppression, ... And do the gentlemen quite forget that Heine is a poet of *lieder* beside whom only Goethe's name can stand, and that the *lied* is a specifically German form of poetry?"

"No Kaddish will be said ... ," no funeral prayer, Heine wrote of himself.

In 1897 the sculptor Ernst Herter (1846–1917) carved a Heine fountain for the poet's birthplace, Düsseldorf. Owing to the many protests it could not be set up there, and it finally found a site in a New York park. The Danish scupltor Louis Hesselries created a seated, meditating Heine figure for Hamburg. The city senate would not have it; Empress Elizabeth of Austria placed it before her castle on the island of Corfu. When Kaiser Wilhelm II bought the property after Elizabeth's death, he indignantly had the statue removed. It found a home in Hamburg in the garden of the Campe family – Heine's publishers. Not until 1928 during the Weimar Republic was it publicly erected in Hamburg – only to be removed in 1933.

When the sculptor Georg Kolbe (1877–1947) raised a memorial to Heine in the form of the figure of a boy, there was uproar throughout anti-Semitic circles and national Defense and Protection leagues. Nevertheless, the statue was installed in a Frankfurt park; in 1934 the poet Georg Binding saved it from destruction.

The anti-Semitic literary historian Adolf Bartels (1862–1945) and the Jewish satirist Karl Kraus (1874–1936) agreed only in their dismissal of Heine. But most of intellectual Germany, from Nietzsche to Gerhart Hauptmann, were admirers and defenders of Heinrich Heine. In 1906, on the fiftieth anniversary of his death, *Simplicissimus* joined them.

East European Jews Seek Work and Freedom

LEFT: The East European Jewish Eisen family, from Galicia: three brothers from a baker's family. The middle one became a textile merchant, one of his sons an orientalist, another an art historian. Munich 1907.

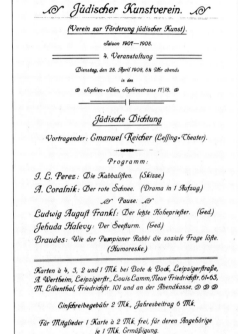

RIGHT: Jewish Art Society: program of an event in Berlin in 1908. There were Jewish cultural societies in all the major cities in Germany. The performer announced in this program, Emanuel Reicher (1849–1924), emigrated from Galicia in 1887 and became a celebrated performer of Ibsen and Hauptmann with the Otto Brahm ensemble.

An unsere russischen Leser!

Wir sind in der Lage, unsere verehrten **Abonnenten in Russland** von folgendem Entgegenkommen der **Kaiserlich-russischen Post-Direktion** in Kenntnis zu setzen:

Nach einer uns soeben zugegangenen, vom 23. November (5. Dezember) datierten Mitteilung des **Kaiserlich-Russischen Ministeriums des Innern** werden vom Januar 1902 ab

sämtliche Central-Postämter in Russland

Abonnements auf „**Ost und West**" entgegennehmen, und zwar:

St. Petersburg, Moskau, Warschau, Odessa, Riga, Wilna, Kiew, Charkow, Nishny-Nowgorod No. I, Kasan und Tiflis.

LEFT: Advertisement for "East and West," 1901: "To our Russian readers." The German language was a link in the East European Jewish culture reaching deep into the Caucasus.

After the Khmelnytsky massacres of 1648, the pogroms in Russia in 1881/82 were the first cause of mass flights to the West in more recent times. Most emigrants – over two-and-a-half million between 1880 and 1914 – traveled on to America via Hamburg and Bremen; a number went to England. Some remained in Germany, however difficult the authorities tried to make it for them. The land of Schiller and universal brotherhood was seen by many Jews from the East as the home of freedom of thought and humane government. Many had come at the invitation of industrialists as skilled workers for new manufacturing sectors, a few as miners and colliery workers; students found places at German universities.

In 1910, 614,000 Jews were living in Germany as members of Jewish congregations. Of these some 79,000 were born in Eastern Europe. These "Eastern Jews" made up for the numerical decline in German Jews (through falling birthrates,

baptism, and emigration) and had a regenerating and activating effect on Jewish life.

The first wave of immigrants consisted mainly of artisans and craftsmen. Many became skilled workers in the Offenbach leather industry, cigarette and tobacco manufacture in Berlin, Dresden, and Munich, and the Leipzig fur industry. Leipzig developed, thanks to eastern Jewish skilled workers, dealers, importers, and exporters, into a world center of the skin and bristle trade, and remained so until 1933. Other Eastern Jews played a part in the import of iron, wood and leather, or in opening up markets in Eastern Europe for German industrial products.

Many Jews from eastern Europe arrived penniless as refugees and survived at first as peddlers, street venders, or "black" workers. But in general, industriousness and intellectual interests in Jews were unwelcome in Germany, in contrast, for example, to America. Another bone of contention was the unusual hunger for education of the new immigrants. Even in the second generation many sons left trade and industry and turned to academic and liberal professions.

Among the artists and writers were violinists such as Bronislaw Huberman, pianist Arthur Schnabel (1882–1951), graphic artist Ephraim Mose Lilien (1874–1925), composer and writer Arno Nadel (1878–1943), and translators Alexander Eliasberg and Berthold Feiwel. Efraim Frisch (1873–1942), from an Orthodox Eastern Jewish family, became the publisher of the literary journal *Der neue Merkur*. Samuel Saenger (1864–1944), the editor of the important literary

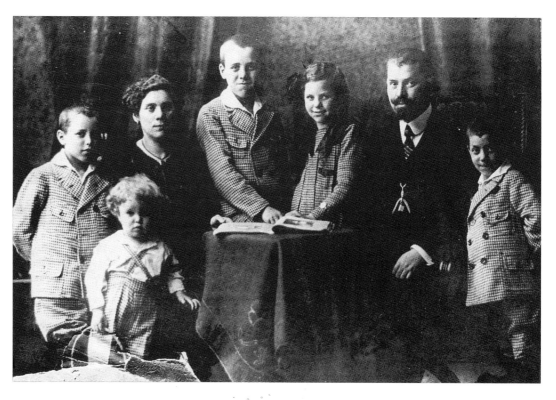

The family of a furrier from Russia who emigrated to Munich in 1905. One son became a furrier, the daughter and her husband also remained in the fur business with their fashion salon. The second son studied biology and became a well-known photo journalist. The third son, the author of this book, became a historian and photo journalist; the fourth a leading fire service engineer in Israel. Photograph 1917.

Russian-Jewish Scholars' Society, Berlin 1889. The splinter group of Jewish-nationalist inclined students separated from the "Russian Students' Society," which – although consisting exclusively of Jews – was uninterested in Judaism. Among the members of the new society were Leo Motzkin, Shmaryahu Levin, Chaim Weizmann, and, the only German Jew, Heinrich Loewe, later a leading Zionist.

monthly *Die neue Rundschau*. Samuel Fischer (1859–1934) from an assimilated family in Liptoszentmiklós in Slovakia, founded the S. Fischer Verlag publishing house. Son of an Eastern Jewish cellist in Frankfurt am Main, Paul Nikolaus Cossmann (1869–1942) published the influential conservative monthly *Süddeutsche Monatshefte*. He converted to Catholicism and in the First World War was a dyed-in-the-wool chauvinist. He died in Theresienstadt concentration camp.

The students were a small but culturally very active group. They studied in Berlin, Heidelberg, Munich, and at other universities and technical colleges, after failing to find acceptance in Russia and Poland owing to the fixed quotas operating there. For instance, the later Nobel Prize winner Samuel Josef Agnon (1888–1970) from Galicia, the Hebrew poets Hayyim Nahman Bialik (1873–1934) and Saul Chernikovski (1875–1943), and publicist Zalman Schazar (1889–1974), later the third president of Israel, spent long years in Germany as students or writers, as did Chaim Weizmann (1874–1952), Israel's first president.

Jewish revolutionaries from Poland and Russia – many of whom had fled from Russia after the failure of the 1905 revolution – attached themselves to German socialist circles. Among them were Rosa Luxemburg, Eugen Leviné, and Leo Deutsch.

Hermann Minkowski (1864–1909), born in Alexotas (Lithuania), mathematician and number theorist, became a professor in Göttingen in 1902. With Lorentz and Einstein he developed the mathematical foundations of the theory of relativity. His brother Oskar (1858–1931) became a professor in Breslau and facilitated the discovery of insulin through his research.

Martin Buber (1878–1965), born in Vienna, came as a three year-old to Lemberg (now Lvov in the Ukraine), where he lived in the house of his grandfather, a rabbinical scholar and merchant. He went to Germany as a student; in old age he said of himself, "I am a Polish Jew" (*Gog und Magog*, 1957)

From Russia, Poland, Galicia, Hungary and Romania came Zionist leaders Victor Chaim Arlosoroff, Nahum Goldmann, and Shmaryahu Levin, actors Alexander Granach, Kurt Katsch, Vladimir Sokoloff, Maria Orska, Elisabeth Bergner, and Rudolph Schildkraut, singers Friedrich Schorr, Hermann Jadlowker, Alexander Kipnis, Josef Schmidt, and many others. Nahum Goldmann (1895–1982) from Visznevo in Lithuania immigrated with his family to Germany in 1900 and grew up in the Eastern Jewish atmosphere of his

ABOVE: Bacteriologist Lydia Rabinowitsch-Kempner (1871–1935) from Kovno, the first woman professor in Prussia in 1912, working with Robert Koch. Her son, Robert Kempner, was one of the American prosecutors in the Nuremberg war crimes trials.

LEFT: Founding of the Jewish Publishing House, Berlin 1902. From the left: Berthold Feiwel (seated), a writer from Moravia; Ephraim Mose Lilien, graphic artist from Galicia; Chaim Weizmann, later world-renowned chemist and president of the World Zionist Organization, from Russia; Martin Buber (seated), who grew up in Poland and David Trietsch, later a Zionist leader, from Russia.

parental home. Together with Arlosoroff and David Ben Gurion he was for a long time a driving force in the radical wing of the Zionist movement. When the British left Palestine in 1947 he worked for the immediate foundation of a Jewish State. Later he became President of the Jewish World Congress, which he himself initiated and after 1948, of the Zionist World Organisation. A brilliant speaker, in Yiddish as well, as an old man he regarded himself as "German and Jewish." His main achievement is still that of putting through the reparations claims of Jews from Germany.

Within the communities, in the decades after the first waves of immigration, there were very few social contacts between the often arrogant "old settlers" and the "foreign" Jews, except in Zionist societies and student bodies. The eastern Jews gathered in regional associations with their own religious schools, and in prayer communities and social clubs. Only in later years did closer relations develop: in aid associations, singing clubs, Zionist gymnastic and sports clubs and in the Zionist and orthodox youth movement, where eastern Jewish youth met German Jews at the same level, both in artistic and literarycircles.

The relationship of the eastern Jews to the authorities was always difficult, with some exceptions. Only in the rarest cases was naturalization allowed.

On the other hand, there were more and more frequent expulsions and deportations. Within the Jewish communities the eastern Jews had to fight for a long time for suffrage. The Central Association of German Citizens of the Jewish Faith excluded foreign Jews for being just that-foreign.

In broad strata of non-Jewish workers and petit bourgeoisie, as well as among the literati and artists, relations with the eastern Jews were often cordial, perhaps because most of them did not try to conceal their eastern Jewishness and the acknowledged difference gave both sides an inner security in mutual contacts.

The eastern Jewish immigration meant a spiritual "pollination" of German Judaism by rabbis and teachers, by men like Martin Buber, the philosophical writer Jakob Klatzkin (1882–1948) and the circles of the Jewish publishing house in Berlin, which published the Talmud, histories, and many books by eastern Jewish authors, including the works of Jizchak Leib Perez (1852–1915) and Sholem Aleichem (1859–1916).

ABOVE RIGHT: Rosa Luxemburg founded the Spartacus League in 1917 with Karl Liebknecht. This pronouncement of hers has become famous: "Freedom only for the supporters of the government, only for the members of one party-however many they are – is no freedom. Freedom is always only the freedom of those who think differently, not from fanaticism for justice, but because all that informs and purifies in political freedom hangs on this nature and fails in its effect, when freedom becomes a privilege."

RIGHT: Marcus Harmelin (right) and his son Joachim Harmelin (left) from Russia, in their firm's brush and bristle store in Leipzig, 1905. The firm of Harmelin was the biggest brush importer and exporter in Europe.

National Renaissance

After the destruction of Jerusalem by Titus in 70 AD, and since Hadrian's ban on the Jewish religion in 135 AD, return to the land of their fathers had been the unshakable hope of the Jewish people in the Diaspora. The phrase "Next year in Jerusalem" is still the promise of the Feast of the Passover.

Toward the end of the 19th century economic pressure, continuing threats to the life of the Jewish masses, especially in Russia (with the state-backed pogroms), and the failed attempts at emancipation in Austria, Hungary, and Germany led to the first steps towards a secular realization of the old Messianic hope of Zion.

The hope of return, of building the land of Israel, now took shape. It was supported by a new Hebrew literature in Russia and a related national and cultural self-confidence.

Moses Hess's *Rom und Jerusalem* ("Rome and Jerusalem"), 1862, and Judah Leib Pinsker's *Autoemancipation! Ein Mahnruf an seine Stammesgenossen von*

ABOVE: Rabbi Zwi Hirsch Kalischer (1795–1874), proponent of religious Zionism.

BELOW: The Kattowitz conference of the "Friends of Zion," 1884.

ABOVE: Title page for "Rome and Jerusalem" by Moses Hess, 1862.

BELOW: "*Autoemancipation!* A challenge to his people from a Russian Jew" by Judah Leib Pinsker (1821–1891), Berlin 1882.

	5. Friedländer. Kattowitz O S.	6. Freidenberg. Bialystok.	10. Moses. Kattowitz O S.	13. Rittenberg. Warschau.	15. Freuthal. Kattowitz.	18. Pines. Rosana.	20. Mirkin. Pultawa.	
1. Rabinowitz. Warschau.	3. Dr. Chasanowitz. Bialystok.	7. Jasinowsky. Warschau.	9. Schalit. Riga.	12. Dr. Drübinowitz. Rostow a. Don.	16. Luntz. Riga.	19. Wollrauch. London.	22. Meyersohn. Warschau.	23. Davidsohn. Warschau.	25. Löbinger. Kattowitz.
2. Wissozki. Moskau.	4. Klewansky. Kowno.	8. Gordon. Lyk O P.	11. Rab. Mohilewer. Bialystok.	14. Dr. Pinsker. Odessa.	17. Rab. Friedmann. Karlin.	21. Zederbaum. St. Petersburg.	24. Dr. Rabbinowitz. Paris.	26. Deiches. Charkow.

BELOW: Prominent participants in the Second Zionist Congress in Basle, 1898. From left: Max Bodenheimer, Theodor Herzl, Max Nordau, and David Wolffsohn. The Cologne attorney Max Bodenheimer (1865–1940) and the merchant Wolffsohn (1856–1914) had founded the "Cologne Society for the Promotion of Agriculture and Farming in Palestine" in 1893.

einem russischen Juden ("Auto-Emancipation! A challenge to his people from a Russian Jew"), 1882, laid the first foundations of the secular movement.

As early as 1861 Zvi Hirsch Kalischer (1795–1874), a rabbi and respected Talmud scholar in Posen, published a book, *Drishat Zion* ("Longing for Zion"), in which the need for Palestine to be settled by Jewish farmers was actually proclaimed as a religious commandment.

In 1864 Kalischer founded in Berlin a Central Committee for Jewish Settlements in Palestine; in 1870, in collaboration with the French philanthropist Charles Netter (1826–1882), he succeeded in founding a school of agriculture near Jaffa. Named Mikveh Israel (Hope of Israel), it is still in

DER

JUDENSTAAT.

VERSUCH
EINER

MODERNEN LÖSUNG DER JUDENFRAGE

VON

THEODOR HERZL
DOCTOR DER RECHTE.

LEIPZIG und WIEN 1896.
M. BREITENSTEIN'S VERLAGS-BUCHHANDLUNG
WIEN, IX., WÄHRINGERSTRASSE 5.

Title page for "The Jewish State. An Attempt at a Modern Solution of the Jewish Question" by Theodor Herzl, 1896.

ABOVE: Theodor Herzl (1860–1904). Photograph by Ephraim Mose Lilien.

ABOVE RIGHT: Grand Duke Friedrich of Baden, who was friendly toward Zionist ideas.

RIGHT: Zionist delegation received by the Grand Duke of Baden when the Second Zionist Congress met in 1898.

existence. Over the course of a century thousands of farmers have been trained there.

Kalischer was a precursor of practical Zionism on a religious foundation. Especially after the pogroms of 1881/82, groups were formed in many places in Russia, Romania, and Galicia, and to a lesser extent in Poland, Germany, and England, of "Choveve Zion" (Friends of Zion), from which a number of students, although without the necessary education, went to Palestine (aliyah – "Ascent to the Land of Israel") and founded agricultural settlements. This movement found its intellectual expression in the book by Judah Leib Pinsker (1821–1891) already mentioned, which appeared in German in Berlin. German was read in many circles of East European Jewry and a number of Eastern Jews studied at German universities. The book was a call to the Jews throughout the world to become a nation once again, with all the appropriate intellectual, cultural, and political attributes.

At Pinsker's suggestion, a conference met in Kattowitz in November 1884 with participants from Russia, Poland, England, and Germany. Even before this conference

the first Jewish village, Rischon le Zion (First in Zion), was founded in Palestine in 1882 by Russian-Jewish pioneers, mostly students.

In 1889 the first Zionist student association was formed in Berlin. Future leaders of the Zionist movement were members, including Leo Motzkin (1867–1933), Shmaryahu Levin (1867–1935), Chaim Weizmann, and also a German Jewish student, Heinrich Loewe (1869–1950).

But these were only isolated phenomena. It was left to the charismatic Theodor Herzl (1860–1904) to create the World Zionist Organization, and hence political Zionism, with the first Zionist Congress in

Basle (1897). He carried the Jewish masses, especially in Eastern Europe, with him. The "Basle program" was proclaimed as the Magna Carta of the Jewish people: "Zionism is working to create for the Jewish people a homeland under public law in Palestine."

Herzl wrote in his diary in November 1897 after this first Zionist Congress in Basle: "Today I have created the Jewish state." He reminded the Jews in his novel *Altneuland* ("Old New Land"), 1902: "If you will it, it is not a fairy tale!" Barely fifty years later, in 1948, the state of Israel was founded.

HATIKWA.

Andantino. M.M. ♩=60.

Bearbeitet von Leo Kopf.

Gesang.

Kol od ba-le-waw pēni-ma Nefesch jē-hu-di ho-mi-ja, Ufe-
faa-te mis-rach ka-di-ma A-jin lē-zi-jon zo-fi-ja.
Od lo awē-da tik-wa-te-nu Ha-tik-wa ha-no-scha-na.
Laschuw lē-e-rez a-wo-te-nu Ir ba-da-wid cha-na.

Klavier.

ABOVE: *Hatikvah* ("the Hope") is the hymn of the Zionist movement, written by Naphtali Herz Imber (1856–1909): "As long as in the inmost heart/A Jewish soul still lives/And forward looks toward the east/One eye toward Zion …/Our hope is not yet lost/The age-old hope:/Returning to the land/Of our forefathers/And to the home of David."

RIGHT: Caricature from the humorous paper *Der Schlemiel* (1903–1905; 1919–1921). "Schlemiel" is a vulgar word for a bird of ill-fortune.

„Das muss ein schäbig Volk sein, das mir den Durchgang neidet Und keinen fremden Mann auf seinem Boden leidet."

(Waltharilied des Ekkehard v. St. Gallen.)

Theodor Herzl opens the Second Zionist Congress in Basle, 1898.

Zionism in Germany

In the 19th century a Jewish religious-secular movement began in Germany whose goal was to return to the land of their fathers (see page 302). Before Theodor Herzl arrived in 1893, Max Isidor Bodenheimer (1865–1940), a lawyer, and David Wolffsohn (1856–1914), a merchant from Lithuania, had founded the "Cologne Association for the Promotion of Agriculture in Palestine." After Herzl's death, Wolffsohn was President of the World Zionist Organization from 1905 to 1911.

After the First Zionist Congress in 1897, the Zionist Association of Germany published its first paper, *Der Zionismus*, which stated, among other things: "Zionism works for a lasting solution of the Jewish question by the foundation of a place of refuge assured under public law for those Jews who cannot or do not wish to remain in the land of their birth. Zionism works for the return of a high proportion of Jews to agriculture in the historically consecrated soil of Palestine. Zionism works for

LEFT: Olive trees, planted to commemorate special events, made a great contribution to the afforestation of Palestine.

RIGHT: Masthead of the Zionist central organ *Die Welt*.

BELOW RIGHT: The Zionist sports club "Bar Kochba," Berlin 1904.

BELOW: The Sixth Zionist Congress in 1903 decided on the practical work of reconstruction in Palestine. Its direction was entrusted to (from right): Selig Soskin, Otto Warburg (president of the World Zionist Organization 1911–1920, 1921 Director of the Agricultural Institute in Rechowot, after 1925 at the Hebrew University in Jerusalem), and agrarian reformer Franz Oppenheimer.

DIE WELT

BERLIN W15, SÄCHSISCHE STR. 8.   ERSCHEINT JEDEN FREITAG

ZENTRALORGAN DER ZIONISTISCHEN BEWEGUNG

Nr. 31   BERLIN, 31. Juli 1914   XVIII. JAHRG.

the revival of Jewish self-awareness, the maintenance of Jewish ideals, the cultivation of Jewish literature and history, the education of the young in the spirit of the Jewish people …

"'Assimilate, then things will be better!' they assured us with feeling. We did so, we assimilated up to our ears. We imitated all the moves and customs of the nations without testing their value, we forgot our own customs, neglected our own culture. What good did it do us? In the eyes of the nations we remained *Jews*, which means not those who profess the Jewish faith but sons of a different race … We have courted the favor of the Aryan peoples long enough, even renouncing our own dignity, but that lady is very disdainful and the more one humbles oneself to her, the less she thinks of one … "

From the beginning German Zionism struggled against assimilation, to which the majority of German and Austrian Jews subscribed. The Central Association of

Max Bodenheimer, chairman of the Zionist Union of Germany, plants an olive tree as a symbolic gesture when visiting a settlement in 1904.

Group photograph of the first visit to Palestine of Zionists from Germany, 1913. In the back row right (hatless) Nahum Goldman; seated in front (with glasses) Arthur Ruppin.

German Citizens of the Jewish Faith, for instance, regarded the colonization of Palestine as purely praiseworthy philanthropic work to save threatened Jews from East European countries. Most German Jews, who had fought so long for their emancipation and equal status, saw in Zionism a threat to their civil status and fought it bitterly, together with many liberal rabbis, "protest rabbis," as the Zionists called them They also prevented the holding of the First Zionist Congress in Munich, and yet the movement slowly gained a firm circle of adherents, especially among academics and students, who later became its leaders.

The Zionist student body and the young people in the youth movement "Blau Weiss", the gymnastic and sporting society "Bar Kochba," and the "Hechaluz" (The Pioneer) saw their goal in self-realization in Palestine, especially as workers and farmers.

Whereas for the Jewish masses in Eastern Europe and most east European Jews in Germany, Zionism was the path of their Jewish life, to those German Jews who joined it, it meant a way back to Judaism, which had become a hollow form for many of their parents. In this way the Zionist movement in Germany, because of the historical and social development of German Judaism, differed from that of Eastern Europe and America, in which an emotional and sentimental element played a considerable role.

The number of Zionists who converted their ideas into action and went to Palestine was at first very small; the Zionists' strength lay in the intellectual arena: Zionism gave them self-awareness and liberated them from their identity crisis. These ideas were formulated especially by Kurt Blumenfeld (1884–1963) and the editor of the weekly *Die Jüdische Rundschau*, Robert Weltsch (1891–1982). Blumenfeld was General Secretary of the Zionist Association for Germany from 1911 and its chairman from 1924. His influence on the intellectual and political development of the younger generation in particular before and after the First World War was decisive;

LEFT: Lawyer Felix Rosenblüth (1887–1978), co-founder of the Zionist youth movement "Blue and White" (1912); in Palestine from 1921. Israeli Justice Minister (now using the name Pinchas Rosen) 1948–1961.

RIGHT: Group of girls of the Zionist ramblers' league "Blue and White," Breslau 1913.

BELOW CENTER AND RIGHT: Extract from the prospectus of the Jüdischer Verlag ("Jewish publishing house"), 1920.

Martin Buber was their educator. The paper *Der Jude* founded by him became the intellectual platform of German Zionism.

Die Jüdische Rundschau, run by Robert Weltsch from 1919 until it was banned in 1938, was a political forum with a decisive influence on the fight against assimilation. In the thirties Zionism was of the greatest significance in fortifying German Jews, and Palestine became a home for tens of thousands.

Die Geschichte des Jüdischen Verlags

1902 Eine jüdische Hochschule. — Jüdischer Almanach 5663. — Palästina. Zeitschrift. Jahrgang I.

1903 Palästina. Zeitschrift. Jahrgang II. — Acher, Mathias: Achad-Haam. Ein Denker und Kämpfer der jüdischen Renaissance. — Herzl, Theodor: Der Judenstaat. — Jüdische Künstler. Herausgegeben von Martin Buber. — Judt, J. M.: Die Juden als Rasse. — Junge Harfen. — Lublinski, S.: Die Entstehung des Judentums. — Jüdische Statistik.

1904 Schechter, Salomon: Die Chassidim, eine Studie über jüdische Mystik. — Toldt: Judenmassakres in Kischinew. — York-Steiner, Heinrich: Der Talmudbauer und Anderes.

1905 Achad-Haam: Am Scheidewege. — Dubnow, S. M.: Die Grundlagen des Nationaljudentums. — Herzl, Theodor: Zionistische Schriften. — Jung Israel. — Loewe, Heinr.: Eine jüdische Nationalbibliothek. — Moses. — Perez, J. L.: Erzählungen und Skizzen. — Pinski, David: Eisik Scheftel. — Protokoll des VII. Zionistenkongresses.

1907 Protokoll des VIII. Zionistenkongresses.

1909 Grünau, Heinrich: Unterwegs. — Kann, J. H.: Erez Israel, das jüdische Land. — Kann, J. H.: Erets Israel. Französische Ausgabe. — Nordau, Max: Zionistische Schriften.

1910 Boehm, Adolf: Der jüdische Nationalfonds. — Eisler, Max: Von jüdischer Kunst. (Joseph Israels.) — Die Judenpogrome in Rußland. — Jüdischer Almanach 5670. — Protokoll des IX. Zionistenkongresses.

1911 Jesser, Dr. Max: Die Juden in der modernen Rassentheorie. — Bialik, Ch. N.: Gedichte. — Loewe, Heinrich: Die Sprachen der Juden. — Nordau, Max: Das Judentum im 19. und 20. Jahrhundert. — Pasmanik, D.: Die Seele Israels. — Ruppin, Dr. Arthur: Die Juden der Gegenwart. — Zionistisches Merkbuch.

1912 Auerbach, Dr. Elias: Palästina als Judenland. — Der zionistische Student. — Hebräische Wandkarte von Palästina. — Loewe, Heinr.: Die Juden in der katholischen Legende. — Trietsch, Davis: Palästina-Handbuch. — Protokoll des X. Zionistenkongresses — Zlocisti, Theod.: Am Tor des Abends. — Die jüdische Gemeinschaft, Heft 1: Moritz Goldstein, Begriff und Programm einer jüdischen Nationalliteratur. Heft 2: Alexander Schueler, Der Rassenadel der Juden. — Vom alten Stamm. Nr. 1. Asch, Schalom: Im Lande der Väter. Nr. 2. Gotelit, Sch.: Die liebe Provinz.

1913 Achad-Haam: Am Scheidewege. Band 1 der neuen Ausgabe. — Kisselhoff, S.: Das jüdische Volkslied. (Die jüdische Gemeinschaft Nr. 3.) — Perez: Volkstümliche Geschichten. (Vom alten Stamm Nr. 3.) — Denkwürdigkeiten der Glückel von Hameln. — Tschlenoff: Fünf Jahre der Arbeit in Palästina.

1914 Chad Gadja, das Peßachbuch. — Herrmann, Leo: Nathan Virnbaum. (Die jüdische Gemeinschaft Nr. 4.) — Asch, Schalom: Kleine Geschichten aus der Vibel. — Friedemann: Das Leben Theodor Herzls. — Blau-Weiß-Liederbuch. — Oppenheimer, Dr. Franz: Gemeineigentum und Privateigentum an Grund und Boden (Nationalfondsbibliothek Nr. 1). — Protokoll des XI. Zionistenkongresses. — Ruppin, Dr. Arthur: Zionistische Kolonisationspolitik. — Scholem Alejchem: Die verlorene Schlacht. (Vom alten Stamm Nr. 4.)

1916 Achad-Haam: Am Scheidewege. Band II. — Buber, Martin: Die jüdische Bewegung. — Das Buch von den polnischen Juden. — Dreibuch. — Erez Israel. Nr. 1. — Meyer, Ludwig Franz: Gedichte. — Treue.

1917 Autoemanzipation. (Die jüdische Gemeinschaft Nr. 5.) — Erez Israel. Nr. 2. — Jontefflieder. Heft I und II. — Oettinger, Ing.-Agr. Jakob: Methoden und Kapitalbedarf jüdischer Kolonisation in Palästina. (Nationalfondsbibliothek Nr. 3.)

1918 Agnon, S. J.: Und das Krumme wird gerade. — Eliot, George: Daniel Deronda — Jiskor. — Jontefflieder. Heft III—XI. — Hatikwah. Dort wo die Zeder. — Hebräisches Quartettspiel. — Moaus-Zur, ein Chanukkahbuch. — Statistik der Juden. — Zum Nationaljüdischen Jugendtag.

The German Palestine Policy

Under the kaisers (1871–1918) Germany pursued an active Eastern policy with the goal of promoting its political, economic and cultural interests in the Near East. This policy was most strikingly expressed in the Baghdad Railway project and the founding of branch banks in the Ottoman Empire. A "Palestine Bank" was also founded, as well as a German shipping line for commerce with Jaffa and Beirut. In the cultural field, Imperial Germany financed German schools, churches, and missions in Palestine. In 1898, Kaiser Wilhelm II was present when the Lutheran Church of the Redeemer was dedicated in the Old City of Jerusalem and the foundation stone for the Roman Catholic Church of the Dormition was laid on Mount Zion; the fortresslike "Empress Auguste Vikt-

RIGHT: Welcome arch erected by the Jewish community of Jerusalem for the imperial couple: "Blessed be he that cometh in the name of the Lord: we have blessed you out of the house of the Lord!" (Psalm 118, 26).

BELOW: Kaiser Wilhelm II with his entourage at Sultan's Pool in the Hinnom Valley. In the background the city walls of Jerusalem. Photograph: American Colony, 1898.

oria" castle was built in a strategically favorable position on Mount Scopus.

Kaiser Wilhelm II's interest in Zionism had been aroused through his uncle, Grand Duke Friedrich I of Baden. During the Kaiser's visit to the East in 1898, Theodor Herzl tried to persuade him to intervene with the Sultan in favor of Jewish settlements in Palestine. After a positive conversation between Herzl and the Kaiser in Constantinople, the subsequent meeting in Jerusalem was a bitter disappointment. Objections from his Chancellor von Bülow, who in turn was influenced by anti-Zionist Jewish bankers, journalists, and rabbis, caused the Kaiser's interest to cool. It became simply an episode in the political history of Zionism.

All the same, Germany played a crucial role for the Jews of Palestine at a critical time.

In the First World War Turkey was an ally of Germany. Richard Lichtheim (1885–1963), a representative of the World Zionist Organization in Constantinople, was able to persuade the German government to save the Jews in Palestine, who were threatened by the policy of the Turkish military governor Djemal Pasha with expulsion and worse.

With the agreement of the Foreign

Jewish colonists' sons as volunteers in the Turkish-German army, 1915.

BELOW: Richard Lichtheim (1885–1963), representative of the World Zionist Organization in Constantinople during the First World War, with his wife and child.

Office, the German ambassador von Wangenheim intervened with the Turkish central government in Constantinople, preventing the worst, although many Jews were deported to Egypt. In cooperation with the German and American ambassadors in Constantinople, Lichtheim obtained wheat and medical aid from the United States, which saved Palestinian Jews from famine and disease.

The Balfour Declaration in November 1917 and the war turning in the Allies'

favor also meant the end of Germany's political role in the Near East. In 1919, freed from considering Turkish interests, the new German government declared its fundamental agreement with the Zionist work of construction in Palestine.

LEFT: Theodor Herzl welcomes the Kaiser in Mikveh Israel ("Hope of Israel") school of agriculture on 28 October 1898.

The First World War

On the outbreak of the First World War, Jewish associations, both non-Zionist and Zionist, encouraged their members to volunteer, which to a great extent actually happened. A total of 100,000 Jews served in the German army in the First World War, 17 percent of all German Jews of all ages. Fifteen hundred received the Iron Cross First Class; some 12,000 died.

One of the popular soldiers' songs was the *Reiterlied* by Hugo Zukkermann (b.1881), Zionist and volunteer in the Austrian army, killed 1914.

"There on the meadow's edge
two jackdaws perching.
If I fall by the Danube,
or die in Poland;
What does it matter.
Before they take my soul,
I fight as a horseman.
Before they take my soul,
I fight as a horseman.
There in the dying sun
two crows are flying.
When comes the reaper death,
our bodies scything?
It is no matter,
If only I see our standards flying
over Belgrade!
If only I see our standards flying
over Belgrade!"

Among the first volunteers was the Social Democrat member of the Reichstag Ludwig Frank, then aged 40. A pioneer of the Labor Youth Movement and supporter of Franco-German understanding, he fell at Lunéville on 3 September 1914.

In October 1916 the German war minister Adolf Wild von Hohenborn ordered a "Jew count," based on a complaint from an anti-Semitic Reichstag member: they wanted statistical proof that fewer Jews than non-Jews were serving at the front and many more Jews than non-Jews were among the "rejected." After this actions were taken in the army which strengthened anti-Semitism throughout the country. The War Ministry did not publish the results when it turned out that very probably the relative number of Jewish soldiers at the

Excerpts from appeals from various Jewish societies and from the *Jüdischer Rundschau* to mobilize.

An die deutschen Juden!

In schicksalsernster Stunde ruft das Vaterland seine Söhne unter die Fahnen.

Daß jeder deutsche Jude zu den Opfern an Gut und Blut bereit ist, die die Pflicht erheischt, ist selbstverständlich.

Glaubensgenossen! Wir rufen Euch auf, über das Maß der Pflicht hinaus Eure Kräfte dem Vaterlande zu widmen! Eilet freiwillig zu den Fahnen! Ihr alle — Männer und Frauen — stellet Euch durch persönliche Hilfeleistung jeder Art und durch Hergabe von Geld und Gut in den Dienst des Vaterlandes!

Berlin, den 1. August 1914.

Verband der Deutschen Juden.
Centralverein deutscher Staatsbürger jüdischen Glaubens.

Deutsche Juden!

In dieser Stunde gilt es für uns aufs neue zu zeigen, dass wir stammesstolzen Juden zu den besten Söhnen des Vaterlandes gehören. Der Adel unserer vieltausendjährigen Geschichte verpflichtet.

Wir erwarten, daß unsere Jugend freudigen Herzens freiwillig zu den Fahnen eilt.

Deutsche Juden!

Wir rufen Euch auf, im Sinne des alten jüdischen Pflichtgebots mit ganzem Herzen, ganzer Seele und ganzem Vermögen Euch dem Dienste des Vaterlandes hinzugeben.

Der Reichsverein der Deutschen Juden · Zionistische Vereinigung für Deutschland

Wir schließen uns dem Aufruf des Reichsvereins der Deutschen Juden und der Zionistischen Vereinigung für Deutschland an.

Wir vertrauen, daß unsere Jugend, durch die Pflege jüdischen Bewußtseins und körperliche Ausbildung in idealer Gesinnung und Mannesmut erstarkt, sich in allen kriegerischen Tugenden auszeichnen wird.

Das Präsidium des Kartells Jüdischer Verbindungen
Der Ausschuß der Jüdischen Turnerschaft

Wir deutschen Juden kennen trotz aller Anfeindungen in den Zeiten des Friedens heute keinen Unterschied gegenüber andern Deutschen. Brüderlich stehen wir mit allen im Kampfe zusammen.

Wir wissen aber auch, daß der Sieg des Moskowitertums jüdische und zionistische Hoffnungen und Arbeit vernichtet. Wir wissen, daß unser Interesse wie im Frieden, so noch mehr jetzt in dem wilden Weltkriege ausschließlich auf deutscher Seite liegt. Denn auf deutscher Seite ist Fortschritt, Freiheit und Kultur. Uns gegenüber stehen härteste Tyrannei, blutigste Grausamkeit und finsterste Reaktion.

Rolph Meyerstein

[handwritten poem in German, "Soldatentraum"]

Umfang: 16 Seiten.

IV. Jahrgang.
No. 48

122. Kriegsnummer

26. November 1916.
Einzelpreis 10 Pfg.

Das Illustrierte Blatt

Verlag der Frankfurter Societäts-Druckerei G.m.b.H. Frankfurt am Main

Leutnant Wilhelm Frankl,
der bisher 16 feindliche Flugzeuge abgeschossen hat und damit nach Boelckes Tod unser erfolgreichster Flieger ist

ABOVE: Mobilization 1914, Unter den Linden (street) in Berlin. A married couple say goodbye to a friend. Fritz and Emma Schlesinger recognized each other when the photograph was exhibited in Naharia, Israel, where they were then living. The cavalryman is Ludwig Börnstein, who celebrated his 100th birthday in Tel Aviv in 1989.

LEFT: Flight Lieutenant Wilhelm Frankl, 1916. After baptism he received the decoration "Pour le Mérite" (shot down April 1917).

Rolph Meyerstein: "Soldiers' Dream." Farmer in Brandenburg after the war, from 1933 near Jerusalem, where he kept 60 dairy cows with one helper. He sold the milk himself to households in Jerusalem. Meyerstein was a grandson of Jeanette (Jettchen) Gebert (see page 234) and Friederike Josephy (see page 235).

front was no smaller than that of non-Jews and that there were more "rejected" non-Jews (popularly known as shirkers) than Jews.

The call by the supreme army command "To the Jews in Poland" immediately led to anti-Jewish excesses in Russia. More than 500,000 Jews, from babies to old people, were transported from western Russia to the interior as "friendly to the enemy," many losing their lives in the process.

About 35,000 Polish and Lithuanian Jews were recruited to Germany for the war industry and the coal mines, where they were nevertheless treated like forced laborers. The writer Arnold Zweig (1887–1968) working in General Ludendorff's headquarters, wrote: "We talked with our brothers and sisters, still in the uniform of a German soldier. They said, 'Your system is disgusting. You regiment and bully for all you're worth, you beat innocent people in hearings, you seize and steal and you enrage us with your contempt. Your forced labor battalions are a kind of Siberia in the middle of the country; your orders are aimed at letting our weak members die of starvation and diseases which were not there before. It was better under the tsar than under you; if only the Russians would come back!...'" (*Das ostjüdische Antlitz* ("The Face of Eastern Jewry"), 1919/20).

ABOVE: Work card for East European Jewish workers. Some 30,000 East European Jews worked in Germany during World War I.

BELOW LEFT: Title page of "East European Jewish Workers in the War" by Julius Berger, 1919.

BELOW CENTER: Book cover "War Letters by Fallen German Jews" published by the Reich League of Jewish Front Line Soldiers.
Against the denigration of Jews in Germany: "12,000 Jews fell in battle!"

BELOW RIGHT: Flyer by the Reich League of Jewish Front Line Soldiers.

RIGHT: Shlomo and Karl Ettlinger from Karlsruhe, radio operators in a flying corps.

Ostjüdische Arbeiter im Kriege

Ein Beitrag zur Arbeitervermittlung unter Juden

Von

Julius Berger

Berlin 1919

Sonderdruck aus „Volk und Land", jüdische Wochenschrift für Politik, Wirtschaft, und Palästina-Arbeit, herausgegeben von Davis Trietsch.

Kriegsbriefe

gefallener Deutscher Juden

AN DIE DEUTSCHEN MÜTTER!

72 000 jüdische Soldaten sind für das Vaterland auf dem Felde der Ehre gefallen

Christliche und jüdische Helden haben gemeinsam gekämpft und ruhen gemeinsam in fremder Erde.

12 000 Juden fielen im Kampf!

Blindwütiger Parteihass macht vor den Gräbern der Toten nicht Halt.

Deutsche Frauen,

duldet nicht, dass die jüdische Mutter in ihrem Schmerz verhöhnt wird.

Reichsbund jüdischer Frontsoldaten E.V.

ABOVE LEFT: Ludwig Frank (1874–1914), from 1906/7 Social Democrat member of the Reichstag. He died in September 1914 as a volunteer at Lunéville.

ABOVE CENTER: Egon Popper, bosun's mate in the Austro-Hungarian navy, 1915.

ABOVE RIGHT: Engineer and front line soldier Leo Loewenstein (1879–1956), founder and first chairman of the Reich League of Jewish Front Line Soldiers, 1919. He survived the Theresienstadt ghetto.

LEFT: Jewish refugees during the German-Russian battles.

After energetic protests, Julius Berger, General Secretary of the Zionist Association for Germany, was appointed representative at the German Central Labor Office in Warsaw, which now set up a "Jewish department." He was assisted in this especially by a few Jewish Social Democrat Reichstag members, the General Secretary of the Trade Union Commission Robert Schmidt and the painter Hermann Struck. In 1918, in collaboration with all Jewish associations, a "Labor Welfare Office of the Jewish Organizations of Germany" was set up and made semiofficially responsible for foreign workers from Eastern Europe.

Berger, who tried to achieve humane and dignified treatment for them, published an eye-witness account of the fearful treatment of the Jewish forced laborers, many of whom died, or survived only as cripples.

At the end of the war most East European Jewish workers, now homeless, having lost their places of work and generally their families in the East through pogroms, starvation, and disease, remained for the time being in Germany.

THE WEIMAR REPUBLIC

German-Jewish Synthesis: the Creative Illusion

Encounter with the World of Eastern Jewry

TOP LEFT: Conversation with an Eastern Jew: Lt Robert Weltsch, editor of the *Jüdische Rundschau*, in a shtetl (village) on the eastern front.

ABOVE: German Jewish soldiers in a Lithuanian village

LEFT: *Ostjuden* ("Eastern Jews"), a special issue of the *Süddeutsche Monatshefte*, Munich, for February 1916. This special issue was intended to win sympathetic support for a victorious Germany in postwar Poland.

When the German Jewish soldiers came across the world of the Eastern Jews on the eastern front in the first years of the war, it was for many of them their first direct encounter with a living Jewish community. The closer the German and East European Jews came into contact, the warmer their human relations generally grew, despite the ingrained prejudices.

This was often true of non-Jews as well. The lithographs of Eastern Jewish life drawn on the eastern front by the painter Max Unold (1885–1964), for example, are comparable only to those of Hermann Struck (1876 1944) in their depth of feeling and understanding. For the majority of German Jewish soldiers in Poland and Lithuania, the first encounter with the Eastern Jews was often a salutary shock, a fundamental, momentous experience.

This was particularly the case with soldiers from the Zionist student circles, who had fed on largely romantic stories about the Eastern Jews and Hasidism and who now saw themselves confronted by the rude reality. What they found, in conditions of poverty thought possible only in Asia, was a people of a rich inner life, unshakable idealistic faith, and wise humor, a people of vitality and optimism despite the great destitution in which they lived. "How much more natural is the social structure ... than in Germany, where the Jews are exclusively either middle class or intellectuals! How much more Jewish and conscious of tradition ...," one of these Western Jews wrote home to his family; his encounter with Eastern Jewry was what led him, as it did many others, back to Judaism. Not a few of the Jewish soldiers from student backgrounds carried a little piece of Eastern Jewry back with them to Germany.

One of the strongest influences in the German Jews' discovery of the world of the Eastern Jews was Fritz Kaufmann (1888–1921). From an assimilated Berlin family, Kaufmann adopted "Mordechai" as his second forename, published Eastern Jewish folk songs, and involved himself with the integration of Eastern Jewish immi-

Hasidim in a small town in Galicia.

BELOW: Members of a German-Jewish delegation and officers of the German police administration in Warsaw at a meeting with Eastern rabbis. In the back row, to the left of the officers, is the German Jewish rabbi Alexander Carlebach.

grants in Berlin. In 1916, the third year of the war, Martin Buber and some friends founded a monthly periodical, *Der Jude*. Through this and the earlier *Ost und West* magazine, founded in 1901, through the performances of the Habima Hebrew theater of Moscow and the Moscow Yiddish Theater, through the Eastern Jewish cultural associations and the new Eastern Jewish immigrants, the German Jews began to learn more about Eastern Jewry, about their philosophy of life, their culture and literature, their social and political movements, and also their religious and spiritual world, the world of rabbinism, Hasidism, and the Enlightenment movement. And not least they also became acquainted with Yiddish folksong and the Eastern Jewish sense of humor, often elegiac, suffused with philosophical self-irony, rather than aggressively witty.

Occasionally in Eastern Jewish anecdotes we also come across a sense of the absurd, reminiscent of the illogicalities of

TOP RIGHT: "The loveliest songs of the eastern Jews," collected by Fritz Mordechai Kaufmann.

CENTER RIGHT: Lines from a Yiddish song, about a laundry girl and her beloved, from the songbook of the Bar Kochba Athletics and Sports Club, Berlin, 1930.

BOTTOM RIGHT: The title page of "A Practical Grammar of the Yiddish Language" by Nathan Birnbaum, 1916.

LEFT: Fetching water in the shtetl. Lithograph by Max Unold, 1918.

ABOVE: "Girl,"
Hermann Struck, 1915.

ABOVE RIGHT: "Boy,"
Hermann Struck, 1915.

LEFT: "Jewish Wagoner,"
Hermann Struck, 1915.
"Newspaper Vendor,"
Hermann Struck, 1915.

the Bavarian humorist Karl Valentin. Two friends are holding a conversation: "You are a scholar, Jonas. Just explain this to me: This morning at 9.12, my aunt in Lemberg handed in a telegram to my father and at 9.13 it arrived at our place in Warsaw. How is that possible? How do the letters travel down the telegraph wire?" – "Now listen here, Meir. Picture to yourself a long dog. Its head is here in Warsaw, the tail is in Lemberg. Your aunt pulls the tail, and the dog barks in Warsaw. That is modern tech-

nology." – "Wonderful! Wonderful! Technology, yes, yes, modern technology! ... But another thing, Jonas. I've heard about a new thing, telegraphy without wires. How does that work?" – "You really don't have the faintest idea about modern technology, do you! It's the same. Only without the dog." – The present writer told Valentin this story and he replied: "The story could be one of mine. Do you know something, it is one of mine, the two Jews took it off me!" – "But excuse me, Mr Valentin, you hadn't heard

that story until a few moments ago." – "Yes, yes. You see, they took it off me *in advance*."

The flavor of authentic Eastern Jewish humor can be gained from the following epigrams: "If a poor man eats a chicken, either the chicken is ill or the man will be." – "People who are ashamed of themselves don't have children." – "You can't joke with God. First, you're not allowed to. And second, he doesn't permit it." – "O God, if you're not going to save us, then at least save the goyim (gentiles)."

The Revolution

LEFT: The first cabinet of the German republic, Weimar, 13 February 1919. From left: Ulrich Rauscher (press spokesman), Robert Schmidt (food, SPD), Eugen Schiffer (finance, DDP), Philipp Scheidemann (chancellor, SPD), Otto Landsberg (justice, SPD), Rudolf Wissell (economics, SPD), Gustav Bauer (labor, SPD), Count Ulrich von Brockdorff-Rantzau (foreign Minister, independent), Eduard David (without portfolio, SPD), Hugo Preuss (interior, DDP), Johann Giesberts (post, Center Party), Johannes Bell (transport and colonies, Center Party), Georg Gothein (without portfolio, DDP), Gustav Noske (armed forces, SPD). Not present: Matthias Erzberger (without portfolio, Center Party).

RIGHT: Special edition of the Social Democrat newspaper *Vorwärts*, 10 November 1918.

LEFT: Kurt Eisner, Bavarian premier, on his way to the state parliament, 1918. His wife is on his right, to his left Minister Hans Unterleitner.

Despite the equal rights legislation of 1871, the German Jews had continued to suffer humiliating restrictions in both state and society, although possibly more painful to them was the knowledge that they were socially not fully accepted. However, the fact that in the revolution of November 1918, which followed Germany's military defeat in World War I and the flight of the Kaiser, a comparatively large number of revolutionaries were Jewish or of Jewish origin aroused more apprehension than enthusiasm in the overwhelming majority of German Jews, who belonged to the middle class and were at the liberal conservative end of the political spectrum. It was true that the new German republic promised the Jews complete and final equality, a promise honored in the 1919 constitution, but the revolutionaries were decried as "typical Jews" by the revolution's opponents, even though these same political rightwingers managed to regard the antirevolutionary, "capitalist Jew" as equally typical of all Jews.

Among the Jewish pioneers of a socialist republic were Kurt Eisner (1867–1919), Rosa Luxemburg (1871–1919), Hugo Haase (1863–1919), and Gustav Landauer (1870–1919), all four of whom died at the hands of assassins, Oskar Kohn (1859–1934) and Otto Landsberg (1869–1957). Landsberg and Haase were members of the Council of People's Representatives, Germany's first republican government after the collapse; in 1919 Landsberg became Minister of Justice. The constitution of the

Weimar Republic was in its fundamentals the work of the democratic member of parliament and constitutional lawyer Hugo Preuss, who from February to June 1919 was Minister of the Interior.

The majority of orthodox and conserva-

revolution gives us Jews the prospect and hope that from a new democratic system ... we will achieve recognition and satisfaction of our demands. Democracy and justice, under whose banner the German people is entering the new era,

previously by 'the Junkers' and 'the student fraternities' ... After all, it is not so unnatural that it should be the Jews, in particular, who, after being shoved into a corner for so long, have now emerged into the front rank. But there are already signs of the backlash. Day

RIGHT: The constitutional lawyer Hugo Preuss (1860–1925), Interior Minister in 1919 and one of the fathers of the Weimar constitution.

LEFT: Hugo Haase (1863–1919), member of the Council of People's Representatives and chairman of the Independent Social Democratic Party, the USPD.

LEFT: The lawyer Bernhard Falk (1867–1944), a battalion commander in World War I and a deputy for the German Democratic Party (DDP) in the 1919 National Assembly. In 1933 he fled to Belgium.

tive Jews and Eastern Jews rejected any kind of violent upheaval. In Bavaria a large number of them remained loyal to the monarchy for many years.

Im Deutschen Reich, the largest circulation Jewish weekly published by the Central Association of German Citizens of the Jewish Faith, struck a note of melancholy in its reaction: "Hindenburg ... now stands a lonely figure on the ruins of shattered hopes."

The Zionist *Jüdische Rundschau*, by contrast, welcomed the revolution: "The

are our strong, invincible helpers."

The attitude of the orthodox press was fundamentally opposed: "Might rules, and the law withholds its blessing ..." (*Jüdische Monatshefte*, 5, 1918.)

Noting the strong Jewish contingent among the leaders of the revolution, the historian Hans Delbrück, an "enlightened conservative" and opponent of the "stab in the back" legend of German defeat, commented that "Germany is governed as little by 'the proletarians' and 'the Jews' now as it was

by day anti-Semitism is gathering force." – "There is a scent of pogrom in the Berlin air," the *Israelitische Gemeindeblatt* of Cologne wrote as early as 13th December 1918. "But the only Jews being attacked are those who do not defend themselves. Only Jews who have no respect for their own Jewishness are despised. But we intend to cling to our Jewishness to our last drop of blood ... The Jews have no need to strike their flag before any civilized nation. We are Jews and intend to remain so for all eternity."

The Munich Soviet Republic

ABOVE: Gustav Landauer (center, with fur hat and beard) at a demonstration on the Theresienwiese in Munich, 16 February 1919.

ABOVE RIGHT: Eugen Leviné, one of the leading minds of the second Soviet Republic in Munich. Executed on 6 May 1919 for resisting the authority of the state.

LEFT: The spot where Count Arco-Valley, whose mother was Jewish, shot Premier Eisner on 21 February 1919.

On 21 February 1919, Kurt Eisner, a Berliner by birth, who for the preceding hundred days had been the socialist premier of Bavaria, was walking down a Munich street on his way to read out his resignation statement when he was shot dead by Count Anton Arco-Valley, an aristocrat who on his mother's side was of Jewish descent. As a socialist revolutionary, Eisner was a founding member of the Independent Social Democratic Party of Germany (USPD) and the driving force behind a Bavarian republic, for the idea of which he had enthused the crowds at a mass demonstration on 8 November 1918. It had been a bloodless coup.

Since then, however, the communists had come to regard Eisner as a tool of the bourgeoisie, while for the right he was a Jewish Bolshevik and "bloody Prussian." Eisner had not the slightest interest in Jewishness or Judaism.

Gustav Landauer held the position of people's delegate for the education of the Masses during the first Bavarian Soviet Republic, in which the mainstream Social Democrats took no part. A socialist, anti-Marxist, and social philosopher, the moving spirit behind Berlin's first cooperative society, cofounder of the Berlin People's Theater and interpreter of Shakespeare's works, Landauer was a friend of Martin Buber and the only leading figure of the revolutionary period in Munich to feel close ties to his Jewishness.

This first Soviet Republic in Munich, led by USPD members and anarchists like the writer Erich Mühsam (1878–1934; tortured in the Oranienburg concentration camp and hanged in the latrines), lasted just six days. On 14 April, after an abortive coup attempt by the Munich garrison, the second Soviet Republic, more communist-minded than its predecessor, was proclaimed. Jewish politicians were as involved in the second as the first.

As early as 16 April, Gustav Landauer ("Marxism is the plague of the world") resigned. After the Soviet Republic was put down by the troops of Hoffmann's Social Democratic government, he was arrested, subjected to dreadful torture, and murdered. "We put four bullets / in the commie Landauer's ass," his murderers sang.

Eugen Leviné (1883–1919) was the chairman of the governing committee during the fourteen days of the second Soviet Republic. Born into a well-to-do Russian Jewish middle-class family, he had taken part in the Russian revolution of 1905, then studied law in Heidelberg and Berlin, graduating in 1914 in political economy. Having become a German citizen, he fought as a soldier in World War I. A friend and party comrade of Rosa Luxemburg and Karl Liebknecht, he became a member of the government of the Munich Soviet Republic. On 6 May 1919, after the victory of the "white guard" in Munich, he was condemned to death and shot for "resisting state authority."

Ernst Toller (1893–1939) was a World War I volunteer and front-line soldier who turned against the war and joined the USPD to work alongside Kurt Eisner. After the failure of the first Soviet Republic, Toller conducted the negotiations with Hoffmann's official Social Democratic government, then with its seat in Bamberg, over the peaceful dissolution of the Soviet. In the second republic he commanded the "red army" to victory over their adversaries, in the only fighting that took place at that time. On 26 April, he wrote a letter announcing his resignation: "[I consider] the present government a disaster for the working people of Bavaria." Among those who spoke up for him after his arrest were Thomas Mann and

BELOW: Wanted poster for Ernst Toller, 15 May 1919.

BELOW: Flyer of the Central Association of German Citizens of the Jewish Faith against anti-Semitic outbursts, 1919.

Max Halbe. His defense was conducted by Hugo Haase. He was sentenced to five years' confinement in a fortress (a more honorable punishment than imprisonment). Toller's poems and plays made a deep impression during the Weimar Republic, particularly on the young.

In politics as in art and literature, it was primarily assimilated Jews who were most eager to embrace revolution as the means to achieve their ethical and social message. Many of these revolutionaries were fighting for a new "inner" home, to replace the Jewish one they had lost. Ernst Toller, for instance, felt his Jewishness as "something painful" even as a child. In 1914 he volunteered as a front-line soldier, to prove by risking his life that he was "a German and nothing but a German." Later, after 1933 and before his suicide in 1939, he asked himself: "Was it all in vain?"

It was the same question that Rahel Varnhagen, Berthold Auerbach, Kurt Tucholsky, Maximilian Harden, and many others had asked themselves before him.

But there were many Jews who disputed the right of their fellow Jews, as members of the very small Jewish minority in Germany, to occupy high political office. As early as November 1918, for example, Martin Buber, writing in the monthly *Der Jude*, had had the following to say about the role of Jews in the German revolution: "Since time immemorial he has believed in renewal, in the 'new dawn,' the 'new earth,' in 'making all things new.' Of course, he often goes astray, he *has to* go astray again and again … he will only cease going astray *when he implements his truth on his own soil and among his own people.* But still, today, we welcome the revolution … not as beneficiaries but as men who share the struggle and the responsibility."

Anti-Semitism and Prosecution

Germany had lost the war. "The Kaiser fled, the generals remained." Those responsible sloughel off the guilt for this inconceivable event on to others, on to the republican and revolutionary parties and on to a minority they had never felt quite comfortable about, the Jews.

In his 1897 pamphlet *Höre Israel* ("Hear, Israel"), Walther Rathenau, the son and heir of the founder of the AEG electrical company, who on 21 January 1922 became Germany's foreign minister, had warned the Jews "not to attract so much attention." But Rathenau, as a Jewish big businessman, the Jewish organizer of wartime raw material supplies, and Germany's Jewish foreign minister, attracted the most attention of all Jews, although like many other Jews before and since who felt they had to distance themselves from "the Jews," he never realized this.

And yet he recognized the tragedy of this denial of identity, when he wrote: "In

ABOVE: "Shock Troops: Hitler Squad," Munich 1923.

RIGHT: "Rathenau murdered!", *Vorwärts*, 24 June 1922.

BELOW: Poster for a Nazi party meeting to be addressed by Hitler, 17 February 1922.

Nationalsozialistische Deutsche Arbeiter-Partei

Freitag, den 17. Februar 1922
im Bürgerbräukeller, Rosenheimer Straße

eine große **Volksversammlung** ab.

Es wird sprechen:

Herr **Adolf Hitler** über:

„Volksrepublik oder Judenstaat"

Beginn der Versammlung 8 Uhr abends.   Juden ist der Zutritt verboten.

Zur Deckung der Saal- und Plakatunkosten M. 1.— Eintritt.
Kriegsbeschädigte frei.

Der Einberufer: Für die Parteileitung A. Drexler.

Sonder-Ausgabe.

Vorwärts
Berliner Volksblatt
Zentralorgan der Sozialdemokratischen Partei Deutschlands

Sonnabend den 24 Juni 1922

Rathenau ermordet!

Um ½,12 Uhr teilte der Reichskanzler den in der Wandelhalle des Reichstags versammelten Abgeordneten mit, daß vor etwa einer halben Stunde der Außenminister Dr. Rathenau ermordet worden sei.

Als Dr. Rathenau heute vormittag 11 Uhr sein Automobil vor seinem Hause in der Königsallee im Grunewald bestiegen hatte, näherte sich von der entgegengesetzten Seite ein elegantes Privatautomobil, das den Wagen des Ministers bis zur Königsallee, Ecke Wallotstraße, verfolgte.

Hier überholte das Privatautomobil, in dem sich drei Leute mit dunklen Brillen befanden, das Automobil des Ministers.

In demselben Augenblick, als das Auto in die Wallotstraße einbog, erhob sich einer der bedrillten Leute und warf eine Handgranate in das Auto des Ministers. Die Granate explodierte. Rathenau richtete sich einen Augenblick auf und brach dann zusammen. Der Chauffeur fuhr mit dem sterbenden Minister sofort in dessen Wohnung zurück, während einige Passanten die Verfolgung des flüchtigen Autos aufnahmen.

In der Wandelhalle des Reichstags sind jetzt die deutschnationalen Abgeordneten nicht zu erblicken, sie haben sich zurückgezogen, um den Verwünschungen und Drohungen der übrigen Abgeordneten zu entgehen.

Ueber die Täter ist Näheres noch nicht bekannt.

Massen, haltet Euch bereit!

DEVTSCHLAND

the youth of every German Jew there is a painful moment, which he will remember as long as he lives: when he realizes fully for the first time that he has been born into the world as a second-class citizen, and that no virtue and no merit can free him from this situation." Many years later, in December 1917, Rathenau wrote to Gertrud Wilhelmine von Hindenburg, the field marshal's sister-in-law: "... even though I and my forefathers have served our country to the best of our ability, as a Jew I am, as you are surely aware, a second-class citizen. I could not become a political official, nor, even in peacetime, a lieutenant." As a Jew in a select regiment, he had been able to rise no higher than the rank of sergeant.

Rathenau rejected baptism as a way out. "I stayed in the Jewish religious community because I had no desire to run away from rebukes or hardships, and I have had plenty of those to experience right up to the present day." He described Prussia's policy toward the Jews as the grossest of insults to one section of the population, misplaced and unethical. "In truly civilized countries, in England, France, Italy, and America, they [the Jews] are one of the groups that are most positive toward the state."

Meanwhile, on house walls in Berlin in 1922, graffiti appeared reading: "Walter Rathenau should be shot / the Jewish pig, whom God rot!" On 24 June 1922, Walther Rathenau was assassinated by "young, nationally minded Germans."

The historian Golo Mann later wrote: "The enormous moral confusion and brutalization that followed the defeat, then the complete impoverishment and loss of social status of many millions of people in the inflation, events that simply surpassed the comprehension of most of them, led for the first time to the cry of 'The Jews are our misfortune' gaining some resonance. I would go so far as to say the following: anti-Semitic passions have never run so high in Germany as in the years 1919–1923. This was the period of the National Socialists' first great success. Almost as soon as the inflation ended and the masses saw a glimmer of hope that their life could be more worthy of human beings, the Nazi movement began to lose support."

The Relief Organization of German Jews

The Relief Organization of German Jews was founded in Berlin in 1901 by a group of businessmen and philanthropists to "promote the moral, spiritual, and economic development of our coreligionists, particularly in Eastern Europe and Asia." A further aim was to parallel the work of the French Alliance Israélite Universelle and establish a relief organization for the German-speaking world, which would represent and promote German cultural interests.

The first major relief action for the wounded and homeless began after the Russian and Romanian pogroms of 1903–1905. However, although the Relief Organization even negotiated with the Russian and Romanian governments, its attempts to improve the situation of the legally unprotected victims of persecution remained largely fruitless.

In Palestine the Relief Organization set up a broad network of schools, from kindergartens to teacher training colleges, and in other parts of the Ottoman Empire, too, it promoted Jewish education and health. From 1904 to 1914, the organization's local committees in Bremen and

A Relief Organization kindergarten in Jerusalem, 1907.

Hamburg looked after more than 200,000 Eastern Jews who were emigrating to America.

During World War I, the Relief Organization started a generous aid operation in the German-occupied areas of Poland and Russia. This continued on a larger scale after the war, in cooperation with American aid agencies, when a wave of pogroms again broke over the heads of the Jews.

After the war the organization also carried on its welfare work for emigrants in Germany and its aid programs in other countries.

ABOVE LEFT: Military doctor Ludwig F. Meyer, who led rescue operations for the Relief Organization of German Jews in Russian Poland during World War I.

ABOVE CENTER AND RIGHT: A letter of thanks to Ludwig Meyer from the Jewish community of Oschmiana, 1916.

BELOW: Refugees in a synagogue in Brest Litovsk, 1922. The Relief Organization and the American Joint Distribution Committee helped in the reconstruction of the wrecked Jewish quarter.

BELOW: After the pogrom in Kiev, 1917: children in a Relief Organization camp.

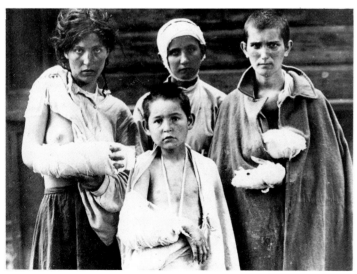

Spiritual and Intellectual Leadership

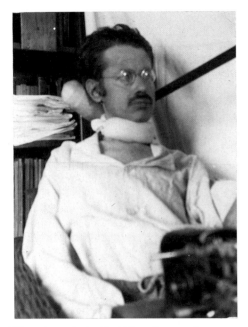

Philosopher and educationist Franz Rosenzweig (1886–1929). From 1922 onward Rosenzweig was seriously ill.

Leo Baeck (1873–1956), the last great rabbi of German Jewry. Portrait painted by Max Westfeld.

While the 19th-century renaissance of Jewish secular and religious life continued after the turn of the century, the catastrophe of World War I called for a new search for meaning. In this the Jews' situation was no different from that of intellectuals in general in the Weimar Republic. Orthodox theologians like Nehemia Nobel, religious philosophers like Rosenzweig and Buber, political thinkers and educationists like Robert Weltsch and Ernst Simon: they all in their own way tried to find an answer to those questions of existence that were troubling young people in particular.

The philosopher and educational theorist Franz Rosenzweig (1886–1929) is remembered particularly for his *Hegel und der Staat* ("Hegel and the State"), 1919, *Der Stern der Erlösung* ("The Star of Redemption"), 1921, and *Zweistromland* ("The Land of Two Currents"), 1926, and his translations of Judah ha-Levi's poems and, with Martin Buber, of the Bible (1926 ff.). In his youth, Rosenzweig became alienated from his assimilated family and, in his search for a living religious faith, came close to converting to Christianity. It was the experience of an Orthodox service on the High Holidays in autumn 1913 that "brought him back to the path" of Judaism. He now became a "Jewish Jew" and in 1921, with Ernst Simon, founded the Free Jewish House of Learning in Frankfurt am Main as a Jewish adult education organization. Rosenzweig presented his students with a choice: "To be Jewish or not to be Jewish!" Assimilation in his view did not have to be an irreversible process. Thousands of young people trying to find a meaning for their Judaism in the modern world looked to Rosenzweig as their guiding light.

Nehemia Nobel (1871–1922), the son of an Orthodox rabbi from Hungary, moved to the German town of Halberstadt as a child. He graduated with a thesis on Schopenhauer's Aesthetic theory and in 1910 became the rabbi of the Orthodox congregation of Frankfurt am Main. His influence, however, extended over the

Martin Buber giving a seminar to students. In the left-hand corner of the photograph is Ernst Akiba Simon, one of the outstanding spiritual leaders of Jewish youth. Simon became professor of education at the Hebrew University of Jerusalem in 1928.

Teachers at the College for the Science of Judaism, Berlin. Right, seated: Leo Baeck. Next to him, standing: Prof. Ismar Elbogen (1874–1943). Between the two, rabbi and philosopher Max Wiener (1882–1950).

Kurt Blumenfeld (1884–1963), president of the Zionist Alliance for Germany and spiritual leader of the Zionist students.

Merchant and publisher Zalman Schocken (1877–1959). Owner of a chain of department stores, in 1931 he founded the Schocken publishing house, and provided spiritual support to the German Jews in the years of persecution.

whole community, thanks first to his lively sermons and Talmud courses but also to his public lectures, some of which he gave in Rosenzweig's school. A supporter of Theodor Herzl from his youth, Nobel was a founder-member of the nationalist religious Mizrachi party. His rulings on Jewish religious law – as, for instance, when he supported the right of women to be elected to Jewish official positions – were also taken with an eye to the construction of a Jewish state in Palestine.

Martin Mordechai Buber (1878–1965), from 1924 to 1933 professor of Jewish religion and ethics at Frankfurt University, the director of the Jewish House of Learning in Frankfurt and the Central Office for Jewish Adult Education, is known in the Western world largely as the author of *Drei Reden über das Judentum* ("Three Addresses on Judaism"), 1911, *Ich und Du* ("I and Thou"), 1923, and *Erzählungen der Chassidim* ("Hassidic Tales"), 1949. In Nazi Germany, he campaigned through the adult education classes for moral resistance. Buber's aim

was the renewal of Judaism through the spirit of the Bible and the Hasidic books.

Buber was also a champion of Jewish-Arab understanding, both on practical political grounds and because of the need for the people and state of Israel to preserve their position, in their Zionist embodiment, among the nations. Buber's philosophy of dialogue influenced philosophy itself, educational theory, psychology, and theology.

Salomon Breuer (1850–1926, from Neutra in Slovakia) studied at Hungarian yeshivas and in 1889 became the rabbi of the Orthodox congregation in Frankfurt am Main. Following in the footsteps of his father-in-law Samson Raphael Hirsch, he pursued the latter's educational program, "What is beautiful is the Torah in combination with general education," although Breuer laid more stress on the Torah and the Talmud. He founded a yeshiva and became a radical leading figure in the orthodox Agudat Israel organization, which during his lifetime was anti-Zionist

in outlook. Later some of its leaders took a more positive interest in the construction of a Jewish Palestine.

Robert Weltsch (1891–1982, born in Prague), a leading Zionist publicist who wrote in German, English, and Hebrew, campaigned with his friend Martin Buber for Jewish-Arab understanding with the purpose of establishing a binational state. From 1919 he was editor of the *Jüdische Rundschau*. After the founding of the Leo Baeck Institute in 1955, Weltsch edited the first 22 volumes of the institute's yearbook, which was devoted to the history of the German Jews in all its aspects, although regrettably only from the time of Moses Mendelssohn onward.

Leo Baeck (1873–1956), the son of a conservative rabbi from Lissa (in the province of Posen), was a leading representative of moderate liberalism. He regarded the "foundations of ethical monotheism" as eternal, but the liturgical forms as transient and changeable.

His major work, *Das Wesen des Judentums* ("The Essence of Judaism") was conceived as a rejoinder to Adolf von Harnack's *Wesen des Christentums* ("Essence of Christianity"), 1900. In it Baeck expressed what Moses Mendelssohn, when challenged by Lavater, had not dared to say. Baeck rejected Christianity because as a Jew he held Judaism to be superior, just as Lavater and Harnack had regarded Christianity as superior.

From 1912 he was a rabbi in Berlin, from 1921 also a teacher at the College for the Science of Judaism in Berlin and the chairman of the German Rabbinical Association. When the Reichsvertretung, the representative body of German Jews, was set up in 1933, he became its president, which he remained until the end. Leo Baeck was thus the chief representative of the Jews in Germany, even after his deportation to the Theresienstadt concentration camp in 1943.

Jewish Writing

Title page of Franz Rosenzweig's "Star of Redemption," 1921.

JÜDISCHES LEXIKON

Ein enzyklopädisches Handbuch
des jüdischen Wissens
in vier Bänden

Mit über 2000 Illustrationen, Beilagen, Karten und Tabellen

Herausgegeben von

Dr. GEORG HERLITZ und Dr. BRUNO KIRSCHNER

Unter Mitarbeit von über 230 jüdischen Gelehrten und Schriftstellern

"Jewish Lexicon" vol. I, 1927 (publisher's advertisement).

ABOVE: Publisher's advertisement for "The Book of Bahir," a "written monument from the early history of the cabala," translated and edited by Gerhard Scholem, 1929.
BELOW: "Addresses on Judaism" by Martin Buber, second edition, 1932 (head of title page).

The oldest surviving Jewish publishing house in 1933 was the I. Kaufmann Verlag in Frankfurt am Main, founded in 1832, which published religious books and prayer books such as the much-read household volume *Bibel und Talmudschatz* ("Bible and Talmud Treasury").

The Jüdische Verlag, the publishing house founded by the Zionist Alliance for Germany, published works by Zionist and Eastern Jewish writers including Theodor Herzl, Martin Buber and Max Nordau, and was known particularly for such multivolume works as the *Jüdisches Lexikon* ("Jewish Lexicon") and Simon Dubnow's *Geschichte der Juden* ("History of the Jews"). The nine-volume German translation of the Babylonian Talmud by Lazarus Goldschmidt (1871–1950) was also published by the Jüdische Verlag.

The Akademie Verlag, Berlin, specialized in Jewish studies; the Eschkol Verlag, founded by Nahum Goldmann and Jakob Klatzkin, put out the *Encyclopedia Judaica*, although only ten of the twenty projected volumes had appeared by 1933. The Philo Verlag produced, in cooperation with the Central Association of German Citizens of the Jewish Faith, mostly apologetical literature, the monthly *Der Morgen*, intellectual works by Franz Rosenzweig and others, and the famous *Philo-Lexikon* (1934). The Benjamin Harz Verlag was known for belles lettres.

In 1931, business magnate and patron of the arts Zalman Schocken (1877–1959) founded the publishing house that was to be the most active in the coming years. Among the titles that appeared here were the Buber-Rosenzweig translation of the Bible, all of Martin Buber's writings, Benno Jakob's commentary on Genesis, and a series of smaller volumes, known as the Schocken Library, aimed largely at the young. Schocken also issued a collected edition of Kafka's works and the books of

Advertisement of the Jüdischer Verlag, Berlin.

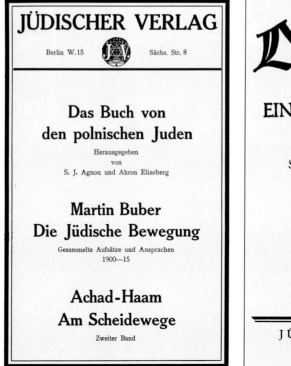

Cover of *Der Jude*, 1923.

Gershom Scholem and other Jewish thinkers. Zalman Schocken's commitment to Jewish literature was thus of crucial importance for the intellectual life of the German Jews in the years after 1931.

Cover of *Jeschurun*, 1927, (detail), a monthly devoted to Jewish "life and doctrine."

Title cover of the "Journal of the History of the Jews in Germany."

Title cover of the bi monthly *Der Morgen*, 1931.

A Stettin Family Album

His parents had a meat-processing business in Mainz but son Nathan Marx (1873–1929) did not like his father's occupation, so around 1890 he became a messenger boy for a bank. Then, wanting a more independent career, he became a rep-

ABOVE LEFT: The Marx family home.

ABOVE RIGHT: Nathan Marx with members of the workforce, outside the factory.

LEFT: The living room with the father's portrait by Max Liebermann.

BELOW LEFT: The five children. From left to right: Lotte, Eva, Hans, Ruth, and Ernst.

BELOW RIGHT: The Purim festival.

resentative for a factory making suit linings and buttons. With his savings he moved, newly married, to Stettin and began building up a firm in which he could put his own ideas into practice: he was the first to introduce into Germany sleeve linings that were not black or white but had colored patterns designed in his own workshops.

The business grew and soon had thirty employees on its staff. The production of the lining patterns was contracted out to small manufacturers. Over the course of the years Nathan Marx became well-to-do and moved into Stettin's residential quarter. He became chairman of the Jewish

community and of various charitable organizations. With his wife Grete he collected drawings by such artists as Hermann Struck, Joseph Budko, Jakob Steinhardt, and especially Käthe Kollwitz, and also paintings by Lesser Ury, whom the couple helped through some financially lean years with their purchases. Nathan Marx had his portrait painted by Max Liebermann.

The Marx family belonged to the Zionist minority in the Stettin community. The five children were members of the Zionist youth movement and the Bar Kochba sports club. After their emigration to Palestine in 1933, the eldest son joined a village community while one daughter became a member of a kibbutz.

RIGHT: Family gathering at Hans's Bar Mitzvah, 13 October 1923.

BELOW: The drawing room.

ABOVE RIGHT: The children's room.

LEFT: Family outing.

RIGHT: Hans (x) with other members of the Bar Kochba sports club, 1929.

The Youth Movement

The Blue-and-White Club's beginnings were romantic in character. A Breslau group.

Rambling in all weathers. A Blue-and-White group from Munich on a hike to Franconia, some 200 kilometers away. Photo Walter Goldstern, London.

Around the campfire. A Blue-and-White group from Frankfurt, 1924.

In 1912 a student, Josef Markus, and some friends in Breslau formed the Blau-Weiss (Blue-and-White) ramblers' club; blue and white were the colors of the Zionist flag. Although interrupted by World War I, when most of the club's young leaders became soldiers, it grew to have over 30,000 members and become the largest Jewish youth group in Germany. Felix Rosenblüth, one of the first members of the Blue-and-White Club and later Israel's first justice minister, wrote in his manual for the club: "Brought up among adults who act and think only materialistically, surrounded by skeptical, ironic, joyless human beings alienated from nature, in an atmosphere of Jewish self-mockery ... the Jewish Blue-and-White Club seeks to lead the younger generation back to nature, in the hope of thereby providing a counterweight to the errors of a false education ... it brings children up in opposition to their elders' ideas of life, not in opposition to the Jewish point of view ..."

The Blue-and-Whites were particularly opposed to the assimilationist middle-class mentality of their parents' generation. In their rejection of the older generation and their embrace of their own people, the Blue-and-Whites had similarities with the German youth ramblers' movement, the *Wandervogel*, which, however, became increasingly nationalist and largely anti-Semitic. Rambling, the experience of nature and community, and the folk song were characteristic of both movements, albeit in the case of the Blue-and-Whites Hebrew songs began to be sung alongside German songs, medieval soldiers' songs, and canons by Mozart. Hesse's *Knulp* and *Siddartha*, Tolstoy's "Folk Tales" and "War and Peace", Keller's *Der grüne Heinrich* ("Green Henry"), Morgenstern's *Galgenlieder* ("Gallows Songs"), and the poetry of Hölderlin, Whitman, and George featured as prominently in the Blue-and-White reading matter as Buber's *Reden über das Judentum* and the stories of Isaac Leib Peretz.

There was never any place in Blue-and-White ideology for the inclination toward the "folk" or "racial" mythology and

Landsknechtsmarsch, 16. Jahrh. Nach Forster.

1. Wir zogen in das Feld, wir zogen in das Feld, da hättn wir weder Säckl noch Geld. Stram-pe-de-mi, a-la-mi pre-sen-te al vostra sig-no-ri.

2. |: Wir kamn vor Siebentod, :| da hättn wir weder Wein noch Brot. Stram-pe-de usw.

3. |: Wir kamen vor Friaul, :| da hättn wir allesamt groß Maul. Stram-pe-de usw.

Wer je die flamme umschritt
Bleibe der flamme trabant!
Wie er auch wandert und kreist:
Wo noch ihr schein ihn erreicht
Irrt er zu weit nie vom ziel.
Nur wenn sein blick sie verlor
Eigener schimmer ihn trügt
Fehlt ihm der mitte gesetz
Treibt er zerstiebend ins all.

ABOVE AND RIGHT: "Blue-and-White" songs. Stefan George's songs were also much read in the Jewish youth movement.

BELOW: Club camp near Elpertshofen, summer 1924. Photo Saul Syman.

Marschlied

Po, be-e-rez chem-dat a-wot, tit-ga-schem-na kol ha-tik-wot, po nich-je u-fo ni-zor cha-je so-har, cha-je d'ror, po te-hi ha-sch'chi-na scho-ra, po tif-rach gam ss'fat ha-to-ra! Ni-ru nir, nir, nir! Schi-ru schir, schir, schir! Gi-lu gil, gil, gil! K'war he-ne-zu ni-za-nim. Ni-ru nir, nir, nir! Schi-ru schir, schir, schir! Gi-lu gil, gil, gil. Od ja-wo-u se-r'o-nim.

Po b'erez.

Hier im Lande der Sehnsucht der Väter werden alle Hoffnungen verwirklicht werden. Hier wollen wir leben, hier wollen wir schaffen ein Leben in Reinheit, ein Leben in Freiheit. Hier soll Gottes Glanz weilen, hier soll auch der Thora Sprache blühen. Zieht Furche auf Furche! Singt Lied auf Lied! Seid freudig, froh! Schon schimmern die Blüten. Zieht Furche auf Furche! Singt Lied auf Lied! Seid freudig, froh! Bald werden auch Früchte kommen.

romantic mystification encouraged by the "Wandervogel," the non-Jewish ramblers' movement. Nor did any of the Jewish clubs indulge in the romantic, nationalist idealization of the "beautiful, supple, naked male body" cultivated in many non-Jewish clubs and later in the Third Reich. The Blue-and-Whites did not subscribe either to the idea that girls were by nature predestined to be mothers and housewives.

In 1923–24, around four hundred members of the Blue-and-White Club completed practical courses in agriculture or training in craft skills in urban workshops.

For an entire generation of young Jews, the Blue-and-White Club meant the first acquaintanceship with the history of their own people, with the particular problems of individual Jews in the Diaspora, and with the national renaissance, whether as the basis of their German-Jewish existence or with the aim of settlement in Palestine.

The attitude of the younger generation that grew up in the Blue-and-White and other Jewish clubs had, with a few minor exceptions, nothing apologetic about it. Confident in their own Jewish values, they did not

ABOVE: Morning prayers at the spring. Photo Walter Goldstern.

ABOVE RIGHT: A girls' group from the Kadima club on an outing to Prague, 1932. Photo Tim Gidal.

CENTER RIGHT: Dancing the hora at meeting of the Kadima-Habonim club, 1932. Photo Tim Gidal.

LOWER RIGHT: Ball games at a Kadima Shavnot camp meeting in the Altmühltal, 1926. Photo Georg Gidal.

depend on the judgment of the hostile world in which they lived but merely noted it with indifference, and often with scorn.

Around 1922–23 the first Blue-and-White groups began to emigrate to Palestine, and were followed by others in the 1930s. The first groups either joined existing kibbutzim or started workshops on a private basis. But these workshops failed to form any ideological links with the country's labor force, and with the economic depression of those years, disillusionment led to returns to Germany and the leadership's decision to dissolve the Blue-and-White club. Immediately, however, a successor organization, Kadima ("Forward"), sprang up.

There were numerous other Jewish youth clubs besides the Blue-and-White. The Young Jewish Ramblers' Club (founded in 1923, around 1300 members) saw itself from the start as a source of new blood for the socialist workforce in Palestine and later amalgamated with another club with similar ideas and parts of the Kadima to form the Habonim club. Their work was based on practical preparation for agricultural or

craft occupations in Palestine. In 1929 club members and friends of theirs from Italy and Czechoslovakia founded the Givat Brenner kibbutz, which with its 1600 inhabitants is today the biggest in the country.

In 1931 the German section of the Hashomer Hazair ("The Young Guard") was formed. Leftwing but anticommunist, it combined German educational ideas (Gustav Wyneken) with Eastern Jewish culture. This club, too, required its members to learn a craft or follow agricultural

LEFT: "Adventure in Tonkin," an amateur theatrical by Martin Luserke performed at a meeting of the Jewish Scouts' Association, Munich, 1926. Photo Georg Gidal.

BELOW: A group from Cologne of the German nationalist Falken ("Falcons"), c. 1930.

training, as preparation for settlement in Palestine.

The "Bund der Kameraden" ("Comrades' League") was founded in 1919 as a national association of Jewish ramblers, sports, and gymnastic clubs. In its statutes it exhorted its members to become "thoroughly acquainted with all the religious, moral, and ethical values of the Jews," to "pledge loyalty to the German fatherland and nationhood," and to "immerse themselves in the German spirit and sensibility." It also called for a "ceaseless struggle against anti-Semitism" and against all attempts to organize German Jews on a Jewish nationalist basis.

Unbridgeable differences appeared as early as the Comrades' first national conference in 1921. A visit to Franz Rosenzweig (see page 330) led to the formation of a group for whom the renaissance of "a new Germany in the spirit of the Middle Ages, Goethe and Stefan George" loomed less large than the Jewish renaissance.

Gradually the search for their own Jewish identity led many Comrades to the religious views of Franz Rosenzweig and Martin Buber, which they combined with socialist thinking. One of these breakaway groups adopted the name "Die Werkleute" ("The Artisans"). It embraced the path of socialist Zionism and later founded the Hazorea kibbutz, both industrially and agriculturally one of the most successful in Israel, close to the fortress of King Solomon at Megiddo.

The Ezra Orthodox youth association (named after Ezra the scribe, who led the Jews out of the Babylonian exile in the 6th century BC) also had about 1000 members, who likewise underwent agricultural training, under the leadership of an Orthodox farmer. In Palestine the association founded Orthodox kibbutzim.

In 1930 the Jewish youth associations in Germany, including the sports clubs (see page 344), had around 40,000 members.

A group of comrades from the town of Oppeln, on a hike.

The Emancipation of Women

Alice Salomon (1872–1948), a social reformer and from 1908 to 1924 the head of the Social School for Women in Berlin.

Rahel Hirsch (1870–1953), the first woman in Prussia to be become a professor of medicine (1913). Photo Alice Matzdorff, 1917.

Bertha Pappenheim (1859–1936), founder of the League of Jewish Women in 1904 (known to the history of psychoanalysis as Anna O).

One of the first, if not the first, woman in Germany to demand female emancipation, in the sense of legal and social equality with men, was Rahel Levin-Varnhagen (see page 142). She rejected male hegemony.

Shortly before her death she was visited by the then 20-year-old Fanny Lewald (1811–1889) from Königsberg. Fanny Lewald wrote her first novel, *Clementine*, under the influence of Rahel Levin-Varnhagen's ideas about women's emancipation, which she saw as being a companion movement to the emancipation of the Jews and the liberation of the workers. In *Clementine* Fanny Lewald also repudiated conventional marriage. In 1870 she made a second public declaration of her views, in *Für und wider die Frauen* ("Women, For and Against"), one of the first clarion calls for unrestricted equality for women.

A year earlier, Friederike Kempner (1836–1904) from Opatow in the province of Posen had published an essay calling for the abolition of solitary confinement in prison. Even as a young girl she had

protested against vivisection. She campaigned successfully for the establishment of mortuaries, to prevent the burial of those only apparently dead, and for an end to solitary confinement for prisoners serving life sentences. Kempner's achievements in the social sphere and in combating anti-Semitism were, however, overshadowed by her fame as the "Silesian nightingale." Indeed, the unintended humor of the poems she published from 1873 onwards aroused great hilarity in her readers.

The literary critic Werner Kraft claims to find genuine poetic force in some of her verses. It is not impossible that she was in fact aware of their comic nature and that she published them in order to annoy her stuffed-shirt bourgeois relations, who looked down on her, half mockingly and half in pained embarrassment, as a bluestocking. Kempner was the aunt of the famous literary critic of Weimar Berlin, Alfred Kerr. He wrote intentionally "comic" verse; when Bertold Brecht once remarked that he had inherited his poetic talent from his aunt, it evoked a suitably

absurd piece of doggerel from Kerr: "Sometimes by night in fields of bones / There
issue braying hee-haw moans, / The ass can
think of nothing new, / Drag in the aunt,
she'll have to do."

One prominent figure in the women's
movement and in social education was
Bertha Pappenheim (1859–1936), a
Viennese and descendant of Glückel of
Hamelin (see page 93): in Frankfurt in
1904 she founded the Jewish League of
Women, which had close links with the
German women's movement. Following
journeys to Romania, Russia, and Poland,
she concentrated on combating prostitu-
tion and discrimination against illegitimate
children. Near Frankfurt she founded a
home for prostitutes, unmarried mothers,
and women who had come into conflict
with the law. Bertha Pappenheim was an
opponent of the Zionist movement,
because in her view, by taking young
people off to Palestine, it was responsible
for breaking up families. She died in 1936,
shortly after an interrogation by the
Gestapo.

Alice Coblenz-Bensheimer (1864–1957)
was the assistant of Gertrud Bäumer, the
leader of the German women's movement,
and was for 25 years the secretary of the
Federation of German Women's Associations. Another Jewish woman to play an
outstanding role in the campaign for
women's rights was the influential Alice
Salomon (1872–1948), who from 1908 to
1924 headed the Social School for Women
and from 1925 to 1933 the Social and
Educational Academy for Women in
Berlin. Henriette Katzenstein-Fürth
(1861–1939) helped to found the prenatal
care movement in Germany and was also
active in Jewish social welfare.

LEFT: Writer and philanthropist Friederike Kempner
(1836–1904), aunt of the critic Alfred Kerr and the
"muse of unintentional humor."

German Jewish campaigners for women's rights. From
left to right: Elisabeth Altmann-Gotheiner, Alice
Coblenz-Bensheimer, the secretary of the Federation of
German Women's Associations, Gertrud Bäumer (non-
Jew), Emma Ender.

Sport

LEFT: Erich Levi, German amateur heavyweight champion in 1924, trained the boxers of the Hakoah Essen club, a division of Maccabi.

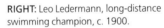

RIGHT: Leo Ledermann, long-distance swimming champion, c. 1900.

Gymnastics and sport played a significant role in the Jewish renaissance years at the end of the 19th century. While for some they were an expression of a new Jewish self-assertion, for others they were also a means of integrating into the non-Jewish environment.

At the first modern Olympic Games in Athens in 1896, eighty-one athletes took part. Among the five Olympic champions from Germany was the gymnast Alfred Flatow, who won gold on the parallel bars, silver on the horizontal bar, and, with his cousin Gustav and the other team members, also won a gold medal for the team gymnastics event.

Ernst Emanuel Simon, of the Bar Kochba club in Berlin. Brandenburg 800 meter champion in 1918 and 1919, Bavarian champion in 1921; from 1924 sports doctor in Palestine; Israeli sport and gymnastics leader.

The first Jewish sports club was founded in Berlin in 1898, in the wave of Zionist enthusiasm following the First Zionist Congress in Basle in 1897; the club was named Bar Kochba, after the leader of the rebellion against Roman rule in Palestine (132–135 AD). The club also played a role in community life through its cultural events, and was a place where indigenous Jews could meet those from Eastern Europe. In 1903 a neutral Jewish Athletics Club for Germany was founded, to attract to a Jewish sports club assimilated Jews who had encountered animosity in non-Jewish clubs. Incidentally, the numerically largest Jewish athletics and sports club was founded in Warsaw in 1915, during the German occupation.

The umbrella organization for all Jewish athletics and sports clubs is still the World Maccabi Association (1921), named after the Maccabees, who recaptured Jerusalem from the Seleucids in 164 BC. Apart from sports and athletics, all Maccabi clubs were united by their wide range of cultural activities: educational programs, musical and hiking groups, literary evenings, and Hebrew classes.

In 1930 the Maccabi sports movement had around 200,000 members. Their relations with non-Jewish athletics and sports clubs were generally friendly.

ABOVE RIGHT: A Bar Kochba team at a sports festival in Berlin, 1930.

RIGHT: Relay race at a Jewish sports day in Berlin, c. 1932.

In Trade and Industry

Industrialization had led in general to an increasing exodus from the land. In accordance with their past and their training, the Jews arriving in the cities tended to join the ranks of small businessmen and the self-employed, as shopkeepers and small factory owners, exporters and importers; as representatives for the big manufacturers and industrial firms, which were almost entirely non-Jewish; as bank employees and bankers; and as workers in, above all, the cigarette, leather, and fur industries. This integration into the urban economy stabilized in the years of the Weimar Republic, but grew harder because of increasing anti-Semitism, particularly in government and administration, and in the cartelized and nationalized industries, where Jews were scarcely employed as white-collar workers.

The number of artisans, workers, and small traders remained constant thanks to immigration from Eastern Europe, while the number of Jews in artistic occupations – musicians, graphic artists, and decorators – grew for the same reason.

In 1925 around two-thirds of all Germany's Jews were living in cities. Proportionately there were twice as many non-Jews as Jews employed in industry and twice the number of Jews as non-Jews in trade and banking, reflecting the historical evolution of the economic activity of the non-Jewish and Jewish sectors.

Jewish involvement in the founding of big new industrial firms had more or less come to an end; that kind of activity was possible only for financial giants like Krupp, Thyssen, and Hugenberg. On the other hand, it was Jewish entrepreneurs who built up the marginal and financially risky film industry.

According to a statistic of 16 June 1933, there were in Germany at that point in time 240,487 Jews in employment, out of a total of 550,000 Jews overall. Some 33,661 were unemployed.

TEILANSICHTEN DER LETZTEN BAUTEN DES SCHOCKEN-KONZERNS
① Zwickau, ② Nürnberg, ③ ⑦ Stuttgart, ④ Waldenburg-Schles., ⑤ Crimmitschau, ⑥ Chemnitz

Art Collectors, Dealers, and Patrons

The Simon Gallery in the Kaiser Friedrich Museum in Berlin. The James Simon Present

Of all the major art collectors in Germany, the most generous patron was the Berlin businessman James Simon (1851–1932). To mark the opening of the Kaiser Friedrich Museum, on whose governing board he sat, Simon made a gift of his worldfamous collection of Italian renaissance paintings, sculptures, medallions, and bronzes. His other donations included the funds to purchase the celebrated Nefertiti bust. Ruined by the great inflation, he turned down an offer of help from the

museum's director, von Bode. Interestingly, most other Jewish patrons collected German art, while non-Jewish collectors concentrated on works of the Renaissance.

Like James Simon, other collectors and patrons sought the advice of art historians and museum directors, then donated their collections or individual works to museums. They included Marcus Kappel, Franz and Robert von Mendelssohn, Alfred Beit, Oscar Huldschinsky, Eduard Arnhold, and Philip Rothschild. In 1910 the banker

Eduard Arnhold (1849–1925) gave the Prussian state the Villa Massimo in Rome, which to this day awards grants to assist young German artists.

The greatest collections of German 19th century painters belonged to Max Böhm and Rudolf Mosse; the greatest collection of Old Master drawings was assembled by Paul Davidson. Leopold Sonnemann (see page 240) bequeathed the greater part of his collection of German and French art to the Frankfurt am Main City Art Institute,

which also inherited Walther Rathenau's collection of paintings. H. H. Meyer donated his collection of 60,000 drawings to the city art gallery in his hometown of Bremen.

Among the major art dealers were Alfred Flechtheim, Herwarth Walden, and Paul Cassirer in Berlin, and Bernheim and Heinemann in Munich. Walden was a spokesman for the Expressionists (Chagall, George Grosz, Otto Dix, Meidner and others); Flechtheim was instrumental in making Picasso, Klee, Carl Hofer, and Max Beckmann more widely known, along with black African art.

The most significant European art dealer and pioneer of modern art (Picasso, Braque, Gris, Léger) was Daniel-Henry Kahnweiler, of Mannheim.

The Jewish museums in Germany, incidentally, remained at the level of small provincial collections, scarcely noticed by the Jewish patrons and collectors.

ABOVE: The art collector Alfred Flechtheim (1878–1937), photographed by Hugo Erfurth.

ABOVE RIGHT: Advertisement for the Flechtheim Gallery, 1926.

RIGHT: The art dealer Daniel-Henry Kahnweiler (1884–1979). His gallery in Paris, opened in 1907, particularly exhibited Cubist art. Kahnweiler's *Der Weg zum Kubismus* ("The Road to Cubism") was published in 1958, followed by *Meine Maler – Meine Galerien* ("My Painters – My Galleries") in 1961. Photo: Pablo Picasso, 1912.

Publishers, Booksellers, and Bibliophiles

LEFT: Advertisement for the works of Franz Kafka, Kurt Wolff publishers, Berlin.

BELOW LEFT: Title page of Elke Lasker-Schüler's "My Heart. A Love Story."

BELOW: Advertisement for the "Propyläen History of Art," Propyläen publishers, 1926.

The Jews' special relationship with books goes back thousands of years. Ever since the Bible was written down on rolls of parchment, the "people of the book" have been busy spreading it far and wide.

The Jews' reverence for the Torah scroll, from the moment of its writing to its preservation and use in synagogue services, is what underlies the Jews' passionate relationship with books. The preoccupation with books is therefore part of the Jewish tradition, and with it the work of the writer of books, the printer, the publisher, the bookseller, and the antiquarian.

Germany's foremost publisher of *belles lettres* in the Weimar years was S. Fischer Verlag, founded in 1886 by Samuel Fischer

(1859–1934) and still going today. Writers published by Fischer included ((J) = Jewish) Henrik Ibsen, Arthur Schnitzler (J), Stefan Zweig (J), Thomas Mann, Gerhart Hauptmann, Walther Rathenau (J), Sigmund Freud (J), Hermann Hesse, Joseph Conrad, Jakob Wassermann (J), Alfred Döblin (J), Hans Carossa, and Wilhelm Lehmann. Equally famous between 1910 and 1933 as a publisher of modern literature and original graphic art was Kurt Wolff, who on his mother's side descended from a Jewish family in Bonn. The authors he published included Georg Trakl, Franz Kafka (J), Heinrich Mann, Karl Kraus (J), Georg Heym, Carl Sternheim (J), Franz Werfel (J), Gustav Meyrink, Joachim Ringelnatz, and Joseph Roth (J).

Georg Bondi (1865–1935) published the books of the Stefan George circle and its *Blätter für die Kunst* ("Pages for Art"). The Propyläen publishing house was renowned chiefly for its editions of the classics and its multivolume *Weltgeschichte* ("History of the World") and *Kunstgeschichte* ("History of Art"). Bote & Bock was Germany's largest music publisher and ran a concert agency as well. Most of the titles published by Wieland Herzfelde's Malik Verlag (from 1917) were by communist writers, and they often appeared with photomontage covers by his brother John Heartfield. They were nephews of Jozef Herzfeld, a Reichstag deputy first for the Social Democratic Party, then the Independent Social Democrats, and finally the German Communist Party.

Jakob Hegner (1882–1962) is credited with the revival of fine printing in the modern era. His editions for the Marées Society are among the most distinguished productions of his press. Hegner also designed books for another Jewish publisher, Zalman Schocken. Paul Cassirer, Erich Reiss, and Fritz Gurlitt produced bibliophile editions with original illustrations.

Both Rütten and Loening in Frankfurt am Main (*Struwwelpeter*, 1847) and the Deutsche Verlagsanstalt in Stuttgart were founded by Jews, as were the later publishing houses of Erich Reiss, Brandus, and a number of specialist presses. Alongside these were houses that published exclusively Jewish books.

The printing and publishing of fine books and works with original illustrations would not have been possible without the book collectors, and a considerable number of Jews were active in this field as founders and members of bibliophile societies. A number of antiquarian booksellers were known throughout the world: Baer in Frankfurt am Main, Martin Breslauer in Berlin, and Jacques Rosenthal in Munich.

BELOW LEFT: The publisher Samuel Fischer (1859–1934).

BELOW: "Incunabula Typographica," Joseph Baer, 1924.

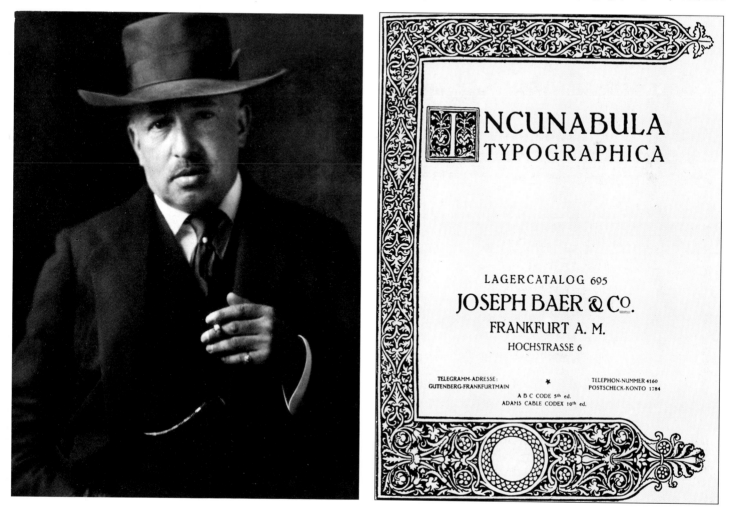

Political, Literary, and Art Magazines

Jewish publishers and editors were also involved in magazines of literary, artistic, and political interest in the Weimar Republic, more so than under the kaisers. But they were not interested in formulating and reflecting a Jewish attitude to the events of the day.

Die Weltbühne (1918–1933) was the left-wing intellectuals' weekly; *Der neue Merkur* was a monthly devoted to literature and contemporary problems; *Die Neue Rundschau* (S. Fischer) was the forum of established literature, *Die Literarische Welt* a weekly open to all literary movements; *Kunst und Künstler* saw itself as a vanguard of modern art; the highbrow *Corona* reflected the literary world of Hugo von Hofmannsthal, Paul Valéry, and Hermann Hesse; *Der Querschnitt* was home to all the contemporary currents in literature, art, and lifestyle and was brilliantly illustrated, with experimental photographs and drawings by artists from many countries.

LEFT: Title page of *Die Weltbühne*, 24 November 1925.

BELOW: Inside page from the journal *Kunst und Künstler*, 1927.

Die Zukunft (1892–1922) and Die Fackel (1899–1936) were the media organs respectively of Maximilian Harden (1861–1927; Harden's real name being Felix Ernst Witkowski), a politically and ideologically committed publisher, and the witty, quarrelsome Karl Kraus (1874–1936), who was revered by his devoted followers as an uncompromising moralist and social critic, and pitiless satirist. Kraus thought of himself as the supreme authority on the German language. Maximilian Harden, a relentless opponent of Kaiser Wilhelm II and his policies and for periods the political mentor of Imperial Germany, survived an assassination attempt in 1922 and emigrated to Switzerland.

RIGHT: Title page of *Die Neue Rundschau*, May 1927.

BELOW: Title page of *Der Querschnitt*, September 1929.

IX. Jahrgang, Heft 9
Berlin, Ende September 1929

PREIS: M 1,50

DER QUERSCHNITT

BEGRÜNDET VON ALFRED FLECHTHEIM
HERAUSGEBER: H. V. WEDDERKOP

IM PROPYLÄEN-VERLAG / BERLIN

FÜNFTES HEFT   MAI 1927

DIE NEUE RUNDSCHAU

XXXVIII. Jahrgang der freien Bühne

Herausgeber: Oskar Bie, S. Fischer, S. Saenger

Inhalt

Rudolf Pannwitz, Der Geist Europas
Hermann Hesse, Traktat vom Steppenwolf
Hermann Hesse, Ein Stück Tagebuch
Hugo Ball, Hermann Hesse und der Osten
W. E. Süskind, Hermann Hesse und die Jugend
Wilhelm Hausenstein, Notizen aus Südfrankreich
François Mauriac, Der junge Mensch
Samuel Saenger, „Religiöse Erneuerung"
Rudolf Kayser, Europäische Rundschau

Anmerkungen:
Martin Gumbert, Totenmasken

S. FISCHER / VERLAG A.-G.
Berlin und Leipzig

Postvertrieb ab Leipzig

The Humanities

The hub of Jewish thought in the Weimar years remained the College for the Science of Judaism in Berlin, among whose teachers were Julius Guttmann, Ismar Elbogen, and Rabbi Leo Baeck (see page 244f.).

One of the most important philosophers of the Weimar period was the neo-Kantian Ernst Cassirer, a professor at Hamburg University from 1919 to 1933. His work ranged from epistemological problems and a philosophy of symbolic forms to the relativity theory of Albert Einstein, which he demonstrated could be reconciled with the neo-Kantianism of Hermann Cohen.

Two other thinkers of far-reaching significance were the philosopher of religion Leo Strauss and the philosopher and cultural critic Ernst Bloch. Bloch's writings- *Der Geist der Utopie* ("The Utopian Mind"), 1918, *Thomas Münzer*, 1922, and *Das Prinzip Hoffnung* ("The Hope Principle"), 1954–59 – enjoyed something of a renaissance in the 1960s and '70s.

In sociology, Karl Mannheim (1893–1947), a professor at the University of Frankfurt, influenced later generations with his sociology of knowledge and theory of democracy (*Ideologie und Utopie* ("Ideology and Utopia"), published in 1928). The legal theorist and constitutional lawyer Hans Kelsen (1881–1973) was the originator of a "pure theory of law." Martin Wolff (1872–1953) taught civil law and international commercial law in Marburg, Bonn, and Berlin. Jewish authors were, as they had been from 1871 to 1918, responsible for many of the commentaries in different areas of the law.

In 1930 Max Horkheimer became the director of the Institute for Social Research at the University of Frankfurt, founded in 1923. In their many books and in articles for the *Zeitschrift für Sozialforschung* ("Journal of Social Research"), he and his colleagues published scientific investigations whose common foundation was a critical evaluation of bourgeois society in the Marxist tradition. Most of the roughly 50 members of the institute's staff were of Jewish origin and for this reason, and also because of their political convictions, had to leave Germany after 1933. Horkheimer escaped first to Switzerland, then to New York and California. In 1949 he returned to Frankfurt University, becoming its rector from 1951 to 1953.

Horkheimer's closest collaborator, the cultural and social philosopher Theodor

Zeitschrift für
Sozialforschung

Herausgegeben vom

Institut für Sozialforschung Frankfurt a. M.

Jahrgang I / 1932

VERLAG VON C. L. HIRSCHFELD / LEIPZIG

IMAGO

ZEITSCHRIFT FÜR ANWENDUNG DER PSYCHO-
ANALYSE AUF DIE GEISTESWISSENSCHAFTEN

IX. BAND   1923   HEFT 1

EINE TEUFELSNEUROSE
IM SIEBZEHNTEN JAHRHUNDERT

Von SIGM. FREUD

An den Neurosen der Kinderzeit haben wir gelernt, daß manches hier mühelos mit freiem Auge zu sehen ist, was sich späterhin nur gründlicher Forschung zu erkennen gibt. Eine ähnliche Erwartung wird sich für die neurotischen Erkrankungen früherer Jahrhunderte ergeben, wenn wir nur darauf gefaßt sind, dieselben unter anderen Überschriften als unsere heutigen Neurosen zu finden. Wir dürfen nicht erstaunt sein, wenn die Neurosen dieser frühen Zeiten im dämonologischen Gewande auftreten, während die der unpsychologischen Jetztzeit im hypochondrischen, als organische Krankheiten verkleidet, erscheinen. Mehrere Autoren, voran Charcot, haben bekanntlich in den Darstellungen der Besessenheit und Verzückung, wie sie uns die Kunst hinterlassen hat, die Äußerungsformen der Hysterie agnosziert; es wäre nicht schwer gewesen, in den Geschichten dieser Kranken die Inhalte der Neurose wiederzufinden, wenn man ihnen damals mehr Aufmerksamkeit geschenkt hätte.

ABOVE: Max Horkheimer (1895–1975), director of the Institute for Social Research in Frankfurt am Main, 1931.

ABOVE CENTER: Title page of the *Zeitschrift für Sozialforschung*, 1932.

ABOVE RIGHT: Title page of the journal *Imago*, 1923.

The Sigmund Freud circle in Berlin, 1922. Standing, from left: Otto Rank, Karl Abraham, Max Eitingon, Ernest Jones. Seated, from left: Sigmund Freud, Sándor Ferenczi, and Hanns Sachs.

W. Adorno (1903–1969), was in his youth a pupil of the composer Alban Berg and for some years a member of Arnold Schoenberg's circle. The description of Schoenberg's "serial music" in the 22nd chapter of Thomas Mann's Dr. Faustus is based on an essay of Adorno's entitled *Philosophie der neuen Musik* ("Philosophy of the New Music"). However, Adorno's chief interest remained his work in the field of the Frankfurt school. Among other collaborators in the Frankfurt project were Friedrich Pollock, Erich Fromm, Leo Löwenthal and Herbert Marcuse.

Aby Warburg (1866–1929), the eldest of Hamburg banker Moritz Warburg's seven children, indicated in his works on art and religion the close connexions between the art of the Renaissance, classical antiquity, early astrology, and Christianity. He founded and expanded the famous Warburg Cultural Studies Library in Hamburg, which provided the basis for research into the links between political history and the history of art and culture. In 1933 the library was successfully transferred to London, where its 60,000 volumes and 20,000 photographs became the core of the Warburg Institute.

Prominent figures in art history were Max J. Friedländer (1867–1958), author of a four-volume work on *Die altniederländische Malerei* ("The Netherlandish Old Masters"), 1924–37, Erwin Panofsky (1892–1968), an expert on Albrecht Dürer and the iconography of German Gothic Art, and Carl Einstein, with his early insights into black African art (*Negerplastik* ("Negro Sculpture"), 1915).

Kurt Koffka (1886–1941) was the founder of Gestalt psychology. Seeing no hope of academic preferment at the University of Giessen, in 1924 he emigrated to the United States, where he received a professorship and published his main work, *Principles of Gestalt Psychology*.

Psychoanalytical research in Germany revolved around the Psychoanalytical Institute in Berlin. Karl Abraham (1877–1925), Max Eitingon (1881–1943) and their colleagues had succeeded in 1920 in founding a psychoanalytical clinic in Berlin, with a research and training institute attached. Researchers famed throughout the Western world were involved in the

The psychoanalyst Siegfried Bernfeld (1882–1953), Photo Tim Gidal.

ABOVE: Reading room of the Warburg Library in Hamburg, 1926.

RIGHT: The psychologist William Stern (1871–1938), Hamburg.

work of this institute, finished their training there, or were invited to give lectures:

Karen Horney, Siegfried Bernfeld, Theodor Reik, Helene Deutsch, Anna Freud, Melanie Klein, Wilhelm Reich, Sándor Radó, and Michael and Alice Balint.

It was also left to Jewish outsiders to venture into areas which academic research still fought shy of: Siegfried Kracauer (1889–1966), for instance, wrote about photography and the sociology of film, Rudolf Arnheim about visual communication.

The Sciences

LEFT: Physicist and 1954 Nobel Prize-Winner Max Born (1882–1970), teacher of Werner Heisenberg and Pascual Jordan.

in 1940 through Spain to the United States, where he was given a visiting professorship at the University of Pennsylvania. The physicist Gustav Hertz (1887–1975), baptized son of a Jewish father, survived the Nazi barbarism in Germany. In 1945 the Russians took him to Sukhumi on the Black Sea, when he returned to (East) Germany in 1954 as a professor at Leipzig University. The biochemist Otto H. Warburg (1883–1970), director of the Kaiser Wilhelm Institute for Cell Physiology in Berlin-Dahlem, a baptized Jew, also survived the Hitler years in Germany.

Richard Willstätter (1872–1942), professor of organic chemistry in Munich, was awarded the Nobel Prize in 1915. He followed in the footsteps of the greatest organic chemist of his time, the 1905 Nobel Prize-Winner Adolf von Baeyer

"If my theory is shown to be true, the Germans will call me a German and the French will call me a Jew. If it should be proved false, the Germans will call me a Jew, and the French a German," said Albert Einstein after the publication of his theory of relativity (1914/15).

Five of the fifteen German Nobel Prize-winners during the Weimar period were Jews: Albert Einstein (Physics, 1921); Otto Meyerhof (Medicine, 1922); James Franck (Physics, 1925); Gustav Hertz (Physics, 1925); and Otto H. Warburg (Medicine, 1931).

The biochemist Otto Meyerhof (1884–1951) emigrated to Paris in 1938, fleeing

RIGHT: The biochemist and Nobel Prize-Winner, Richard Willstätter (1872–1942).

358

(1835–1917), who was of Jewish descent on his mother's side.

In 1924, when his recommended candidate for the chair of organic chemistry was rejected by a majority of the professorial council because he was a Jew, Richard Willstätter resigned his chair in protest; in 1939 he emigrated to Switzerland.

James Franck (1882–1964), a professor at Göttingen University from 1920 to 1933, was awarded the Nobel Prize for physics in 1925. From 1933 he worked as an atomic physicist in Baltimore, and in his 1945 "Franck Report" he declared himself against any use of atomic energy for military purposes and protested at the dropping of atomic bombs on the Japanese cities of Hiroshima and Nagasaki. Franck died 21 May 1964 in Göttingen, during a visit to Germany.

RIGHT: The physiologist Otto Meyerhof (1884–1951), winner of the Nobel Prize for Medicine in 1922.

BELOW RIGHT: Atomic physicist Gustav Hertz (1887–1975), Nobel Prize-Winner for Physics, 1925.

BELOW: Physicist and Nobel Prize-Winner James Franck (1882–1964).

Painters, Sculptors, and Graphic Artists

The Jewish painters, sculptors, and graphic artists of Germany lived and worked within the general artistic currents of the time. Only a few took Jewish subjects as their theme, among them Hermann Strunk, Ephraim Mose Lilien, Joseph Budko, Jakob Steinhardt, Lesser Ury and Jankel Adler (see page 368).

Otto Freundlich (1878–1943, murdered in Lublin or Majdanek) sought "for a cosmic harmony destined to overcome the alienation between man and nature and bring external occurrences into harmony with the feeling and conduct of men. In Freundlich's view, art is an expression of 'cosmic morality'." His painting *Die Mutter* ("The Mother") evokes the "meditative harmony of organ music." Nikolaus Braun's *Berliner Strassenszene* ("Street Scene in Berlin"), 1921, "is a typical example of Berlin art in the period after World War I. Expressionist verve in the brushwork combines with an inclination to realism in the depiction of the subject – big city painting. The extreme agitation of the composition gives an impression of profusion, of fast and furious activity ... The viewer is also invited voyeuristically into the interiors of rooms."

"The theme of the organ-grinder (see page 363) in the work of Felix Nussbaum (1904–1944, murdered in Auschwitz) is pure Berlin. It belongs to the Berlin of the workers' quarters, of the backyards, the Berlin of the little men. There is a sad look in his eyes. The organ-grinder's heart is turned in upon itself ... Strangely, the atmospheric charm of the melancholy flowing from the picture is one of the characteristics that bewitches the old Berlin hand again and again," (Eberhard Roters).

Rudolf Levy, born in Stettin in 1876, was trapped in 1944 by two Gestapo agents disguised as art dealers and murdered in a concentration camp. In the Weimar period, he was regarded as a wise opposite pole to Expressionism. In 1907 in France he became a friend of Matisse, in whose studio he worked for many years. In the Café Dôme in Paris, then later in Berlin and Florence, he was the witty, stimulating center of a circle of artists that included Oskar Kokoschka, Albert Weisgerber, Jules Pascin, and many others.

A memory of their night-long discussions was preserved in some mock-serious comic verse (a parody on a well-known

LEFT: Benno Elkan (1877–1960): "To the Victims," a memorial in bronze in to those who fell in World War I (Frankfurt am Main).

RIGHT: Lesser Ury (1861–1931): "Self-Portrait in Old Age," 1931.

poem to autumn by German poet Johann Gleim):

"Place the sweet-scented still lifes on the
    table,
Bring that last tube of zinc white over here,
And let's talk of Cézanne …
As we did in spring and summer – and do
    all year."

The sculptors mostly remained tied to classical forms. Benno Elkan (see page 368f.) after his flight from Germany devoted himself largely to Jewish themes. Sculptor Arnold Zadikow (1884–1943, murdered in Theresienstadt), was one of the pioneers in developing modern sculptural forms in glass and crystal.

LEFT: Rudolf Levy (1876–1944), pupil and friend of Matisse: "Still Life," 1924.

RIGHT: Felix Nussbaum (1904–1944): "The Organ-Grinder," 1931.

Artistic Revolution

ABOVE: Nelly and Herwarth Walden, the editor of *Sturm*. On the walls, paintings by Marc Chagall, 1920.

LEFT: Ludwig Meidner: "Apocalyptic Vision", pen, ink, and opaque white, December 1913.

Herwarth Walden who was born 1878 in Berlin, and married to the poet Elke Lasker-Schüler, disappeared without trace in the Soviet Union in 1941. He was a composer, playwright and critic, and editor of literary magazines. In 1910 he started the magazine *Der Sturm* ("Storm"); in 1912 he opened the Sturm art gallery with an exhibition that introduced the works of the Blaue Reiter Group to the public; that same year he also exhibited the artists of French and German Expressionism. With his magazine and his gallery, Walden became an important promoter of modern art. Among the artists whose works could be seen at his gallery were Paul Klee and Oskar Kokoschka, Marc Chagall, Lyonel Feininger, Wassily Kandinsky, Franz Marc, and August Macke.

Of the painter and poet Ludwig Meidner (1884–1960), Willi Wolffradt wrote that in him "the volcanic epoch of Expressionism has its hottest crater, spitting out a lava of visions … as if in a torment of furious passion." The title of his book *Im Nacken das Sternemeer* ("The Sea of Stars at my Heels"), 1918, became one of Expressionism's distinctive metaphors.

The publishing house at the center of Expressionist literature was the Kurt Wolff Verlag in Leipzig and Munich. Kurt Wolff (1887–1963) was of Jewish descent on his mother's side. Wolff's *Der Jüngste Tag* ("The Day of Judgment"), the most important series of Expressionist poetry books, which ran to 86 volumes, published many Jewish writers: Mynona (pseudonym of Salomo Friedländer), Oscar Baum, Max Brod, Albert and Carl Ehrenstein, Carl Einstein, Franz Kafka, Ludwig Rubiner, and Ferdinand Bruckner (Theodor Tagger). The first volume was *Die Versuchung* ("The Temptation") by Franz Werfel (1890–1945), whose earlier collection of poems, *Der Weltfreund* ("Friend to the World"), had been an appeal for brotherhood and peace, similar to that half a century later by the flower children of the 1960s. Werfel's cry of enthusiastic hope recalls Schiller's "Ode to Joy":

"So I belong to you and to all!
Let no one, please, stand in my way!
Oh, if only it could happen, one day,
That we like brothers
Into each other's arms might fall!"

The programmatic poem of 1920s expressionism was *Weltende* ("End of the World") by Jakob van Hoddis (1887–1942). The poem was written in 1911 and published in a collection bearing the same title in 1918:

"The citizen's hat flies off his pointed head/The winds echo with noises like cries.

"The tilers fall off the roofs and are split in two,/And on the coasts – we hear – the floods are rising.

"The storm is here, the wild seas hop/onto the land, flatten thick dykes.

"Most people have a cold./The railways fall from the bridges."

This poem, which reads today like a schoolboy prank, struck supporters of the Expressionist movement as "the poem that would usher in a colossal renaissance of mankind," in the words of the poet Johannes R. Becher. It emerged later that Hoddis had it actually written to make fun of people's fear of Halley's Comet. In 1942, Jakob van Hoddis was deported from a mental hospital and murdered.

The Dada movement, "which began as a piece of tomfoolery" (Hans and Paul Citroen), was formally launched in 1916 at the Café Voltaire in Zurich; it later came to be regarded as a general protest against all concepts of art, as a "reaction to the puffy white cloud tendency of so-called fine art" (George Grosz).

Other Dadaists were Paul Citroen (1896–1983), his brother Hans, John Heartfield (Helmut Herzfeld), and Hans Richter, later a director of avant-garde films.

The early work of the architect Erich Mendelsohn (1887–1953), his famous Einstein tower in Potsdam (1920), for instance, clearly shows the Expressionist-Symbolist influence. As he struggled with

RIGHT: Arthur Segal: "Heligoland," oil, 1923.

ABOVE: Hans Citroen: "Wilson's Fourteen Points," shown in Berlin's first Dada exhibition, 1920. Hans Citroen was the youngest Dadaist, only 14 at the time.

building materials (glass, cement, brick) and the traditional forms of construction, he visibly developed a more functional and severe architecture, without abandoning his original intentions and inspiration. Mendelsohn's successes began after 1925: his buildings included among others the Schocken department stores in Stuttgart (1927) and Chemnitz (1928), the Universum film theater (1928) and the Union of Metalworkers' building in Berlin, the Hadassah hospital on Mount Scopus overlooking Jerusalem (1938), and synagogues in St. Louis (1950), Cleveland (1952), and St. Paul (1954), in the United States.

The painter Arthur Segal (1875–1944) began as an Expressionist but moved, after

studying optics and esthetic theory, to naturalistic painting. His book *Licht-probleme der bildenden Kunst* ("Light Problems in Visual Art") influenced painters like Delaunay, Noland, and Vasarely. In 1933 Segal fled via Spain to England.

Jankel Adler (1895–1947) from Lodz was a painter who followed his own path, an individualist within the group of Düsseldorf artist friends around Otto Dix. Although he loved his second home, Germany, Adler always retained a feeling for his Eastern Jewish roots; in 1933 he fled first to Paris, then England.

Constructivism was the passion of both the Hungarian László Moholy-Nagy (1895–1945) and his wife Lucia. He worked first in Berlin, then from 1923–1928 as a teacher at the Weimar Bauhaus and coeditor of the Bauhausbücher ("Bauhaus Books"). In 1933 he emigrated via England to the United States, where he became one of the founders of modern "kinetic art." Through his important theoretical writings on photography and film, he also influenced industrial design and advertising.

El (Eliezer) Lissitzky (1890–1941) was originally from Smolensk but studied architecture in Darmstadt. Under the influence of Kasimir S. Malewitsch and in association with the Bauhaus, from 1925 to 1928 he worked in Hanover as an important Constructivist typographer, stage designer, interior designer, photographer, and painter. With the painter Kurt Schwitters he published the magazine *Merz*; at the PRESSA exhibition in Cologne in 1928 and the "Foto & Film" exhibition in Stuttgart in 1929, he was responsible for designing the Russian halls. With Surrealist film director Hans Richter, he worked on the magazine *G* (for *Gestaltung*, "Design"). In 1929, El Lissitzky returned to the Soviet Union.

BELOW: Cover page of the avant-garde magazine Merz, published by El Lissitzky and Kurt Schwitters.

The Theme of Jewishness as Seen by the Artist

Ephraim Mose Lilien (1974–1925): "Yesterday …:"
"The Crossing to America." Drawing, 1923.

Jewish art, like Christian art, takes its themes from the contents and the emotions of religion, in our case the Jewish religion and its history, including the history of the Jewish people in the Diaspora and their hopes for its ending.

Ephraim Mose Lilien (1874–1925), born in Galicia, joined the staff of the Munich art magazine *Jugend* in 1895. In 1900 in Berlin, he illustrated Münchhausen's volume of poems, *Judak*, in the Art Nouveau style, which remained his form of artistic expression from then on. In 1902 he illustrated Morris Rosenfeld's *Lieder des Ghetto* ("Songs of the Ghetto"). Lilien, who moved in the Zionist circle of friends centered on Martin Buber, fell, like other exponents of Art Nouveau, into oblivion, and has only been re-discovered in recent years. Unknown to the public at large, Lilien, with his photographs of Jerusalem, was also one of the greatest photographers of his time.

In his etchings and lithographs, Hermann Struck drew landscapes and portraits of which the series *Das ostjüdische Antlitz* with texts by Arnold Zweig (see page 318) remained the most powerful. He advised Max Liebermann, Lesser Ury, Lovis Corinth and many other painters. His book *Die Kunst des Radierens* ("The Art of Etching"), which has gone through numerous editions since 1909, is regarded as a standard work. An orthodox Zionist and a leading light of the nationalist religious party Mirachi ("Spiritual Center"), he occupied himself with Jewish themes his whole life long. In 1924, he emigrated to Palestine, whose landscapes he captured in numerous pictures.

Jakob Steinhardt (1887–1968, from Posen) developed as an Expressionist artist into an illustrator of works ranging from the Bible to the tales of life among eastern European Jews by Isaac Leib Peretz. From 1933 he was a teacher, later the principal of the Bezalel Art Academy in Jerusalem, which had been cofounded by Lilien. Working primarily in the medium of the woodcut, his themes were the crooked alleys of the Old City of Jerusalem, the harsh Judaean mountain scenery, and the figures of Jews at prayer.

ABOVE: Joseph Budko (1888–1940): "I shall not flee, not I." Woodcut.

RIGHT: Jankel Adler (1895–1949): "King David Plays the Flute." Painting.

The portraits of Benno Elkan (1877–1960) were on show in numerous galleries until 1933, and his large-scale sculptures were to be found in public places in many German towns and cities. After emigrating to England in 1933, Elkan was best known for his seven-branched candlestick with its numerous figures, which was commissioned by the British parliament and set up in Westminster Abbey. A second example stands in front of the Knesset building in Jerusalem.

A particularly Jewish art form is the micrograph, a special form of calligraphy in which texts in the form of minute Hebrew letters are playfully arranged to form symbols, portraits, cabalistic formulas and pictorial charms (see pages 23 and 234).

Film: Producers, Directors, and Actors

Jewish names were numerous among the pioneers of film and the film industry.

Paul Davidson (1866–1927) founded, with Hermann Fellner (1878–1936), whom he met up with later, the Universum-Film-AG, known as UFA, the first German film company. In Mannheim Davidson built the first German cinema. In 1921 UFA merged with film producer Erich Pommer's Decla-Bioscop; Pommer (1889–1966) was responsible for *Das Kabinett des Dr. Caligari* ("The Cabinet of Dr. Caligari") and Fritz Lang's *Der müde Tod* ("Destiny"), 1921, and *Metropolis*, 1926.

LEFT: Fritz Lang directing the masses in the film *Metropolis*, 1926.

BELOW: Max Pallenberg (1877–1934) examining a reel from a silent film.

A man who played a major part in building up the American film industry was Carl Laemmle, from Laupheim. He emigrated to the United States in 1893, opened his first movie theater in Chicago in 1906, and in 1909 began distributing films commercially. His Universal Picture Company also established a German arm, which produced the Harry Piel films among others.

An outfit known for more artistically ambitious films was S. Nebenzahl's Nero Film Company, producers of, for example, *Das Testament des Doktor Mabuse* ("Dr. Mabuse"), 1930, and *M*, 1931.

There was a large number of Jewish film directors, starting with Lupu Pick (1886–1931), whose first career was as a stage

LEFT: Scene from the "The Nibelungen," 1923/24, by Fritz Lang, with Paul Richter as Young Siegfried.

BELOW: Scene from "The Cabinet of Dr Caligari," 1920, the best-known and most influential Expressionist film. The screenplay was written by Carl Mayer and Hans Janowitz, the director was Robert Wiene. The film's producer was Erich Pommer, the director of the Decla-Bioscop company.

and film actor. His films *Scherben* ("Fragments"), 1921, and *Silvester* ("New Year's Eve"), 1923, were low-budget studio theater plays, but with striking effects of light and shadow. Ghost stories with Expressionist features, a favorite theme of the time, crystallized in the film *Der Golem* ("The Golem"), 1914, after the novel of the same name by Gustav Meyrink, which was adapted for the screen by Henrik Galeen and Paul Wegener. Galeen also wrote the screenplay for *Nosferatu – eine Symphonie des Grauens* ("Nosferatu – A Symphony of Horror"), 1922. Still remembered today are the films of Ernst Lubitsch (1892–1947), among them *Madame Du Barry* (1919), *Das Verbotene Paradies* ("The Marriage Circle"), 1924, *Lady Windermere's Fächer* ("Lady Windermere's Fan"), 1925, *Krach im Paradies* ("Trouble in Paradise"), 1932, and *Ninotchka*, 1937. Paul Leni

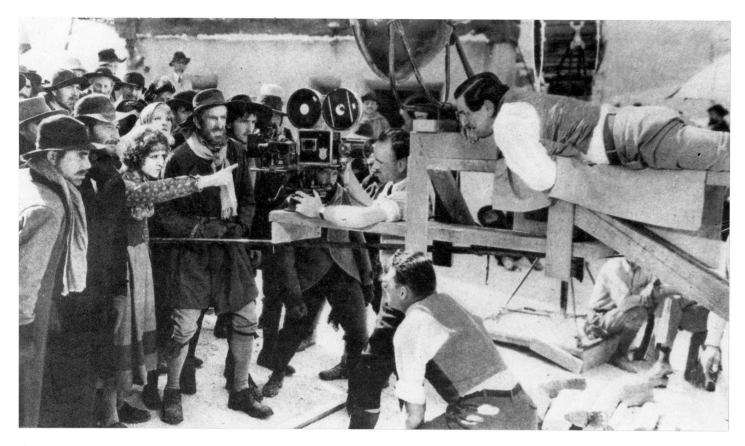

ABOVE: Film director
Ernst Lubitsch
(1892–1947) at work.

(born 1885) directed *Das Wachsfiguren-kabinett* ("Waxworks"), 1924. Ludwig Berger (1892–1969) is remembered for *Der verlorene Schuh* ("The Lost Shoe"), *Das Glas Wasser* ("The Glass of Water"), and *Pygmalion* (1936).

One successful collaboration was the husband-and-wife team Paul Czinner and Elisabeth Bergner. From 1924 onward Czinner directed a series of films with his wife in the lead role, the best known of which is *Fräulein Else*, 1929. Josef von Sternberg (1894–1969) worked mostly in America. His film *Der Blaue Engel* ("The Blue Angel"), 1930, with Marlene Dietrich, is still frequently shown; *Shanghai Express*, 1932, has proved equally popular.

Jewish scriptwriters as well as directors, among them Robert Liebmann (born 1890) who wrote the screenplay for "The Blue Angel," contributed to the success of German films in those turbulent years of the Weimar Republic, when unconventional ideas and forms were still allowed. Nor are the many actors forgotten: Julius Falkenstein, Kurt Gerron, Fritz Kortner, Alexander Granach, Ernst Deutsch, Grete Mosheim, Lucie Mannheim, Rosa Valetti, and many others.

RIGHT: Elisabeth
Bergner in the film "The
Florentine Violin Player,"
1926. Paul Czinner
directed the movie.

New Photography

In the 20th century photography finally won its place among the contemporary arts, not just as a means of visual communication but as a creative medium. In advertising, illustrated magazines, exhibitions and books, it became a part of daily experience.

Creative forces from various fields contributed to the widening of photography's potential: the new vision of the photographic avant-garde in Germany, the development of small cameras, the Russian film.

These endeavors reached a high point, along with the new picture reports in the mass media, in the landmark exhibition "Foto & Film" in Stuttgart in 1929, where new directions in postwar photography

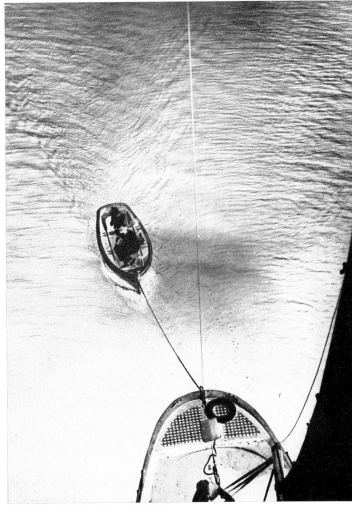

ABOVE: Helmar Lerski (1871–1856): "Yemeni Jewess."

RIGHT: László Moholy-Nagy: "Boat," Berlin 1928.

throughout the world were brought together for the first time.

An extract from the exhibition catalog reads: "What was important was to show what could be created only by the means of photography, the means that are essential and exclusive to it ... The aim of the exhibition was to obtain works by the individuals who first recognized the camera as our most contemporary creative medium and worked with it in a corresponding way." The new press photographers were not represented, however, for at the time of the exhibition, in May 1929, publications using modern photojournalism were still a rarity.

ABOVE: The actress Lotte Lenya, photographed by Lotte Jacobi, c. 1928.

LEFT: Martin Munkaczi: "The Hansom Cab," Berlin, 1928.

The avant-garde of the new photography in Germany included Paul Citroen, Georg and Ignaz (Tim) Gidal, Lotte Jacobi, John Heartfield (Herzfeld), Helmar Lerski, László and Lucia Moholy-Nagy, Aenne Biermann, and Sasha and Cami Stone. Paul Citroen moved on from Dadaist fragmentation to the symbolism of his city montages. Georg Gidal, in his *Kopenhagener Tagebuch* ("Copenhagen Diary"), developed new elements of photographic form, his ideas of the "camera unleashed" similar to those of the Russians Pudovkin and Rodschenko. Ignaz (later Tim) Gidal, less concerned with formal experimentation, tried to reproduce common patterns of human gesture. Lotte Jacobi humanized the portrait and in her photographs caught the depth of character of the human face. Helmar Lerski, in complete contrast, attempted to completely transform the human countenance, with the aid of mirrors, lighting, and vaseline, like a maker of theatrical masks.

John Heartfield remains the supreme master of political photomontage, through which, often oversimplistically, he revealed the contradictions of bourgeois society and the background to the events of the day in all their brutality. His montages appeared mostly on the covers of the *Arbeiter Illustrierten Zeitung* and the books of the Malik publishing house.

László Moholy-Nagy and his wife Lucia together discovered a new esthetic idea in

John Heartfield: "The Face of Fascism," 1928.

scenes that were not posed, and conducted playful, pseudophilosophical experiments in photomontages and in photograms, where pictures were produced in the dark-room without the aid of a camera. The result was often bizarre black-and-white effects on the developed and fixed photo-graphic paper.

Paul Citroen: "The City." Photomontage 1923.

Tim Gidal: "Kafka in Prague." Photomontage, 1932.

Modern Photojournalism

The invention around 1925 of the small camera and more sensitive film meant that moving scenes in interiors lit only by electric light could be captured photographically. It thus became technically possible to create a more intimate visual record of events and moments of general interest in rooms and halls. This was made appreciably easier by the fact that the small camera – first the Leica, then others – allowed thirty-six photographs to be taken in quick succession on one roll of film.

In the late 1920s, with the help of receptive editors such as Kurt Korff, the genius in charge of the *Berliner Illustrirte Zeitung*, a small group of "New Photojournalists" developed modern photojournalism, which by the 1930s had spread from Germany via France to America and England. Competition for circulation and advertising among the

ABOVE: Erich Salomon (1886 Berlin – 1944 Auschwitz) with his legendary Ermanox camera. Photo Lore Feininger, 1929.

ABOVE LEFT: Kurt Korff (1876–1938), editor in chief of the *Berliner Illustrirte Zeitung*, taken c. 1927.

LEFT: The German chancellor, Heinrich Brüning, and his Foreign Minister, Julius Curtius, visiting Benito Mussolini in Rome, Hotel Excelsior, August 1931. From left: Benito Mussolini, Heinrich Brüning, Graf Dino Grandi, and Julius Curtius. Photo by Dr. Erich Salomon.

Der alte Vagabund
Vertraut um die Erde, und immer noch gut auf den Beinen

SERVUS KUMPEL

Die Bruderschaft der Vagabunden trifft sich in Stuttgart

Kaffeeküche nach dem Zeitung durch die Stadt

Mittagspause auf dem Rasen:
Beim dießjährigen Vagabundentreffen in Stuttgart

Aufnahmen: Ignaz Gidal

Servus Kumpel! Das ist der Ruf der Armen und doch auch Reichsten der Welt, der Landstreicher, die von ewiger Unruhe getrieben die Straßen der Welt entlang trotten. Jetzt hat Gregor Gog, der „Vaga-" bundenkönig" die Brüder von der Landstraße zu einem Treffen zusammengerufen. Zu einem riesigen Garten hoch über Stuttgart waren sie 3 Tage lang zusammen. Dann tippelten sie wieder in alle Himmelsrichtungen hinaus. J. G.

„Freut euch des Lebens, weil noch das Lämpchen glüht"
Der Vagabundendichter verabschiedet sich am Mandolind

Landstreicher aus Überzeugung:
Ein seltsamer innerer Entschluß, der seit 20 Jahren auf der Landstraße lebt

"Greetings, Comrade!." A photoreportage by Tim Gidal for the *Münchener Illustrierte Presse*, June 1929.

like Kurt Korff a Jew. As editor of London's *Picture Post* from September 1938 to May 1940, Lorant brought modern photojournalism to its full flowering.

Chronologically, the first of the German photo-reporters in the new photojournalism was the still unrivaled Erich Salomon (1886–1944, Auschwitz). And Salomon achieved this pinnacle despite not taking photo sequences but by capturing, at times with the expressive power of a Daumier, the mood and content of diplomatic meetings or artistic and social events in one single image, perpetuating the moment for ever. Salomon and a few others, the pioneers of modern photojournalism, had this gift of human communication. This select group numbered as many Jews as non-Jews: Martin Munkaszi, Georg and Ignaz (Tim) Gidal, Alfred Eisenstaedt, Zoltan Kluger, Kurt Hübschmann-Hutton, Max Seldow, Erich Comeriner, Kurt and Margot Lubinsky, and best known for his sculpture photography, Hans Casparius.

What interested these avant-garde photographer-journalists equally were the new possibilities of human communication, not unlike the quest for new dimensions in the art, science, and politics of that time. The fact that the disproportionately high number of Jews among the photo-reporters were almost exclusively Jews

illustrated papers was also a considerable factor in giving photojournalism the wide opportunities it enjoyed.

The old reports illustrated by pictures from various sources were replaced by photo series, photoreportage and photo essays. Photoreportage allowed the photographer to encapsulate an individual experience in visual form, with the camera seeing and fixing the event in a series of pictures, as if it were an extension of the eye.

The main publications that cultivated the new style of photojournalism, alongside the *Berliner Illustrirte Zeitung*, or *B.I.Z.* as it was known, with its circulation of 1,870,000 in 1930, were the *Münchener Illustrierte Presse* in Munich, which had a circulation of 650,000 that year; the *Republikanische Illustrierte*; the *Kölnische Illustrierte Zeitung*, based in Cologne and the Catholic-inclined *Feuerreiter*. The picture editor of the *Münchener Illustrierte Presse* from mid-1932 to March 1933 was Stefan Lorant, who was from Budapest and

"Rendezvous: The Zoo Station Clock," by Hans Casparius, Berlin, 1930.

Im Banne des Vortrags... — Professor Mollier, der bedeutende Münchner Anatom, doziert   Aufnahmen: Weltrundschau

Wie kaum ein andrer weiß Professor Mollier seine Hörer durch seine wundervolle Sprache zu packen; seine hinreißenden Schilderungen sind vom Leben durchglüht, durch anschauliche Vergleiche bringt er die schwierigsten Erläuterungen leicht faßlich zum Vortrag. Eine Vorlesung von ihm zu hören, ist ein Erlebnis, an das sich die Studierenden immer mit Begeisterung erinnern

"...Das erhabenste Wunderwerk der Schöpfung, das wir wahrnehmen können, ist der menschliche Körper, sein Aufbau und seine Funktionen... — Die Funktion dieses Muskels ist zweifach: verkürzt er sich, so bringt er die Kinnlade..." Professor Mollier ist ein sehr gewandter Zeichner, der seine Vorträge laufend mit farbigen Kreidezeichnungen illustriert

PROFESSOR MOLLIER DOZIERT...

"Professor Mollier lecturing," photo-reportage by Georg Gidal, *Kölnische Illustrierte Zeitung*, 1929.

from assimilated backgrounds may be no accident. Without any vital relation to the people of their origins, assimilated Jews in the Diaspora became spokesperson for and supporters of new ideas and ideals in many fields.

Playing an important role as middlemen between the editors and photoreporters, and giving them constant stimulation, were the picture agencies, like the *Deutscher Photo Dienst*, or Dephot and *Weltrundschau* in Berlin, which specialized in the new field of photoreportage. Rudolf Birnbach, the head of *Weltrundschau*, gathered around him a circle of young photographers, including Neudatschin-Neudin, Joffe, Seldow, and Comeriner, whom he trained in modern photojournalism. He found them contemporary subjects and negotiated sales and commissions with the editors of the illustrated papers.

Dephot was run by Simon Guttmann, who inspired his in-house photographers and the editors to many an interesting reportage. He also advised the photojournalists who sold photographs they had taken abroad through the Dephot. Later other picture agencies, like Mauritius (Ernest Meyer), began to produce photoreportage.

LEFT: "Newsvendor in Berlin," photo Tim Gidal, 1930.

"London Slum," a photo-reportage by Alfred Eisenstaedt, *Münchener Illustrierte Presse*, 1932.

The World of Music

Arnold Schönberg (1874–1951), the inventor of the twelve-tone system, was the most influential force in modern music. His disciples included Alban Berg, Anton Webern, and Hanns Eisler. In 1898, under the spell of Richard Wagner, he had himself baptized.

In 1922 the painter (and composer) Wassily Kandinsky, who had been a friend of Schönberg's, joined a group of anti-Semitic teachers at the Bauhaus in Weimar which had stopped Schönberg being given a post there. Schönberg wrote to Kandinsky on 20 April 1923: "What I have been made to learn over the last year, I have now finally grasped, and won't ever forget. Namely, that I am not a German, not a European, perhaps even scarcely a human being (at least the Europeans prefer the worst of their race to me), but that I am a Jew ... I have heard that even Kandinsky sees only bad in the actions of Jews and in their bad actions sees only Jewishness, and so I give up any hope of an understanding. It was a dream. We are different kinds of people. Definitively!" And two weeks later, on 4 May 1923, he reproved Kandinsky: "And you play along with them and 'reject me as a Jew.' When did I apply to you for

RIGHT: Arnold Schönberg. Photo Man Ray, c. 1930

BELOW: Friedrich Schorr (1888–1953), one of the great Wagnerian singers, as Wotan.

RIGHT: Performance of the "Threepenny Opera" by Kurt Weill and Bert Brecht. Photos Georg and Tim Gidal, *Münchener Illustrierte Presse*, 1929.

The Jewish Youth Orchestra of Dresden, 1927. The violinist in the foreground is Max Weiner-Varon, later Israeli ambassador to Burma (see also page 401).

anything? How can a Kandinsky ... fail to fight a system which aims at Saint Bartholomew's Day?"

In 1933, in a Paris synagogue, he identified himself publicly with Judaism: "We Jews ... know that we have been chosen to preserve, and think through to the end, the idea of the one, eternal, unimaginable, invisible God!" That same year Schönberg emigrated to the United States, where in the final years of his life he suffered the direst poverty.

An early fan of Schönberg was Arnold Josef Rosé (1863–1946) from Jassy in Romania. The members of his Rosé Quartet were regarded for many years as model

RIGHT: The virtuoso violinist Bronislaw Hubermann (1882–1947). In 1935 he founded the Palestine Symphony Orchestra.

OPPOSITE BOTTOM: Artur Schnabel (at the piano, far left) playing at a family celebration, c. 1927.

BELOW: Lieder and opera singer Richard Tauber (1891–1948), Electrola record sleeve.

interpreters of chamber music from Haydn to Schönberg. Occasionally Rosé was also conductor at the Bayreuth Festival.

Der Protagonist ("The Protagonist"), 1926, *Der Zar lässt sich fotografieren* ("Royal Palace"), 1927, these two based on texts by Georg Kaiser, *Die Dreigroschenoper* ("The Threepenny Opera"), 1928, and *Aufstieg und Fall der Stadt Mahagonny* ("The Rise and Fall of the City of Mahagonny"), 1928, both with libretti by Bertold Brecht, were the international successes of a cantor's son from Dessau, Kurt Weill (1900–1950). After his emigration to America in 1933, he composed mainly musicals. Operetta and film composers whose music was often played were Oscar Straus, Friedrich Holländer, Paul Abraham, and Richard Heymann.

Bronislaw Hubermann, one of the greatest violinists of this century, came from Poland to Berlin, where as a child prodigy he attracted the attention of Brahms and Bruckner (see also page 283). In 1935, after his emigration from Germany, he founded the Palestine Symphony Orchestra in Tel Aviv. Other Jewish musical virtuosi of this time were Rudolf Serkin, Fritz Kreisler and Artur Schnabel.

Among the greatest conductors of the Weimar period were Leo Blech, Bruno Walter, and Otto Klemperer (see also page 283).

Outstanding among Jewish singers were the bass baritone Friedrich Schorr, one of the great Wotans at Bayreuth (see also page 283); the Wagnerian singers Alexander Kipnis, Emmanuel List and Margarete Matzenauer; the soprano Maria Ivogün ("The Nightingale") at the Munich opera house; Fritzi Massary, the most popular operetta star of the German-speaking stage; and the lyric tenor Richard Tauber from Dresden (1891–1948), an equally outstanding singer of Mozart and operetta. Joseph Schmidt (1904–1942), a cantor from Romania, achieved fame primarily through the song *Ein Lied geht um die Welt* ("A Song Goes Round the World"). The Hamburg singer Karl Salomon emigrated from Germany and became an important composer and conductor in Israel.

The World of the Theater

During the Weimar years, fear of Jewish competition gave way in a number of fields to cooperation and, often, to ungrudging recognition. This was true above all of literature, science, and the theater. An age free of prejudice seemed to have dawned in many walks of life.

Max Reinhardt, the pioneer of modern theater in Imperial Germany (see also page 284), director (until 1933) of the German Theater and the Kammerspiele (Studio Theater) in Berlin, was also involved with the Salzburg Festival, which he had helped to found, from 1920, and from 1924 directed plays at the Viennese Theater in the Austrian capital. A master of musically orchestrated crowd scenes, he captivated audiences particularly by his productions of the classics. In 1933 he fled to Vienna, then in 1938 to the United States, where he filmed Shakespeare's *A Midsummer Night's*

Fritz Kortner (1892–1970) as Shylock in Shakespeare's *The Merchant of Venice*.

BELOW: Max Reinhardt (1873–1943) at a rehearsal of *Oedipus*. Drawing by Emil Orlik.

RIGHT: Therese Giehse as Mother Wolffen in *Der Biberpelz* ("The Beaver Fur"), at the Münchener Kammerspiele, 1928.

FAR RIGHT: Dolly Haas as the youngest member of the *Berliner Prominenten* ("Berlin Celebrities"), 1930.

LEFT: Alexander Granach (1890–1945), one of the most powerful character actors of the German stage.

RIGHT: The great character actor Ernst Deutsch (1890–1969), c. 1930.

Dream in Hollywood. Bitter years of fruitless struggle for a new existence followed.

"What Max Reinhardt has given the German stage is immense, and it owes him immense thanks. He brought in an age of inspired openness, after the severe, closed world that was inevitably associated with the name of Otto Brahm: new methods, a newfound style were applied with magisterial freedom to the whole of German theater, and developed in the most surprising way." This how the playwright Gerhart Hauptmann summed up his view of Reinhardt.

The productions of Leopold Jessner (1878–1945) at the Berlin Playhouse were regarded in Germany as pioneering examples of modern stagecraft.

Mutual respect perhaps came more easily to actors and directors, Jewish or non-Jewish, because they all made their own particular contribution to the success of the ensemble: the quiet intensity of Lucie Höflich, the scintillating Maria Bard, the cold, pent-up fire of Gustav Gründgens contrasted with the stirring passion of Fritzi Massary, Orska, Elisabeth Bergner, Alexander Granach, or Fritz Kortner. Among all the actors and actresses of Jewish descent we can mention only a few: Therese Giehse, Grete Mosheim, Dolly Haas, Lucie Mannheim, Lilli Palmer, Eleonore von Mendelssohn, Rosa Valetti and her brother Hermann Vallentin, Ernst Deutsch, Max Pallenberg, Kurt Horwitz, Adolf Wohlbrück, Felix Bressart, Kurt Gerron, Peter Lorre.

Program for a special performance, in memory of Albert Steinrück, of a play by Frank Wedekind.

ABOVE: Ludwig Hardt (1886–1947), famous for his public recitals of classical German poetry. Painting by Eugen Spiro.

ABOVE LEFT: "The Weintraub Syncopators": actors Max Pallenberg on saxophone and Fritzi Massary on drums at the memorial evening for Albert Steinrück, 28 March 1929.

LEFT: Elisabeth Bergner and Ernst Deutsch in "Amphytrion 38" by Jean Giraudoux, German premiere at the Berlin Theater in the Stresemannstrasse on 15 January 1931. Directed by Victor Barnowsky.

Jews in German Literature

The Weimar Republic gave the Jews a sense of complete civil liberty. For the first time in history they faced the anti-Semites, now less feared than despised, as equal citizens. Yet over many of them even in these years lay the shadow of an identity crisis. There was still no dialogue between Germans and Jews. Jews of all literary persuasions – but hardly any non-Jewish Germans – were conscious of their inner synthesis of Germanness and Jewishness. So this synthesis remained one-sided. Many Jewish writers were able nevertheless to pursue careers as German writers in the illusion of a German-Jewish synthesis.

Jewish themes and German-Jewish problems loomed large in the works of Arnold Zweig, Jakob Wassermann, Lion Feuchtwanger, and Max Brod; Karl Kraus and Kurt Tucholsky were notable for their hatred of their Jewish origins.

The Berlin doctor and novelist Alfred Döblin (1878–1957), the son of Eastern Jewish immigrants, first discovered his Jewishness on a visit to the Jews in Poland.

The result was his book *Reise in Polen* ("Journey into Poland"), 1926. Shortly afterward he began work on *Berlin Alexanderplatz* (1929), his epic of working-class Berlin, the milieu in which he worked as a doctor. In 1941 in America, fleeing from the German army, he converted to Catholicism.

Arnold Zweig (1887–1968), from Glogau in Silesia, wrote as a committed German and was also, until his return to East Germany in 1948, a conscious Jew of Zionist sympathies. An anti-Jewish horror story was the inspiration for his play *Ritualmord in Ungarn. Jüdische Tragödie* ("Ritual Murder in Hungary: A Jewish Tragedy"), for which in 1915 he received the Kleist Prize. World War I led him, too, to a profound understanding of Eastern Jewry, which found expression in his *Das Ostjüdische Antlitz* ("The Face of Eastern Jewry"), 1919–20. Zweig became best known for his novel *Der Streit um den Sergeanten Grischa* ("The Case of Sergeant Grischa"), 1928, which centers

A meeting of the literary section of the Prussian Academy of Arts, 1929. Seated, from left: Hermann Stehr, Alfred Mombert, Eduard Stucken, Wilhelm von Scholz, Oskar Loerke, Walter von Molo, Ludwig Fulda, Heinrich Mann. Standing, from left: Bernhard Kellermann, Alfred Döblin, Thomas Mann, Max Halbe.

on the fate of a Russian prisoner of war who is wrongfully executed.

Lion Feuchtwanger (1884–1958), in his *Thomas Wendt*, a novel in the form of a dialogue, gave Brecht the inspiration for his theory of epic theater. In *Erfolg* ("Success"), Feuchtwanger drew a bitingly ironic portrait of the Munich of the during the soviet republic (see page 324f.) and of the provincial, hypocritical, avaricious bourgeoisie which provided the breeding ground of Nazism. Fame came to Feuchtwanger through his historical novels *Jud Süss* ("Jew Süss," in U.S. title "Power"), 1925, and the *Josephus-Trilogie* ("Josephus Trilogy"), 1932–45.

Ernst Toller's plays were impassioned

appeals for social justice. Ferdinand Brückner (1891–1958) was the founder of the Berlin Renaissance Theater in 1923, a director who experimented with modern stage techniques and a playwright remembered for his *Die Verbrecher* ("The Criminals"), 1929, *Krankheit der Jugend* ("The Sickness of Youth"), 1929, and *Elisabeth von England* ("Elizabeth of England"), 1930. Emil Ludwig (1881–1948) was a successful writer of historical reportage and biography. Alfred Neumann (1895–1952), a master of the psychological novel, also published novellas in the style of Heinrich von Kleist. Hermann Broch (1886–1951) wrote novels portraying the decay of bourgeois society. Rudolf Borchardt (1877–1945), a cousin of Georg Hermann (who wrote *Jettchen Gebert*, see page 288), was a lyric poet, essayist and inventive translator associated with Hugo von Hofmannsthal's circle and the New Romantics. The writings of cultural philosopher and essayist Walter Benjamin (1892–1940), a friend of Gershom Scholem, Ernst Bloch, Max Horkheimer, and Theodor W. Adorno, attempted a synthesis of Jewish mysticism, Zionism, and Marxist thought.

Bruno Frank, Hermann Kesten, Wilhelm Speyer, Vicky Baum, Jakob Wassermann, Martha Karlweis (Wassermann's second wife), and Mascha Kaléko were popular writers of the time. Kurt Tuchol-sky fought a fruitless battle in his satires and songs against the growing tide of militarism and fascism.

Ludwig Strauss, Nelly Sachs, Trude Kolmann, Manfred Sturmann, Margarete Susman, and Arno Nadel circled, like Else Lasker-Schüler, around and around their Jewish self-understanding, even when singing hymns to their German surroundings.

Other Jewish writers who must be counted as belonging to the German literature of the Weimar period are those who lived in Vienna and Prague. Foremost among the Viennese were Arthur Schnitzler, Peter Altenberg, Raoul Auernheimer, Felix Salten, satirist Karl Kraus, and the "master of the miniature," Alfred Polgar; Stefan Zweig lived from 1919 in Salzburg. Joseph Roth (1894–1939) died in exile in Paris in 1939. His stories and novels, among them *Juden auf Wanderschaft* ("Wandering Jew") 1927, *Hiob* ("Job"), 1930, and *Radetzkymarsch* ("Radetzky March"), 1932, were those of a psychological and stylistic master. Many were mirrors of old Austrian society, and his theme was man's isolation, which he revolts bitterly against, but finally, with the humor of wisdom, accepts.

Despite all the collaboration between Jews and non-Jews in the cultural sphere, part of the surrounding non-Jewish world regarded the Jews' literary productions as "un-German." Signs of cultural insecurity leading to an aversion to the "otherness" of the Jews were already evident in the final quarter of the 19th century. Anti-Semitic circles were characterized by a fear of "Überfremdung" ("being swamped by foreigners"), a fear which was sometimes real, sometimes demogogically blown up as a result of envy. Thomas Mann tried to analyze this fear of otherness in an essay on the writer Theodor Storm. Whereas Gottfried Keller, a Swiss, had despised anti-semitism as vulgar, the north German Theodor Storm from Holstein reacted with pointed anti-Semitism to Jewish critics: the "nordic paganism" naturally made him, Storm, "a bit of an anti-Semite," Mann wrote. "It is as well to establish the emotional connections clearly and objectively: that between the blonde North German homeland cult and anti-Semitism is unswerving."

All cultural and artistic experimentation, all critical comment and even satire was dismissed in advance by "völkisch" (German racial nationalist) circles as "Jewish." It was a problem that the majority of Jews simply failed to register, which, as the events of 1933 made mercilessly apparent, was a dangerous self-deception.

LEFT: Joseph Roth (1894–1939). Lithograph by Georg Eisler.

RIGHT: Else Lasker-Schüler (1869–1945). Drawing by her son Paul Lasker-Schüler.

BELOW: Else Lasker-Schüler's poem *Ein alter Tibetteppich* ("An Old Tibetan Rug"). Woodcut by Josua Reichert.

ein alter Tibetteppich

Deine Seele , die die meine liebet ,
Ist verwirkt mit ihr im Teppichtibét .
Strahl in Strahl , verliebte Farben ,
Sterne , die sich himmellang umwarben .
Unsere Füße ruhen auf der Kostbarkeit ,
Maschentausendabertausendweit .
Süßer Lamasohn auf Moschuspflanzenthron ,
Wie lange küßt dein Mund den meinen wohl
Und Wang die Wange buntgeknüpfte Zeiten schon ?

The Jewish Community in Berlin

The first documentary mentions of the fishing village of Berlin and the presence of Jews there are almost contemporaneous: Berlin in 1237; the first Jewish settlement in 1295. The latter continued until 1571, when the Jews were expelled.

The modern history of the Jews in Berlin begins a hundred years later, in 1671, when for economic reasons a tolerant Great Elector granted fifty well-to-do Jewish families driven from Vienna a temporary right of settlement in Brandenburg (see page 112). By the year 1812, the Jewish congregation had grown to 3,300 members; another hundred years later, in 1912, it numbered 165,000. Many had come from Silesia, after its conquest by Frederick the Great, and many from Breslau and its surroundings; others came from West and East Prussia. The Jewish proportion of the total Berlin population fluctuated between two and four percent; the highest Jewish population for Berlin was recorded in 1925, when the community had 172,000 members (out of the city's total population of around four million).

By that time most Jewish organizations in Germany had their headquarters in Berlin. It was also the seat of the Prussian Regional Association of Jewish Congregations, to which 655 communities belonged. The German-Israelite Community Federation had its seat here, as did the College for the Science of Judaism, the Association of German Jews, the Central Association of German Citizens of the Jewish Faith, the Orthodox Rabbinical Seminary, the Union of German Zionists, the League of Jewish Combat Veterans, the Maccabi/Bar Kochba Zionist athletics club, and many others.

Politically the Berlin community was the home of liberal Judaism in the Weimar years, with Orthodox Jews and Zionists having less political weight in the community. For its many areas of activity, the leadership of the Jewish community had an annual budget in 1930 of around ten million marks. State funding was given to the Jewish community from the ten percent of general income tax allocated to established religions, and this was supplemented by considerable sums in the form

City plan, 1922: a guide to Jewish Berlin.

1 School
2 Orphanage
3 Old Age Home
4 Jewish Hospital
5 Cemetary
6 Uniform store
7 Synagogue (old/new)
8 Society of Jewish Culture
9 Administration
10 Synagogue, Welfare and School

✡ Welfare services
📖 Schools and religious colleges

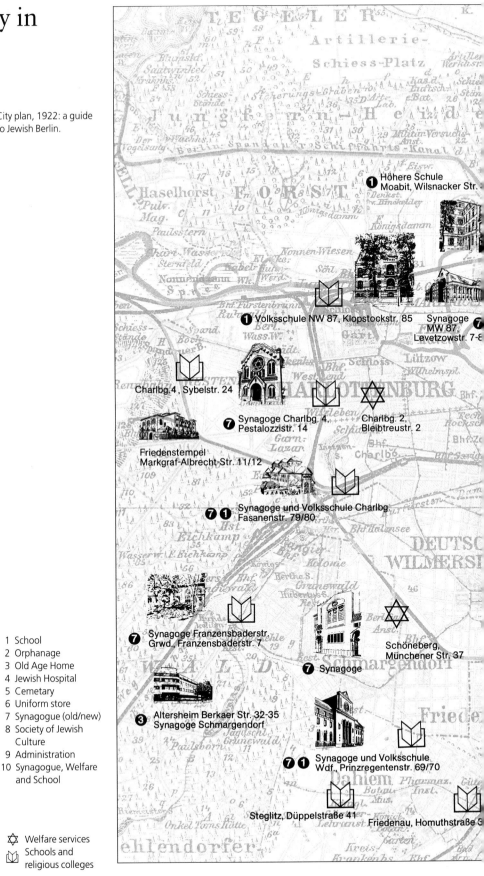

1 Höhere Schule Moabit, Wilsnacker Str.
1 Volksschule NW 87, Klopstockstr. 85
7 Synagoge NW 87, Levetzowstr. 7-8
Charlbg 4, Sybelstr. 24
7 Synagoge Charlbg. 4, Pestalozzistr. 14
Charlbg. 2, Bleibtreustr. 2
Friedenstempel Markgraf-Albrecht-Str. 11/12
7 1 Synagoge und Volksschule Charlbg. Fasanenstr. 79/80
7 Synagoge Franzensbaderstr. Grwd., Franzensbaderstr. 7
Schöneberg, Münchener Str. 37
7 Synagoge
3 Altersheim Berkaer Str. 32-35 Synagoge Schmargendorf
7 1 Synagoge und Volksschule Wdf., Prinzregentenstr. 69/70
Steglitz, Düppelstraße 41
Friedenau, Homuthstraße 3

394

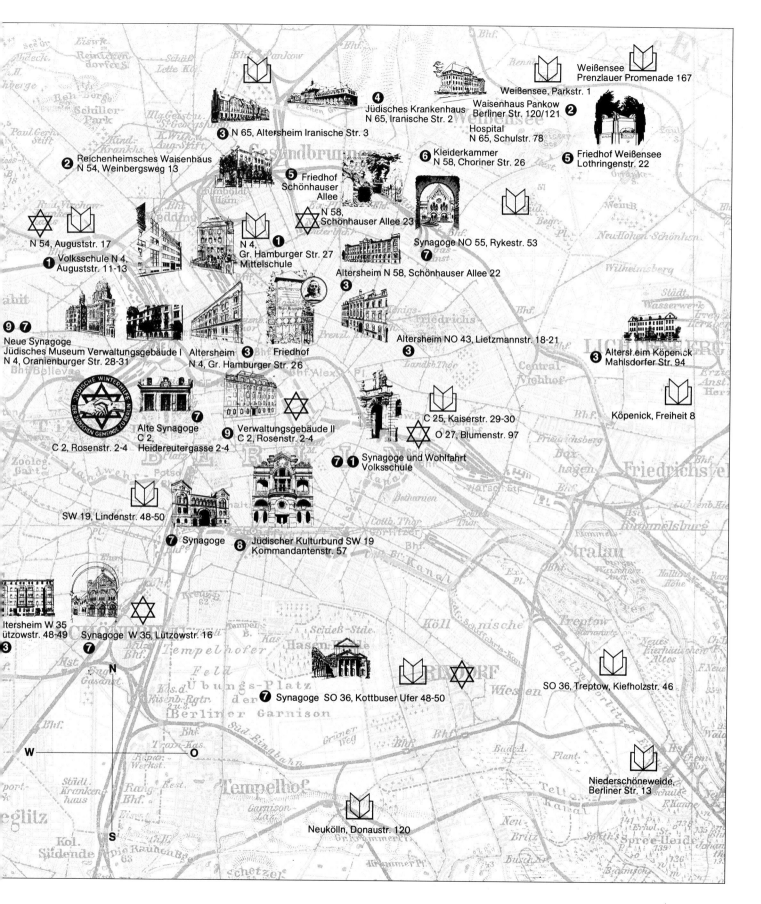

Weißensee
Prenzlauer Promenade 167

Weißensee, Parkstr. 1

Waisenhaus Pankow
Berliner Str. 120/121 **2**

4 Jüdisches Krankenhaus
N 65, Iranische Str. 2

Hospital
N 65, Schulstr. 78

3 N 65, Altersheim Iranische Str. 3

6 Kleiderkammer
N 58, Choriner Str. 26

5 Friedhof Weißensee
Lothringenstr. 22

2 Reichenheimsches Waisenhaus
N 54, Weinbergsweg 13

5 Friedhof
Schönhauser
Allee

N 58,
Schönhauser Allee 23

Synagoge NO 55, Rykestr. 53

N 54, Auguststr. 17

1 Volksschule N 4,
Auguststr. 11-13

N 4, **1**
Gr. Hamburger Str. 27
Mittelschule

7

Altersheim N 58, Schönhauser Allee 22

3

9 7

Neue Synagoge
Jüdisches Museum Verwaltungsgebäude I
N 4, Oranienburger Str. 28-31

Altersheim **3**
N 4, Gr. Hamburger Str. 26

Friedhof

Altersheim NO 43, Lietzmannstr. 18-21

3

3 Altersheim Köpenick
Mahlsdorfer Str. 94

Köpenick, Freiheit 8

Alte Synagoge
C 2,
Heidereutergasse 2-4

7

9 Verwaltungsgebäude II
C 2, Rosenstr. 2-4

C 25, Kaiserstr. 29-30

C 2, Rosenstr. 2-4

7 1 Synagoge und Wohlfahrt
Volksschule

O 27, Blumenstr. 97

SW 19, Lindenstr. 48-50

7 Synagoge

8 Jüdischer Kulturbund SW 19
Kommandantenstr. 57

Itersheim W 35
ützowstr. 48-49

Synagoge W 35, Lützowstr. 16

3

7

N

W ────── **O**

S

7 Synagoge SO 36, Kottbuser Ufer 48-50

SO 36, Treptow, Kiefholzstr. 46

Niederschöneweide,
Berliner Str. 13

Neukölln, Donaustr. 120

LEFT: Masthead of the *Gemeindeblatt der Jüdischen Gemeinde zu Berlin*, the newspaper of the Berlin Jewish community.

Wir helfen Tausenden

durch

Brotverteilung,
Kohlenversorgung,
Kleider-, Schuhe- und Wäsche-
Beschaffung,
Speisung unserer Kinder,
Wärme-Räume.

Helfen Sie uns durch Spenden!

*Wohlfahrts- und Jugendfürsorgeamt der
Jüd. Gemeinde, Berlin C.2, Rosenstraße 2-4*
Norden 6711   Postscheckkonto: Berlin Nr. 29640

*Kleiderkammer der Jüdischen Gemeinde
(PEAH), Berlin N, Choriner Straße 26*
Humboldt 0789 und Norden 6711   Postscheckkonto:
                                                    Berlin Nr. 29640

SYNAGOGEN-KONZERT

veranstaltet vom

Vorstand der Jüdischen Gemeinde zu Berlin

Mittwoch, den 29. Januar 1930, abends 7,30 Uhr
NEUE SYNAGOGE, ORANIENBURGER STRASSE 30

MITWIRKENDE:

Kammersänger HERMANN JADLOWKER

Professor ALBERT EINSTEIN
Professor ALFRED LEWANDOWSKI ｝ Violine
Der verstärkte Chor der Neuen Synagoge, Dirigent: Janot S. Roskin
An der Orgel: Arthur Zepke

MA TOWU C-Dur . . . . . . Sulzer
MAARIW
ADON OLOM . . . . Würfel

VORTRAGSFOLGE

1. a) Sonate 2, B-Dur . . . . Händel
   b) Adagio aus dem Doppelkonzert C-Moll . . . . J. S. Bach
      für zwei Violinen mit Orgelbegleitung
   (Professor Einstein und Professor Lewandowski, Orgel: A. Zepke).
2. Kol-nidre . . . . Jadlowker
3. Socharti-loch . . . . Rosowsky
4. B'rosch Haschonoh . . . . Sulzer
5. Uw'chen jissakdasch . . . . Goldstein
6. Ki ono t'schimcho . . . . Weintraub
7. Ono towo . . . . Naumburg
8. Ato niglesso . . . . Jadlowker
9. Hallelujah . . . . Lewandowski

Der Reinertrag fließt dem Wohlfahrts- u. Jugendamt der Jüdischen Gemeinde zu

---

GESCHICHTE DER JUDEN IM UMRISS
EIN ZYKLUS VON ACHT EINZELVORTRAEGEN

Unsere bisherigen Geschichtskurse stießen auf ein unverhältnismäßig geringes Interesse. Gerade der vorstehende Aufsatz Martin Bubers wird zeigen, wie wichtig für das von uns erstrebte Anschluß-Finden eine genaue Kenntnis der jüdischen Geschichte ist. Um hier eine erste Beziehung anzubahnen, veranstalten wir in diesem Trimester einen Kurs in Einzelvorträgen. Wir möchten auf diese, von hervorragenden Sachkennern vermittelte Einführung ganz besonders hinweisen.

1. Der Aufstieg des Reiches
   Israel   *Dr. Elias Auerbach*
   Am 3. Februar

2. Der Untergang des jüdischen
   Reiches   *Dr. Elias Auerbach*
   Am 10. Februar

3. Die Juden in der römisch-helle-
   nistischen Zeit   *Prof. Dr. Ismar Elbogen*
   Am 17. Februar

4. Die Juden im islamischen Mittel-
   alter   *Prof. Dr. Julius Guttmann*
   Am 24. Februar

5. Die Juden im christlichen
   Mittelalter   *Prof. Dr. Ismar Elbogen*
   Am 2. März

6. Von Reformation zu Revolution
   im westlichen Europa   *Dr. Georg Landauer*
   Am 9. März

7. Juden im Westen seit der fran-
   zösischen Revolution   *Dr. Gustav Krojanker*
   Am 16. März

8. Die osteuropäischen Juden seit
   dem Ausgang des Mittelalters   *Dr. Aron Steinberg*
   Am 23. März

Die Vorträge finden jeweils Mittwoch um 8 Uhr abends in der Aula des Schulgebäudes, Auguststraße 11—13, statt. Hörergebühr: für den ganzen Zyklus 2,— M., für den einzelnen Vortragsabend 50 Pf., Angehörige der Schule 30 Pf.

ABOVE LEFT: "We help thousands … .": an appeal for charitable donations for the poor, 1930.

ABOVE CENTER: Notice of a synagogue concert with Albert Einstein and Hermann Jadlowker, 1930.

ABOVE RIGHT: Lecture schedule (Jewish history) at the Jewish Youth School, January to March 1932.

RIGHT: The Fasanenstrasse synagogue after a service. Photo by Hans Casparius, 1928.

LEFT: Budget allocations for the various departments of the congregation, 1930.

Verwaltung	5,36%
Friedhofswesen	9,76%
Bildungswesen	12,51%
Vermögensverwaltg. einschl. Zinsendienst u. Grundst.-Abgaben	15,17%
Kultuswesen	17,66%
Wohlfahrtswesen	39,55%

ABOVE: Interior of the Jewish Museum (1933). On the left, bust of Moses Mendelssohn.

RIGHT: The cemetery at Weissensee.

of voluntary donations for the welfare departments.

The community's administration costs were also met from this budget, the largest item of which were sixteen synagogues with their thirty rabbis, then seven old people's homes, a hospital with 300 beds, the cemetery, sports grounds, kindergartens, youth hostels, religious colleges, a general secondary school, two orphanages, a library of 67,000 volumes, an art gallery and museum, a higher educational institute, and several elementary schools. There were comprehensive counseling services available. Notable were the extensive welfare arrangements for the poor and unemployed, whose number was high in relation to the general population.

The Eastern Jews

Short story writer and essayist Efraim Frisch (1873–1942), editor of the literary monthly *Der neue Merkur* in Munich from 1914 to 1916 and 1919 to 1925.

SCHRIFTEN DES ARBEITERFÜRSORGEAMTES DER JÜDISCHEN ORGANISATIONEN DEUTSCHLANDS

HEFT II

OSTJUDEN IN DEUTSCH= LAND

PHILO=VERLAG / BERLIN S.W. 68
1921

Title page of "Eastern Jews in Germany," a publication put out by the Workers' Welfare Office of Jewish Organizations in Germany.

Nahum Goldmann (1894–1982), president of the World Jewish Congress (1949–1977) and the World Zionist Organization (1956–1968). Photo Tim Gidal.

Restaurant in the Grenadierstrasse in Berlin, c. 1924.

For rightwing circles and anti-Semites in Germany, the term "Eastern Jew" (*Ostjude*) was a stick that could also be used to beat the German Jews. A consequence was that for many assimilated German Jews, "Eastern Jew" was at best a condescending term for foreign Jews, who it was hoped with financial assistance would rapidly move on to other countries. There was little social contact even with those already resident in Germany. An exception were Eastern Jews who had integrated into literary, artistic, or scientific life in Germany, who, it has to be said, were accepted by the assimilated Jews.

Most German Jews were of a liberal persuasion, which was also true of the synagogues to which they belonged. They had achieved equal legal and political rights for themselves, yet when it came to positions on the boards of the Jewish congregations, they restricted these rights to those who were German citizens.

The stereotype of the "dirty and uncultivated Eastern Jew," taken from the literature of anti-Semitism, also persuaded many assimilated Jews, who considered themselves culturally superior to the Eastern Jews. For their part, the Eastern Jews remained unimpressed by both the anti-Semitism of the anti-Semites and the prejudices of the Western Jews. They took anti-Semitism as a sign of moral inferiority and looked down scornfully on the Germanizing pretensions of many German Jews and their ignorance of things Jewish. After the anti-Semitic waves from 1919 to 1924, which were directed against "the" Jews, relations between the Eastern and Western Jews improved.

In one poor quarter of Berlin, the "Scheunenviertel" ("barn quarter") as it was known, there was one group of

Police raid in Berlin's Scheunenviertel ("barn quarter"), February 1920. Those found without valid identity cards – mostly women brought to Germany by their husbands – were taken into custody by the police.

Eastern Jewish immigrants who continued to wear their traditional dress, their beards and ringlets. They were at the most five or six hundred people, but because of their exotic appearance they were taken as typical of all Eastern Jews, not only by the anti-Semites but by many Western Jews as well. Theodor Wolff, for instance, the editor of the *Berliner Tageblatt* newspaper, Georg Hermann, the author of the best-selling novel *Jettchen Gebert* and others exploded in tirades of hatred against the foreign undesirables.

In the communities, the wrangles over voting rights for Eastern Jews lasted for decades, and there was always a latent mutual hostility. In November 1933, however, the chairman of the Central Association of German Citizens of the Jewish Faith, Ludwig Holländer, whose

position had always been that of mediator, wrote that the Eastern Jews were "Jews like us" and that penurious German Jews in Western countries were often regarded as Eastern Jews.

However belatedly, Holländer had put his finger on the root of the prejudice. It was the poverty of the majority of Eastern Jews which inspired the stories of their low morals. What underlay the superciliousness of many non-Jewish and Jewish Germans toward the Eastern Jew was largely the class difference between the *arrivés* and these latecomers, who had to struggle for their daily bread and were not always choosy about the means they employed. The condescension remained even after the Eastern Jews had risen into the working or middle classes.

With the exception of the numerically small but visually conspicuous group of Orthodox believers, the Eastern Jews very rapidly assimilated to their German surroundings in language, dress, manners, and cultural interests, and even in their style of beard. In Berlin, not a few acquired a Kaiser Wilhelm mustache, while in Munich many sported full, well-kempt beards in the manner of the Bavarian prince regent, Luitpold. Many Eastern Jews played a part in the artistic and literary life of Germany, while others became scientists, engineers, and architects. This did not, however, prevent most of them, even the second generation, from remaining members of their Eastern Jewish congregations (see page 300f.). Even religiously indifferent Eastern Jews like Elisabeth Bergner or the biologist Lydia Rabinowitsch-Kempner made no attempt to hide their Eastern Jewish origins.

There are no detailed descriptions of the Eastern Jewish congregations in Germany. Only one attempt was made, on the occasion of the consecration of a modest synagogue in Munich in 1931, the construction of which resulted from agreement between the Galician, Polish, and Russian Jews of Munich. Years earlier, despite the gibes between the various nationalities, they had joined together to form a General Council of Eastern Jews, in order to defend them-

Report from a Talmud Torah school. Children at these schools, where attendance was voluntary, were given instruction in the Talmud and Talmudic commentaries.

selves against the arbitrary actions of the anti-Semitic Bavarian state commissioner Gustav von Kahr. In 1923, shortly before Hitler's attempted putsch, von Kahr and his police chief Ernst Pöhner began deporting Eastern Jews from Bavaria. Many were assembled in camps, then taken to the border and dumped on the other side. The General Council of Eastern Jews succeeded in demonstrating the illegality of these actions to the Bavarian government and getting many of the deportations reversed. Hitler declared at the time that the deportations were "too mild." Only a brutal nationalist dictatorship, he said, could solve the Jewish question. His intention was "to string all Jews up."

There were around 500 Eastern Jewish families living in Munich at that time, or roughly 2000 individuals out of a total population of some 500,000. There were two Eastern Jewish cultural associations; and in the Jewish Choral Society and the Bar Kochba Athletics Club, the majority of the members were from Eastern Jewish families. A mutual aid society, to which all Eastern Jews contributed financially, made interest-free loans. Another important Eastern Jewish institution was the voluntary arbitration court. Disputes were brought before this court, to avoid the necessity of confronting prejudiced German judges.

The men, and often the women, worked as tobacco workers, furriers, traveling salesmen, small manufacturers, teachers, representatives, and businessmen; bakers, butchers, joiners, and cobblers; as musicians, carpet importers, jewelers, and goldsmiths; second-hand clothes dealers and market stall holders. But the Eastern Jewish community also included the owner of a small department store, the proprietor of a cigarette factory, the owners of the EMELKA film company, which later merged with UFA, and a number of well-to-do cloth merchants and furniture dealers.

By the second and third generation, there were already 50 academics in those 500 families. Among the best-known names were the physicist Arno Penzias, who won the 1978 Nobel Prize for

Certificate awarded to Max Weiner, from an Eastern Jewish family in Dresden, on the occasion of his victory in the triathlon at the 1927 Reich Youth Games.

physics, Alexander Schindler, son of a Jewish poet and later president of Jewish organizations in the United States, and Saul Eisenberg, who built up an international business in Japan, Korea, America and Israel. A prominent figure in politics was Arnold Wadler, a lieutenant in World War I and housing commissar in the Munich soviet republic. Sentenced to seven years' imprisonment, he began to study linguistics in his cell. After fleeing to Switzerland in 1933, he published two works, *Der Turm von Babel* ("The Tower of Babel") and *Germanische Urzeit* ("Germanic Prehistory"), in which by linguistic comparison he sought to show that all the world's languages originally belonged to one family.

One revealing sociological fact is that the hostility of non-Jews to the Eastern Jews was often connected to their social status. Hostility was least evident within

Jüd.-Literarischer Abend
Kultur-Verein Progress
Sonnabend, den 5. Januar 1924, 7½ Uhr abds findet im gr. Saal des zion. Heims, Landsberger Str. 89 ein
Vortrag des Herrn Prof. Dr. Stermann
über das Thema „D i e K l a c z e" von Mendele Mocher Sfarim, statt. **Die Kultur-Kommission.**

LEFT: Notice of a meeting of an Eastern Jewish cultural society in Berlin, 1924.

BELOW: The Eastern Jewish "Progress" Cultural Society, 1923/24. In the back row on the right is Abraham Pisarek, later renowned for his photographs of Jewish daily life in Berlin under Hitler.

the working class, as was illustrated in the Ruhr during and after World War I, when thousands of Eastern Jews worked in the mines and heavy industry there. The Jews were only rarely subjected to verbal or physical abuse, and once the Eastern Jews had shown themselves to be loyal trade unionists, cooperation in the unions proceeded very harmoniously.

Internal Jewish Conflict

The majority of German Jews identified with the aims of the Central Association of German Citizens of the Jewish Faith. This was as true of the Orthodox as it was of the Liberals, who had been joined by many supporters of reform. It was also true of most of those who were indifferent to religion. The religious tendencies had reached a modus vivendi based on mutual respect.

LEFT: The journalist Robert Weltsch, from 1919 to 1938 editor of the Zionist *Jüdische Rundschau* in Berlin. On the wall a portrait of the Hebrew poet Hayyim Nahman.

RIGHT: The lawyer Ludwig Holländer (1877–1936), from 1908 to 1930 director of the Central Association of German Citizens of the Jewish Faith, and from 1896 chairman of the "Kartell Convent" (K.C.) of German Students of the Jewish Faith.

The German Pro-Palestine Committee, 1928. From right, standing, front row: the chairman, Count Heinrich Bernstorff, Prof Chaim Weizmann, and Carl von Schubert. To the left behind Schubert, Albert Einstein; between Schubert and Weizmann, the secretary, Katharina von Oheimb. Behind Count Bernstorff and to his right, the banker Oskar Wassermann, and next to him Kurt Blumenfeld, president of the German Zionist Association.

ABOVE: The masthead of the paper *Der Nationaldeutsche Jude*. This small but active organization was close to the German National People's Party (DNVP) and was anti-Zionist.

LEFT: Advertisement for the *Jüdisch-liberale Zeitung*, a weekly for liberal Jews.

RIGHT: Election poster of the Poale Zion for local elections in Berlin.

The conflicts were now transferred to the political plane. Here there were serious clashes between the Central Association, the League of Jewish Ex-Combatants, and the Association of National-German Jews (a small group) on the one side and the Zionist groups and the social democratic Jewish People's Party on the other. The Eastern Jews, even naturalized ones, belonged mostly to the Zionists and Social Democrats. The Association of National-German Jews identified with the aims of the German National People's Party (DNVP), the Jewish People's Party with the socialist workers' parties and the social democratic workers' organization Poale Zion ("Zion's Workers"). Only in the Jewish People's Party, the Poale Zion, and the Zionist organizations did the Eastern Jews enjoy equal rights of representation with the Western Jews.

The Eastern immigrants' struggle for equal rights in the Jewish communities also went on for decades. Leading members of the Central Association were, however, involved in measures to assist the economic integration of the Jewish foreigners, demanding for them the same rights enjoyed by non-Jewish foreigners. The Central Association meanwhile regarded its active participation in the non-party umbrella organizations for construction in Palestine as an unpolitical, strictly economic contribution: the Union rejected Zionism's political aims.

A further forum for cooperation was the Pro-Palestine Committee, which, with the benevolent support of the Foreign Ministry, served the same ends. Its membership comprised, alongside non-Jewish friends of Palestine like Count Bernstorff and Katharina von Oheimb, scientists such as Albert Einstein, Central Association members like the banker Oskar Wassermann, and leading Zionists like Kurt Blumenfeld.

LEFT: "Declaration of German Jews" in response to the violent clashes between Arabs and Jews in Palestine, August 1929.

A Light Interlude: Walter Trier

The painter and cartoonist Walter Trier (1890–1951), who had been a pupil of Knirr and Stuck at the Munich Academy, was the most popular illustrator for the Ullstein magazines *Die Dame*, *Die Koralle*, and *Der Uhu*.

He also illustrated a large number of books, among them Erich Kästner's children's stories. After his emigration to England in 1936, he worked on *Lilliput* magazine, for which he drew the title page. From 1947 onwards he lived in Toronto. This is what he said of himself:

"I was born in Prague in 1890, when the exchange rate was 80 pfennigs to the crown. My father was a misanthrope by profession. 'Eight days late! That's just like you!' he said to me, and went off for a coffee.

"While he was away I made a number of valuable acquaintanceships. There were already five brothers and sisters. We had an animated conversation and I discovered lots of new things. Including in particular that WAC Vienna had beaten DFC Prague 3:0. This news got me fearfully excited. I was given valerian and fennel. They had no effect. I only calmed down when one of

ABOVE: "Me." Self-portrait by Walter Trier.

ABOVE RIGHT: "Fritz Kortner." Cigarette card, c. 1930

LEFT: "Einstein." Caricature by Walter Trier.

Kintopp ("The Flicks"), 1920.

my brothers threw a football into my tummy.

"This was how my interest was aroused in the sport of football, to which I sacrificed all my powers for the next fifteen years. I would undoubtedly have become a major international player in that field, if my school had not plunged a dagger in my back. Determined at all costs to make a scholar of me, it taught me the two times table. A little of it remains in my memory to this day. Later I became an art student. When, at my matriculation into the Prague Academy of Arts, the secretary looked through my final school report and saw the 'satisfactory' in drawing and the 'excellent' in gymnastics, he asked me, with tears in his eyes: 'Wouldn't you rather go and be an acrobat?' My abysmal lack of talent could not be concealed forever. With one mighty swing I flew out of the School of Arts and Crafts and the Academy. All the way to Munich!"

German Jews Go to Palestine

One of the first German Jews to follow his Zionist convictions and settle in Palestine was the political economist and sociologist Arthur Ruppin (1876–1943). From 1908 onward he was the head of the Zionist Palestine Office in Haifa and afterward directed the establishment of the first agricultural cooperative settlements.

LEFT: Drainage work on Lake Huleh in Galilee, 1930. The swampy land was almost entirely drained. Today there are some 20 kibbutzim there.

BELOW: A number of Jews, mostly academics and members of the Blue-and-White youth movement, went to Palestine in 1923/24. Most of them joined a kibbutz, as here in En Harod.

He continued these activities after World War I and in 1933 conceived a policy for a planned immigration and settlement of Jews from Germany.

Siegfried Lehmann (1892–1958) was a founder of homes for young people and children, which encouraged a sense of responsibility and cooperation in the

LEFT: Arthur Ruppin (1876–1943), originator and promoter of the kibbutz movement.

RIGHT: The botanist Otto Warburg (1859–1938), member of the Zionist Organization's action committee, from 1921 the director of the agricultural institute in Rehovot.

BELOW: The settlement of Nahalal, designed by the architect Richard Kaufmann.

young. After 1918 he brought pogrom orphans and refugee children from Lithuania to Berlin, and from 1927 to Palestine. There he set up the Ben Shemen children's village.

Among the academics who as Zionists emigrated to Palestine long before 1933 were the historian Fritz Baer, ethnologist Erich Brauer, mathematician Abraham Fränkel, geologist Leo Picard, geologist and archaeologist Adolf Reifenberg, natural scientist Samuel Sambursky, Cabala scholar Gershom Scholem, philosopher Hugo Bergmann, educationist Ernst Akiba Simon and others. Jerusalem's first modern bookstore was opened in 1911 by Ludwig Mayer from Breslau.

Even before World War I, a new Palestine style of architecture had been developed by Alex Baerwald (1878–1930), among whose buildings was the technical school in Haifa. Architect Richard Kaufmann designed the sites of collective settlements such as Nahalal, the prototype of the cooperative village, and some kibbutzim.

A number of German Jewish doctors laid the foundations of a modern health service in Palestine. In 1919, doctor and historian Elias Auerbach established the first practice for Jews, Arabs, and German Knights Templar in Haifa. Albert Ticho started an eye clinic in Jerusalem, and Ernst Treu the first orthopedic clinic; Ernst Emanuel Simon became the leading physical educationist in the country.

In 1924, groups of craftsmen and members of the Blue-and-White youth movement went to Palestine and set up workshops there. Other Blue-and-Whites joined kibbutzim or work groups, which in pursuit of their ideals ("Conquest of Work") constructed roads and drained

ABOVE: Jewish orphans on the way to the children's village of Ben Shemen in Palestine, founded by Siegfried Lehmann (center left, with hat).

LEFT: Ludwig Mayer's bookstore in Jerusalem. The couple came to Palestine from Breslau in 1924.

①   ②

swamps. The Givat Brenner kibbutz was established in 1928 by a group of young Zionists from Germany and other countries (see page 416). Walter Moses, the leader of the Blue-and-Whites, set up the Dubek cigarette factory. Large areas in the bay of Haifa were purchased on the initiative of Joseph Loewy: settlers from Germany established light industry and residential settlements there.

Before 1933, about two thousand German Jews emigrated to Palestine for idealistic reasons. They helped in many fields to prepare the ground for the mass immigration after 1933.

ABOVE: Geologist Leo Picard (born 1900) from Wangen, head of the department of geology of the Hebrew University, Jerusalem, from 1924. Photo by Tim Gidal.

ABOVE RIGHT: The technical school in Haifa, designed and built (1910) by government architect Alexander Baerwald, an immigrant from Germany. Photo Ben Dov, 1924.

BELOW: Professors and other teaching staff of the Hebrew University of Jerusalem, 1927. Seated in the front row, from left: mathematician Prof. Abraham Fränkel from Munich, rector 1938–40 (1); Prof Judah Leon Magnes, from San Francisco, the university's first president and an early campaigner for Jewish-Arab understanding (2); botanist Prof Otto Warburg from Hamburg, cofounder of the Hebrew University of Jerusalem (3); historian Prof Yizhak Fritz Baer from Halberstadt (4); political economist and sociologist Dr Arthur Ruppin from Rawitsch (5); scholar of the Cabala and Jewish mysticism Gershom Scholem from Berlin (6); geologist Prof. Leo Picard from Wangen (7); agronomist and art historian Prof. Adolf Reifenberg from Berlin (8); philosopher Prof. Hugo Bergmann from Prague (9).

Hakhsharah and Aliyah

On the Winkel training farm in Brandenburg: milking, leisure time, a gramophone concert. Photos Tim Gidal.

Hakhsharah means "making fit or preparation"; Aliyah in biblical times meant a "going up" to the land of Israel and the temple in Jerusalem. In its modern sense, it means immigration for national or religious reasons. Always associated with the term was also the idea of advancing to a higher plane of spiritual life.

It was the Zionist movement and the Zionist Labor Party of Germany which looked after the preparation of young people for life in the kibbutz. Generally the training took place on teaching farms. There like-minded young people lived and worked together, not only learning an agricultural trade but also familiarizing themselves once more with Jewish culture and history and the Hebrew language: an ideal preparation for resettlement in Palestine

TOP: Grain harvest at the farm in Winkel.

RIGHT: A group of Orthodox Jews on the training farm at Rodges, 1930. The group founded the Tirat Zvi kibbutz in the Jordan Valley.

Enzo Sereni, founder member of the Givat Brenner kibbutz, as a deputy of the socialist workers' organization. At a meeting of Habonim groups from Germany in 1932 he argued for prompt hakhsharah and aliyah.

Sereni, son of the king of Italy's physician, became a Zionist in his early years. Parachuted into Yugoslavia during the war, he was captured by the Germans and killed in Dachau concentration camp in 1945.

BOTTOM LEFT: In the Sha'ar Hanegev kibbutz. The soil there proved too saline and the kibbutz was later resettled in upper Galilee. The kibbutz members received financial support from the Jewish National Fund to enable them to remove the blocks of basalt from the fertile soil. Fruit and olive plantations and a carpenter's shop were the foundation of the new Kfar Szold kibbutz's economic existence. Photo Tim Gidal.

BELOW: In 1933, members of the Habonim group founded the Sha'ar Ha-negev (Gate of Negev) kibbutz. Photo by Tim Gidal.

and integrating into the kibbutz movement. This went on despite the resistance of many parents, who saw it as a rebellion against their allegedly secure middle-class existence in Germany, which they regarded as their homeland. Several training farms ran out of money and had to be abandoned. But these young Zionists did not give up: they hired themselves out to farmers as agricultural laborers.

After the hakhsharah came the aliyah, emigration to Palestine, with or without a religious motivation. In either case, aliyah was the embodiment of deliverance from the dispersion among the nations, with all its humiliations and persecutions and demands for self-surrender never made of any other people.

Ever since the early Middle Ages there had been Jews in Germany who had gone on aliyah on religious grounds. At the end

of the 19th century one or two people began to emigrate to Palestine for secular, Zionist reasons (see page 306). The first wave of halutzim (pioneers) from Germany of any size came after World War I, primarily from the Blue-and-White youth movement (see page 338). The overwhelming majority joined existing kibbutz. There is no private property in the kibbutz; the community is responsible for the needs of its members and their families. The guiding principle of the kibbutz communities is social justice, which includes complete

equality between men and women. This was in practical terms the only way in which, in the most difficult living conditions – years of living in tents, no electricity, often little to eat – barren and marshy ground could be transformed into fruitful land. Over the years, most kibbutzim developed into prosperous villages.

The role played by the kibbutz movement, in the economy, in politics and culture, and particularly in securing a Jewish homeland in Palestine and later in the State of Israel, was crucial.

The Givat Brenner Kibbutz south of Tel Aviv, founded in 1928 by halutzim from Germany and Italy, and today, with over 1,500 residents, the country's largest. Apart from intensive farming, the kibbutzim run a fruit-canning factory, a large carpenter's shop, a factory for making agricultural sprinklers, a factory for essential oils, and a hotel. Photo by Tim Gidal, 1930.

On the Eve

Performance of *Jeremias* by Stefan Zweig (second row, center right, with mustache) by an amateur theatrical group, on the occasion of a conference of the Jewish Youth Associations in Munich, June 1930.

Bruno Walter conducting. Photo Dr Erich Salomon.

ABOVE: Appeal by the welfare office of the Jewish community of Berlin, winter 1932.

The economic slump of 1929 spread from America to Europe and Germany. Large sections of the population were thrown into distress, with Jews, especially in the middle classes, hit more severely than the non-Jews, as almost no Jews were in permanent state employment or had land holdings of any value. In Berlin, the welfare agency had now to extend its work into areas in the west of the city previously regarded as wealthy. Thousands were given the means to pay their rent arrears, to avoid being thrown out on the street; thousands received at least one meal a day.

In Berlin, Jews were already being beaten up in broad daylight. Interior Minister Wirth issued a statement to

ABOVE: The Bar Kochba group parading after the Grünwald-Munich relay races in 1932. Photograph taken at the corner of Arcis Strasse and Brienner Strasse by Tim Gidal.

The last foundation laying of a synagogue in Germany took place at the end of 1930 in Munich, where four small Eastern Jewish congregations got together to construct a joint synagogue. Photo Georg Gidal.

LEFT: The Jewish Baum family in the garden of their house in Solln near Munich, 1932. Dr. Erich Baum, holder of the Iron Cross military decoration and a member of the Central Association of German Citizens of the Jewish Faith, worked as a chemist at the Wacker works in Munich. In 1934 he and his family emigrated to Haifa. Photo Tim Gidal.

RIGHT: The German presidential elections of 13 March 1932. The painter Max Liebermann leaving the polling station.

BELOW: "Vote German!" An election poster of the Association of National German Jews for the Reichstag elections of 31 July 1932.

Deutsche Volksgenossen jüdischer Abstammung!

Der Wahltag ist der Tag, unser Deutschtum zu bewähren.

Man verspricht uns von der einen Seite, daß wir Juden geschützt werden, wenn bestimmte Parteien zur Regierung kommen.

Man droht uns von anderer Seite, daß wir entrechtet werden, wenn bestimmte Parteien oder Gruppen zur Macht gelangen. Jedem, der so unsere Gesinnung und unsere Wahlstimmen zu kaufen versucht, sei gesagt, daß wir bei Erfüllung unserer vaterländischen Pflicht nicht durch Drohungen und nicht durch Versprechungen zu beeinflussen sind.

Nicht „ubi bene", nicht wo es uns gut ergeht, ist unser Vaterland.

Unser Vaterland ist dort, wo unsere Seele ist.

Mit Deutschland sind wir verbunden durch die deutsche Kultur, die seit Jahrhunderten in unseren Familien heimisch ist, durch die deutsche Muttersprache, durch die Liebe zum deutschen Heimatboden, durch das Wissen um unsere Zugehörigkeit zum deutschen Volke. Wir sind Deutsche nicht um irgendwelcher Vorteile willen, sondern durch den Zwang des Gefühls.

Diese unverbrüchliche Verbundenheit mit dem deutschen Volke kann uns nicht geraubt werden, nicht durch Drohungen irregeleiteter Judenfeinde, nicht durch Hirngespinste einiger dem Deutschtum künstlich entfremdeter Zionisten, nicht durch Angstpolitik einer kleinen wurzellosen Zwischenschicht.

Das Volksgefühl gibt den Ausschlag, nicht die sogenannte „Rasse".

Wer in seinem Gefühl zum deutschen Volke gehört, wählt am 31. Juli nicht für den vermeintlichen Vorteil der Juden, er wählt für die deutsche Kultur und die deutsche Zukunft.

Wählt deutsch!

Verleger bzw. Verfasser oder Herausgeber: **Verband nationaldeutscher Juden e. V., Bln. W 35, Blumeshof 9**
Berek - Druck, Berlin SW 19, Grünstraße 17-26. Telefon: B 2 Lützow 5355

"The Only Solution. A Play about Jewish Distress and Jewish Construction" by Sally Lewin (text) and Daniel Sambursky (music), directed by Benno Fränkel, 1932.

BELOW: Announcement of a lecture by Jakob Wassermann: "German Jews in the German Landscape," from the *Jüdische Gemeindezeitung*, the paper of the Jewish community, Berlin, 12 February 1933.

Amtliche Bekanntmachungen
Religiöser Vortrag
Sonntag, den 12. Februar 1933, vorm. 11.30 Uhr, Synagoge Prinzregentenstr. 69/70
Jakob Wassermann
Deutsche Juden in deutscher Landschaft
Chor — Orgel
Eintritt frei! ————— Vorstand der Jüdischen Gemeinde

restore calm, saying there was no reason for concern about a supposed anti-Semitic threat, as the government would take any measures that proved necessary. The Central Association of German Citizens of the Jewish Faith pledged that it would make sure Jews' legal rights were safeguarded.

Generally speaking, however, Jewish life in Germany proceeded on its customary path.

RIGHT: The Purim celebration of the Jewish Choral Society of Munich, 1932.

1933

"Heil!"

The year 1933 brought an end to the hope of a German-Jewish synthesis, a hope that essentially existed on only one side and was harbored mostly only by the German Jews. The small number that emigrated, thus escaping the persecutions to come in Europe, succeeded in making a new beginning in Palestine and in the other countries that were prepared to take them.

What happened then was something which the poet Heinrich Heine had feared a century earlier. In 1834 he warned: "Do not smile at the fantasists ... and when one day you hear a cracking such as was never heard before in the history of the world, then you will know: the German thunder has finally reached its target ... Germany will stage a performance next to which the French Revolution will seem a harmless idyll." For the Jews of Europe, the path led from the burning of their places of worship and their holy scriptures to Dachau, Belsen, Buchenwald, Maidanek, Treblinka, and Auschwitz ...

Debatte im Oberhaus

Einzelnummer 0,25 Goldmark

JÜDISCHE RUNDSCHAU

Erscheint jeden Dienstag u. Freitag. Bezugspreis bei der Expedition monatlich 2.— Goldmark, vierteljährlich 5,75 Goldmark. Auslandsabonnements werden in der Währung der einzelnen Länder berechnet. Anzeigenpreis: 8 gesp. Nonpareillezeile 0,50 G. M. Stellengesuche 0,25 G. M.

Redaktion, Verlag und Anzeigen - Verwaltung: Jüdische Rundschau G. m. b. H., Berlin W15, Meinekestr. 10. Telefon: J 1 Bismarck 7165-70. Anzeigenschluß: Dienstag und Freitag nachmittags 4 Uhr Redaktionsschluß Sonntag und Mittwoch nachmittag.

Postscheck - Konten: Berlin 173 92, Basel V 9355, Belgrad 680 32, Brüssel 394 33, Budapest 596 93, Danzig 1973, Haag 140 470, Prag 594 10, Riga 4155, Straßburg 164 30, Warschau 190 708, Wien 156 030. Bank Konten: Dresdner Bank, Deposien Kasse Berlin, Kurfürstendamm 52. Rumänische Kreditbank, Cernaut (Rumänien); Anglo Palestine Co. in Haifa, Jerusalem, Tel-Aviv.

| Nummer 27 | Berlin, 4. IV. 1933 | XXXVIII. Jahrg. |

Der Zionismus erstrebt für das jüdische Volk die Schaffung einer öffentlich-rechtlich gesicherten Heimstätte in Palästina. „Baseler Programm."

Tragt ihn mit Stolz, den gelben Fleck!

Der 1. April 1933 wird ein wichtiger Tag in der Geschichte der deutschen Juden, ja in der Geschichte des ganzen jüdischen Volkes bleiben. Die Ereignisse dieses Tages haben nicht nur eine politische und eine wirtschaftliche, sondern auch eine moralische und seelische Seite. Ueber die politischen und wirtschaftlichen Zusammenhänge ist in den Zeitungen viel gesprochen worden, wobei freilich häufig agitatorische Bedürfnisse die sachliche Erkenntnis verdunkeln. Ueber die moralische Seite zu sprechen, ist unsere Sache. Denn so viel auch die Judenfrage jetzt erörtert wird, was in der Seele der deutschen Juden vorgeht, was vom jüdischen Standpunkt zu den Vorgängen zu sagen ist, kann niemand aussprechen als wir selbst. Die Juden können heute nicht anders als als Juden sprechen. Alles andere ist völlig sinnlos. Der Spuk der sogenannten „Judenpresse" ist weggeblasen. Der verhängnisvolle Irrtum vieler Juden, man könne jüdische Interessen unter anderem Deckmantel vertreten, ist beseitigt. Das deutsche Judentum hat am 1. April eine Lehre empfangen, die viel tiefer geht, als selbst seine erbitterten und heute triumphierenden Gegner annehmen.

ist eine nationale Frage, und um sie zu lösen, müssen wir sie vor allem zu einer politischen Weltfrage machen, die im Rate der Kulturvölker zu regeln sein wird."

Man müßte Seite um Seite dieser 1897 erschienenen Schrift abschreiben, um zu zeigen: Theodor Herzl war der erste Jude, der unbefangen genug war, den Antisemitismus im Zusammenhang mit der Judenfrage zu betrachten. Und er erkannte, daß nicht durch Vogel-Strauß-Politik, sondern nur durch offene Behandlung der Tatsachen vor aller Welt die Besserung erzielt werden kann. Gegen nichts hat er so leidenschaftlich Stellung genommen als gegen das, was ihm jetzt untergeschoben wird, nämlich gegen den Gedanken, die Juden könnten eine nichtöffentliche Weltverbindung herstellen oder irgend etwas tun, was bei den anderen Völkern irrtümlicherweise solche Vorstellungen erwecken könnte. In seiner Schrift „Leroy-Beaulieu über den Antisemitismus" schreibt er:

„Wir Zionisten sind auf das deutlichste und entschiedenste gegen jede internationale Vereinigung von Juden, die, wenn sie wirksam wäre, den mit Recht verpönten Staat im Staate vorstellte und, da sie machtlos und nichtssagend ist, nur Nachteile bietet. . . . Nur das sei gesagt, daß wir

gedacht. Wir nehmen sie auf, und wollen daraus ein Ehrenzeichen machen.

Viele Juden hatten am Sonnabend ein schweres Erlebnis. Nicht aus innerem Bekenntnis, nicht aus Treue zur eigenen Gemeinschaft, nicht aus Stolz auf eine großartige Vergangenheit und Menschheitsleistung, sondern durch den Aufdruck des roten Zettels und des gelben Flecks standen sie plötzlich als Juden da. Von Haus zu Haus gingen die Trupps, beklebten Geschäfte und Schilder, bemalten die Fensterscheiben, 21 Stunden lang waren die deutschen Juden gewissermaßen an den Pranger gestellt. Neben anderen Zeichen und Inschriften sah man auf den Scheiben der Schaufenster vielfach einen großen Magen David, den Schild König Davids. Dies sollte eine Entehrung sein. Juden, nehmt ihn auf, den Davidsschild, und tragt ihn in Ehren!

Denn — und hier beginnt die Pflicht unserer Selbstbesinnung, — wenn dieser Schild heute befleckt ist, so sind es nicht unsere Feinde allein, die dies bewirkt haben. Viele Juden gab es, die sich nicht genug tun konnten in würdeloser Selbstverhöhnung. Das Judentum

FRANKFURTER ISRAELITISCHES GEMEINDEBLATT

Amtliches Organ der Israelitischen Gemeinde

| 11. Jahrgang | Frankfurt a. M., April 1933 | Nr. 8 |

An die Gemeindemitglieder

In dieser schweren Zeit ist es uns ein tiefes Bedürfnis, ein Wort an unsere Gemeinde zu richten. Jeder darf überzeugt sein, dass wir mit unserer ganzen Kraft bemüht sind, in Verbindung mit den anderen Gemeinden Deutschlands für die staatsbürgerliche Gleichberechtigung der deutschen Juden einzutreten, den in Not Geratenen beizustehen und den Fortbestand unserer Gemeinde zu sichern.

Nichts kann uns die tausendjährige Verbundenheit mit unserer deutschen Heimat rauben, keine Not und Gefahr kann uns dem von unseren Vätern ererbten Glauben abspenstig machen. In Besonnenheit und Würde wollen wir für unsere Sache einstehen.

Wenn keine Stimme sich für uns erhebt, so mögen die Steine dieser Stadt für uns zeugen, die ihren Aufschwung zu einem guten Teil jüdischer Leistung verdankt, in der so viele Einrichtungen vom Gemeinsinn der Juden künden, in der aber auch das Verhältnis zwischen jüdischen und nichtjüdischen Bürgern stets besonders eng gewesen ist.

Verzagt nicht! Schliesst die Reihen! Kein ehrenhafter Jude darf in dieser Zeit fahnenflüchtig werden. Helft uns, das Vätererbe zu bewahren, und wenn die Not der Zeit den Einzelnen hart anfasst, so gedenkt der Worte, die wir am bevorstehenden Pessachfest, dem Fest der Befreiung, von altersher sprechen: „Von Geschlecht zu Geschlecht sind sie gegen uns aufgestanden, uns zu vernichten. Aber der Heilige, gelobt sei Er, hat uns aus ihrer Hand errettet."

Frankfurt a. M., 30. März 1933

Vorstand der Israelitischen Gemeinde

Jüdischer Rechtsanwalt erschossen

Nach Redaktionsschluß erreicht uns folgende erschütternde Meldung:

In der Nacht zum Dienstag wurde in Chemnitz Rechtsanwalt Dr. Weiner in seiner Wohnung von drei Männern, die grüne Uniformen mit SA.-Binden trugen, festgenommen und im Kraftwagen gewaltsam entführt. Dienstag vormittag fand man seine Leiche auf der Wiederauer Flur mit einem Kopfschuß auf. Bei der Leiche wurden Wertsachen und 400 RM Bargeld gefunden. Die Chemnitzer Leitung der SA. erklärt, daß es sich um die Tat von Provokateuren handelt.

Dazu teilt das Polizeipräsidium u. a. mit: Unter Vorlegung eines Ausweises haben die Täter dem Rechtsanwalt in seiner Wohnung erklärt, daß er verhaftet sei. Der Rechtsanwalt hat den Ausweis geprüft und auf eine Frage seiner Frau erklärt, daß die Sache in Ordnung sei. Tatsächlich hat kein Schutzhaftbefehl bestanden. Weiner war nicht in der Boykott-Liste jüdischer Rechtsanwälte enthalten, weil er den Weltkrieg mitgemacht hatte und Offizier geworden war. Die Täter sind in einem Kraftwagen nach einer in der Nähe von Wiederau befindlichen Sandgrube gefahren, wo der Rechtsanwalt erschossen wurde. Das Polizeipräsidium hat für die Aufklärung der Bluttat eine Belohnung ausgesetzt.

Nachruf!

Unsere Israelitische Religionsgemeinde ist von einem schweren Verluste betroffen worden.

Am 10. April cr. wurde unser stellvertretender Vorsitzender Herr **Rechtsanwalt Dr. jur.**

Arthur Weiner

ganz plötzlich aus unserer Mitte gerissen.

Länger als zwei Jahrzehnte hat der Heimgegangene unserer Gemeindevertretung angehört.

Seine hervorragenden Geistesgaben hat er unermüdlich für das Interesse und Gedeihen unserer Gemeinde eingesetzt. Sein vornehmer Charakter und sein stets ausgleichendes, sympathisches Wesen werden uns immerdar vorbildlich bleiben.

Sein Andenken wird in unserer Gemeinde allezeit in Dankbarkeit und hohen Ehren genannt werden.

Der Vorstand der Israelitischen Religionsgemeinde zu Chemnitz.

LEFT: A message from the leaders of the Frankfurt am Main Jewish community, promising to stand by its members and recalling the Jewish contribution to Frankfurt's history. From the *Frankfurter Israelitisches Gemeindeblatt*, April 1933.

BELOW LEFT: "Jewish lawyer shot dead," a report in the *Israelitisches Familienblatt* Hamburg, 12 April 1933, on the killing of Dr. Arthur Weiner by Nazi storm troopers in Chemnitz.

BELOW: An obituary notice for Arthur Weiner in the *Israelitisches Familienblatt*, 12 April 1933, placed by the board of the Chemnitz congregation.

The last photograph of the writer and philosopher Theodor Lessing (1872–1933). In April 1933 he fled to Czechoslovakia, where he was murdered by National Socialists in Marienbad on 31 August 1933.

The composer Arnold Schönberg and many other baptized Jews now publicly declared their return to Judaism. The architect Erich Mendelsohn declared: "We Jews are caught in the vise of national passions and can find our own right to existence only as a nation, as an independent people."

BELOW: Peter and Lisl B. at the station of a German town. Employed by a rare books store in Munich, Peter B. was rescued from a concentration camp by influential Christian friends. He obtained an entry and residence visa to Kenya as a supervisor on a tea plantation. Photo Tim Gidal.

Declarations of Leo Baeck and Albert Einstein

"For us Jews from Germany, an historical epoch has come to an end. Such an epoch ends whenever a hope, a belief, a trust has finally to be buried. Our belief was that the German and the Jewish spirit could meet on German soil and through their marriage become a blessing. This was an illusion – the Jewish epoch in Germany is over, once and for all."

Rabbi Leo Baeck in New York 1945, after his liberation from the Theresienstadt concentration camp.

The declaration (right) was made by Albert Einstein in 1933. Translated, it reads:

"A striving for knowledge for its own sake, a love of justice bordering on fanaticism and a striving for personal independence – these are the elements of the tradition of the Jewish people which have always made me consider my membership of it as a gift of fate.

Those who today fulminate against the ideals of reason and individual freedom and try to impose by methods of brutal violence a mindless state slavery, are right to see in us their irreconcilable foes. The struggle history has given us to fight is a hard one; but so long as we remain the devoted servants of truth, justice and freedom, we will not only continue to survive as the oldest of earth's living peoples, but also carry on by our productive work the creation of values that contribute to the nobility of the human race."

DÉCLARATION
D'ALBERT EINSTEIN

Streben nach Erkenntnis um ihrer selbst willen, an Fanatismus grenzende Liebe zur Gerechtigkeit und Streben nach persönlicher Selbständigkeit — das sind die Motive der Tradition des jüdischen Volkes, die mich meine Zugehörigkeit zu ihm als ein Geschenk des Schicksals empfinden lassen.

Diejenigen, welche heute gegen die Ideale der Vernunft und der individuellen Freiheit wüten und mit den Mitteln brutaler Gewalt geistlose Staats-Sklaverei durchsetzen wollen, sehen mit Recht in uns ihre unversöhnlichen Gegner. Die Geschichte hat uns einen schweren Kampf auferlegt; aber solange wir ergebene Diener der Wahrheit, Gerechtigkeit und Freiheit bleiben, werden wir nicht nur fortbestehen als ältestes der lebenden Völker sondern auch wie bisher in produktiver Arbeit Werte schaffen, die zur Veredelung der Menschheit beitragen.

A. Einstein

Select Bibliography

This select bibliography makes no claim to completeness. A comprehensive bibliography of available works on Jews and Judaism will be found in *Literatur zum Judentum*, an occasional publication edited by Rachel Salamander (obtainable by writing to: Literaturhandlung, Fürstenstrasse 17, 80333 Munich, Germany).

The following three books give some idea of Jewish life during the Hitler regime (not covered by this volume): Victor Klemperer's *LTI. Notizbuch eines Philologen.*, 15th ed., Frankfurt, 1996, and two illustrated books, *Jüdischer Alltag in Deutschland 1933–1945* by Günther Bernd Ginzel, 2nd ed., Düsseldorf 1993, and *Der Gelbe Stern. Die Judenverfolgung in Europa 1933 bis 1945* by Gerhard Schoenberner, Frankfurt 1995. *Publisher's Note*

General Works

BEIN, ALEX: *Die Judenfrage. Biographie eines Weltproblems*, 2 vols., Stuttgart 1980

BEN-SASSON, Chayim Hillel (ed.): *Geschichte des jüdischen Volkes*, 3 vols., Munich 1980

CLAUSSEN, DETLEV: *Grenzen der Aufklärung. Zur gesellschaftlichen Geschichte des modernen Antisemitismus*, Frankfurt 1987

Der Babylonische Talmud. selected, translated and explained by REINHOLD MAYER, Munich 1963 (the best single-volume German edition)

Deutsche und Juden. Beiträge von NAHUM GOLDMANN *et al.*, Frankfurt 1967

DUBNOW, SIMON: *Die neueste Geschichte des jüdischen Volkes*, 3 vols., Berlin 1920–23

DUBNOW, SIMON: *Jüdische Geschichte, ein geschichtsphilosophischer Versuch*, Frankfurt am Main 1921 (short work, fundamental)

EHRLICH, ERNST LUDWIG: *Geschichte der Juden in Deutschland*, Düsseldorf 1957

ELBOGEN, ISMAR/STERLING, ELEONORE: *Geschichte der Juden in Deutschland. Eine Einführung*, Frankfurt 1966

FINKELSTEIN, LOUIS (ed.): *The Jews. Their Role in Civilization.* New York, 1949

FRANZHEIM, LIESEL: *Juden in Köln*, Köln 1984 (documentary in words and pictures)

FUCHS, EDUARD: *Die Juden in der Karikatur. Ein Beitrag zur Kulturgeschichte*, Berlin 1984

GAMM, HANS J.: *Das Judentum. Eine Einführung*, Frankfurt am Main 1979

GOLDING, LOUIS: *The Jewish Problem*, London, 1938

Leo Baeck Yearbooks, 1956–1997. Ed. by ROBERT WELTSCH and ARNOLD PAUCKER.

MASSING, PAUL: *Rehearsal for Destruction; a Study of Political Antisemitism in Imperial Germany.* New York, 1949.

ROTH, CECIL: *A Short History of the Jewish People.* London, 1948.

RUBENS, ALFRED: *A Jewish Iconography*, London, 1981

SCHOLEM, GERSHOM: *Major Trends in Jewish Mysticism.* New York, 1961.

ibid.: Judaica, Frankfurt am Main 1963

SIEVERS, LEO: *Juden in Deutschland*, Munich 1983

STEINHAUSEN, HERMANN: *Die Judenfrage – eine Christenfrage*, Lucerne 1939

STEMBERGER, GÜNTER: *Geschichte der jüdischen Literatur. Eine Einführung*, Munich 1977

STRAUSS, HERBERT A./HOFFMANN, CHRISTHARD: *Juden und Judentum in der Literatur*, Munich 1985

STRAUSS, RAPHAEL: *Die Juden in Wirtschaft und Gesellschaft. Untersuchungen zur Geschichte einer Minorität*, Frankfurt am Main 1964

TREPP, LEO: *Das Judentum. Geschichte und lebendige Gegenwart*, Reinbeck 1987

WELTSCH, ROBERT: *Die deutsche Judenfrage. Ein kritischer Rückblick*, Kronberg 1981

WILHELM, KURT (ed.): *Jüdischer Glaube. Eine Auswahl aus zwei Jahrtausenden*, Bremen 1961

ZUNZ, LEOPOLD: *Namen der Juden. Eine geschichtliche Untersuchung*, reprint of 1837 Leipzig edition, Hildesheim 1971

Middle Ages and Early Modern Period

ARONIUS, JULIUS: *Registern zur Geschichte der Juden im fränkischen und deutschen Reiche bis 1273*, Berlin 1902 (the fundamental documentary work)

BEN SASSON, CHAYIM HILLEL: *The Reformation in Contemporary Jewish Eyes*, Jerusalem, 1970

BERLINER, ABRAHAM: *Aus dem Leben der deutschen Juden im Mittelalter, zugleich ein Beitrag zur deutschen Culturgeschichte*, Berlin 1900

BLUMENKRANZ, BERNHARD: *Juden und Judentum in der mittelalterlichen Kunst.* 1973 Delitsch lecture, ed. by Karl H. Rengstorf, Stuttgart 1965

BREUER, NATASCHA: *Das Bild der Juden in den Passionsspielen und in der bildenden Kunst des deutschen Mittelalters*, Frankfurt 1986

CARO, GEORG: *Sozial- und Wirtschaftsgeschichte der Juden im Mittelalter und in der Neuzeit*, Frankfurt 1924

Germania Judaica. Vol. I: Von den älteren Zeiten bis 1238, Tübigen 1934; Vol. II: From 1238 till the middle of 14th century; Vol. III/I (A-L), from 1350–1519, Tübingen 1987

HAVERKAMP, ALFRED (ed.): *Zur Geschichte der Juden im Deutschland des späten Mittelalters und der frühen Neuzeit.* Monographien zur Geschichte des Mittelalters, Vol. 24, Stuttgart 1981

KELLENBENZ, HERMANN: *Sephardim an der unteren Elbe. Ihre wirtschaftliche und politische Bedeutung vom Ende des 16. bis zum Beginn des 18. Jahrhunderts*, Wiesbaden 1958

KIRSCH, GUIDO: *Forschungen zur Rechts- und Sozialgeschichte der Juden in Deutschland während des Mittelalters*, 2nd edition. Sigmaringen 1978

MARCUS, JACOB R.: *The Jew in the Medieval World*, Cincinnati, 1938

METZGER, THÉRÈSE and MENDEL: *Jüdisches Leben im Mittelalter nach illuminierten hebräischen Handschriften vom 13. bis 16. Jahrhundert*, Würzburg 1983

POLIAKOV, LÉON: *The History of Antisemitism. Four vols.* London, 1965–85

SCHUBERT, KURT: *Die Kultur der Juden*, Teil II: Judentum im Mittelalter (Handbuch der Kulturgeschichte), Wiesbaden 1979

SEIFERTH WOLFGANG: *Synagoge und Kirche im Mittelalter*, Munich 1964

STERN, SELMA: *Josel von Rosheim; Befehlshaber der Judenschaft im Heiligen Römischen Reich Deutscher Nation*, Stuttgart 1959

STOBBE, OTTO: *Die Juden in Deutschland während des Mittelalters in politischer, sozialer und rechtlicher Beziehung*, Brunswick 1866 and Berlin 1923

VEITSHANS, HELMUT: *Kartographische Darstellung der Judensiedlungen der schwäbischen Reichsstädte im Mittelalter*, Arbeiten zum Historischen Atlas von Südwestdeuschland. Heft 6. Stuttgart 1970

WENNIGER, MARKUS J.: *Man bedarf keiner Juden mehr. Ursachen und Hintergründe ihrer Vertreibung aus den deutschen Reichsstädten im 15. Jahrhundert*, Vienna 1981

Enlightenment, Emancipation, Assimilation

ALLERHAND, JACOB: *Das Judentum in der Aufklärung*, Stuttgart – Bad Cannstadt 1980

ARENDT, HANNAH: *Rahel Varnhagen: The Life of a Jewess.* London, 1957.

BERLIN, JESAYA: *The Life and Opinions of Moses Hess*, Cambridge, 1959

Das Judentum in der deutschen Umwelt 1800–1850. Studien zur Frühgeschichte der Emanzipation. Ed. by HANS LIEBESCHÜTZ and ARNOLD PAUCKER, Tübingen 1977

Der Jude, Monatsschrift. Ed. by MARTIN BUBER, Berlin 1916–24 (Spezialhefte 1925–28)

GLANZ, RUDOLF: *Geschichte des niederen jüdischen Volkes in Deutschland. Eine Studie über historisches Gaunertum, Bettelwesen und Vagantentum*, New York 1968

GLÜCKEL VON HAMMELN: *Denkwürdigkeiten.* Ed. by L. Feilchenfeld, Berlin 1923, Reprinted Königstein/Taunus 1980

GRAB, WALTER/SCHOEPS, JULIUS H. (ed.): *Juden in Vormärz und in der Revolution von 1848*, Stuttgart/Bonn 1983

Herz, Henriette: Ihr Leben und ihre Zeit. ed by HANS LANDSBERG, Weimar 1913

HESS, MOSES: *The Revival of Israel: Rome and Jerusalem, the Last Nationalist Question.* Nebraska, 1995.

JERSCH-WENZEL, STEFFI: *Juden und "Franzosen" in der Wirtschaft des Raumes Berlin-Brandenburg zur Zeit des Merkantilismus*, Berlin 1978

Judentum im Zeitalter der Aufklärung. Wolfenbütteler Studien zur Aufklärung, vol. IV. Presented to Günther Schulz on his 70th birthday, Wolfenbüttel 1977

KOBLER, FRANZ: *Das Zeitalter der Emanzipation. Jüdische Geschichte in Briefen aus Ost und West*, Wien 1938

KOBLER, FRANZ: *Napoleon and the Jews*, Jerusalem, 1975

MAHLER, RAPHAEL: *Jewish Emancipation*, New York, 1941

NEBEL, THEOBALD: *Die Geschichte der jüdischen Gemeinde in Talheim*, Talheim 1963

OPPENHEIM, MORITZ: *Erinnerungen*, Frankfurt am Main 1924

POLIAKOV, LÉON: *The History of Antisemitism. Four vols.* London, 1965–85

REISSNER, HANNS GÜNTHER: *Eduard Gans. Ein Leben im Vormärz*, Tübingen 1965

RICHARZ, MONIKA (ed.): *Jewish Life in Germany: Memoirs from Three Centuries.* Bloomington, 1991.

RICHARZ, MONIKA: *Der Eintritt der Juden in die akademischen Berufe. Jüdische Studenten und Akademiker in Deutschland 1678-1848*, Tübingen 1974

SCHOEPS, JULIUS H.: *Moses Mendelssohn*, Königstein/ Taunus 1979

STERN, SELMA: *Der preußische Staat und die Juden*, 4. vols., Tübingen 1962–1975

STERN, SELMA: *Jud Süss, ein Beitrag zur deutschen und jüdischen Geschichte*, Munich 1973

TOURY, JAKOB: *Der Eintritt der Juden in das deutsche Bürgertum. Eine Dokumentation*, Tel Aviv 1972

Imperial Germany and the Weimar Republic

ADLER, HANS GÜNTHER: *Jews in Germany: From the Enlightenment to National Socialism.* Notre Dame, 1973.

ADLER-RUDEL, S.: *Ostjuden in Deutschland 1880–1940*, Tübingen 1959

BAB, JULIUS: *Schauspieler und Schauspielkunst*, Berlin 1926

BOEHLICH, WALTER (ed.): *Der Berliner Antisemitenstreit*, Frankfurt 1965

BÖHM, ADOLF: *Die zionistische Bewegung*, Berlin 1920

BORRIES, ACHIM VON (ed.): *Selbstzeugnisse des deutschen Judentums 1870–1945*, Frankfurt 1986

BUBER, MARTIN: *Reden über das Judentum*, Berlin 1923

Der Schlemiel, Jüdische Blätter für Humor und Kunst, Berlin 1903–1905 and 1919/20

DUNKER, ULRICH: *Der Reichsbund jüdischer Frontsoldaten 1919–1938. Geschichte eines jüdischen Abwehrvereins*, Düsseldorf 1977

ELON, AMOS: *Morgen in Jerusalem. Theodor Herzl; sein Leben und Werk*, Vienna/Munich/Zürich 1975

GIDAL, TIM: *Modern Photojournalism: Origin and Evolution.* [N.Y.? - publisher is Macmillan], 1974. New York, 1974.

GIDAL, TIM: *Jerusalem in 3000 Years*, Cologne, 1996

GRAB, WALTER and JULIUS SCHOEPS (eds.): *Juden in der Weimarer Republik*, Stuttgart/Bonn 1986

HAMBURGER, ERNST: *Juden im öffentlichen Leben Deutschlands. Regierungsmitglieder, Beamte und Parlamentarier in der monarchischen Zeit 1848–1918*, Tübingen 1968

HAMMER-SCHENK, HAROLD: *Synagogen in Deutschland. Geschichte einer Baugattung im 19. und 20. Jahrhundert*, 2 vols. In: Hamburger Beiträge zur Geschichte der deutschen Juden, vol. 8, Hamburg 1981

HERZL, THEODOR: *The Jewish State.* London, 1896.

HUBMANN, FRANZ: *Das jüdischen Familienalbum,*

Vienna/Munich/Zürich 1974

KAPLAN, MARION A.: *Die jüdischen Frauenbewegung in Deutschland. Organisation und Ziele des jüdischen Frauenbundes 1904–1938.* In: Hamburger Beiträge zur Geschichte der deutschen Juden, Vol. VII, Hamburg 1981

KRONJAKER, GUSTAV (ed.): *Juden in der deutschen Literatur,* Berlin 1922

KUPISCH, KARL et al.: *Judenfeindschaft im 19. Jahrhundert. Ursachen, Formen und Folgen,* 2. ed. Berlin 1982

LIEBESCHÜTZ, HANS: *Juden im Geschichtsbild von Hegel bis Max Weber,* Tübingen 1967

LIEBESCHÜTZ, HANS: *Von Georg Simmel zu Franz Rosenzweig. Studien zum Jüdischen Denken im deutschen Kulturbereich,* Tübingen 1970

MAURER, TRUDE: *Ostjuden in Deutschland 1918–1933.* In: Hamburger Beiträge zur Geschichte der deutschen Juden, vol. XII, Hamburg 1986

Menorah, Jüdisches Familienblatt für Wissenschaft, Kunst und Literatur, Vienna 1923–1933

MOSSE, GEORGE L.: *Germans and Jews,* New York, 1970

MOSSE, WERNER E.: (ed.) *Juden im wilhelminischen Deutschland 1890–1914. Ein Sammelband,* Tübingen 1976

MOSSE, WERNER E. and ARNOLD PAUCKER (eds.): *Deutsches Judentum in Krieg und Revolution 1916–1923,* Tübingen 1971

MÜHLEN, ULRIKE: *Yiddish Elements in German Colloquial Speech.* Dissertation, Columbia University, New York 1982

OPPENHEIM, MORITZ DANIEL: *Bilder aus dem alt-jüdischen Familienleben, nach Original-Gemälden.* With an introduction by Leopold Stein, Frankfurt am Main 1882

OPPENHEIMER, FRANZ: *Die Judenstatistik des preussischen Kriegsministeriums,* Munich 1922

PAUCKER, ARNOLD: *Der jüdische Abwehrkampf gegen Antisemitismus und Nationalsozialismus in den letzten Jahren der Weimarer Republik.* In: Hamburger Beiträge zur Zeitgeschichte, Vol. IV, 2nd ed. Hamburg 1969

POLIAKOV, LÉON: *The History of Antisemitism.* Four vols. London, 1965–85

PRINZ, ARTHUR: *Juden im deutschen Wirtschaftsleben. Soziale und wirtschaftliche Struktur im Wandel 1850–1904,* Tübingen 1984

PULZER, PETER: *The Rise of Political Antisemitism in Germany and Austria.* New York, 1964

RUBENS, ALFRED: *A History of Jewish Costume,* London 1973

RUBENS, ALFRED: *A Jewish Iconography,* London 1981

SCHOEPS, JULIUS: *Theodor Herzl,* Wien 1996

SILBERGLEIT, HEINRICH: *Die Bevölkerungs- und Berufsverhältnisse der Juden im Deutschen Reich,* Berlin 1930

THEILHABER, FELIX A.: *Der Untergang der deutschen Juden. Eine volkswirtschaftliche Studie,* Berlin 1921

TOURY, JACOB: *Soziale und politische Geschichte der Juden in Deutschland 1874–1871,* Düsseldorf 1977

WASSERMANN, JACOB: *My Life as German and Jew.* New York, 1933.

ZEICHLIN, EGMONT: *Die deutsche Politik und die Juden im Ersten Weltkrieg,* Göttingen 1969

ZELINSKI, HARTMUT: *Richard Wagner – deutsches Thema. Eine Dokumentation zur Wirkungsgeschichte 1876–1976,* Frankfurt 1976

ZIELENZINGER, KURT: *Juden in der deutschen Wirtschaft,* Berlin 1930

ZWEIG, ARNOLD: *Bilanz der deutschen Judenheit 1933. Ein Versuch,* Amsterdam 1934. Reprinted Cologne 1961

ZWEIG, ARNOLD: *Das ostjüdische Antlitz. Zu 50 Steinzeichnungen von Hermann Struck,* Berlin 1920

ZWEIG, ARNOLD: *Juden auf der deutschen Bühne,* Berlin 1927

Index

Page numbers in *italic* refer to illustrations

Picture Credits

Privatalbum Nina Adler, Munich 403 b.; ADN-Zentralbild, Berlin 399; Archiv Kibbuz Hasorea 415 a.; Archiv fur Kunst und Geschichte, Berlin 140 b., 143 b., 207 l.b.; Leo Baeck Institute, New York 31 l., 31 a.r., 98 b., 107 r., 141 M., 142 r., 168 b.r., 178, 182 b., 198 a.r., 228 a., 241, 246, 247 b., 248 a., 262 a.l., 281 b., 291 a., 292 a.l., 295 a., 315 a.r., 323 r., 330 b.l., 344 a.r., 352 a.r., 354 r., 358 r., 390 a.r., 398 a.l., 423 a.l.; Bayer. Hauptstaatsarchiv, Munich 84 b.; Bayer. Nationalmuseum, Munich 38 b.r., 41 r.; Bayer. Staatsbibliothek, Munich 36 r., 37 r., 66, 67, 68 b., 82 b.l.; Archiv Behr, London 202 b.r.; Sammlung Dr. Alex Bein, Jerusalem 219 l., 267 a.l.; Ben Zwi Institute, Jerusalem 85 a.; Berlin Museum, Berlin 228 b., 386 b.; Berlinische Galerie, Berlin 249 a.r., 283 a.l., 286 r., 360, 361, 363, 364 a., 365 b., 378 b., 381 a., 384 b., 418 b.l.; Biblioteca Apostolica Vaticana, The Vatican 24 b., 35; Bibliothek der Universiteit van Amsterdam 93 a.; Bibliothèque Nationale, Paris 68 a., 382 a.; Bibliothèque Royale Albert Iᵉʳ, Brussels 50 b.; Archiv Marcus Bier, Berlin 284 a.r., 389 a.l.; Bildarchiv Foto Marburg, Marburg 38 a., 43, 82 a.l.; Bildarchiv PreuBischer Kulturbesitz, Berlin 59 a.l., 59 a.r., 218 b., 274 M.r., 281 a.r., 282 a.r., 332 a.l., 342 b.; Bischöfliches Ordinariat, Augsburg 34 l.; Ludwig Bloch Archiv, Basle 205 a.r.; Courtesy Peter Bock, London 176 a.; Bodleian Library, Oxford 54, 62 a.; The British Library, London 31 b.r., 33 M.l.; The British Museum, London 61 b.; Martin Buber Archiv, Jerusalem 324 a.l.; Lichtbildstelle der Bundesbahndirektion, Nürnberg 164 b.; Sammlung Dr. Werner Cahnmann, New York 239 a.l., 261 b.l., 390 a.l.; Dr. Alexander Carlebach, Jerusalem 319 b.; Archiv Karoline Cauer 114 a.l.; Central Archives, Jerusalem 50 a.r., 99 a.r., 171 r., 181 a., 183 b.l., 184, 187 a., 230 a., 244 b.; Elishewa Cohen, Jerusalem 205 b.; Columbia University Library, New York 79 a.r.; Brunhilde Dahn, Krefeld 262 b., Erich David, Jerusalem 341; Deutsches Museum, Munich 274 a., 275 a.l., 275 a.r., 279 b.; Sammlung Alexander Furst zu Dohna-Schlobitten, Basle 141 l.; Dr. Ruben Eisen-Eytan, Jerusalem 298 a.l.; Sammlung Hermann Elbin, Jerusalem 330 b.r.; Ruth Ettlinger, Kfar Saba 314 M.; S. Fischer Verlag, Frankfurt am Main 351 b.l.; Dr. Benno Fränkel, Jerusalem 415 b., 421 a.; Fremdenverkehrsverband Württemberg, Stuttgart 171 l.; Stefan George Archiv, Stuttgart 290 a.l., 290 b.; Germanisches National-museum, Nürnberg 81, 101 a.l., 109 b., 113 b.l., 169 a.r., 177 b.l.; Helmut Gernsheim, Castagnola 106 r.; Archiv Gerstenberg, Wietze 147; Emmi Ginsburg-Horovitz, Giwat Chaim 239 a.r., 250 b.r.; Walter Goldstern, London 336 M., 339 a.l.; Ruth Gorny-Lessing, Hannover 425 b.; Gerd Granach, Jerusalem 387 b.l.; Privatsammlung Irene Guggenheim, Jerusalem 336 b.; Sammlung Luba Halevy, Jerusalem 337 b.; Claus & Liselotte Hansmann, Stockdorf 172 a., 173 a.; Hilde Harmelin, London 301 b.; Hauptstaatsarchiv, Stuttgart 125 b., 250 a.; The Hebrew Union College Gallery of Art and Artifacts, Cincinnati 126 b.; Heinrich-Heine-Institut, Düsseldorf 216, 296 a.l.; Hessische Landes- und Hochschulbibliothek, Darmstadt 70, 71, 97 a.; Historisches Museum am Hohen Ufer, Hannover 107 a.l.; Historisches Museum, Frankfurt am Main 146 r., 158 M.l., 160, 162 a.r., 162 b.r., 200 l.; Sammlung Inge Höchberg-Gerster, Basle 100 a.; Sammlung Peter Hunter, Den Haag 391; Institut fur die Geschichte der deutschen Juden, Hamburg 156 b., 174; Internationales Institut fur soziale Geschichte, Amsterdam 203 a.r., 223, 236 a.l., 243 a.l., 315 a.l., 324 b.; The Israel Museum, Jerusalem 23 b., 61 a., 69, 99 a.l., 102 b., 103 a.l., 166, 167 b., 185, 192 b.r., 193 a.r., 193 b., 194 a., 195 a., 200 r., 201 r., 277, 286 b.l.; Jerusalem City Museum, Jerusalem 311 a.; The Jewish Museum, London 127, 188, 189, 190, 191; Jewish National and University Library, Jerusalem 37 l., 78 b.l., 80 a., 100 b.l., 114 b.r., 120 M., 120 b., 121 a.r., 122, 123 l., 135, 145 l., 145 r., 151 r., 151 l., 154, 155 r., 161, 197, 213 r., 220 a., 245 a.l., 253 l., 259 b.r., 270 l., 270 M., 274 a.l., 277 a., 277 M., 281 M.r., 300 b., 302 a.l., 303 a.r., 304 a.l., 329 b.l., 333 a., 342 a.l., 404 a.r., 405 r., 424 a.l., 424 b.r.; Dr. Jakob Katzenstein, Jerusalem 211 b.l., 237 a.; Alfred Knopf Verlag, New York 164 a.; Kösel-Verlag, Munich/Holzschrift von Josua Reichert zu dem Gedicht Der Tibetteppich 393 b.; Kunsthistorisches Museum, Vienna 29 b.; Ruth Kuski-Marx, Giwataim 287 a.l., 320 M.r., 334, 335; Landesbildstelle, Berlin 114 b.l., 137 a., 143 a., 176 b.l., 218 a.r., 247 a.r. 248 b., 252 a., 260 a.l., 301 a., 322 b.l., 327 b., 379 b., 387 b.r.; Sammlung Harald Lechenperg 84 a.l.; Library of Congress, Washington 213 l.; Ursula Liebstädter, Jerusalem 234 b., 235 a.l., 306, 313 a.r.; Makkabi Museum, Ramat Aviv 344 a.l., 345 b.; Märkisches Museum, Berlin 114 a.r.; Hermann Mayer, Jerusalem 412 b.; Archiv Familie Mendelssohn 118 M.a.l.; Prof. Heinrich Meng, Basle 280 b.; Dr. Peter Meyer, London 329 M.a., 329 a.r.; Privatbesitz Meyerbeer Erben 124 a.r.; Mindener Museum für Geschichte, Minden 231, Titelbild; Sammlung Prof. George L. Mosse, Madison 272 a.l.; Sammlung Murczinskaja, Cologne 366 a.l.; Museum der Stadt Worms b. Städt. Gemäldegalerie, Worms 32 a., 58 a.; Museum Folkwang, Essen 349 a.l., 375 a., 380, 381 b.; Museum für Hamburgische Geschichte, Hamburg 210 a.; Museum für Kunst und Gewerbe, Hamburg 204; Museen für Kunst und Kulturgeschichte, Lübeck 177 a.; Museum of the Jewish Diaspora, Tel Aviv 198 a.l., 259 b.l., 411 a.l.; Museum des Landestheaters, Hannover 285 a.l.; Österr. Nationalbibliothek, Vienna 40 a., 48 a.r., 284 b.r., 289 a.l., 392 a.r.; Bildarchiv Pisarek, Berlin 402; Prentenkabinet der Rijksuniversiteit, Leiden 376 r.; Privatbesitz Rabinowitz 300 a.; Grete Rapp, New York 315 M.a.; Max Reinhardt Forschungs- und Gedenkstätte, Salzburg 285 b.r.; Rheinisches Bildarchiv, Cologne 29 a., 170 b., 192 b.l., 202 b.l., 219 r., 259 a.; Rheinisches Landesmuseum, Trier 24 a., 51 l.; Sammlung L. Rosenberg 235 b.; Rosgarten Museum, Konstanz 52; Sammlung Alfred Rubens, London 90 a.l., 92 M., 92 b., 95 b., 99 b., 105 a.r., 116, 123 r., 132 a., 136 b.l., 136 b.r., 146 l., 168 a., 175 b.r., 177 b.r.; Sammlung Mirjam Sambursky, Jerusalem 235 a.r.; Sammlung Joint Distribution Committee, Genf 329 b.r.; Prof. Gershom Scholem 354 l.; Jacques V. Sichel, Union City 238; E. E. Simon, Giwataim 344 b.; Sotheby's, Tel Aviv 369 r.; Schocken Library, Jerusalem 36 l., 56 r., 331 r., 347; Staatsgalerie moderner Kunst, Munich 295 b.r.; Staatl. Graph. Sammlung, Munich 150 a., 150 b., 169 a.l.; Staats- und Universitatsbibliothek, Hamburg 33 a.l., 38 b.l., 74 b., 75 b.; Stadt- und Kreismuseum, Landshut 47 b., 48 a.l.; Stadtarchiv Bamberg 42; Stadtarchiv Frankfurt am Main 50 a.l., 90 a.r., 90 b., 98 a., 133 a., 133 b., 149 a.l., 158 b., 158 r., 159, 162 b.l., 163, 165 b., 165 a., 199 a., 206 l., 207 a.l., 207 M.l., 208 a., 225, 236 a.r., 240, 249 a.l., 287 a.r., 346 b., 362 a.l., 423 a.r., 424 a.; Stadtarchiv Konstanz 47 a.r.; Stadtarchiv Mainz 33 b.l., 104 b.; Stadtarchiv Mannheim 187 b., 205 a.l., 230 b., 343; Stadtarchiv Munich 203 a.l., 221 l., 290 a.r., 322 b.l., 325 l.; Stadtarchiv Nürnberg 60; Stadtarchiv Speyer 48 b.; Stadtbildstelle Essen 249 b., Städt. Kunstsammlungen, Augsburg 170 r.; Städt. Museum, Gottingen 152 a.l., 195 b.r.; Stadtmuseum, Cologne 58 b.r., 195 M.b., 222, 323 b.l.; Dr. Karl Steinorth, Stuttgart 374 r.; Eva Michaelis-Stern, Jerusalem 357 b.; Stiftung Deutsche Kinemathek, Berlin 372, 373; Privatsammlung Daniel Tal, Jerusalem 318 a.l.; Technisches Museum, Vienna 274 M.l.; Theatermuseum, Munich 387 a.l., Archiv Prof. Treu, Göttingen 226 a.; Ullstein Bilderdienst, Berlin 157 a.l., 268 a., 278 b.r., 313 a.l., 348, 359 a., 359 b.r., 378 a.l., 393 a.l., 420 a.r.; Universität Koln/Martin Buber Institut 247 a.l.; Universitätsbibliothek, Freiburg 45 a.; Universitätsbibliothek Heidelberg 33 r., 49; University of London, The Warburg Institute 357 a.; Rosi Varon, Jerusalem 401; Verw. der Staatl. Schlösser und Gärten, Berlin 113 a.; Eric Warburg, Hamburg 237 b.; Geschenk von Dr. Robert Weltsch 289 b.; Wiener Library, London 355 a.l., 422; Leo Wissmann, Jerusalem 251 b.; Prof. Bernhard Witkop, Washington 278 a.l.; Privatsammlung Ilse Yallon, Jerusalem 329 a.l.; YIVO Institute, New York 318 a.r.; Zentralbibliothek Zürich 44, 45 b.; General Zionist Archives, Jerusalem 258 b., 299 b., 302 b.l., 305 b., 307 a.l., 307 b.r., 308 a., 308 b., 309 a.l., 311 b.l., 312, 328 M.l., 331 l., 404 b., 411 a.r., 411 b., 413 a.r.

Almost all the illustrations are from the Dr N. Gidal Collection or Archive. For the reproduction of illustrations of works of art by members or copyright holders of the licensing agencies S.P.A.D.E.M./Paris, S.A.B.A.M./Brussels, BEELDRECHT/Amsterdam, V.A.G.A./New York, and S.I.A.E./Rome, copyright clearance has been granted by the licensing agency BILD-KUNST/Bonn.

The author and publisher have not been able to trace all owners of rights to the images reproduced. Owners of such rights are requested to address any claims arising from them to the publisher.